THE
PEOPLE CALLED SHAKERS

A SEARCH FOR THE PERFECT SOCIETY

———◆———

By EDWARD DEMING ANDREWS

1368

NEW ENLARGED EDITION

DOVER PUBLICATIONS, INC.
NEW YORK

This new Dover edition, first published in 1963, is an unabridged republication of the work first published by the Oxford University Press, Inc., in 1953, to which has been added an Appendix of Notes supplying background and bibliographical information for over three hundred text references and for all the illustrations in the book. This new material has been prepared by the author especially for this Dover edition.

Library of Congress Catalog Card Number: 63-17896

Manufactured in the United States of America

Dover Publications, Inc.
180 Varick Street
New York 14, N.Y.

TO *ANOTHER SEEKER—MY MOTHER*

Preface to the Dover Edition

FOR thirty-five years the culture of the American Shakers has been, for me and my wife, an absorbing and expanding interest. First to engage attention was their economy and the products of their industry. Next it was their craftsmanship in furniture, and after this the various manifestations of their religious beliefs: their songs, dances and curious rituals. Little research had previously been done in these fields; it was pioneer work, with the excitement of continuous discovery.

In the course of gathering data (as well as artifacts) for monographs on the above subjects, it became increasingly evident how abundant were the sources, primary and secondary, all throwing light, in one way or another, on the topic at hand. Manuscripts and notes accumulated. As we became ever more deeply immersed in the subject, the idea evolved of writing a definitive history of the movement. The Shaker society, we came to realize, was a closely integrated, a homogeneous culture. We had been treating of its various facets; now we wanted to bring together all its parts.

When I felt that the extensive literature by and about the Believers had been properly assimilated, the question arose as to how much of this fascinating material, particularly that in manuscript, should be incorporated into the history. I wanted the narrative to move along without the distraction of foot-notes. On the other hand, I felt it important to document events, to let the Shakers speak for themselves, and in general to enrich the account with commentary.

In the first edition of *The People Called Shakers* it was decided to dispense with the notes. I am pleased that in the present edition they have been retained, for I feel that they add immeasurably, for the general reader as well as for the student of American communitarianism, to the value of the work. They help to define the culture, in all its complexity and diversity. Made clearer, I think, is its impact on individuals and its relationships to the prevailing *American* culture.

Though the Shakers were separatists, their protest against the world's wrongs and their search for a more perfect form of social organization were a part, more influential in its fruits than we may suspect, of the American heritage. It is the author's hope that this fuller record of their productive experiment in association will deepen appreciation of a way of life and work that is surely meaningful to us as it was, in another context, to the Believers themselves.

Pittsfield, Massachusetts   E. D. A.
February 1963

Table of Contents

List of Illustrations

Introduction

I found a spirit-level on the window
seat, a very good emblem for the Society.

—*Emerson's Journals*

THE Shaker society was a unique experiment in association. By virtue of its communal principles, its status as a separatist sect, and its diverse social and economic contributions, the united order of Believers, or Shakers, forms a significant chapter in our history. As old as the Republic itself, the order evolved a distinctive culture which has played an unobtrusive but important part in America's development.

Independence, in thought and action, marked the course it ran. Its relationship to such early Old World heretical sects as the Montanists, the Manicheans, the Albigenses, the Waldenses, and others — whom the Shakers regarded as forerunners of a new 'dispensation' — was one of spiritual affinity only. Their connection with the Camisards, or French Prophets, and in England the Society of Friends, was tenuous. In America their antecedents were the Labadists, a Dutch Separatist sect, who established a short-lived order, practicing community of goods, at Bohemia Manor about 1683; the small colony of brethren called 'The Woman in the Wilderness,' set up by the Pietist Johannes Kelpius in Pennsylvania later in the seventeenth century; and Ephrata, the celibate order of men and women founded by Johann Konrad Beissel, a Seventh Day Baptist, in 1735. But these communal undertakings apparently exercised no influence on Shaker doctrine or practice.

Once rooted, with branches extending into many parts of northeastern America, the Shaker movement exhibited a surprising inner vitality, so much that in the end it outlived even those subsequent experiments in idealistic association, religious and transcendental, Owenite and Fourieristic, which flourished, mostly for brief periods, during the first half of the nineteenth century. The cloisters at

Ephrata are empty. Zoar, Ohio, and Economy, Pennsylvania, the homes of the German-origin societies of Separatists and Harmonists founded in the first quarter of the last century, are now deserted. The members of the Society of True Inspiration at Amana, Iowa, and of Noyes' Perfectionist colony at Oneida, New York, both founded before the middle of the century, no longer share their goods in common. The phalanxes are gone, and Icaria is only a dream. But the United Society of Believers, still clinging to its principles, has seen the passage of over a hundred and seventy years.

Its extinction, however, seems imminent. Adherence to the basic dogmas of celibacy and 'joint interest' has handicapped adjustment to a rapidly changing world. Loss of a once progressive spirit and leadership, together with a gradual depletion of numbers, has slowly weakened a one-time robust economic and social structure. Before the Civil War eighteen prosperous colonies proclaimed the vitality of a unique system of thought and life. Today but three remain, with a combined membership of less than fifty. The essential character of the Shaker movement has long been manifest; its ideals have been tested by experience; its influence has been exerted, and its chief contributions made. Though a few years yet will pass before the last Believer leaves the last community, the historical record of one of the purest, most successful, and in many respects most creative of new world socialisms is virtually complete. The time is right, therefore, for the full story to be told.

That this venture in socio-religious separatism was, to a degree, representative of the character and growth of America itself, invests the movement with special interest. 'The impulse towards communal organization,' as Constance Rourke has pointed out, 'formed a conspicuous strain in our history.' The 'single-minded community' (whether Pilgrims, Mennonites, Dunkers, Shakers, Fourierists, or the frontier hamlet) was a common type of settlement, representing 'wide-spread popular concerns' and reflecting a major aspect, therefore, of America's early social character. Such organizations produced, in Giedion's words, many of 'the constituent facts from which the future was to take its structure.' The religious communities, in particular, were manifestations of a spirit fostered by conditions in a new land. The human urge to remake life anew, to seek perfection, to bring heaven to earth, engendered many unorthodox doctrines and sectarian experiments which were free to work themselves out in terms of whatever merit they possessed. The ideas of plain people, touched by inspiration, found expression, over and over again, in utopian undertakings which in the aggregate do much to illuminate the temper of the young country.

These ideas and experiments attracted a lively contemporary interest and a continuing curiosity. Thousands joined such communities. The extensive literature about the Shakers, in particular, a literature running from the 1780's up to the present time, is evidence of the attraction this people has exercised to travelers from near and far, to legislators and theologians, to sociologists, economists, and historians, to artists and humorists, even to plain people — farmers, mechanics, and housewives — who recorded their impressions in the printed word. A wealth of information, aside from the profuse publications of the Shakers themselves, is here available: notably the early eye-witness records of the Rathbuns, West, Taylor, Plumer, and others; the accounts of such apostates as Brown, Haskett, and Lamson; the experiences of Elkins in the Senior Order; the travelogues of the Englishmen Buckingham, Finch, Combe, Dixon, and Baker; Nordhoff's *Communistic Societies of the United States;* the notes of the itinerant Scotch printer, A. J. Macdonald, discovered and later used by Noyes in his *History of American Socialisms, Shakerism — Its Meaning and Message,* by the eldresses Leila Taylor and Anna White; Robinson's *Concise History;* Hinds' *American Communities;* MacLean's pioneer studies in Shaker bibliography and the annals of the western societies; and recently, Melcher's *Shaker Adventure.* The early books and pamphlets by and about the Shakers were likely to be doctrinal or polemic. But as the United Society became established as part of the American scene, it attracted increasing attention as a social institution deserving of serious appraisal. Many accounts continued to be biased. Others were sympathetic, even laudatory: Hepworth Dixon, for instance, found in the movement a 'distinct genius' which was helping 'to shape and guide, in no slight and unseen measure, the spiritual career of the United States.' 'We are indebted to the Shakers,' was Noyes' considered belief, 'more than to any or all other Social Architects of modern times.'

Their writings were essential to research. A definitive history could not have been written, however, without recourse to the profuse but neglected material in manuscript: such sources as the original Shaker covenant, Benjamin Youngs's and Issachar Bates's western journals, Joseph Meacham's 'way-marks' on communal organization, Isaac Youngs's authoritative history or 'Concise View,' the influential 'Millennial Laws,' the letters, autobiographies, order books, accounts of meetings, and so forth. In such records the Shakers speak for themselves; not only do the records yield data nowhere else to be found, but in reading them we gain fresh insight into the forces motivating the behavior of these New World seekers: their strong convictions, their loyalty to certain ideals, the affirmations which were the fruit of dissent.

Had it not been for the inspiration furnished by the Believers themselves, however, this history might never have been written. A new world opened on that memorable day, in the fall of 1923, when Faith, my wife, and I stopped at the Hancock, Massachusetts, community to buy a loaf of Shaker bread. As we went on, from bread to chairs, from chairs and other forms of furniture to tools, from tools to the multiple things made by tools, and from these to books and manuscripts, prints and paintings, we found the Shakers the friendliest of people — sincere, hospitable, and once their confidence was won, helpful beyond measure. Led to believe that isolation had made them a 'peculiar' folk, and that the routine of the years had stereotyped them, we found them a very human people; nor had individuality been obliterated by the communal system. There was humor here, and breadth of interest, and above all, a quality best described as simple goodness. There was Sister Sadie Neale, for example — orchard deaconess, teacher, and postmistress at Mount Lebanon — who one day would sell us asparagus, cherries, or potatoes, on another, a collection of miscellaneous items she called 'trumpery,' and on a third, some unique document — delighting always in recounting an anecdote of the early days (she was 98 when she died), or singing and 'stepping' an early Shaker dance. There was Sister Alice Smith, of Hancock, who would stop her weaving to guide us into the remotest corners of the dwellings and shops, and who, one morning, produced from a chest in her 'retiring-room' the first inspirational painting we had ever seen, explaining how, as a young sister, she had sensed its significance, rescued it from destruction, and now wanted it (and others) to be forever preserved. There was Eldress Sarah Collins of the South Family, New Lebanon, left with the Shakers during the

Civil War, whose fingers were knotted by decades of seating chairs;
Elder Walter Shepherd, reserved but kind, whom we remember at
work in his carpentry shop, or sweeping the stone steps in front of
his dwelling; Eldress Emma Neale, a Shakeress for over ninety years,
and known to many in the world as a trustee of the Church; Eldress
Rosetta Stephens, a lover of flowers and songs, who walked firmly in
the spirit of the faith; Sister Marguerite Frost of Canterbury,
friend and guide in that lovely New Hampshire village; Eldress Fan-
nie Estabrook of the Hancock Church, quietly ministering now to her
family of six; Sister Jennie Wells, also at Hancock, from whom we
have received many treasures; the saintly Eldresses Anna Case of
Watervliet and Prudence Stickney of Sabbathday Lake. These, and
many more, most of them now gone, were personalities in their own
right. It was they, more perhaps than the material of their environ-
ment, who kindled in us a profound affection; they animated these
materials and made us aware of the kinship between the spirit of the
people and the quality of their craft. 'A history of the Shakers,'
wrote Hawthorne, 'will be a very curious book.' It will be seen that
misunderstanding, derision, and often persecution were their lot.
But today many would join with us, as latter-day witnesses, in testifying to their humanity and rectitude.

Since all the absorbing activities of research, collection, and pres-
entation have been jointly pursued, it is right that my wife should
be considered a close collaborator in consummating this work. In-
estimable encouragement was given us, in the beginning, by the late
Homer Eaton Keyes, the first editor of *The Magazine Antiques*,
whose imaginative scholarship always stood at the service of others.
Practical support, here gratefully recorded, came from the late
Mrs. Juliana Force, director of the Whitney Museum, and subsequently from the American Council of Learned Societies, the American Philosophical Society, and the Guggenheim Foundation. The
Western Reserve Historical Society, with its fine Shaker library, has
been a source of substantial aid. Valuable assistance was given by
Dr. Louis C. Jones, director of the New York State Historical Association; under his auspices the manuscript received constructive
criticism and the award by the Association of a Dixon Ryan Fox fellowship. Most earnestly, in conclusion, do I avow my indebtedness to
the Believers themselves. They will know, I am sure, that only by an

honest treatment of all data may the heritage of the order be most clearly revealed.

E.D.A.

Richmond, Massachusetts
April 1953

THE PEOPLE CALLED SHAKERS

We believed we were debtors to God in relation to Each other, and all men, to improve our time and Tallents in this Life, in that manner in which we might be most useful.

—Shaker Covenant, 1795

CHAPTER I

Ann Lee Leads the Way

At Manchester, in England,
This blessed fire began,
And like a flame in stubble,
From house to house it ran:
A few at first receiv'd it,
And did their lusts forsake,
And soon their inward power
Brought on a mighty shake.

— *Millennial Praises*, 1813

O N 14 July 1772, the constable of the manor of Manchester, England, entered in his expense account a bill for seventeen shillings which he had expended to quell a 'disturbance' — noted in the record as a 'breach of the Sabbath.' The outlay represented payment 1* of six pence to each of the twenty-four assistants required for the occasion, plus five shillings, sixpence for ale consumed after peace had been restored.

Five persons had been arrested, among them one John Lees, a blacksmith living on Toad Lane (now Todd Street), and his daughter Ann. The melee must have been rather violent, for charges of assault were later entered against the five, as well as a claim for damages for breakage of the ironwork on the house of a certain widow Shapley. They were arraigned the following day before Justice Peter Mainwaring, a physician serving on the commission of the peace, at the Mule Inn, where ale drinking again accompanied the proceedings. On the twenty-third the constable paid out one shilling, sixpence of the public moneys to the 'Jurors Baillif on prosecuting John Lees and his Daughter Ann,' and a week later presented a 'Bill of expenses

*The marginal reference numbers refer to the Notes which begin on page 299.

at the Mule when Justice Mainwaring attended to examine the Shak-
2 ers.' At the ensuing quarter sessions of the court, the blacksmith and
his daughter were sentenced to a month in prison.

Members of the sect thus popularly designated continued, however,
to disturb the peace. On 3 October of the same year, the constable
again had to summon aid to disperse a 'mob' which was threatening
to pull down the Cannon Street house of John Townley, a bricklayer
who had recently joined the order. Obviously a noisy Shaker meeting
was in progress, such as occurred two weeks later when the same
officer had to break into the Lees house on Toad Lane 'to apprehend
the gang' — damaging the 'breaches' to the extent of five shillings,
sixpence. One result of that affair was the detention of Ann's brother
James until he could find sureties.

Conflict with the law reached its climax late the next spring when
'Ann Lees a shaker' was re-arrested, this time for 'disturbing the
Congregation in the old Church,' an offense described in the *Man-
chester Mercury* of 20 July as follows:

Saturday last ended the Quarter Sessions, when John Townley, John
3 Jackson, Betty Lees, and Ann Lees (Shakers), for going into Christ
Church, in Manchester, and there wilfully and contemptuously, in the
time of Divine service, disturbing the congregation then assembled at
morning prayers in the said church, were severally fined £20 each.

Inability to pay the fine resulted in a prison term of unrecorded
length. The constable's accounts for 30 May state that Ann was detained in the 'Prison room for two days with an attendant, and maintained with meat and drink.' A later reference (28 July) recorded the
expenditure of three shillings for 'attending Ann Lees two whole
nights.' In a testimony many years later, the blacksmith's daughter
said she was kept in a 'stone prison' for two weeks and then transferred to the 'house of correction.'

At the time of these incidents Ann Lees was in her middle thirties,
a short, rather stout woman with a fair complexion, blue eyes, and
light chestnut-brown hair. 'Her countenance was mild and expressive,' writes one biographer, 'but grave and solemn. Her glance was
keen and penetrating; her countenance inspired confidence and respect. Many called her beautiful.'

Up to this period, her life had been uneventful, and even the annals of her family are obscure. The registry of the fifteenth-century Manchester cathedral, the 'old Church' mentioned before, has no record of her birth — which Shaker tradition places on or about 29 February 1736 — but contains an entry of her private baptism on 1 June, 1742. She was the second eldest of eight children, five sons, and three daughters. Her mother receives little notice in Shaker history, and we do not even know her given name, only that she was 'esteemed as a very pious woman.' Her father supplemented his earnings by tailoring. An uncle may have been a London sheriff and an alderman of Algate ward. Ann herself had no schooling, and early in her teens went to work in a textile mill, first as a cutter of velvet and a helper in preparing cotton for the looms, and later as a shearer of hatters' fur. At the age of twenty she was serving as cook in a public infirmary, perhaps the 'house with twelve beds' which had been planned at a meeting in the Old Coffee House in 1752 and for which one 'John Lees' had been appointed, among others, to receive donations. The fact that this institution also received mental cases may account for the rumor, later circulated in the manor, that the 'Lees woman' was once 'confined to a madhouse.'

The turning-point in her life came in 1758, when she was twenty-two. In September of that year she joined a society of religious dissenters led by Jane and James Wardley (or Wardlaw), Quaker tailors living in Bolton-on-the-Moors, a bleak little town twelve miles northeast of Manchester. Some ten years or so before, the Wardleys had come under the influence of the French Prophets, or Camisards, a radical sect of Calvinists from the mountains of the Cevennes, numbers of whom, after the revocation of the Edict of Nantes in 1685, had sought civil and religious freedom and refuge from persecution in England. Scattered groups of Prophets continued to hold semi-secret meetings in various parts of the British Isles, loosely federated under the leadership of Benjamin du Plan, Antoine Court's associate in France, who had settled in London in 1738. Six years later, according to Tylor, there still existed in that city 'a remnant of the Cevenol prophets, or of their descendants, who, though despised and derided by almost all classes, had even succeeded in gaining some new adherents.' Among these were the Wardleys who, about the year 1747, received from the exiled Prophets that 'further degree of light and power' by which they were separated from the Society of Friends.

Apparently the Bolton tailors had been affected, through du Plan or others, by the more extreme beliefs and practices of the Camisards. In France, Court had dissociated himself from the prevalent fanaticism and disorderly behavior of the so-called *inspires*, calling for their suppression and the restoration of discipline. But the earliest Shaker worship of which we have a record duplicates, in its ecstasy of spirit and various manifestations, the marvels reported from the Cevennes: the fasts, the trances, the agitations of head and limbs, the prophecies concerning the end of the world and the Second Coming of Christ, the calls for repentance, the miracles of heavenly voices, lights in the sky and other 'signs,' the testimonies of supernatural succor in times of distress. A Wardley meeting might begin in true Quaker fashion, the worshippers sitting awhile in silent meditation. Then they would be taken

. . . with a mighty trembling, under which they would express the indignation of God against all sin. At other times they were affected, under the power of God, with a mighty shaking; and were occasionally exercised in singing, shouting, or walking the floor, under the influence of spiritual signs, shoving each other about, — or swiftly passing and
6 repassing each other, like clouds agitated by a mighty wind.

Like their antecedents, these early Shakers, or 'Shaking Quakers' as they were sometimes called, had no clearly formulated doctrine. Their prophecies — often, as with the Camisards, the passionate utterances of women — partook of the same millennial, apocalyptic, and anti-clerical character. Thus Mother Jane, the leading spirit of the English movement, would exhort her followers to

. . . amend your lives. Repent. For the kingdom of God is at hand. The new heaven and new earth prophesied of old is about to come. The marriage of the Lamb, the first resurrection, the new Jerusalem descending from above, these are even now at the door. And when Christ appears again, and the true church rises in full and transcendant glory, then all anti-Christian denominations — the priests, the church, the pope — will be swept away.

England at this time was entering an era characterized by forces of change and popular unrest. The energetic Pitt was assuming political power, and the zealous evangelism of George Whitefield and the Wesleys was producing a revival of religion in marked contrast to the indifference and lethargy which had previously existed. Lancashire was a center of the 'great awakening': the only propertied member of the Wardley order, John Hocknell, had formerly been a Methodist; and Ann herself had been one of Whitefield's 'hearers,' holding him to have 'great powers and gifts of God.' One cannot help but feel that this new spirit, beginning to arouse the common people to an increasing awareness of their rights, may have had its influence on the discontented toiler in the mills, accounting in part for her defection from the Anglican faith.

For some time after joining the Wardley society Ann Lees does not appear to have been a very active member. But four years later an event occurred which was largely instrumental in confirming her faith, and ultimately in elevating her to the position of leadership. This was her marriage, on 5 January 1762, to Abraham Standerin (or Stanley), a Manchester blacksmith who may have worked for her father, a lusty, good-humored fellow, 'kind according to nature,' but temperamentally unsuited to the woman he had wed. Ann had apparently not yet renounced the Anglican faith, for the banns were published in the cathedral on the three consecutive weeks of 20 and 27 December 1761, and the following January third. Two days later, in the presence of James Shepherd and Thomas Hulme, the ceremony took place, the illiterate principals signing the registry with crosses. There is no evidence that Ann desired the marriage. Perhaps she took the step on the importunity of parents anxious to win their daughter away from the heresies of the Wardley faith.

The next few years were critical ones. Four children were born of the marriage, all of whom died in infancy. The deliveries were difficult, and in the case of the last child, Elizabeth, forceps had to be

Banns of Marriage _Abraham Standerin and Ann Lees were Published on Sunday Decr 20th 27th and January 3^d 1762 this said_

N° 7 _abraham Standerin_ – of _this_ Parish _and Town of Manchester_

Blacksmith — and _Ann Lees_ — of _this_ Parish _and Town of Manchester_ _Spinster_ — were Married in this _Church_ by _Banns_ this _fifth_ — Day of _January_ — in the Year One Thousand Seven Hundred and _Sixty One_ — by me _Maurice Griffith_

This Marriage was solemnized between Us { abraham Standerin mark / ann Lees mark

In the Preference of _James Shepherd_ _Tho^o Hulme_

BANNS OF MARRIAGE, ABRAHAM STANDERIN AND ANN LEES

7 used, the patient lying for hours 'with but little appearance of life.'
The tragic experiences of these years not only undermined Ann's
health, both physical and mental, but strongly conditioned her views
toward sex and the institution of marriage. Her first reactions were
guilt, shame, and aversion. She saw the deaths of her children as a
series of judgments on her 'concupiscence.' Fearing to stir up the
affections of her husband, her testimony reads, she began to avoid
her bed 'as if it had been made of embers.' She was afraid to sleep lest
she 'awake in hell'; and night after night she walked the floor in her
stocking feet, laboring for a sense of the word of God. So great was
her anguish, in this struggle against the flesh, that 'bloody sweat'
pressed through the pores of her skin, tears flowed down her cheeks
until the skin 'cleaved off,' and she wrung her hands until the blood
'gushed from under her nails' — her only comfort being the thought
that when weariness came she would be 'released by the refreshing
operations of the power of God.' Groans and cries in the night made
the family tremble, and once her agitation was so great that her bed
rocked violently and her husband was 'glad to leave it.'

Remorse and misgivings developed in time into the conviction that
only by a full mortification of the body could her soul be purified. She
not only abstained from sleep but denied herself 'every gratification
of a carnal nature,' eating and drinking only what was 'mean and
poor' — that her soul 'might hunger for nothing but God.' Her flesh
wasted away, and she became so weak that she had to be fed and supported by others. The 'last remains of human depravity' being finally
discarded, Ann experienced a complete conversion. 'My soul broke
forth to God,' her testimony continues, 'which I felt as sensibly as ever
a woman did a child, when she was delivered of it.' She had been born
into the spiritual kingdom, she affirmed, feeling at first like an infant
8 bewildered by the colors and objects of a strange world.

Following the death of her last child in October 1766, Ann Lees
assumed a more zealous role in the Wardley order. During her ordeal
the Wardleys had been a source of personal comfort, and their meetings a means of emotional release. But once her health was restored,
participation was infused with a sense of mission. What she had un-
dergone as an individual, she came to believe, was really a universal
struggle. In retrospect, the deaths of her children were 'a particular
means of increasing her conviction of the deplorable loss of the human

race.' 'Cohabitation of the sexes' was the cardinal sin, the source of all evil. Even before she proclaimed this doctrine in the Wardley meetings, she had had violent arguments with Abraham, who complained of his wife's conduct to the cathedral authorities; had antagonized her brothers by outspoken diatribes against 'sin'; and had incurred her father's wrath by warning her mother against acts of 'carnal indulgence.'

Though several years were to elapse before Ann replaced Mother Jane as head of the Shaker sect, its moral discipline gradually became more strict, its testimony against the flesh more pointed. The temporal condition of the order, already strengthened by the advent of the propertied Townley, was also improved, about this time, by the admission of one John Hocknell of Cheshire, his wealthy brother-in-law; John Partington of Mayor-town (Mereton); James Shep-herd, the witness at Ann's marriage; and the Whittaker family — Jonathan, his wife Ann Lee (a distant cousin of the blacksmith), and their son James. Particularly surprising was the conversion of two members of Ann's own family, her father and her younger brother William — the tall, powerful Father William of Shaker history, who after an apprenticeship with his father had served as an officer of horse in a regiment of the King's guard, the Oxford Blues. Two relatives had also joined, Nancy Lees, a niece of the blacksmith, and Betty Lees, his cousin or sister-in-law. Hocknell supported a number of poor members at his own house, which alternated with the Townley and Partington homes, and later with the Lees's, as gathering places of the 'church.'

Increased membership and sharpened convictions — the open condemnation of lust, criticism of the established church for 'condoning' marriage, denunciation of worldliness of every kind — resulted in more tempestuous meetings, conclaves which often lasted well into the night, disturbing the neighborhood and provoking widespread resentment and suspicion. Tales of the strange worship, with its shakings, tongue-speaking, and dark prophecies, spread throughout the manor and surrounding towns. Charges of fanaticism, heresy, even of witchcraft, were raised against the sect, breeding a spirit of intolerance and leading, eventually, to overt acts of oppression. As narrated by Ann and others, the accounts of such persecution, reminiscent of those told of the French Prophets, throw considerable light on the comparable Shaker mind — the faith in a protective Providence, the belief in miracles and signs, the delusions of grandeur. Witness her testimony of an encounter with one of her brothers who sought to 'overcome her will':

So he brought a staff, about the size of a large broom handle; and came to me, while I was sitting in my chair, and singing by the power of God. He spoke to me; but I felt no liberty to answer. Will you not answer me? said he.

He then beat me over my face and nose, with his staff, till one end of it was much splintered. But I sensibly felt and saw the bright rays of the glory of God, pass between my face and his staff, which shielded off the blows, so that he had to stop and call for drink.

While he was refreshing himself, I cried to God for His healing power. He then turned the other end of his staff, and began to beat me again. While he continued striking, I felt my breath, like healing balsam, streaming from my mouth and nose, which healed me, so that I felt no harm from his stroke, but he was out of breath, like one which had been running a race.

10

On another occasion, a mob which had set out to stone Ann and four companions fell into contention when the missiles failed to find their target. 'While they were throwing their stones,' she recalled, 'I felt surrounded with the presence of God, and my soul was filled with love.' Providence interceded again when a 'rabble' bound her hand and foot and tried to throw her from an upper window. Escaping a third time, she lay all one night on the ice of an isolated pond, 'in great peace and consolation and without taking cold.'

Intervention was sometimes human. Once, as she was being driven out of a town by 'a great mob' — who knocked her down with clubs, kicked and abused her for nearly two miles — 'a certain nobleman, living at some distance, who knew nothing of what was passing . . . being remarkably wrought upon in his mind,' ordered his horse and, arriving at the scene, commanded the crowd to disperse. In another crisis a friendly neighbor concealed the prophetess in an attic room by covering her with wool.

When the church authorities finally took cognizance of the Shaker heresy, they brought charges of blasphemy against Ann, summoning her before a council of four 'learned ministers.' But again the Lord succored her. Her accusers had threatened, she said, to brand her cheek and bore her tongue with a hot iron but, being moved to speak to them 'in many tongues of the wonderful works of God,' they saw she was truly inspired and released her. In one version of the story, she spoke in twelve languages, including French, Hebrew, Greek, and Latin; in another, in seventy-two different tongues, 'so perfectly that they flattered me with an offer to teach the languages.' This examination may have been the immediate aftermath of the incident in which the Lees 'wilfully and contemptuously' disturbed the congregation in the 'old Church.'

The imprisonment of Ann Lees in the house of correction marked her ascendancy to leadership in the sect. To her associates she had now become a martyr as well as a saint, an inspired leader on whom had fallen the mantle of Christ. A kind of apotheosis accompanied her release. The Shakers placed full credence in her story of the 'cruelty' of the jailers, who had detained her for fourteen days in a cell so small she could not straighten herself, who had locked the door and given her nothing to eat or drink, keeping her there 'four days longer than they could reasonably expect that anyone could live without food.' They marveled at the means by which she had escaped starvation — the devoted, youthful James Whittaker once in every twenty-four hours, under cover of darkness, injected the stem of a pipe through the keyhole, pouring wine and milk into the bowl to nourish his beloved leader. Like other tales of the prophetess, these were exaggerations. Prisoners were not starved to death for breaking the Sabbath. Furthermore, in the Manchester house of correction the inmates were kept on the second floor, where there could be no keyhole accessible to the street. Such legends have significance, however, as examples of the persecutory complex which in the early years of the movement frequently characterized Shaker testimony.

It was in prison that Ann Lees beheld the 'grand vision of the very transgression of the first man and woman in the Garden of Eden, the cause wherein all mankind was lost and separated from God.' Here Christ appeared to her, comforting her with His presence and commissioning her to preach the gospel of the stainless life. Indeed, the concept, central in Shaker thought, that the spirit of Christ had so suffused her being that she regarded herself as His special instrument, seems to have taken form at this time. 'It is not I that speak,' she told her followers, 'it is Christ who dwells in me.'

The sublimation of spirit which was the outcome of this mystic experience was attested by many witnesses. 'I converse with Christ!,' she cries on one occasion, 'I feel him present with me, as sensibly as I feel my hands together!' And again: 'I have been walking in fine vallies with Christ, as with a lover . . . I am married to the Lord Jesus Christ. He is my head and my husband, and I have no other! I have walked, hand in hand, with him in heaven . . . I feel the blood of Christ running through my soul and body, washing me; Him do I acknowledge, as my head and Lord.' Emerging from the 'dark dungeon' by the Irwell River, Ann could say to her companions, 'I am Ann the Word.' The 'candle of the Lord,' they saw, had passed from Mother Jane — now recognized as a 'John the Baptist in the female line' — into the hands of a new witness, enabling her, 'by the light thereof, to search every heart and try every soul.' She took the title of 'Mother,' or 'Mother of the new creation' and, in the house of John Townley on Cannon Street, formally assumed the leadership of the order.

No theology had yet been formulated, no organization effected. At this stage the movement revolved about a single personality, presenting a situation strikingly similar to that created by Ann's English contemporary, Joanna Southcott, the servant girl of Devonshire, who had also escaped from the reality of sex to find satisfaction in fantasy, who likewise had read in Eden's sin the fall of man and burden of woman, and as 'Mother' or 'the woman clothed with the sun,' in like manner had heard the call to redeem the race. Mother Ann's doctrine was simple: confession was the door to the regenerate life, celibacy its rule and cross. Her contribution to the Wardley faith was the concept that the world's wrongs — war, disease, slavery, famine, poverty, the inequality of the sexes, human 'depravity' — were all the result of 'concupiscence.' Into the nature of humankind the deceit of the devil had been craftily diffused. To expose that 'ugly serpent,' and by sharp reproof rend 'the glossy covering which like a mantle covered the doleful works of the flesh' — this was the mission of the true church. For only by freeing oneself absolutely from such bondage could one achieve complete salvation.

The Shakers were unmolested in the ten-month period between Ann's release from prison and the departure for America. Evidently their exuberant worship — 'singing and dancing, shaking, and shouting, speaking with new tongues and prophesying, with all those various gifts of the Holy Ghost known in the primitive Church' — was tolerated as long as the gospel was not publicly proclaimed in the streets or churches. No increase in numbers, however, is recorded.

With the exception of Townley, Hocknell, and Partington, the members of the sect were poor laborers — mill hands, mechanics, housewives, and servants — who worked during the day and assembled in the evenings for worship. Their leader's decision to go to America was doubtless conditioned by the restrictions on her preaching and the failure of the society to progress in the country of its birth.

To the Shakers, however, it was a divine call. In repeated revelations the prophetess had seen a chosen people awaiting her in New England. One night, when the little group of Believers in Christ's Second Appearing were resting by the roadside on their twenty-mile walk to the Hocknell and Partington homes, James Whittaker had a vision of the church of Christ in America, which was like a large tree whose leaves 'shone with such brightness, as made it appear like a burning torch.' A meeting was appointed to discuss the venture, at which 'there were so many gifts in confirmation of our coming . . . that some could hardly wait for others to tell their gifts; and we had a joyful meeting, and danced till morning.' In the spring of 1774, the mission chosen and their temporal affairs settled, Mother Ann delegated Hocknell to make arrangements for the passage to the new world.

On board the ship *Mariah* (Captain Smith of New York), which sailed from Liverpool on 10 May, were eight members of the original Shaker order: Ann and William Lees, James Whittaker, James Shepherd, John Hocknell and his son Richard, Mary (the wife of John Partington), and Nancy Lees. Also on board, strange to relate, was Ann's husband, the enigmatic Abraham Standerin, the shadowy antagonist in the drama. Abraham may have maintained a tenuous connection with the movement, but his motive in joining the hegira was more likely an economic one. Hesitancy to leave an established occupation, together with the fact that Ann's mother was never a confirmed Shaker, probably accounts for the absence of John Lees. On the Wardleys, who left the society either as an aftermath of Ann's rise to power or in protest against its radical doctrines, and on the early Shaker, John Townley, at whose house the Wardleys had taken lodgings, the curtain also falls. The Quaker tailors who had pioneered the movement were soon to seek refuge in the almshouse, and the remnants of the society drifted back into the 'common course' of the world.

CHAPTER II

Opening the Testimony in America

Near Albany they settled,
And waited for a while,
Until a mighty shaking
Made all the desert smile.
At length a gentle whisper,
The tidings did convey,
And many flock'd to Mother,
To learn the living way.

— *Millennial Praises*, 1813

THE SHIP *Mariah* nearly foundered on the voyage. During a storm she sprang a leak, owing to a loosened plank, and though the crew and passengers together worked hard at the pumps, the ship filled with water and appeared to be doomed. At this critical juncture, Ann told the captain to be of good cheer. 'Not a hair of our heads shall perish,' she promised, 'and we shall arrive safely in America. For I was just now sitting by the mast, and I saw a bright angel of God, through whom I received the promise.' As she spoke a great wave, striking the vessel, forced the loose plank back into place, and soon after all were released from the pumps.

After a three-month voyage, Ann and her disciples disembarked in New York harbor on 6 August 1774. It was a quiet Sabbath afternoon. The townsfolk were sunning themselves outside their doors, gazing idly at the passers-by, when the little body of Believers, detached from the other passengers, came marching resolutely up 'Broad Way.' Turning in at Queen-street (now Pearl Street), they continued their pace until they came to a house occupied by a family named Cunningham. Here the group came to a halt, the leader went up to the

14

mistress of the house, who was sitting outside, and addressing her by
name made the startling announcement: 'I am commissioned of the
Almighty God to preach the everlasting Gospel to America, and an
Angel commanded me to come to this house, and to make a home for
me and my people.'   13

So goes the story. Whether the woman's name was Cunningham, or
Smith, as related in another version, is irrelevant. The austere bearing of the stranger aroused respectful sympathy. The company was
taken in and kindly treated. Ann herself was given domestic employment in the Queen-street house, and Abraham worked as a journey-
man in the husband's smithy.

Although they had now gained their first objective, the Shakers
lacked an immediate plan of action. Even at this early stage of the
movement it was their Quaker-like custom to wait for inspiration to
direct their steps. Each went his or her own way. A mutual desire existed, however, for a permanent base of operations and, when they
were informed by some Friends of a tract of cheap land near Albany,
Hocknell, William Lee,* and Whittaker went up the Hudson River
to investigate. The section, in a district known by the Indian name
of Niskeyuna, about eight miles northwest of Albany, proved to be   14
chiefly wooded and low swampland, a desolate wilderness country. But
the enterprising river town of Albany offered a convenient means of
subsistence for William, the blacksmith, and James, who was a
weaver; and with the capital provided by Hocknell the three took a
short-term lease from Peter Van Stuyvesant, the owner of the property. After a piece of land had been cleared, a crude log cabin was
erected, with a room on the first floor for the 'sisters' and one on the
second floor for the 'brethren.' Lee and Whittaker traveled back and
forth to Albany, where the former was taken into the employ of one
Jesse Fairchild. In the spring, under Whittaker's supervision, work
was begun on a small farm, which was tended by Shepherd, the two
Hocknells, Nancy Lees, and Mary Partington. After the settlement
was under way John Hocknell returned to New York, where he embarked for England to fetch his wife Hannah and his friend John
Partington.

In the meantime, except for one or two visits to Niskeyuna, Mother

---

* After the Believers reached America the family name of the prophetess and her
brother was shortened, in Shaker usage, to *Lee*. The civil and military authorities, however, used her married name, Ann(e) Standerin.

Ann remained in New York, earning her living by washing and ironing. Whether or not she shared her lodging with Abraham we do not know, and the mystery surrounding their relationship persists. Did Ann stay behind in the city because it was imperative that every Shaker be gainfully employed? Did she hope that she might still win her husband to the divine fellowship? Or was the flesh still in contention with the spirit? She retained her married name and, when the blacksmith fell ill, was sufficiently loyal to give up work to nurse him back to health. But the bond was obviously weak. Abraham frequented the taverns, led a debauched existence, and once brought to Ann's room a woman of the streets, threatening to desert her for this creature unless she renounced her celibate vows. For the prophetess, on the eve of realizing her splendid dream of a New Jerusalem, there was but one alternative, and sometime in the year 1775, after thirteen years of unhappy wedlock, her final tie with the 'world' was severed. For the remainder of the year she lived alone in the direst poverty, being reduced to such necessity that once her only shelter was a small, unheated, bedless room 'with only a cold stove for a seat and her only morsel . . . a cruse of vinegar.' Conditions improved about Christmas time, when the Hocknells and John Partington arrived from England, and by spring the colony up the river was in shape to house the entire company.

Settlement was probably speeded by the political excitement and unrest then prevalent in New York, the town to which George Washington had shifted his troops when the British, after their evacuation of Boston in March 1776, embarked on plans to gain control of the Hudson-Champlain route to Canada. Before the Howes appeared off the strategic post, however, Ann had joined her companions at Niskeyuna.

There was little opportunity for the English messiah to preach the gospel in a wilderness inhabited only by roving Iroquois and the scattered families of white settlers. The immediate problem was sustenance, which imposed on the pioneers a rigid discipline of hand labor; trees had to be felled, swamps drained, land tilled, and buildings erected for present and future needs. But with the money brought in by blacksmithing, weaving, and shoemaking — the first trades in the church — and the aid supplied by Hocknell, the small community gradually improved its domain, and in 1779 a frame house was completed, only to burn to the ground quite soon after it had been raised.

Hardships of manual toil these early believers patiently endured, but the failure of the faith to attract attention was a great tribulation. Ann's followers had anticipated no difficulty in the spreading of the Word, and when year after year passed with little accomplished, they approached the point of being bitterly disillusioned. But the divine promise upheld their leader. 'O my dear children,' she would tell the family, 'hold fast, and be not discouraged. God has not sent us into this land in vain; but he has sent us to bring the gospel to this nation, who are deeply lost in sin; and there are great numbers who will embrace it, and the time draws nigh.' Again, when William Lee asked his sister if she believed the gospel would ever open to the world, she answered: 'Yea brother William, I certainly know it will; and the time is near at hand when they will come like doves.' But Ann was often dispirited; and it is told how she would wander alone into the woods and by the streams, in deep anguish crying out: 'O, that the fishes of the sea, and fowls of the air, and all things that have life and breath, yea all the trees of the forest and grass of the fields would pray to God for me!' Only by daily, sometimes hourly, worship were the hopes of the Niskeyuna society sustained and its union preserved.

Though only one stranger, a neighbor by the name of Eleanor Vedder, gave her allegiance to the church, preparations to receive the 'great numbers' never slackened. Three years after the first cabin was 15 built, the temporal condition of the settlement was one of 'comfort.' In the spring of 1779, Ann gave orders to lay up surplus stores of provisions, saying, 'We shall have company enough, before another year comes about, to consume it all.' The following winter she had repeated visions of people flocking to hear the Word.

The feeble church at Niskeyuna drew its initial support from the religious excitement known in New England as the Great Awakening. Starting back in 1734, when Jonathan Edwards of Northampton, Massachusetts, began to preach his powerful sermons on justification by faith alone, and further stimulated by the popular evangelistic tours of George Whitefield in the 1740's, revivalistic outbreaks were 16 still common when the Shakers founded their first colony. People still debated the issues of free will, human responsibility, vital piety, the part played by good works in the scheme of salvation. Groups of people still looked forward to an imminent judgment day. In the

Congregational Church the schism between the 'Old Lights' and the 'New Lights,' or Separatists, who believed in good works and conditional salvation, remained as irreconcilable as ever, with the Baptists constantly enlisting under their Arminian banner large numbers from the Separatist congregations.

In June 1779, one such revival broke out among the New Light Baptists in New Lebanon, New York; Hancock, Massachusetts; and adjacent towns. The leaders of the movement were Joseph Meacham, a lay preacher from Enfield, Connecticut, and the Reverend Samuel Johnson, who had been the first pastor of the Presbyterian church in New Lebanon. During the summer, meetings were held in the barn of George Darrow, a prosperous farmer living on the slope of the Taconic mountain range in the eastern part of New Lebanon township. Here there was a nightly scene of wild, exalted preaching; of visions, signs, operations, and prophetic utterances; of shouting, screaming, and the falling of men and women 'as if wounded in battle.' The revival was hailed as an event immediately precedent to the millennium itself, when all systems of religions, it was proclaimed, would fall before the triumphant second coming of Christ. The excitement lasted until the late fall, when the ardor abated, leaving the people exhausted by excess of emotion and in despair over the continued absence of their Lord.

On a March day of the new year, two disillusioned subjects of this revival, Talmadge Bishop and Reuben Wight, were on their way westward to seek new fortunes when by chance they came upon Mother Ann's obscure community. Cordially welcomed and invited to stay for the night, the wayfarers witnessed the strange Shaker worship and were deeply impressed by the testimony that the Christ for whom they had waited in vain, had already made His appearance. The resurrection, they were told, was not a day of reckoning coming with catastrophic suddenness to all mankind. When any man confessed his sins, then he was personally saved and resurrected; when he entered into the life of the spirit, then for him the 'world' was at an end. For those nourished on the belief of a universal judgment day, this was revolutionary doctrine. And when Bishop and Wight expressed their astonishment, Ann told them 'that we are the people who turn the world upside down.' *

* 'The World Turned Upside Down' was an old English song with which Mother Ann was undoubtedly familiar. It was dolefully played by British bands on the occasion of Cornwallis' surrender at Yorktown.

With minds vacillating between skepticism and belief, the couple hastened back to New Lebanon to recount their experience to Joseph Meacham, who straightway delegated one of his ablest associates, Calvin Harlow, to investigate the new religion and, in particular, to put this query to its female head:

Saint Paul says, Let your women keep silence in the Churches; for it is not permitted unto them to speak; but they are commanded to be under obedience, as also saith the law. And if they will learn any thing, let them ask their husbands at home; for it is a shame for a woman to speak in the Church. But you not only speak, but seem to be an Elder in your Church. How do you reconcile this with the Apostle's doctrine?   18

When Harlow reached Niskeyuna, he duly interrogated the prophetess, whose answer represents the first official expression of her Messianic pretensions:

The order of man, in the natural relation [she explained], is a figure of the order of God in the spiritual creation. As the order of nature requires a man and a woman to produce offspring; so, where they both stand in their proper order, the man is the first, and the woman the second in the government of the family. He is the father and she the Mother; and all the children, both male and female, must be subject to their parents; and the woman, being second, must be subject to her husband, who is the first; but when the man is gone, the right of government belongs to the woman: So is the family of Christ.   19

While it was difficult to accept without reservations the contention that any mortal, especially a woman living unknown in the woods, should be invested with the authority of Christ, Harlow also fell under the spell of Ann's magnetic personality and persuasive logic, succumbed to the enchantment of the Shaker worship, and departed virtually convinced that this was indeed the long-awaited Coming. So enthusiastic was his report that Meacham, accompanied by Amos Hammond, another Baptist elder, and Aaron Kibbee, decided to see for himself the mysterious 'woman of the new birth.'

The meeting of the New Light and Shaker leaders was as momentous to the destiny of the sect as that earlier occasion when the flickering torch of the Camisards was passed on to the Wardleys. 'Divinely informed' of the time of the strangers' arrival, sensing the great opportunity before her, Ann had made special preparations for the reception of 'the first man in America.' As the delegation entered the

Shaker dwelling on that historic May morning, the tableau presented must indeed have been striking: in one group the Americans, with the tall, erect, slim figure of Meacham in the lead, his high forehead and pale countenance sterner than ever, his brooding hazel eyes glancing curiously about the assembly; and facing them the standard-bearer of a new dispensation, Ann, 'the elect lady,' calm and grave, with her chief disciple, the dynamic Whittaker, by her side, and her small band of faithful followers grouped eagerly behind her.

After greetings had been exchanged and the travelers given refreshment, Meacham opened the interview by asking Whittaker, whom Ann had appointed as her spokesman, why the church at Niskeyuna maintained such a singular faith and manner of life.

'We have been laboring for years,' replied the young Shaker, 'in the work of the regeneration. We have actually risen with Christ, and travel with Him in the Resurrection.' And Whittaker went on to explain the nature of sin and the imperative role of confession and abnegation.

The argument must have carried conviction, for Meacham finally admitted: 'If you have attained to that of God, which we have not, we should be glad to share with you; for we want to find the best way to be saved.'

'If you are ever saved by Christ,' Whittaker warned him in reply, 'it must be by walking as he walked. And if you have committed sins, you must confess them to those witnesses in whom Christ has taken up his abode.' To find a relation to Christ, he insisted — citing the law of Moses and the cases of Achan, Joshua, and John the Baptist — it was necessary to come first to His witnesses.

Then from Meacham came the challenge: 'Are *you* perfect? Do *you* live without sin?'

'The Power of God, revealed in this day,' Whittaker answered, 'does enable souls to cease from sin; and we have received that power; we have actually left off committing sin, and we live in daily obedience to the will of God.'

But the cost was high. 'You must forsake the marriage of the flesh,' Ann admonished the visitors, 'or you cannot be married to the Lamb, nor have any share in the resurrection of Christ.'

As the day-long interview progressed, interrupted once by a period of worship, all objections in the minds of Meacham and his companions vanished. They had been presented with a specific program of salvation far more satisfying than the theoretical vagaries of the revival. As heirs to the Manichaean and Puritan traditions of the conflict of flesh with spirit, it was not difficult for them to accept the premise that to purify the soul all carnal thought and practices must be repudiated. Did not Christ set, in this respect, a supreme example? Why was it not possible to raise oneself from the generative plane to a superior order, a spiritual plane, His plane of living? The doctrine of works, the remarkable 'gifts' of worship, the peace and harmony of the Shaker fellowship seemed to set the seal of truth on the claim that the millennium was here and now. Though the 'cross' was great, the reward was membership in a divine order akin to the primitive church of Jerusalem. Next to Talmadge Bishop, Meacham became Ann's first American convert, her 'first-born son,' to whom, she foretold, would fall the lot of 'gathering' the Church after her own decease.

On the famous 'dark day' of 10 May 1780 — 'though there were neither clouds nor smoke in the atmosphere, the sun did not appear all that day through parts of New England, and people were out wringing their hands and howling, "The day of Judgment is come" ' [20] — the first public opening of the testimony was held at Niskeyuna. Subjects of the New Lebanon revival, still anxious over the problem of salvation, had been deeply affected by the reports of their leaders and the corroborating tales of miracles, gifts of healing, mysterious 'signs,' and singular rituals. That the group near Albany were 'Europeans,' that they had settled in the wilderness, that they were led by a woman with apparently supernatural powers, roused the curiosity even of people not religiously disposed. The log house which served both as dwelling and church was therefore crowded on that inaugural day in May; and for the next two months, as Ann had prophesied, people came 'in droves.' There was need for the surplus provisions, and house room was so limited that often the prophetess and her family slept on the floor.

In the early public meetings and 'interviews' with individuals, the subject of lust — 'the lust of the flesh, the lust of the eye and the pride of life' — was the constant theme. 'The deceitful wantonness of both male and female,' Ann preached, was at the root of hatred, envy, jealousy, and murder among individuals and of destruction, rapine, and war among nations. It brought 'distress and poverty, shame and dis-

grace upon families and individuals, and fills the earth with wretched-
ness and misery.' Unless such 'filthy gratifications' were denied, there
could be no travel toward perfection. Frank and searching was her
testimony. In words 'quick, sharp and powerful as lightning' she reproved young men for tempting and seducing young women, young
women for artfully attracting and ensnaring young men, and parents
for 'building up' their children 'to allure the eyes of the different sex.'
If passions were not overcome in this world, she warned, they would
become more powerful in the world of spirits. In hell sinners would
be 'bound and tormented in the same parts where they have taken
their carnal pleasure.' The fearful consequences of departure from
God's ordinances were not more vividly presented by Jonathan Edwards himself.

James Whittaker, who had been subject to Mother Ann's influence
from early youth, was obsessed with this theme. A gifted speaker, he
swayed his listeners, both young and old, with his fierce diatribes
against the seat of sin. Shouts of approbation greeted his impas-
sioned pleas: 'Blessed are all those that are not defiled by women.'
'Blessed are all those young virgins that never were defiled by men.'
'There is no need of any person's trying the flesh, in order to know
what it is. We have a blessed altar, and it is placed in the garden of
Eden! No one has a right to eat thereon, but such as hate lust.' As
for himself, Whittaker thanked the Lord that he had never had 'carnal knowledge of any woman.' So completely had he subdued the flesh,
he said, that he had 'no more lust than an infant' or 'a child unborn.'

Disapproval of marriage was a logical concomitant of such doctrine. The typical attitude was that expressed by Ann to Jonathan
Slosson, who was in love with a certain young woman: 'The marriage
of the flesh is a covenant with death, and an agreement with hell *
. . . if you want to marry, you may marry the Lord Jesus Christ.'
Censure embraced all marital relations. Laboring with those who were
'bound in their affections' to their married children, the witnesses
bluntly told them their real duty was to the 'believing children.' Elder
James — whose peculiar gift it was 'to wean the affections of the
Believers from natural relations and earthly ties' — used to tell his
audiences that 'your natural relations are very much sunk in an old
rotten profession; and if you do not separate yourself from them,

* The abolitionist, William Lloyd Garrison, later applied this same phrase to the
Constitution when reminded by the South that it recognized slavery.

their sins will become your sins. If you give your minds to labor upon the things of the world, they will become corrupted.' Confession itself was only the first step of salvation: one must forsake sin and those who sinned. Inherent in such doctrine was the necessity of physical as well as spiritual separation from the world.

That marriage was not utterly condemned, however, is indicated by a conversation between Ann and one Daniel Moseley, to whom she said:

Do not go away and report that we forbid to marry; for unless you are able to take up a full cross, and part with every gratification of the flesh, for the Kingdom of God, I would counsel you, and all such, to take wives in a lawful manner, and cleave to them only; and raise up a lawful posterity, and be perpetual servants to your families: for of all lustful gratifications that is the least sin.   21

Until experience could contribute to the formulation of a system of belief, it is not strange that enthusiasm for what they believed to be divinely revealed truths led the early Shaker leaders into doctrinal inconsistency. Thus, Ann could speak at one time of the torments of those who will be 'finally lost,' and at another of souls in the world of spirits traveling 'by sufferings, passing from prison to prison, until they find the mercy of God.' Her statement that rejection of the gospel in this world will not be followed by another chance is hardly consistent with her preaching of the gospel to departed spirits. The three   22 witnesses were not theologians; they were moved by one dominant idea which, as the basis of a religious theory and practical economy, needed the interpretation later accorded it by their successors.

At first, therefore, many elements of their doctrine were presented only in outline. The book of Revelations, more often quoted than any other part of the Bible, furnished the leaders with a basis for certain theological conceptions, notably those of 'the two witnesses' (the Wardleys); the 'beast' of anti-Christ, Babylon, and the mother of harlots (the Catholic church); 'a new heaven and a new earth'; the hundred and forty-four thousand which were sealed; the marriage of   23 the Lamb; and 'a woman clothed with the sun' (Ann Lee) who 'fled into the wilderness, where she hath a place prepared of God, that they should feed her there a thousand two hundred and three score days' — the approximate time that Ann was at Niskeyuna before the opening of her testimony. Such prophecies were common talk in the early order.

Balancing the mysticism and heterodoxy of Shaker thought, however, was a sense of the realities of the situation: at the outset the prophetess was aware that no holy order could be permanent which did not rest on exacting domestic labor. 'If you are not faithful in the unrighteous mammon,' she exhorted her followers, 'how can you expect the true riches?' 'Labor to make the way of God your own; let it be your inheritance, your treasure, your occupation, your daily calling.' No charity could be given, no economic independence won, no order achieved except on the foundation of industry. 'You must be faithful with your hands,' she said, 'that you may have something to give to the poor.' 'The people of God do not sell their farms to pay their debts; but they put their hands to work, and gather something by their industry, to pay their debts with, and keep their farms.' 'Go home, and take good care of what you have. Provide places for your things, so that you may know where to find them at any time, by day or night; and learn to be neat and clean, prudent and saving, and see that nothing is lost.' 'Bring strength to the church, not weakness.' 'Do all your work as though you had a thousand years to live, and as you would if you knew you must die tomorrow.'

Economy, the handmaid of industry, was likewise the theme of many a conversation between Ann and the members of the new church. 'Use the things of this world as not abusing them,' she would say; or, 'Evil management will forever be a loss to the soul.' 'I am as saving of every temporal blessing,' she testified, 'as though I had labored for it with my own hands.' Frequent were the warnings against pride in appearance, superfluity in dress and furniture, wastefulness in food, and indulgences of all kinds, even to the keeping of dogs and cats and 'useless' beasts.

Emphasis was laid on hospitality and charity. 'You must be kind to strangers,' Mother said, 'for that is the only way that you can reward me.' 'Never have one hard feeling towards each other, but live together, every day, as though it was the last you had to live in this world.' 'You must remember the poor and needy, the widow and the fatherless; and deal out your bread to the hungry and your clothes to the naked.' Homely sayings these, but in practice they were the basis of an economy which in the end won wide commendation.

Though public meetings were held two or three times a day, Shaker proselytism was largely an individual procedure. How Ann and the

Elders 'labored' with earnest seekers of salvation is illustrated by the testaments of scores of men and women, of which these are typical:

Prudence Hammond: Mother asked me if I was sick of sin. I told her I saw no way out of sin. She repeated the question, 'Are you sick of sin?' I knew not what to say. She turned to some who were present and said, 'You can find no way out of sin till you confess your sins.' She then told me of some circumstances, and mentioned a number of the transactions of my childhood and youth, which I knew it impossible for her to know but by divine inspiration. I said within myself, 'Is not this the anointed?' . . .

Richard Treat: We were kindly received, and seated by a fire to dry our clothes: for we were very wet and muddy. Mother Ann said, 'James, go fetch some water and wash these men's feet' . . . He then washed our feet and dried our stockings . . . At length John Partington came suddenly up to me, and with his finger made the sign of a cross upon my breast, saying, 'Thou art neither cold nor hot: I would thou wert cold or hot. So because thou art lukewarm, and neither cold nor hot, I will spew thee out of my mouth' . . . I fainted and fell to the floor. — When I came to myself, I heard Mother say, 'Come, James, let us go in; for that man prays.' She . . . said to Elder William, 'Take this man and hear him open his mind.' I told him I believed I had sinned against the Holy Ghost. 'Nay child, (said he,) you cannot do that until you have received the Holy Ghost' . . .

Thankful Barce: When I arrived, Mother Ann met me at the door, took hold of my hand and led me into the house. Her first salutation to me was in these words: 'Being a daughter of Zion, how camest thou hither without a cap on thy head?' She sat down in a chair, and I sat down by her side. Her eyes were shut, and it appeared that her sense was withdrawn from the things of time. She sung very melodiously, and appeared very beautiful . . . The graceful motion of her hands, the beautiful appearance of her countenance, and the heavenly melody of her voice, made her seem like a glorious inhabitant of the heavenly world, singing praises to God. As I sat by the side of her, one of her hands, while in motion, frequently touched my arm; and at every touch of her hand, I instantly felt the power of God run through my whole body . . . 24

Concentrating their collective power in such ways on one individual after another, the Shaker leaders rapidly won converts. The atmosphere of mystery was pervasive. As Job Bishop, later the 'father' of the Canterbury community, wrote: 'The wisdom of their instructions, the purity of their doctrine, their Christ-like deportment, and the simplicity of their manners, all appeared truly apostolical.'

A miraculous power allegedly exercised by the Shaker leaders was that of perceiving unconfessed guilt. In one of many accounts in the *Testimonies* (1827), Father James, at a meeting in Niskeyuna, suddenly cried out, 'There is sin in this assembly,' and turning to a young woman, who fell upon her knees before him, said, 'I see the spirit of a young man, looking over your shoulder. There is something between you and him which you have not confessed.' The woman thereupon told the elder how, two years before, she had jilted a young man who, in despondency, had ridden into a mill pond and drowned himself.

Tales of the 'gift of healing' also helped to confirm Ann's spreading reputation as the female Messiah. When Samuel Johnson, the New Light preacher at New Lebanon, first heard the testimony, a fever and ague which had made him lame 'immediately' left him so that he was able to go to Niskeyuna the next day on foot. In July 1780, Noah Wheaton of New Lebanon, while jumping off a fence, dislocated his ankle and split a bone in his leg. After several hours of suffering he finally crawled home, where he refused to have the bone set or applications made to the swollen part of his leg. Wheaton had recently joined the sect and, believing in the 'gift of miracles,' waited for his faith to effect the cure. The evening of the second day after the accident, as the family was assembled in worship, 'the power of God came suddenly to him and he was instantly hurled from his seat, upon his feet, and whirled swiftly round like a top, for the space of two hours, without the least pain or inconvenience — he then retired to rest, well and comfortable . . .'

Another case was Sarah Kibbee, who as a child had had a 'withered' foot and leg. The day after she had confessed her sins, Elder William Lee came into the room, took hold of her foot and, stroking it with his hands, said: 'According to thy faith, so be it unto thee.' Soon after, Mother Ann entered and bade her 'put away her wooden staves, and lean upon Christ.' The afflicted foot and leg, which had been 'one quarter less than the other,' was immediately restored to perfect soundness so that the girl was able to work and go forth in the worship of God. Elder John Hocknell was credited with effecting several such cures, and the 'gift' was exercised even by Shaker converts: Hezekiah Hammond, Calvin Harlow, Eleazer Rand, Joseph Markham, and others. Ax wounds, fever sores, canker rashes, cancer of the mouth, infections of the jaw, lameness, broken ribs — all were allegedly healed by faith in the new gospel.

To comprehend fully the lure of Shakerism and its hold on increasing numbers of devotees, we must pass, however, beyond the
warnings, the promises, the miracles, the ideals, even the powerful
appeal of the prophetess herself, to the strange mode of worship practiced by the Believers; this form of worship was able to cast a peculiarly potent spell on prospective adherents, attracting them into
ecstatic movements, subtly enticing them into the sacred communion.
In America Shaker ritualism became even more extravagant than in
the Manchester meetings, assuming at times unpredictably fantastic
forms, at times an utter formlessness, and always, for certain people,
an irresistible fascination.

The personalized technique of conversion, in which the rites of
worship played a culminant role, was graphically described in the
earliest eye-witness account of a Shaker meeting, one that took place
at Niskeyuna a week after the first public assembly. The date was
26 May 1780. The writer was Valentine Rathbun, Sr., the founder
and minister of the Baptist church at Pittsfield, and a prominent citizen who had been a delegate to the Massachusetts General Court and
to the assembly that had framed the state's constitution. A man of
'radical' ideas, he had at first been attracted to the Shaker movement,
but for reasons undisclosed, perhaps disgruntlement over his failure
to attain a position of leadership, soon apostatized to become its bit-
ter and prejudiced opponent. In his *Brief Hints of a Religious
Scheme*, Rathbun tells of his reception by 'five males and seven females,' who assured him they had known of his coming the day before.   27
After preparing some victuals for him, one of them sat down by
him and, addressing him by his Christian name, began 'to speak
many good words, saying, I must hate sin, love God, and take up
my Cross, &c. then went on to tell about a new dispensation, and
that they had got into it . . .' After a while they started their worship:

They begin by sitting down, and shaking their heads, in a violent manner, turning their heads half round, so that their face looks over each
shoulder, their eyes being shut; while they are thus shaking, one will
begin to sing some odd tune, without words or rule; after a while another
will strike in; and then another; and after a while they all fall in, and
make a strange charm . . . Some singing without words, and some with
an unknown tongue or mutter, and some with a mixture of English: The
mother, so called, minds to strike such notes as make a concord, and so

form the charm. When they leave off singing, they drop off, one by one, as oddly as they come on . . .

With the meeting well under way, restraint was cast to the winds:

In the best part of their worship every one acts for himself, and almost every one different from the other: one will stand with his arms extended, acting over odd postures, which they call signs; another will be dancing, and some times hopping on one leg about the floor; another will fall to turning round, so swift, that if it be a woman, her clothes will be so filled with the wind, as though they were kept out by a hoop; another will be prostrate on the floor; another will be talking with somebody; and some sitting by, smoking their pipes; some groaning most dismally; some trembling extremely; others acting as though all their nerves were convulsed; others swinging their arms, with all vigor, as though they were turning a wheel, etc. Then all break off, and have a spell of smoaking, and some times great fits of laughter . . . They have several such exercises in a day, especially on the Sabbath . . .

Except for the introductory 'spell' of singing 'odd tunes, and British marches,' et cetera, no regular form was followed in their meetings, nor was there public prayer or preaching. The Believers told Rathbun they chose 'to be singular lest . . . they should be connected with Babylon,' that 'their actions in worship is according to the dictates of the spirit that governs them.' The writer's further impressions bear out the contention:

When they meet together for their worship, they fall a groaning and trembling, and every one acts alone for himself; one will fall prostrate on the floor, another on his knees and his head in his hands; another will be muttering over articulate sounds, which neither they or any body else understand. Some will be singing, each one his own tune; some without words, in an Indian tune, some sing jig tunes, some tunes of their own making, in an unknown mutter, which they call new tongues; some will be dancing, and others stand laughing, heartily and loudly; others will be druming on the floor with their feet, as though a pair of drum-sticks were beating a ruff on a drum-head; others will be agonizing, as though they were in great pain; others jumping up and down; others fluttering over somebody, and talking to them; others will be shooing and hissing evil spirits out of the house, till the different tunes, groaning, jumping, dancing, druming, laughing, talking and fluttering, shooing and hissing, makes a perfect bedlam; this they call the worship of God.

In agreement with this account is the description of the meetings at Harvard, Massachusetts, a year or so later, by one Amos Taylor, 'late of their Number, and acquainted with them in five different Governments for ten Months.' According to this witness, worship was held every night until two in the morning, and often until break of day. The singing meetings came first, 'until they had got some footing, when it was immediately turned into heavy dancing, generally about forty or fifty men together, and as many women separate by themselves in different rooms.' The dancing was performed

. . . by a perpetual springing from the house floor, about four inches up and down, both in the men's and women's apartment, moving about as thick as they can crowd, with extraordinary transport, singing sometimes one at a time, and sometimes more than one, making a perfect charm . . . This elevation draws upon the nerves so as that they have intervals of shuddering as if they were in a strong fit of the ague. — They sometimes clap hands and leap so as to strike the joyce above their heads. They throw off their outside garments in these exercises, and spend their strength very cheerfully this way . . .   30

The letters of William Plumer, later governor of New Hampshire and United States senator, who attended a meeting at Harvard in 1782, corroborate the statements of Rathbun and Taylor, throwing further light on the reason why Mother Ann's followers were called 'Shakers' and 'convulsioners.' He wrote:

About thirty of them assembled in a large room in a private house, — the women in one end and the men in the other, — for dancing. Some were past sixty years old. Some had their eyes steadily fixed upward, continually reaching out and drawing in their arms and lifting up first one foot, then the other, about four inches from the floor. Near the centre of the room stood two young women, one of them very handsome, who whirled round and round for the space of fifteen minutes, nearly as fast as the rim of a spinning-wheel in quick motion . . . As soon as she left whirling she entered the dance, and danced gracefully. Sometimes one would pronounce with a loud voice, 'Ho, ho' or 'Love, love,' — and then the whole assembly vehemently clapped hands for a minute or two. At other times some were shaking and trembling, others singing words out of the Psalms in whining, canting tones (but not in rhyme), while others were speaking in what they called 'the unknown tongue,' — to me an unintelligible jargon, mere gibberish and perfect nonsense. At other times the whole assembly would shout as with one voice, with one accord. This exercise continued about an hour.

An intermission followed, then another dance, then another intermission. After an 'impressive' talk by an elder with 'a strong, clear, distinguishing mind,' the former exercises were renewed for an hour or more:

This done, several of the young people, both men and women, began to shake and tremble in a most terrible manner. The first I perceived was their heads moving slowly from one shoulder to the other, — the longer they moved the quicker and more violently they shook. The motion proceeded from the head to the hands, and the whole body, with such power as if limb would rend from limb. The house trembled as if there were an earthquake. After this several young women embraced and saluted each other; two men embraced and saluted each other; a third clasped his arms around both, a fourth around them, and so on, until a dozen men were in that position, embracing and saluting. I did not
31 observe any man salute or embrace a woman, or any woman a man . . .

'The Shakers are seized with their movements at any time,' ob-
32 served François, Marquis de Barbé-Marbois, who visited the Niske-yuna settlement in 1784. The shakings might come on 'while they cultivate the earth, while they are cutting trees, while traveling on foot, or on horseback':

The convulsion [he notes] does not interrupt anything; the most usual movement is to turn the head from left to right, with eyes closed or raised towards the sky, with an expression which proclaims ecstasy, anguish, and pain. We noticed that the women shed tears, were pale and downcast, and that their face reanimated itself only when the convulsion was at an end. The men raised their arms, trembling; their knees gave way and knocked together. Often while all their members shook, they would seem to have a seizure under which they would succumb, but it was the end of the ecstasy. The head turned less rapidly, and when the crisis was over, they sighed deeply, like people relieved at length of
33 excessive anxiety, or coming out of a painful swoon.

The frenzy of worship sometimes passed into 'signs.' According to Rathbun,

. . . the power will take their hand, stretch it up, pull the other down, they interpret it — the hand up, is a sign of mercy, the hand down, of judgment: Sometimes their hand is stretched out forward, then away they run after it; if it leads to some person, they lay their hand on his head, — then cross their arms, one across the other, — then say he must take up his cross, and renounce the works of the flesh, — then they stretch both hands behind them, and say he must leave the world behind him: Sometimes their hands will be cramped up, one finger stretched out straight, another down into their hand . . . Sometimes their hand will stretch out, and after it they run, — through woods — cross lots — over fences, swamps, or whatever, till they come to a house; perhaps they will be stopt, several times, in their course, and head turn round, as though they had lost their way; then take a new set off, and run again; perhaps, when they get to the house, they will lie down on the ground — make a round ring with their finger, among the dirt — puther about in it — then start up — double their fist at it — run away from it — come at it again — show the looks of vengeance at it — threaten it with postures — then run and jump into it, and stamp it all to pieces: — This sign they interpret it to be the Old Heavens, which are to pass away with a great noise — When he goes into the house, he flutters round with his hands flying, and hissing as if he intended to drive all the flies out of the room — but this, he says, is to hunt the evil spirits out, which the house is full of. ³⁴

Rathbun's reference to signs, especially the act of following an outstretched hand, is confirmed by other sources. Plumer recounts two such incidents, one of a Shaker brother stretching out his arm, with hand shut, to a woman, opening the hand, asking her to shut it again and saying, 'Receive this gift from God.' When the woman asked what he had given, he answered, 'The Holy Ghost.' The other story tells of a Shaker elder whose arm was suddenly outstretched in the direction of a hoe and a stump. He was moved, thereupon, to dig up some ants, put them in a box, and carry them to a certain 'lazy man,' with the injunction, 'Go to the ant, thou sluggard! consider her ways and be wise.' Brown relates the tale of an elder who followed his outstretched arm to a house, and then the room, where a man lay with three broken ribs. His hand was irresistibly moved to rest on the fractured parts, which were 'instantly cured.' Allusions to this operation ³⁵ occur in the Shakers' own literature: Hocknell was guided to the site of the first colony at Niskeyuna by the involuntary pointing of his arm, and had been similarly led to Mother Ann during the persecution at Harvard. Occasionally the account is on the ludicrous side: President Timothy Dwight of Yale, in his travels through New England, became acquainted with a Shaker whose right arm had led him 'to a hog-trough, by the side of which he dropped upon his knees, and made a hearty draught of the swill, with a number of pigs.' ³⁶

Sometimes when Mother or the elders were 'at work with a person,' they would slyly stroke him, mark parts of his body with the sign of

the cross, or putting their hands on his head, prophesy great things
37 for him. 'If the person seems to be sober,' Rathbun wrote, 'then one
takes him by the hand, and round the floor with him, and make him
run and skip about, and laugh heartily at him, and will tell him he
must not be melancholy' — this to the accompaniment of humming
or singing in 'nuptial voices' and speaking in unknown tongues.

If current reports be credited, those who opposed the testimony or
fell away after once embracing it, were treated quite differently. In
reply to difficult questions of doctrine the Shakers would say, 'We
have no gift of God to answer thee,' 'Thou art full of vain philosophy,' or 'The world by wisdom knows not God.' 'If a man's arguments are unanswerable,' asserted Plumer, 'they will without ceremony call him a "liar." ' The 'warring gift' was exercised against
those who expressed doubt or disillusionment. They surround such a
person, asserted one witness, 'threaten him with damnation, storm and
stamp at him, stare open their eyes, pucker up their mouths, and cry
oh! oh! oh! at him, and act all the postures of vengeance, which is
38 enough to frighten a Hercules out of his wits.' Apostates were called
heretics, impostors, reprobates, or more commonly, 'backsliders.'

Such was the manner in which the Shaker gospel was first propa-
gated in America. On one hand arose a body of Believers, the common
people of the day, representative of every stage of intelligence, cre-
dulity, and ability; on the other, a group of skeptics and opposers. In
the resulting clash of opinion a relatively isolated culture was spread
until it became known throughout eastern New York and New England.

The first conflict between the American Shakers and the world,
however, was not on the issues of doctrine or form of worship. The
spring and early summer of 1780 saw many people flocking to Niskeyuna, where they often remained for days and weeks as in the camp
revivals of a later period. The problem of food was acute, especially
since the country was then at war with the British, so people often
took provisions with them and made their first contributions to the
church in stock and the produce of their farms. On 5 July three such
donors — David Darrow, brother of George Darrow, Daniel Green,
and Joseph Potter, Shaker farmers of New Lebanon — were round-
ing up a number of sheep preparatory to driving them to the New
York colony when they were seized by some patriotic neighbors and

taken before Matthew Adgate, justice of the peace in what was then known as King's District. Adgate reported the incident to the Commissioners for Detecting and Defeating Conspiracies in the State of New York, then meeting in Albany, informing them that 'there is the greatest reason to suppose from their [the Shakers'] disaffection to the American Cause that they mean to convey them [the sheep] to the Enemy or at least bring them so near the Frontiers that the enemy may with safety take them.'   *39*

When the farmers were arraigned before the commissioners, Green and Potter satisfactorily proved that their intentions were not treasonable. But Darrow denied the authority of the board and all civil jurisdiction in the state, stating that 'by his religious principles he is restrained from taking up Arms in defence of the Country and that he does not intend to do any kind of Military duty whatsoever nor does not in any instance intend to abide by the Laws of this State.' John Hocknell and Joseph Meacham, who were present at the hearing, acknowledged 'a Concurrence of Sentiment' with the accused, 'declaring that it was their determined Resolution never to take up arms and to dissuade others from doing the same.' As these principles seemed to the commissioners 'highly pernicious and of destructive tendency to the Freedome (and) independence of the United States of America,' the three were committed to the jail at the old city hall — being subsequently removed to a prison in the fort above the town. Ten days later Joel Pratt and Hezekiah Hammond were imprisoned on the same charge.

Complaints continued to reach the commissioners that the family of 'shaking Quakers' was a hive of pacifist agitation. On 24 July, therefore, they issued a warrant for the arrest of 'John Partherton, William Lees and Ann Standerren.' Two days later the trio was brought to Albany, together with 'James Whiteacre, Calven Harlow, and Mary Partington,' whom the deputy had found in the Lees' company. Being questioned on the issue of bearing arms, the dissenters affirmed that they preached a gospel of peace, whereupon all six were committed to jail. On 26 August, Mother Ann — 'the grand actress' as she was termed — and Mary Partington were sent down to the commissioners at Poughkeepsie 'for the purpose of their being removed within the Enemies Lines.'   *40*

It was natural that the colonial authorities should have suspected the English-bred Shaker leaders of pro-British proclivities, especially when the latter were found to be counseling non-resistance. Zadock Wright, who was ordered to appear before the Albany board on 7 July because of his 'affiliation with the shaking Quakers,' was an avowed Tory; and what was probably an inflammatory letter regarding the prisoners was received from Valentine Rathbun in October. Yet it soon became apparent that the sect, though 'infatuated,' was harmless. On the request of his father-in-law, Captain Jarvis Mudge, Darrow was released in October because of the illness of his wife. William Lee, Whittaker, and Hocknell were discharged 15 November 'on entering into a Recognizance' for their good behavior and the posting of a bond of two hundred pounds each. During the next few days all but Ann and Mary were freed on similar terms.

Soon after his release William Lee applied to the military commander at Albany, Lieutenant General James Clinton, for the discharge of his sister at Poughkeepsie. In response to the plea, Clinton wrote a letter to his brother, Governor George Clinton, on 19 November, in which he said: 'You are better acquainted with the circumstances relating to her, than I can be; you can best determine what is to be done with her, and if nothing material has been proven against her, I shou'd suppose she may [be] released agreeable to their requisition.' The letter, followed by a personal interview between James Whittaker and Governor Clinton, had its effect. On 4 December it no longer appeared that the Shaker 'persuasion' tended to 'alienate the minds of the People from their Allegiance to the State,' but that said persuasion seemed to have been 'reformed.' Ann was freed the day after William Lee and Whittaker had bonded two hundred pounds 'for her good Behaviour and not saying or consenting to any Matters or Things inconsistent with the Peace and safety of this the United States.'

The imprisonment of the Shaker leaders publicized what had previously been a relatively isolated movement. It is possible that Ann and the elders had been allowed to preach through the 'prison grates' at Albany and Poughkeepsie. It is certain that many thoughtful people were disturbed by the inconsistency of persecuting a harmless sect for its religious faith at a time when the country was engaged in a struggle for freedom and personal rights. The interest and sympathy thus awakened undoubtedly contributed to the decision of the Shakers to undertake a tour through Massachusetts and Connecticut that was to lay the foundations of a federated communal order.

———◆◆———

CHAPTER III

Mission into New England

The reapers first appeared,
With sickles sharp and keen,
And thousands were alarmed
At such a solemn scene:
The field they now have enter'd,
No more to slack their hand,
Till all the wheat is gather'd,
And shock'd, and thresh'd, and fan'd.

— *Millennial Praises*, 1813

'THE INCREASE of the work was great beyond expression' in the six months of unmolested preaching following Ann's release. Calls to take the testimony eastward, the direction from which most of the converts had come, continued to pour into Niskeyuna: from Joseph Meacham's brother, David, an influential citizen of Enfield, Connecticut; from Daniel Wood of Upton, Massachusetts, who had carried the Word into that section; from residents of Grafton, Harvard, Shirley, Bolton, Petersham, and many other towns in the central and eastern parts of the Bay State. So rapidly did interest spread that the Shaker leaders resolved to postpone no longer the projected mission; late in May 1781, the three 'witnesses,' accompanied by Mary Partington, Samuel Fitch of Richmond, and Wood's sister Margaret Leeland, set out on horseback from their colony in the woods. Their immediate destination was Benjamin Osborne's home in Mount Washington, an isolated hill town in the southwestern corner of Massachusetts, where they tarried ten days, 'laboring' with the Believers in that neighborhood.

Opposition was first encountered at David Meacham's house in

43

Enfield. Charges of witchcraft and delusion swept into the town on the heels of the Shakers, but an open outbreak was avoided when they decided to heed the warning of the selectmen to discontinue their meetings. Turning northward, they spent several days at John Maynor's in Grafton, the Sabbath at Daniel Wood's, and the following night at the home of Zaccheus Stevens in Stillwater. Ann's objective was Harvard, where she arrived the next day, establishing the mission at the house of Isaac Willard.

As a base of operations this town was a shrewd choice, having been for ten years the scene of the fantastic operations of the New Light preacher, Shadrack Ireland, one-time follower of George Whitefield and advocate of the Shaker-like doctrines of perfection, celibacy, and the millennium. With Ireland, however, celibacy had been only an *ad interim* condition, to be discarded when perfection was attained ; children could then be born as perfect beings into the 'new creation.' Claiming to be the second Messiah, Shadrack had taken unto himself a spiritual bride, Abigail Lougee — he had deserted his own wife and children years before in Cambridge — and built himself a retreat, a house (raised in the night) with a square roof, a cupola where he could look out and see when strangers approached, and a trap door and secret staircase leading from the cupola to the cellar. Ireland had boasted that if he died at all he would arise on the third day, and when he did die, his adherents faithfully awaited the resurrection. As in the case of Jemima Wilkinson, the 'Public Universal Friend' who founded 44 her short-lived community of Jerusalem at Seneca Lake, New York, shortly after this period, disillusionment was retarded by deep-seated delusion, and only after weeks had elapsed was the body taken from 45 the cellar of the 'Square House' and, to avoid the hostility of the townsfolk, secretly buried at night in a cornfield.

When Ann took up her abode in the same house, she probably had in mind the successful aftermath of a similar revival in New Lebanon. Here was another field apparently ripe for the harvest : a people poor, unsettled in their convictions, yearning for true salvation. Already she had won the support of such men of means as Zaccheus Stevens and Isaac and Jeremiah Willard. From near-by Shirley and Littleton, from Woburn to the east and Petersham to the west, serious inquirers flocked to hear the testimony. So in spite of a 'cavilling spirit' which occasionally arose in their meetings, Mother and the elders decided to make Ireland's home their church. Provisions were stored in the house for an extended stay.

Notwithstanding the fact that here the infant society suffered its most severe persecutions, Harvard remained the center of Ann's ecclesiastic labors for a full two years. In December 1781, she preached at the homes of Thomas Shattuck and David Hammond in Petersham. Late in February of the next year she again visited Enfield. In March she traveled up the Connecticut River into Massachusetts, stopping at Amaziah Clark's house in Granby, Jonathan Bridges' in Belchertown, and Peter and Abigail Bishop's in Montague. On the farm of Asa Bacon in the remote hill town of Ashfield the travelers relaxed somewhat from their labors; but in May, after a visit to Jonathan and Aaron Wood's in Shelburne, they were on their way back to Harvard.

The early summer of 1782 found Mother Ann, Father James, and other leaders preaching at Harvard, Shirley, Still River, Bolton, and Woburn. The conversion of four prosperous farmers in Shirley — Elijah and Ivory Wilds, John Warren, and Nathan Willard — precipitated that year the first schism in the Congregational Church of the town. In August the mission against set out to nourish the faith among scattered Believers: first to Morrell Baker's in Rehoboth, then on to William Morey's in Norton. In October they were in Stonington, Connecticut, laboring at the homes of Joshua Birch and Joseph Cole. On the way back to the important station at Enfield they granted the appeals of certain people in Preston, Windham, and Stafford to visit those Connecticut towns. Enfield again was hostile and, as winter was approaching, the company continued northward, tarrying a while at Joseph Bennett's in the town of New Providence (Cheshire, Massachusetts), then pushing on to their refuge in Ashfield.

The mission thus briefly outlined laid the foundation for the establishment of communities in all the New England colonies, not only those subsequently established at Harvard, Shirley, Enfield (Conn.), Hancock, and Tyringham, but indirectly the four in New Hampshire and Maine. In the latter states the Shakers again profited from Baptist revivalism, their unwitting benefactor in this case being Benjamin Randall of New Durham, New Hampshire, who under the influence of Whitefield's preaching had recently organized the Free Will

Baptist Church. Like other New Light orders, Randall's congregations rebelled against the strictures of Calvinism and, like the Shakers, were 'free to speak or sing as the spirit gave utterance.' In the freedom they felt 'in being extricated from the shackles and bondage of anti-Christian bigotry,' this radical branch of the New Lights would often express their joy so boisterously that they won the name of 'Come-Outers' or 'Merry Dancers.' One of the most active churches served Canterbury and Loudon, New Hampshire, not far from New
46 Durham; another was at Gorham, in what was then the province of Maine.

Contact between the Shakers and Free Willers came about in the following manner. One summer day in 1782 a pedlar by the name of Benjamin Thompson, passing through Canterbury, roused the interest of members of the Free Will church with a description of the Niskeyuna colony of Shakers. The doctrines of these people seemed to the New Lights even more liberal than their own, and the Shaker manner of worship an unrestrained glorification of God. Curious to know more, they commissioned two members of the church, Edward Lougee and John Shepherd, to visit Mother Ann Lee, who was then at Harvard. What these men reported is not known, but in September the prophetess delegated two of her ablest preachers, Ebenezer
47 Cooley and Israel Chauncey, to carry the gospel to Canterbury.

Their efforts were successful. Benjamin Whitcher, owner of a large farm in East Canterbury, and Henry Clough, son of a landowner in the western part of the town, were among the first to take up their crosses against 'the flesh and the Devil.' In spite of the efforts of Randall, 'Father' Tingley, and other New Lights, the 'infection' soon became deep-seated in the Canterbury-Loudon district, most of the Baptist leaders going over to Shakerism. In October the emissaries,
48 accompanied by Zadock Wright of Hartford, Vermont, rode to Enfield, New Hampshire, where James Jewett, a well-to-do farmer, was added to the fold. For eleven years this man's property, known as Shaker Hill, was the scene of a growing movement which eventually took organized form in the Enfield society.

The communities in Maine may trace their origin to this same Enfield yeoman. For it was Jewett who welcomed John Cotton of Alfred, Maine, a member of the Free Will order in near-by Gorham, as the latter traveled into the 'new state,' knapsack on back, to purchase a farm. The journey had led Cotton to Canterbury, where he noticed

a great change in his New Light brethren, and on to Enfield, where
Jewett confided to the stranger the reason for the change. 'You are
planning to enlarge your material possessions,' he told the sojourner,
'restlessly moving from one state to another, mapping for yourself a
proud career. Are you not aware that you are also moving away from
the state of the spirit? You profess the life of Christ, but do you actually live it? Do you not know that in Christ's Kingdom there can
be no rich nor poor, no high, no low — that all are equal brethren and
sisters in Christ?'

For days Cotton stayed on at the Jewett farmstead, eager to learn
more of the wonderful news. One morning after breakfast, having
finally unburdened his sins, the faith of the man from Maine was
'scaled.' He testified:

> The power of God came upon me, filling my soul and controlling my
> whole being. It raised me from my chair and under its influence I turned
> around, swiftly, for the space of half an hour. The door of the house was
> open. I was whirled through the door-way into the yard among the
> stones and stumps, down to the shore of the Mascoma Lake, some rods
> distant. On reaching the shore of the lake that same power that led me
> to the water whirled me back again in like manner, and I found myself
> in the same chair that I had been taken from.   49

Thus was John Cotton baptized. Soon he turned homeward. Arriving at Alfred one midnight about the first of June, he went immediately to the house of an old friend, John Barnes, rapped for admittance, and shouted with all his might. When John and his wife Sarah
let him in, 'the good news of great joy' was eagerly communicated,
and before sunset the next day these two had also accepted the testimony. Later in the month Barnes, 'dressed in the style of a gentle-
man,' came down to Harvard to pay his respects to Mother Ann, who,
on seeing his brightly polished boots, his gay silk kerchief, and 'profusion of ruffles,' rebuked him with the words: 'You are a proud and
haughty young man; you should kneel where you are, and humble
yourself before God, then pray for a spirit of humility.'   50

The faith spread rapidly in the south of Maine. Leaders of the
church exchanged visits with converts from Alfred, Gorham, Lyman,
Waterborough, Windham, and Falmouth. Before the summer was
over the nucleus of a society had been formed at the Alfred home of
Benjamin and Mary Barnes; and in November meeting places were

established at Eliphaz Ring's in Poland and at Gowen Wilson's in
New Gloucester — then called Thompson's Pond Plantation or Sabbathday-Pond, and later West Gloucester and Sabbathday Lake.
John Barnes was appointed 'first in the lead' over these incipient
orders.

So zealously did the Shakers propagate their doctrines that the
Free Will Baptists, at a quarterly meeting in 1784, 'agreed to observe
a day of fasting and prayer, that God would cut short this delusion
51 and give peace to the churches.'

But the protest of the 'Come-Outers' was mild in comparison with
the defamation and open persecution suffered from the authorities
and citizens of certain New England towns. The fact that the Believers had been absolved of the charge that they were British spies
did not free them from calumny; and when Valentine Rathbun, ex-
ploiting the incident, began to feed popular prejudice with his at-
52 tacks on Shaker doctrine, disapproval found expression in lawless
forms. Despite the fact that this doctrine outlawed all warfare and
that Ann had often prophesied the triumph of the patriot cause, the
wildest rumors against the sect were credited. When, for instance, the
report was circulated at Harvard, in the summer of 1781, that the
'shaking Quakers' had brought seventy wagons and six hundred
stands of arms and had secreted a curious chest of firearms in the
'Square House,' the captain of the local militia ordered a committee
to search the building; and even when it was clear that the mission
was a peaceful one, an ultimatum was issued to the newcomers to leave
the town before a prescribed day.

When the strangers returned to Harvard the following summer,
the smoldering distrust burst into flame. Early on the morning of 19
August a mob of about four hundred gathered around the 'Square
House.' Word went abroad, and soon the Harvard Shakers, with the
exception of Mother Ann, who was at Woburn, joined their brethren
and sisters. The Shaker version of the ensuing events is graphic:

Elder Hocknell now gave orders for all the Believers to assemble in
one large room, fronting the mob . . . He then desired them all to kneel
down and pray to God, for his protection, in such a trying time as
this . . .
The mob no sooner discovered that the Believers were on their knees,
than they rushed upon the doors, which were shut and barred, burst

them open, and began to seize upon the brethren and sisters . . . Richard Treat, being next to the door, was the first that fell into their hands. They seized him by the collar, with such rage and fury, that they nearly severed it from his shirt . . . Thus they seized one after another, some by their collars, some by their throats, and some by the hair of their heads; and wherever they clinched, they kept hold, till they dragged the person out of the room . . .   53

The leaders of the mob ordered home those who lived in the vicinity, and gave the rest an hour to leave town. When the time expired with no action taken, the Shakers were placed in a body between an advance and a rear guard mounted on horseback. The sisters were permitted to ride; but the brethren, accompanied by many of the Harvard men who refused to leave, were forced to march afoot. If any of the aged or infirm Believers did not travel with sufficient speed, 'their pace was soon quickened by a severe stroke of a whip or cudgel.' Dyer Fitch was 'cruelly beaten' over the head for praying, and Abijah Worster was struck with a good-staff for clasping James Shepherd in his arms.

They drove on about three miles, till they came to a level, open plain, near Still-river, where they were ordered to halt. 'Now, (said the leaders of the mob) we will have a little diversion'; and orders were given for James Shepherd to be soundly whipped. James was the only person whom they had taken, of those who came from England, and against whom their enmity was the most pointedly leveled . . .

They accordingly formed a ring, and sent one of the mob into the bushes, to cut sticks for that purpose. He soon returned with his arms full, and distributed them among the company appointed to whip him, and each one was ordered to give him a certain number of strokes. James was then ordered to strip, and accordingly pulled off his coat and jacket, and kneeling down, he said, 'Be of good cheer, brethren; for it is your heavenly Father's good pleasure to give you the Kingdom.'

On hearing these words, one of the ruffians . . . gave him a number of severe strokes, with his horse-whip . . .

Eleazer Rand, later the first minister at Harvard, leaped on Shepherd's back to protect him. The persecutors doubled their efforts, assaulting Rand and others who came to the stricken man's assistance. Someone drove his fist against Eleazer's neck, then hurled him against a stone wall. When a Harvard citizen, William Morey, reproved the captain of the militia, he was answered with a violent blow on the side of his face. Finally the mob proceeded, though another disturbance occurred at the Harvard-Bolton line when the Harvard brethren refused to leave their companions.

From the place where the mob halted, to whip James Shepherd, to Lancaster, a distance of seven miles, was one continued scene of cruelty and abuse; whipping with horse-whips, pounding, beating and bruising with clubs, collaring, pushing off from bridges, into the water and mud, scaring the sisters' horses, with a view to frighten the riders, and every kind of abuse that they could invent without taking lives . . .

And so it continued. If the aged attempted to mount their horses for relief, they would be harried with the butt of a whipstock; one old man was beaten from his horse with a fence rail. Even after the arrival at Lancaster, when the Shakers had been dismissed with the warning never to enter Harvard again, the mob was said to have become so enraged at the sight of a group kneeling in prayer that the Shakers were again lashed 'as tho' they had been a herd of swine.' The Harvard brethren encountered the same treatment on their return: 'a large rough looking man who had placed himself in the road' horse-whipped all he could reach; Jonathan Clark was beaten with a loaded whipstock; and Abijah Worster, who was charged with 'going about and breaking up churches and families,' was stripped, tied to a tree, and lashed.

Mother Ann herself had been 'shamefully and cruelly abused' in Petersham the preceding winter. At an evening meeting in the home of David Hammond, Whittaker was reading the Bible in a chamber filled with attentive listeners, among whom 'a company of lewd fellows,' styled the 'Blackguard Committee,' had quietly distributed themselves. Suddenly someone cried, 'Knock out the lights.' In the darkened room, feebly lit by the one candle still burning in Elder James' hand, three 'ruffians,' painted black, attempted to drag out the prophetess; but though they ripped her dress, her companions held her tightly, and finally the 'Blackguards' retreated. Later in the evening, the meeting having dispersed, 'the house was again assaulted by about thirty creatures in human shape.' Doors were broken open, Hammond and his wife and small child were knocked down, and Elder James was felled to the floor and left for dead. All the candles had been hidden, but the 'wretches' seized fire-brands and, searching the house, located Ann in an upper bedroom:

They immediately seized her by the feet, and inhumanly dragged her, feet foremost, out of the house, and threw her into a sleigh, with as little ceremony as they would the dead carcase of a beast, and drove off, committing at the same time, acts of inhumanity and indecency which even savages would be ashamed of. In the struggle with these inhuman wretches, she lost her cap and handkerchief, and otherwise had her clothes torn in a shameful manner. Their pretence was to find out whether she was a woman or not.

Similar incidents marked the conclusion of the New England tour. When the Shakers returned to Harvard violence broke out again, and Father James was again scourged 'till his back was all in a gore of blood and the flesh bruised to a jelly.' They left Ashfield in the face of rumors that Ann was a British emissary in a woman's habit. At Richmond and Hancock the leaders were fined for disturbing the peace, and three members jailed for 'blasphemy.'

The 'beastly power of anti-Christ' reached a climax at New Lebanon. Preparatory meetings had been held in several farmhouses, at one of which Father William was moved to speak to several Indians in their native tongue. The two hundred people assembled at the opening meeting in John Bishop's orchard witnessed, according to legend, a re-enactment of the miracle of the loaves and fishes: 'though no victuals were cooked' there seemed to be more left than when the 'multitude' began to eat. Citizens of the town, fearing that the infection was getting out of hand, and long annoyed by 'the war between Michael and the dragon' which nightly 'made the forests ring,' obtained a warrant against two of the leading Shakers, David Meacham and George Darrow, charging them with abusing Meacham's daughter. A mob battered down the doors of Darrow's farmhouse, in which the Shakers had barricaded themselves, and, breaking through the ceiling of the room in which Mother Ann was hiding, dragged her to the door and pitched her headlong into a carriage. On the way to Eleazer Grant's, the local magistrate, the 'ruffians' tried to upset the carriage. Several of Father James's ribs were fractured when he was pulled from his horse onto a rock. At Grant's, after a 'mock trial' which was a 'mob tribunal,' the leaders of the sect were finally released on the bond of the Darrow brothers, but the mob followed them threateningly until they were out of town.

Wet and cold, the missionaries spent the night in the cabin of a poor settler, went forth to worship early the next morning, and un-

54

derwent a final tribulation at the house of Nathan Farrington, a Believer, when members of the 'Indian Club' — 'heathenish creatures, of the baser sort,' from Chatham — stoned the house, pulled off clapboards, and made life miserable for the occupants. The next day Ann and her companions departed for Niskeyuna, reaching their wilderness home on the night of 4 September 1783, two years and four months after they had set forth.

In the minds of eighteenth-century New Englanders, Shaker dissent from orthodox beliefs and practices was so extreme as to be heretical: hence the prejudice, alarm, and violent opposition. Intolerance was increased by a persistent propaganda which capitalized on many facets of the strange religion: the refusal of the Believers to take oaths or bear arms, which made people suspect them of aiding the British; the tenet of obedience, which was represented as un-American, pro-Catholic, and particularly pernicious because in this case it involved 'subjection' to English-born leaders; the doctrines of confession and celibacy, which carried added implications of Catholicism; and a mode of worship which lent itself to misinterpretation and the wildest rumors. The chief propagandists were Valentine Rathbun and his son Daniel.

55   The former's 'Discovery of the wicked machinations of the Principal Enemies of America' — published, according to its title page, both in England and America in 1782 — was a calculated appeal to 56 anti-British sentiment, with the Shakers as victims. In this curious document Valentine assembles, in an imaginary conversation, Lords North, Germaine, Bute, and Mansfield; 'a well known toryistical Bishop'; and 'His Majesty George the Third.' North remarks that 'My Lord Germaine has lately had intelligence from some agents we have lately sent to America, to work upon the superstition of the people there.' Whereupon Germaine, addressing the King, reports that 'our accounts from the persons who were sent to propagate a new religious scheme in America are very flattering. They make converts daily, and it is merry to hear of the weakness and folly of their tenets, and how aptly adapted to work on the foolish and superstitious passions of the most ignorant of the Americans.' He calls the Shaker leaders 'our agents,' and proposes, as a means of weakening the rebellion, that these people be 'increased'; their minds, he argues, are so 'weak' and so susceptible to the dictates of their leaders, that they

'might be worked up to anything . . . only let them have a divine revelation to take up arms and destroy rebels to God, and rebels to man.' 'We are almost too late in this affair,' he concludes, 'but it may be that we may yet use these Shaking Quakers . . . to good advantage — I look upon them at least as *late* recruits for Britain.' The Bishop agrees that the Shaker leaders should be encouraged, but on the grounds that the pacifism they advocate will play a part in undermining colonial resistance. 'If we can but get this scheme to go down,' he remarks, 'it will have, I believe, a good tendency to cut the sinews of their rebellion, as the numerous converts will refuse to bear arms against the forces sent to subdue the Americans by Your Majesty.' Lord North, in his turn, feels 'that great things have and may still be done' to bring a people so 'deluded by an appearance of supernatural power . . . under a proper subjection to government, when the force of arms have failed . . . We may see by the easy manner in which the Americans are taken and duped by those Shakers that the bulk of the people there were never fitted by wisdom and virtue for freemen.'

Another attack in the name of American patriotism was made the same year by the apostate Amos Taylor. A discipline based on the alleged perfection of European leaders and the unquestioning obedience of 'American labourers,' Taylor argued, was a dangerously alien doctrine:

When we consider the infant state of civil power in America, since the revolution began, every infringement on the natural rights of humanity, every effort to undermine our original constitution, either in civil or ecclesiastical order, saps the foundation of Independency. To see a body of more than two thousand people, having no will of their own, but governed by a few Europeans conquering their adherents into the most unreserved subjection, argues some infatuating power . . .   57

To these early American charges of subversion was added that of papacy. In the Rathbun pamphlet — which, significantly, gives an account of the Gordon 'No Popery' riots in London in 1780 — the Bishop is made to declare: 'If I am right informed, this new [Shaker] scheme bears a strong resemblance in many particulars to the catholick church — for instance, their profession of being perfect, infallible, confessions of sin, bodily aggitations, out-side shews, etc. this answers directly to the mother papal church, together with their

power of working miracles, Etc.' In the preface to a *Letter* to James
58 Whittaker published by his son Daniel Rathbun in 1785, Valentine
renews the attack with references to the 'papist' doctrines of an
earthly tribunal, with a supreme head, to judge the world; of 'the
resurrection day being now come . . . and the dead rising by thousands'; of atonement in hell; of celibacy and 'a new dispensation, in
which they are beyond the bible.' In the body of the letter the apostate Daniel also takes up the charge. Quoting Joseph Meacham 'that
God would not hear us but by secondary mediators,' he compared the
usages of confession to that of the 'Papists,' who worship and pray
to the Virgin Mary, St. Peter, St. Paul, and the saints 'as interces-
sors with Christ.' Revelations and 'apparitions,' the gifts of healing and casting out devils were likewise termed medieval supersti-
tions.

The *Letter* includes new allegations against the sect. Though now
'in a decaying and dying state,' the vindictive Valentine asserts, the
members of the order are rigorously driven by 'hard hearted Pha-
raoh-like masters, while their leaders live on the spoils of their disciples, and wallow in wealth and ease, and regale themselves in rioting
and drunkenness, in chambering and wantonness.' Daniel also accused the Shakers of dancing naked and other perversities: 'The first
thing that ever stumbled me was, that I saw in the mother at Elijah
Wiles' she look'd very red, and acted to my acceptation as tho' she
had drink'd too hard.' At Woburn Elder William appeared 'as if he
had been drinking very hard'; and Whittaker himself, to whom the
letter was addressed, was accused of being 'so much amiss with liquor'
at a certain place that he 'fumbled' in his speech and 'acted very
oddly.' The assertion that men and women, parents and children
59 danced and bathed 'stark naked together' — a rumor apparently
based on the fact that in warm weather the sisters were 'lightly
clothed' when worshipping, and the brethren discarded their coats or
'outside garments' — was offered in support of the contention that
the new dispensation was quite different from that of Moses or Christ.
In her 'discipline' against fleshly lust, the writer asserted that Ann
performed and encouraged sensual and sometimes sadistic acts of
mortification; and by forbidding marriage, imposed such a 'restraint'
on nature that it took its course in 'habitual' filthiness. So scathing
was her testimony that no one dared disobey. Children dishonored and
disowned their parents. All joined in calling their opposers 'boogers.'

devils and Sodomites; besides pushing, hunching, pulling hair, striking, biting, and spitting in their faces.' 'Can such like,' Rathbun asked, 'be found in the gospel of Christ?' 60

The trend toward a community of interest was dictated by both convenience and necessity. In embracing the unworldly doctrine of celibacy, the followers of Ann Lee committed themselves to living apart from the world. But it is doubtful, since Ann herself had no clear institutional program, whether these first adherents to the new religion fully realized its social implications. Communal experience on the one hand, and persecution and condemnation on the other, convinced all, however, that *in* the world the gospel of regeneration could not prevail. Ann was still on her mission through New England when her disciples began to organize into 'family' units, consecrate their goods to the holy cause, and 'entertain' their converts at 'free cost.'

The early establishments at Niskeyuna, Harvard, and Ashfield were really incipient communities, where circumstances forced the pooling of resources and strict obedience to leadership. Darrow's sheep were a free will offering to the Niskeyuna church. Grain, flour, and cheese were brought from New Lebanon to Harvard, which was short of provisions. At Ashfield, where they maintained from fifty to three hundred people, large supplies had to be purchased in the neighborhood. Though no definite organization was at first instituted in these places, the preservation of the church was dependent on donations of money and food.

Public utterances by Ann Lee and James Whittaker also indicate that a 'common interest,' initiated by property grants, was a half-articulated aim. As early as 1780 the prophetess predicted a great increase of the gospel. 'It will be like a man's beginning in the world,' she told Samuel Fitch, 'raising up a family of children, gathering an interest and then dying, and leaving his interest with his children, who will improve thereon and gather more.' Job Bishop related that she often foretold 'the gathering of the people into a united body, or church, having a common interest.' Her insistence on industry was further proof that Ann thought of the church as an organization having socio-economic as well as strictly religious functions. At the 'beginning,' Daniel Rathbun wrote, 'they taught us the necessity of laying all at the apostles' feet . . . and give up all to their disposal for the relief of the poor.' Rathbun was the first to compare the Shaker order with the Catholic convent.

The first documentary evidence of community planning is found in a letter — the earliest Shaker manuscript extant — written by Whit-
61 taker in February 1782, from the hill town of Ashfield. It was a plea to Josiah Talcott of Hancock to shake off sloth and idleness and get his farm in readiness — 'For you have Land enough [Whittaker said] to maintain three families or more, well improved.' Here, in the winter of 1782–3, Father James made the historic announcement: 'The time is come for you to give up yourselves and your all to God — your substance, your temporal property — to possess as though you possessed not.' 'We shall have one meeting together,' he promised, 'which will never break up.' Without giving the date, Reuben Rathbun credits Whittaker with the order that the people 'sell their
62 possessions and give to the poor'; and it seems probable, from the substance of many of his remarks, that Ann's 'first apostle' was the original promulgator of the community principle.

In a letter from Canterbury dated 19 February 1783, Plumer asserted that at that time the elders were preaching 'the exploded doctrine of having all things in common, and bringing the money to their
63 feet, as successors of the apostles.' Already several valuable properties had been sold:

> The Elders dispose of the people at the different houses [the letter continues]; they are then constantly employed in labor by the heads of houses, who are treated and reverenced as fathers. The common class receive only their food and clothing; the Elders do no labor, nor take any care to provide for their substance; they live freely, travelling from place to place.

Plumer's picture is one of harsh discipline:

> The women and children are under the most abject submission to the master of the house where they live; the laborers and men to the tutors and Elders; and those to the church. A woman cannot give away a meal's victuals to a friend or relative without the express permission of the governor of the house, — even though he is her husband.

More sympathetic is Calvin Harlow's account, written about 1782, of the operation of the principle of 'joint interest':

> The Church at Niskayuna (now Watervliet) before our acquaintance with them, as we were informed, held the property which they had there,

as a Joint Interest. And after we became acquainted with them, and be-   *64*
lieved their testimony, they gave what they had gained by their industry,
with the use and improvement of their farm, for the good and benefit
of the whole society, to be improved in the following manner. Viz. That
there should be a free table kept there, and other necessaries for the
entertainment of those that went to see them — that the poor might have
an equal privilege of the gospel with the rich; and all those who went
there to see them, that were able, had liberty to contribute according
to their own faith, towards supporting table expenses, and the poor that
went there, and other necessary expenses.

None were compelled, nor even desired to contribute, but such as could
do it freely, believing it to be their duty; and they were often cautioned
and taught to deal justly with all men: and were examined whether they
were not in debt, or whether their families did not stand in need of what
they offered to give.

So the doctrine implied plainly, to every rational understanding, that
those that went to see the Church, that were able to support ourselves,
it was our duty to do it, or give as much as we received, and those that
were able to do more, it was their duty to give more than what was sufficient to support themselves while at the Church: For if none were to do
more than to support themselves, the poor could not have an equal privilege of the gospel with the rich.   *65*

The final allusion to Shaker communism as it existed in Mother
Ann's time is contained in a letter to England written February 1784
by Father James: 'I now live with my kind Mother in Israel Ann Lee
and have all things in common with others that have come in to us.'   *66*

Mother Ann died at Niskeyuna 8 September 1784 — a year after
her return from the eastward journey. Four years of persecution and
privation, incessant laborings and a constant expenditure of passionate energy had taken their toll. Harassed in body and tortured in
soul since early youth, the mill girl with the strange obsession was no
longer able to bear her burden; and when her brother William died   *67*
21 July, her hold on life was fatally relaxed. 'She continually
grew weaker in body, without any visible appearance of bodily disease.' She brooded over her loss, and just before her 'departure' was
heard to say, 'I see Brother William coming, in a golden chariot, to
take me home.'

News of the passing of the 'Mother of Zion' was published by the
Albany *Gazette*, and carried by messengers to New Lebanon and
Hancock. A great concourse, Believers and unbelievers alike, at-

tended the funeral, at which Father James expressed the sense of
tragic loss which was felt by the faithful. To the world he said: 'This
that we so much esteem, and so much adore, is a treasure worth labouring for: it is the only means of salvation that will ever be offered
68   to sinners; it is the last display of God's grace to a lost world.'

The passing of their leader was a severe shock to Ann's followers,
many of whom believed — in spite of her rejection of the doctrine
69   that the physical body was immortal — that her ministry, like that
of Shadrack Ireland's, would be endless, or at least a thousand years
long. Numbers lost their faith and fell away, and even the loyal were
assailed by doubts and fears. The gospel was attacked with renewed
zeal, and for a time there was danger that the order would be dissolved. But in Whittaker the church still had one of the three original
'witnesses,' the most gifted preacher in the society. Though certain
members, including James Shepherd and John Partington, refused
to serve under his leadership, and though his foes charged he was the
'champion of that phase of Shaker fanaticism which could find nothing good or beautiful in family life,' nevertheless the faith of Ann's
chief English disciple, dynamic and rigidly consistent, as he saw it,
with the teachings of Jesus, carried conviction wherever he went.
Christ was ever present in his mind, the supreme Mentor whom he de-
lighted to glorify:

O I love him! I love him! I love him! [he exclaims in one of his letters].
He is the chief among ten thousand unto me, and is altogether lovely!
His brightness, His beauty is so great, that the most elegant description that can be given of Him by language is mere deformity before Him.
O! his love . . . how transcendent bright it is! filling all things with
comfort wherever it goes, and one glance of it can happify ten thousand
worlds, and turn hell into Paradise. How happy then will be the over-
70   comer in the fruition and open vision of such an unsearchable beauty!

On this zealot the mantle of authority naturally fell. After the
funeral, Meacham, Harlow, Hocknell, and others 'came forward, and
acknowledged him as their Elder, and that the gift of God rested
upon him for their protection.' In accepting leadership, Father
James assured the people that Ann's entry into the world of spirits
was required for the further increase of her work on earth and, at the
same time, warned that those who opposed or forsook the gospel

would never prosper or 'die the natural death of other men' — a prophecy documented in Shaker annals by accounts of the misfortunes and 'awful' deaths of certain 'reprobates' and the 'curse' that fell on the town of Petersham. Three days later Whittaker took up 71 the unfinished work of gathering together the scattered groups of Believers. For over a year he vigorously promoted these labors, personally visiting the churches in Maine and Massachusetts, delegating such lieutenants as Reuben Rathbun and David Meacham to organize the Connecticut Shakers. So great was the enthusiasm that a ship, named the *Union*, was built and fitted out at Rehoboth, under the command of Morrell Baker, to bear the testimony to foreign lands. Though this project failed after a dispute over Baker's captaincy, the *Union*, with a crew of Shakers and a cargo of horses, flour, et cetera, is said to have made one voyage to Haiti and Havana and back to Boston.   72

MEETING-HOUSES, NEW LEBANON. FIRST CHURCH IN BACKGROUND

Culminating the upsurge of renewed fervor was the raising at New Lebanon, on 15 October 1785, of the first meeting-house, a plain gambrel-roofed structure which was nevertheless the symbol of a faith established, the beginning of the church as 'an outward visible order.' It was Whittaker who had ordered its building, at the place where the gospel was most firmly entrenched. And it was Whittaker who dedicated the edifice, communicating to the people the 'covenant' of the Lord and giving to the society its first 'gospel orders':

Thus saith the Lord, this is the Covenant that I make with you this day. If ye will hearken to the voice of the Lord your God, and do whatsoever I command you, then I will be your God, and you shall be my people; and I will protect you in this House. But if ye refuse to hearken to my Covenant, which I make with you this day, then I refuse your protection.

And these are the Orders that ye are to observe and Keep: Ye shall come in and go out of this house with reverence and godly fear; — all men shall come in and go out at the west doors and gates; and all women at the east doors and gates. Men and women shall not intermix in this house or yard, nor sit together; neither shall there be any whispering, or talking, or laughing, nor unnecessary going out and in, in times of public worship. Neither shall there be any buying or selling, or bargaining done in this house or yard: For ye shall not make this house a place of merchandize; for it was built to worship God in, and to repent in.

Furthermore, ye shall do no servile labor in this house, except to wash and clean the house, and to keep it in order.

73

Experience had shown that missionary labors diffused effort and stirred up opposition at the cost of internal order. Once a house of worship had been erected, therefore, Whittaker and his associate ministers decided to 'withdraw the testimony' from the world and devote their time to consolidating the work of Mother Ann's tour and winning Believers progressively from their 'fleshly relations.' On the Sabbath, 29 January 1786, Whittaker officiated at the first regular assembly in the new meeting-house, where for a year he continued to be the leading preacher. He wrote to his parents, relatives, and friends, trying to induce them to emigrate to this 'spacious country' — where 'any prudent man may make a good living' and where the 'soil is good . . . especially remote from the sea.' In May he made plans to return to England to make a personal appeal but arrived in New York after his ship had sailed. For the rest of the year he traveled constantly among the New England societies, holding so arduously to the task that by January of the new year, though only thirty-six years old, his strength began to fail and he was forced to bid farewell to New Lebanon and seek repose at the Meacham home in Enfield. In March, he visited the Believers in Harvard, Shirley, and Woburn but was unable to go further, and after his return to Enfield his life ebbed slowly away.

Father James's funeral was held on 21 July. 'The season was very affecting to all the Believers, who viewed him as their Elder and Father, and the last of those faithful Ministers of Christ, who had brought the gospel to this land, and had been called to stand in the Ministry.'

74

CHAPTER IV

Early Shaker Communism

Forthi cristene men scholde been
in commun riche, no covetise to hymselve.

— Piers Plowman

'PROCESSIONS OF Juggernaut, camp-meetings, the excitements of
a revival . . . rarely leave any noble or permanent result.' So observed Charles Eliot Norton in his notes on the building of Orvieto
Cathedral in Italy. 'But it was the distinctive characteristic of this
period of religious enthusiasm,' he continued, 'that there were men
honestly partaking in the general emotion, yet of such strong individuality of genius, that, instead of being carried away by the wasteful current of feeling, they were able to guide and control to great
and noble purposes the impulsive activity and bursting energies of
the time.'

Not dissimilar was the turn taken by the Shaker movement after
the deaths of the 'three witnesses.' For at that critical stage there
arose a high-minded leader, possessed of a genius for organization,
who dedicated his unusual gifts to the task of bestowing vitality, order, and direction to what till then, in spite of Whittaker's labor, had
been an amorphous fellowship. Eliminate the influence of Joseph
Meacham, and the church would probably not long have survived the
death of its founder, or merited more than a footnote in the social,
economic, or religious history of America.

Father Joseph, as he was commonly known among the Believers,
was born in Enfield (Conn.) on 22 February 1741. His father, Elder
Joseph Meacham, awakened by the famous Enfield sermon of Jonathan Edwards, founded the first Baptist church and society in that

54

town; and his son, heir to the liberalism of the New Lights, eventually became the leading lay preacher of the denomination at New Lebanon. Here, with his wife and sons, he led the life of a yeoman and an eloquent exhorter of the New Light faith.

Meacham's part in the opening of the Shaker testimony has been told. When Whittaker died, the choice of a successor lay between Joseph, his younger brother David, and Calvin Harlow. It is told 75 that in the first assembly after Father James's death, the Shakers, with one thought uppermost in their minds, waited prayerfully for some manifestation of divine wisdom. When certain leaders were finally inspired to speak, the 'chosen one' listened meekly, no evidence of supernatural power being vouchsafed to his burdened spirit. Then 'the voice of a youth, Job Bishop, was heard, calm and decided, declaring with power which left not the shadow of a doubt on the mind of any one present, that the silent listener, Joseph Meacham, was the 76 anointed of God, to lead his people.'

The Shakers were in fact already prepared for Meacham's leadership. Mother Ann had publicly named him 'the wisest man that has been born of a woman for six hundred years.' 'God has called and anointed him to be a Father to all his people in America,' she said on one occasion; on another: 'the lead will be given to Joseph Meacham'; and again: 'Joseph is my first Bishop; he will have the keys of the Kingdom; he is my Apostle in the Ministry . . . what he does, I do.' The preacher's emotion at Whittaker's grave — where 'he shook and trembled all over, from head to foot,' and spoke with marvelous power — profoundly impressed all witnesses; and his able administration of affairs following that event convinced both David and Calvin that he alone was qualified for the supreme lead. Elder Joseph's accession to the 'second foundation lot' was confirmed, as were all successive appointments to office, by what the Shakers termed the 'mutual approbation of the people.' 77

One of the first acts of his administration was the elevation of Lucy Wright to the lead 'in the female line.' This remarkable woman, who later, for twenty-five years, was to guide the destinies of the sect, was born in Pittsfield 5 February 1760. Her parents, John and Mary (Robbins) Wright, had some means and standing in the town, and Lucy probably received as good an education as the conditions of the time allowed. Possessed of exceptional intelligence and a strong will, her nature was nevertheless restrained, refined, and essentially wom-

anly. At eighteen she was married to Elizur Goodrich, a young mer-
78 chant in the neighboring town of Richmond.

If Ann Lee, as her enemies charged, had been a common charlatan,
it is difficult to see how persons like the Goodriches, Meachams, and
others could have bestowed on her their loyalty and affection. Lucy
and her husband were happily married. Both were prudent and practical. Yet we find them intimately attached to the prophetess and absorbed in the doctrine at the outset — Elizur confessing his sins at an
early period; Lucy sending gifts to Mother Ann in the Poughkeepsie
jail, attending her during the trying days at Harvard, ministering
to the imprisoned elders at Albany. Recognizing in turn the talents
of the young wife, Ann had said that gaining Lucy Wright to the
gospel was 'equal to gaining a nation.' After the death of the foundress, Lucy assumed additional responsibilities at Niskeyuna, while
Elizur played a prominent part in organizing the societies at Hancock and New Lebanon.

In appointing a woman to lead the Shaker sisterhood, Meacham
took the initial step in forming a dual order based on the equality of
the sexes. The decision, it was asserted, came to him as a 'gift,' not as
part of a preconceived policy. Though deeply significant, the assignment was a natural one. Women preachers existed among the English, American, and Continental Quakers; and in Jane Wardley
and Ann Lee the precedent of female leadership had been firmly established. 'Perfect equality of rights,' as between man and woman,
was a logical attribute of the doctrine of a male and female messiahship. Moreover, if the principles of confession and celibacy were to
be preserved under communal conditions, it was imperative that the
sexes be separated and organized along independent yet parallel
lines. There was need, in short, for the 'Mother Gift.'

In September, 1787, Joseph and Lucy — acknowledged now as
'beloved Parents in Church relation, and first in relation to the whole
visible body of the Believers' — decided the time had come for all true
Shakers to separate themselves from the world. Word went out that
those who were prepared should gather together at New Lebanon. A
meeting-house already awaited their coming. David Darrow, John
Bishop, Hezekiah Hammond, Jonathan Walker, and others had dedicated their houses and lands to the cause. During the fall and early
winter of the year, scores of Believers came into the incipient community, occupying huts, cabins, barns, and the few houses on the con-

secrated farms. On Christmas day they sat down together for the first communal meal.

That supper marked the beginning of Shaker communism as an actual institution. In 1788, the year in which most of the Believers were gathered at New Lebanon, the preliminary organization of the church was begun. Meacham patterned the first Shaker family after the Jewish temple, with three 'courts': an inner sacred order, a junior order, and an outer court. For the first or inner court he accordingly gathered about a hundred of those who had 'the greatest faith and abilities in things spiritual,' chiefly unmarried persons of middle age or under — former merchants, tradesmen, mechanics, and other 'indoor workers' — free from debt and family involvements. 'The second 79 in their faith and abilities' composed the second court, or 'family,' mostly young men and women used to outdoor work such as farming and teaming. A few children, on consent of their parents, were also included, for it was Father Joseph's conviction that 'by living longer after the flesh' elderly people were farther from the Kingdom than the young. Those older members — 'such as by age or infirmity, or any other cause were not able to travel with the young people' — he placed in the third or outward court, together with the brethren — 80 David Meacham, Jonathan Walker, and others — selected to carry on business relations with the world. On 27 August 1788, a 'great house' was raised to accommodate the tripartite church.

When the courts were formed, the members entered into an oral agreement 'to stand as one joint community.' As the *Testimony* puts it, 'they freely gave themselves and services, with all their temporal interest, for the mutual support and benefit of each other, and for other charitable uses, according to the light and revelation of God which they had received.' Even before the written covenants were 81 signed, from 1795 on, records were kept of properties consecrated to the church — dedications which stand today as eloquent testimonials of the sincerity of a faith.   82

Also expressive of the will to *re-form* was the early commitment to industry. Though swayed by an essentially romantic ideal, the Shakers were practical New Englanders at heart, knowing that no utopia could be gained without unremitting effort. It is significant that occupational activities were under way even before 'gospel order' was established or appointments of ministers and elders made. As soon as the three courts were formed, Joseph Meacham appointed his

83 brother David as first deacon and trustee of the church. The members of this order put their hands to work, pursuing the same occupations they had once followed for private gain. By 1789 a tannery, fulling mill, clothing shop, chair factory, blacksmith shop, and cobbler's shop were in full operation, manufacturing such articles as saddles and saddlebags, harnesses, leather mittens, whips and whiplashes, dressed cloth, felt hats, chairs, coopers' ware, wrought nails, hoes, shoe and stock buckles, boots, and shoes. Many of the pursuits were housed in the brethren's shop built that year. The Shaker garden-seed industry was also started in 1789, and the farm produced, among other crops, three thousand bushels of potatoes. Meanwhile the sisterhood was occupied with various household arts, chief among which were the spinning and dyeing of yarn and the weaving and dressing of cloth. A 'spin-shop' was erected in 1791. On 21 April of the same year an office building known as the East House was raised for the accommodation of the outer court and a clearing house for Shaker products consigned to the world.

Out of Meacham's three-court arrangement of the New Lebanon church evolved the 'family' system of this and other Shaker communities. An 'order of families,' originally called the 'old believers order,' holding spiritual union with the New Lebanon church but managing its own temporal affairs, was instituted by Joseph and Lucy in 1791. Six separate families, made up of elderly persons and people whose circumstances would not permit them to enter the church proper, were loosely united in this order, each group organized under some prominent leader and called by his name: viz. Rufus Clark's family, Israel Talcott's family, et cetera. Members of these groups often sold their farms and possessions before coming together, though the principle of common stock or united interest was not adopted until the 'old believers order' became the Second family in 1815. Eventually all Shaker societies were organized into 'family' branches or circles (called Second family, East family, Hill family, etc.) around a

84 Church or Center family.

85 With the appointment of elders and eldresses in 1792, 'gospel order' was considered fully established. According to the principles of social practice as outlined by Father Joseph, supreme authority over the whole United Society was vested in the central ministry at New Lebanon (originally Joseph and Lucy but soon to be made up of two elders and two eldresses), who appointed the branch ministries of

other societies, usually grouped into 'bishoprics.' In the families themselves, 'government of all matters . . . both in things spiritual and temporal,' was entrusted to the eldership — composed of two elders and two eldresses, who received their orders directly from the ministry. The temporal affairs of each family was the specific responsibility of the 'lot' of deacons or trustees, generally two of each sex, who took their instructions from the elders. Appointments, according to this system, moved always 'from head to foot.' Meacham wrote in his *Way Marks:*

It is the work of the first Lot in the Ministry to appoint all the rest of the foundation Lots in the Ministry, for the gathering and building of all the Churches, except the first in the present travel, and to give them the principles of Church Order and Law, in their own order . . . the first lot in the Ministry is to give order and counsel to the second lot in the same Ministry, and to the Elders of the first family, in their own Order. But all immediate order or counsel that is given by the Ministry, to any other lots in the Ministry, or any lots back of the first family, ought to be given by the second lot in the Ministry . . . Foundation Lots are called to keep the foundation . . .

86

As first deacon of the Church family in New Lebanon, Elder David Meacham was cautioned 'to receive nothing into the joint property of the Church but what is free and clear of all just claims from those who are without.' Mother Ann had insisted on this rule, and Meacham foresaw the dangers of its infraction. Whoever comes with demands against the Church, labor to settle with them, he advised, rather than try 'to overcome them by the laws of men,' for such was the 'Law of Christ.' 'But if after due labors made with them,' he went on, 'they still hold a demand against the Church, it may be necessary to make them a consideration, in order for a settlement — not as acknowledging or paying a debt on our part, or as justifying them in their demands, but as a settlement for peace sake, that the Church may be blameless; and they that do us wrong may be without excuse in the day of trial.'

On the subject of equal rights and privileges, Father Joseph made the following pronouncement:

All the members of the Church have a just and equal right to the use of things, according to their order and needs; no other difference ought to be made, beween Elder or younger in things spiritual or temporal, than that which is just, and is for the peace and unity, and good of the whole.

Equality between male and female, he held, was according to the order of God in the creation: 'For altho our Blessed Lord and Redeemer, Jesus Christ, was complete in his own glorious person, and laid the foundation for the salvation of all souls, yet as God hath created man of two parts, the male and female, it was necessary that he should make his second appearance in the second part of man, that the order might be complete, in the new creation.'

Meacham's repeated use of the words 'order' and 'use' indicate how important he considered these values. Elder David's office, he wrote, was 'to establish order for the protection and support of the Church . . . to oversee all outgoings . . . to establish trades, or the order of trades . . .' Deacon Jonathan Walker was called 'to the chief care and oversight relating to the order of buildings, yards and fences': his work was 'to lay out the order of the buildings, and to see that the foundations are laid well, that the buildings are not exposed to be damaged by the frost in winter, and to see that the materials for buildings are suitable for their use, according to the order and use of the buildings, and that the work is done in due order.' Concluding his instructions to the deacons, he wrote: 'All work in the church ought to be done plain and decent, according to the order and use of things, neither too high nor too low, according to their order and use.'

The Shaker doctrines of utility and the golden mean were here given their first expression:

All work done, or things made in the Church for their own use ought to be faithfully and well done, but plain and without superfluity. All things ought to be made according to their order and use; and all things kept decent and in good order, according to their order and use. All things made for sale ought to be well done, and suitable for their use . . .

All ought to dress in plain and modest apparel, but clean and decent according to their order and calling, and suitable to their employ, and to the season and state of the weather, neither too high nor too low, but in a just and temperate medium, suitable for an example to others.

Instructions were also given for the education of youth, the proper use of worldly inventions, the stand to be taken relative to military requisitions, and the duty of Believers in relation to the world of mankind in general. Meacham, in conversation with his co-ministers, whom he was training for leadership of the branch societies, gave out many bylaws and orders which at a later date were written into the so-called *Millennial Laws* of the United Society. And in the 'union 87 meetings' which he instituted in 1793, the brethren and sisters, coming together for social or religious discourse, repeated many of these orders until they became the ingrained tradition of communal procedure. At the very beginning of a new social experiment, Meacham, it seems, had an unusual conception of its manifold problems, setting the stamp of a noble spirit on the institution.

Individuals and families, many of whom had adopted the faith in Ann Lee's time, flocked to New Lebanon, Niskeyuna, and other centers during the five-year period, 1788–92. Late in 1790, Father Joseph appointed Calvin Harlow to gather the Believers at Hancock, 88 Tyringham, and Enfield (Conn.) ; and following the example set when Lucy Wright was placed first 'in the female line,' two weeks later the ministry selected a native of Richmond, Sarah Harrison, to assist him in the organization of the sisterhood. Similarly, Eleazer Rand and Hannah Kendal were delegated in 1791 'to stand as the immediate parents' to the Shakers in the bishopric of Harvard and Shirley. The following year Job Bishop and Hannah Goodrich were appointed as ministers to Canterbury and Enfield (N.H.) ; and a year later John Barnes and Sarah Kendal undertook the organization of the churches at Alfred and Sabbathday-Pond. New Lebanon and 89 Niskeyuna, which is now known as Watervliet or Water Vliet, formed the first bishopric, with its affairs administered by the central ministry. The bishopric ministries were required to visit the New Lebanon church at least once each year.

Written covenants — precedents for which may be found in the practices of the Congregationalists and Free Will Baptists — were signed in the church or first families of all the societies during 1795–6. The original compact, whose essential form was preserved in each 90 branch of the society, was drafted by Joseph Meacham in 1795, a year before his death, and signed by twenty-one brethren and twenty-two sisters in the New Lebanon Church family governed by Elder David Darrow and Eldress Ruth Farrington. In it the theory and implications of 'a joint interest' were given specific form:

For it was and is still our Faith [reads the preamble], and confirmed by our experience, that there could be no Church in Complete order, according to the Law of Christ, without being gathered into one Joint Interest and union, that all the members might have an equal right and privilege, according to their Calling and needs, in things both Spiritual and temporal. And in which we have a greater privilege and opportunity, of doing good to each other, and the rest of mankind, and receiving according to our needs, Jointly and Equally, one with another, in one Joint union and interest . . .

The articles of covenant were five:

Firstly, The Conditions on which we were received, as members of the Church, were in Substance as follows. All or as many of us as were of age to act for ourselves, who offered ourselves as members of the Church, were to do it freely and Voluntarily as a Religious duty, and according to our own faith and desire.

Secondly, Youth and Children, being under age, were not to be received as members, or as being under the immediate care and government of the Church, But by the request or free consent of both their parents, if living, except they were left by one of their parents to the care of the other, then by the request or free Consent of that parent, and if the Child have no parents, Then by the request or free Consent of such person, or persons, as may have Just and Lawful right, in Care of the Child; Together with the Child's own desire.

Thirdly, All that should be received as members, being of age, that had any substance or property that was free from debt, or any Just demand of any that were without, either as Creditors or Heirs, were allowed to bring in their Substance, being their natural and Lawful right, and give it as a part of the Joint Interest of the Church, agreeable to their own faith and desire, to be under the order and Government of the Deacons, And Overseers of the Temporal Interest of the Church, for the use and Support of the Church, and any other use that the Gospel requires, according to the understanding and discretion of those members with whom it was Intrusted, and that were appointed to that office and care.

Fourthly, All the members that should be received into the Church, Should possess one Joint Interest, as a Religious right, that is, that all should have Just and Equal rights and Privileges, according to their needs, in the use of all things in the Church, without Any difference being made on account of what any of us brought in, so long as we remained in Obedience to the Order and Government of the Church, and are holden in relation as members. All of the members are likewise Equally holden, according to their abilities, to maintain and support one Joint Interest in union, in Conformity to the order and Government of the Church.

Fifthly, As it was not the duty or purpose of the Church, in uniting into Church order, to gather and lay up an Interest of this World's goods; But what we become possessed of by Honest Industry, more

*Gather into order according to our own
faith, but also we believed it to be
the duty of as many of us that believed,
as might be for the good of the Whole,
to gather into the order and Covenant
in which we now are. We believed we
were debtors to God in relation to
Each other, and all men, to improve
our time and Tallents in this Life,
in that manner in which we might be
most useful. And we have had the
Experience of Seven years Travel and
Labour, and Received a greater Confirm
ation and Establishment in our faith,*

PAGE FROM FIRST WRITTEN COVENANT, NEW LEBANON, 1795

Than for our own support, to bestow to Charitable uses, for the relief of the poor, and otherwise as the Gospel might Require. Therefore, it is our faith never to bring Debt or blame against the Church, or each other, for any interest or Services we should bestow to the Joint Interest of the Church, but Covenanted to freely give and Contribute our time and Talents, as Brethren and Sisters, for the mutual good one of another, and other Charitable uses, according to the order of the church.

Affirmation of the Shaker faith concludes the brief constitution: 'We believed we were debtors to God in relation to Each other, and all men, to improve our time and Tallents in this Life, in that manner in which we might be most useful.' Seven years of 'Travel and Labour' had convinced all that the order represented the highest spiritual state of mankind, one that had the acceptance of God. Solemnly the subscribers affixed their names.

Though not a perfect protection against demands on the 'united inheritance,' this first written instrument gave it status as an institution — not a corporate body, but an established religious denomination whose property, held in trust by appointed trustees, was a possession consecrated to God. The covenant was soon to meet its first legal test, and in the light of further experience, to be further refined.

Quite possibly a serious falling away from the faith, sometime in 1794 or 1795, had convinced Meacham that the oral agreement of 1788 should be committed to writing. The apostasies, lasting several months, were chiefly among the young, being led, in fact, by the elder of a children's order. That Father Joseph was deeply concerned by this breach is evidenced in a letter he wrote to Mother Lucy:

> I believe the late and present troubles among the young, in the Church, are the chief cause of my present weakness and sufferings. As they were young and not able to receive that planting of faith in their understandings . . . as the adults were, I always expected there would be more trouble with them, as they come to ripe age . . . It hath been, and still is my hope and expectation that the greater number of the young will keep their faith, and if weak in the present travel, compared with the older, they may be more useful in the next, and we be compensated for our labors and troubles with them.

Tremendous effort was involved in the organization of eleven distinct communities. Meacham constantly traveled from one society to another, planning and exhorting. His energy was boundless, his faith in the institution exalted. Not only did he lay the secular foundation of Shakerism, but in *A Concise Statement of the Principles of the Only True Church* (Bennington, Vt., 1790) gave it, for the first time in printed form, a rationale. The first light of salvation, he held, was made known to the patriarchs, typified by Abraham; the second appeared in the Mosaic law; the third dispensation of God to man was in the doctrines of Christ; and the fourth, foretold by Daniel and St. John as beginning in 1747, was the 'completing work' of Ann Lee. Deeply spiritual and naturally diffident, Father Joseph often secluded himself from his fellows, meditating and praying in the iso-

A
CONCISE STATEMENT
OF THE
PRINCIPLES
OF THE
ONLY TRUE CHURCH
ACCORDING TO
THE GOSPEL
OF THE
PRESENT APPEARANCE
OF
CHRIST.
As held to and practifed upon by the true
followers of the LIVING SAVIOUR,
at NEWLEBANON, &c.

TOGETHER WITH A LETTER FROM
JAMES WHITTAKER,
Minifter of the Gofpel in this day of CHRIST's
fecond appearing—to his natural relations in
England. *Dated October 9th,* 1785.

Printed at Bennington, Vermont,
By HASWELL & RUSSELL—1790.

TITLE PAGE OF FIRST SHAKER PAMPHLET

lation of his room in the meeting-house. Here he had visions of angels
dancing around the throne of God; here, by himself, he practised by
hours those sacred steps, imparting them to the Believers in their frequent assemblies. The heavy shuffling marches and 'laborings for
mortification' were his contribution to the fundamental ritual of the
Shaker worship — gifts gratefully received, for what Joseph gave
seemed to have come directly from the prophetess herself.

Ceaseless labors, conscientiously pursued for nearly twenty years,
slowly weakened the constitution of this greatest seer of the sect. Returning to his home in Enfield in the early summer of 1796, he fell ill
suddenly and died on the sixteenth of August, leaving Mother Lucy
Wright as the supreme head of what was now an established order. In
less than ten years he had brought together a scattered, somewhat
purposeless fraternity and elevated it to a position of security and
abundant vitality. With his death passed the second phase of the

Shaker movement, a period of entrenchment and construction in which the church was practically undisturbed by the world.

It was Meacham's sensible policy, in giving the church a communal-industrial foundation, to gain the good will of a hitherto critical society: for the church's market, after all, had to be the world of generation. Accordingly he frowned on the practice of denouncing the world and discouraged exaggerated expressions of ceremonial zeal. The way to perfection, he would say, was by inward travel, by warring with evil in one's own soul. Better than condemnation was the creation of a faultless social order as an example to all mankind. As Joseph brought his followers more and more into Gospel Order, their attention was turned increasingly to internal affairs.

A more amicable outward opinion was the reward. On 3 December 1792, the town of Enfield (Conn.) voted to give the Shakers their school money, after a period of depriving them of this privilege. A vote disapproving the conduct of the 'Shaking Quakers' of Shirley in 1782 was followed three years later by the abatement of their minister rates, and eventually (1810) by a vote giving them their proportion of school money. 'Philo,' in a letter published in *The Theological Magazine* in 1796, wrote regarding the sect:

They themselves are plain, decent, and grave in their dress, language, and deportment. As to integrity, their character is established among all considerate people in this quarter, but the very vulgar still entertain idle and shameful stories of this virtuous, honest, and industrious society. The contortions, grimaces, and promiscuous dancings, which marked and disgraced their conduct, when they first arose among us, have given way to a mode of worship, which tends to inspire sentiments of solemnity, 94 rather than derision.

Even the critical President Dwight admitted that, by 1799, policy was taking the place of extravagance.

One policy was obligatory, or at least expedient, if relations with the world were to be harmonious. Before the society was organized it had been criticized for appropriating original bequests and making no allowances for services if a member chose to withdraw — justifying the action by insisting that these goods and services had been given to God, and it would be sacrilege, therefore, to return their value to the seceder. Besides, it was highly unjust, these critics said, that the children of Believers or seceders should suffer loss of property on account of 'belief or disbelief in matters of religion.'

So that the church might be blameless in such cases, it adopted, immediately after the first oral covenant in 1788, Father Joseph's advice regarding 'settlements.' In the Meacham-written covenant, it declined to accept money or other property unless the donor were free from the demands of creditors or heirs. If families were divided in their belief and questions arose about the disposition of revenue from the sale of farms or other property, 'it was felt right for the Father to have twice as much as the Mother, the Mother twice as much as the Son, the Son twice as much as the Daughter.' Further protection against moral blame and possible legal entanglements was provided by the 'discharge,' a form of arbitration in which the seceder, in return for a consideration, signed a document releasing the deacons from any subsequent demand he might make for property or services. The following 'discharge,' signed by Pitman Collins Cooke on 14 March 1789, is a typical document:

Whereas I Pitman Cooke have heretofore professed myself to be of the Religious Society of Christians called Shakers and have frequently visited the Elders of the Church and have from time to time freely Contributed for the Support of the Ministry and Table Expenses for myself and others that have Visited the Elders and for the Support of the poor of said Church and Society which I acknowledge I gave or Contributed freely and Voluntarily according to my own Faith and that it hath been Consumed in the Manner and for the purposes for Which I gave it. Notwithstanding since I have departed from them I have Conceived that I have Contributed more than my Just and equal proportion While I professed to be in union with them, And upon that Consideration I have applyed to the present Elders of the Church to Consider me on that account And have Received of Elder David Meacham in behalf of the Church and Society the Sum or Value of Twenty one pounds two shillings New York currency as a Matter of Gratis on their parts Which together with what I have heretofore Received I do acknowledge myself fully Satisfyed with, and I do believe and acknowledge it to be a Just and equal ballence. Therefore I do by these presents acquit and Discharge the said Church and Society Jointly and Severally from any further Request, Charge or Demand of any Kind or Nature Whatever . . .   95

Seceders were granted sums from twenty to several hundred dollars, and usually clothing, tools, and other articles, all carefully

billed. When anyone joined the society, a careful inventory was taken
of his or her contributions, the equivalent of which was returned if
the member left the order. Thus, a shoemaker departing from the
society was given the complete kit of his trade, a carpenter his, a
cooper his, and so on. Angell Mathewson was paid six dollars for a
swarm of bees which she had consecrated to the united interest. Mary
Dayley received fifty dollars as a charitable gift, together with some
'soallleather,' six chairs, a little wheel, a great wheel, a wheel head,
calf skins, two sides of upper leather, and a cow. Zadock Wright, for
his services, was given a horse, saddle, saddlebags, bridle, a new
'rasor,' fur hat, silk handkerchief, pocket handkerchief, new boots
and shoes, a pair of brass buckles, a short coat, an under Jacket, a
surtout, and other articles of clothing, besides money and a 'money
purse' — the whole amounting to £35-1-1. Because the Hamlin family had lived 'in common' with him for three years, Reuben Wight was
paid £52. Nathan Commins was allowed thirty dollars, besides clothing, for the labor of his son David, a minor. And so it goes on through
paper after paper. Thousands of dollars in cash, property, and
manufactured products were expended by David Meacham, Jonathan Walker, and David Osborne in the effort to dispense justice and
avoid trouble.

Fearing that the original covenant was weak as a legal instrument,
most of its signers, in the last years of the century, devised authorized
wills and testaments in which they confirmed the dedications of property made in that compact. Two types appeared, those in which the
whole estate was to be placed at death in the hands of the deacons or
overseers of the church, and those in which some provision was made
for wife, children, or heirs.

In spite of such attempts to protect the united interest, it was soon
seen that only a more explicit covenant could resist encroachment. In
March 1799, notwithstanding the fact that three years earlier he had
signed a Shaker 'discharge,' Benjamin Goodrich brought suit against
Jonathan Walker, representing the New Lebanon church, for $3000
which he claimed represented wages that were not paid him while he
was a member of the order. Though the case, tried in the New York
supreme court, resulted in a victory for the society, the ministry realized that the covenant should be reframed. Accordingly, on 24 June
1801, a new instrument was adopted in which the section that begins —

Therefore, it is our faith never to bring Debt or blame against the Church, or each other, for any interest or Services we should bestow to the Joint Interest of the Church —

was superseded by the following amendment:

And we do, by these presents, solemnly covenant with each other, for ourselves, and assigns, never hereafter, to bring debt or demand against the said Deacons, nor their successors, nor against any member of the Church, or community, jointly or severally on account of any of our services, or property, thus devoted and consecrated to the aforesaid sacred and charitable uses.   97

Organization of the New Lebanon community was virtually complete by the end of the century. Once the meeting-house was complete, the testimony which had been withdrawn during Whittaker's regime was re-opened 'to such as were in a special manner awakened.' The various 'children's orders,' and the novitiate or 'gathering' order instituted late in 1799, with Ebenezer Cooley as elder, were the result of an increasing number of people seeking 'to find union with the people of God'; and in March 1800, the dwelling north of the church ('the North House') was given over to these 'young believers who were sick of the world.' Here probationers were taught the principles of the faith while still retaining family ties and property. If, after such instruction, they wished to progress, they were moved to a junior order or 'family relation,' a family to which they would devote their services free, but where the grant or retention of all or part of their property was optional. Acceptance into the third class, or senior order, was solemnized by signing a covenant in which one consecrated self and services and all one possessed to the cause.*

* Early in the century a disciplinary 'backsliders order,' for the reclamation of penitents, was instituted but then abolished in 1828.

CHAPTER V

Expansion Westward

It is no matter to me what a tree is called
if its fruit is good . . .

Was it not reasonable for the subjects of the
revival to expect that God would shake the heavens
and the earth with his *Shakers?*

— Richard McNemar: *The Kentucky Revival,* 1808

IT WAS EVIDENT by 1800 that a new kind of monasticism had arisen in America. Eleven colonies in the northeastern states, each divided into an ever-increasing number of 'family' units, were successfully developing an unprecedented form of association. With celibacy went sex equality. Separated into distinct orders, brethren and sisters nevertheless lived under the same roofs, held 'union meetings' together, and often worked in the same shops. The affections of these Yankee monks and nuns were fixed on transcendental glories. Before them was the ideal of individual and communal perfection. Yet they stood firmly on the land, busily creating an earthly paradise. No time was spent in idle dreams. Order and use were sublimated conceptions. The Believers cloistered themselves behind a protective covenant, bulwarked their rights by wills, indentures, and discharges, but left ways open whereby the world itself could help them on their way.

Having secured its foundations, the church resumed its active proselyting, dispatching two of its ablest preachers to those places where groups of 'seekers' were reported. One of these, Elder Benjamin Seth Youngs, or 'little Benjamin' as he was affectionately called, was a member of an old Connecticut family which had entered the Watervliet community in 1794. The other, Issachar Bates, had been a fifer in the Revolution. In 1778 he had married Lovina Maynard, by whom he had had eleven children. Deeply concerned about the problem of salvation, in 1801 Bates had joined the Shakers, 'the only people who did not live after the flesh.' 'My whole stay at Lebanon was not much over an hour,' he wrote about his conversion, 'for we did business quick. I ate quick and talked quick, heard quick and started home quick, for I was quickened.'

One of the first missions of these stalwarts was to Pittsford, Vermont, where a revival was in full swing about 1802, and where they converted twenty-six persons in one evening. In Bates' words:

They had a wonderful revival, caused by a marvelous light, seen on the top of one James Wicker's house; the whole neighborhood was awakened . . . And when we came on the ground, (or before we came,) behold there was an appointment for a Circuit rider to preach at that very house where the light was seen, and we went to the meeting. And as God would have it, the man was taken sick on the way and could not come; and after they had waited long enough, they called on us to speak. I arose first, and felt zeal and freedom; for I felt confident that this effectual door was opened by divine Providence, and I could feel that the word was a vale in a sure place. When I was thro' Elder Benjamin arose, with the same impulse, and clinched the nail completely. And when he was thro' a man rose up, & looking me right in the face, putting his hands upon my shoulders, said, 'I want you to go with me and hear me confess my sins.' Another went to Elder Benjamin in the same manner, & so they kept it up, one after another, till I think there were twelve, (male and female,) who confessed their sins that evening.

At the close of these openings there came one into the room, and told us there was a wonderful sight to be seen in the Sky; We all went out; and there was a bright road across the centre of the Horizon from east to west, about two rods wide, as it appeared, of a palish red, with a bright border on each side. O how soon we interpreted this sign: that this same light and power was going to reach those waiting souls in the west; but not one thought that *we* had got to travel this bright road. *100*

A number more were gathered at Guilford in New Hampshire. When the same brethren were dispatched to Otsego, New York, 'many lovely souls' confessed their sins. And so the work went on until by 1803 over sixteen hundred Believers had been collected into the eastern communes, a population which was to double itself in a score of years.

Watchful to the saving of souls everywhere, the ministry at New

Lebanon had been avidly following newspaper accounts of an extraordinary revival that had been gaining momentum in Kentucky and neighboring states since 1799. Youngs and Bates often discussed the subject on their travels, wondering why the church did not investigate. All the societies so far formed had had their roots in revival movements — why, they asked, had this great awakening been ignored? They recalled, perhaps, the sign in the Pittsford sky; they may have remembered that Ann, on several occasions, had prophesied that the next opening of the gospel would be in 'a great level country in the southwest.' Finally, in December 1804, Elder Ebenezer Cooley summoned Issachar to the central order to ask him how he felt 'towards those precious souls that God was at work with in the West.'

'I told him,' Bates wrote in his autobiography, 'that I had wondered why they had not been visited before this time. He said the Church could never feel a gift till now: but now the door is opened.'

The three men entrusted with this historic undertaking — Bates, 101 Youngs, and John Meacham, the eldest son of Father Joseph — set out from New Lebanon at three o'clock on the wintry morning of 1 January 1805. They were driven as far as Peekskill and then continued on foot, with one horse to carry their baggage. Following the main stage routes, stopping wherever evening overtook them, they passed through New York, Philadelphia, Baltimore, and Washington — where 'the popular and lofty spirit of the reigning government,' Youngs wrote in his journal, 'was as plain to be felt as heavy weights of lead on a person's head, or as blazing fire to a fresh burn.' From there they set their course southwestward through Virginia.

No precise destination was in mind. They were tracing to its source those tremblings and spasmodic movements of the Kentucky revivalists which seemed so like the shakings of their own people as to offer a natural opening for the Shaker doctrine. At Leesburg, Strasburg, New Market, Staunton, Lexington, and Abingdon they were always questioning travelers about the 'jerks.' Random reports came of a new sect called *Christians*, who in their clamorous worship were seized with strange paroxysms which caused them to pace the floor with closed eyes, fall in trance-like states, jerk the head and body, and shout, sing, and bark like dogs. On 15 February they crossed into Tennessee; and on the twentieth, in a society meeting of *Christians*

near Bulls Gap in Bays mountain, they witnessed for the first time
the curious phenomena of the Kentucky Revival. Though deeply impressed, the mission failed, however, to find the sought-for opening,
and hearing that the chief centers of the new movement were in southern and central Kentucky and southern Ohio, they finally turned
northward through Cumberland Gap into the wilderness beyond.

Kentucky and Ohio were sparsely populated at the time of the
Shaker mission. The settlements of farmers and woodsmen which had   *102*
sprung up in the latter part of the eighteenth century were widely
scattered along the creeks or runs, the salt licks and ridges after which
they were so often named. Reading and recreation were almost unknown. Religion was the 'chief intellectual food,' and the frequent
revival meetings, initiated just before the end of the century by such
preachers as James McGready and John McGee, served as centers of
both social intercourse and spiritual stimulation. People drove for
miles not only to hear the Methodist, Baptist, and Presbyterian
preachers harangue from their crude backwoods pulpits, but to hear
the latest news of the neighborhood and the outside world. Lasting for
several days, such gatherings were often marked by the wildest ecstasies of body and spirit.

By 1803, however, a reaction had become manifest. Denominational rivalries and doctrinal contention had divided the churches
and reduced their adherents. In September of that year a schism
among the Presbyterians resulted in the rise of a new sect, called
New Lights, Schismatics, or *Christians,* who withdrew from under
the jurisdiction of the Synod of Kentucky to unite in a body known
as the Presbytery of Springfield, with headquarters at Cane Ridge
in northern Kentucky. Among the leaders of the New Lights — who   *103*
wanted to escape from the ministerial authority of the Presbyterian
system, to develop a 'real spirit of communion,' and to follow the
Holy Scriptures as the 'only rule of faith and practice, the only
standard of doctrine and discipline' — were the scholarly Richard
McNemar, in charge of the congregation at Turtle Creek, the largest
Presbyterian church in southern Ohio; Malcolm Worley, a landowner
of Turtle Creek; Barton W. Stone, the most prominent leader of the
revival in north-central Kentucky, whose station at Cane (Cain)
Ridge was later to become the center of an anti-Shaker movement;
John Dunlavy of Eagle Creek, several miles east of Turtle Creek;

Matthew Houston of Paint Lick in central Kentucky; David Purviance, Robert Marshall, and John Thompson.

Though the Presbytery of Springfield was dissolved in June 1804, many of these New Lights, notably McNemar, Worley, and Houston, soon went further away from orthodoxy to establish a new church. Since God and Christ had their abode in the soul of man, they believed that if they were moved by God's 'irresistible' power in times of worship, whatever exercises were 'congruous' to their inward feelings of joy and love were acceptable to Him. Accordingly they united in common acts of worship in which they would take each other by the hand, shake their whole bodies 'like one churning,' shudder with indignation against their 'soul enemies,' sing spiritual songs, and praise God in the dance. Among their involuntary acts of worship were the rolling exercise, the jerks, and the barks. General confession of sin was a cardinal practice of these new dissenters, who appropriated the name *Schismatics* for their own use.

It was this group — which had captured the spirit of the Revival, adopted a form of worship similar to that of the Believers, and formed some fifteen societies in Ohio, Kentucky, Tennessee, North Carolina, and western Pennsylvania — that was to provide the missionaries with their hoped-for opening.

In his initial observance of the New Lights in Tennessee, Bates had written that though some were 'exercised with the power and gift of the holy Spirit,' most were still solidly 'on the old ground.' It was at Paint Lick, Kentucky, where they heard Matthew Houston 'pound away at old Calvin,' that the easterners had their first opportunity to 'open in some degree' the Shaker faith. At Cane Ridge, near Paris, Elder Stone welcomed them warmly and invited them to attend his next camp meeting. At John Thompson's church in Springfield (Springdale), Ohio, north of Cincinnati, they found 'an abundance of chaff, and but very little wheat'; in the society meeting about ten persons were subject to a sort of jerking and dancing, but these exercises were 'abundantly mixed with their own stuff.' Youngs observed that among the *Christians* all things were common, but that they had 'the same faculty for construing the true form of it that all antichristians have, and just so in relation to the flesh.' 'The first rest for the soles of our feet,' Bates wrote, was at Malcolm Worley's, whose land lay in Turtle Creek between the Little Miami and Great Miami rivers.

Here, after a journey of more than twelve hundred miles from New
Lebanon, the mission arrived on Friday evening, the twenty-second
of March.   *104*

Worley was the first convert to Shakerism in the West. Of all with
whom the 'witnesses' had labored, this man was found to have the
deepest light on the foundation of evil; and it was a matter of only a
few days and nights of earnest discourse before he and his family confessed their sins. They were followed by a Negro slave, Anna Middle-
ton, and shortly after by Richard McNemar himself, with his wife
and children.

McNemar's first impression of the delegates had been a favorable
one. He liked their plain, neat, old-fashioned dress; their white fur
hats, gray coats, blue waistcoats, and 'beautiful brown' overalls.
Their walk and general carriage was 'sprightly, yet majestically
grave, and their affability in conversation banished every idea of superstition or sly deceit.' The regard was mutual. Issachar was a   *105*
keen judge of character, and 'little Benjamin' was alert to every evidence of sound theological thought. McNemar's tall gaunt figure, his
earnest piercing eyes, his broad intelligence, and his command of
the Latin, Greek and Hebrew tongues commended the backwoods
preacher to the esteem of these eastern men.

At McNemar's church the following Sunday, Youngs read the
letter which had been entrusted to him by David Meacham, Amos
Hammond, and Ebenezer Cooley of the New Lebanon church:

The Church of Christ [it read in part] unto a people in Kentucky
& the adjacent states, sendeth greetings. We have heard of a work of
God among you, who worketh in divers operations of his power, for which
we feel thankful, as we have an ardent desire that God would carry on
his work according to his purposes . . .

The loss of man and the way and work of salvation by Christ in the
present witnesses appearing so unspeakably great, that altho we had
been a people greatly wrought upon by the spirit of God, and were looking for the coming of Christ, yet the light manifested in the witnesses
showed us that we were unspeakably short of salvation and had never
travelled one step in the regeneration towards the new birth; for it
showed us that it was impossible for them who lived in the works of
natural generation, copulating in the works of the flesh, to travel in
the great work of regeneration and the new birth.

And as these witnesses had received the revelation of Christ, in this last display of the grace of God to a way of God, which is a way out of all sin, in the manner following.

First. To believe in the manifestation of Christ and in the messengers he had sent. Secondly, To confess all our sins; and Thirdly, To take up our cross against the flesh, the world, and all evil; which we, by receiving and obeying from the heart, have received the gift of God which separated us from the course of this world & all sin in our knowledge, for 20 years past and upwards . . .

We have had a great desire that some of you might have visited us before now, as we have been waiting for some time to know the mind of God in relation to you: we now out of duty to God and our fellow creatures, have sent three of our brethren viz., John Meacham, Issachar Bates and Benjamin Youngs, who we trust will be able to declare these things more particularly and open the way of eternal life unto you, which is a way out of all sin, a way which the vulture's eye never saw, the lion's whelp never trod, and the furious lion never passed by it. Receive them, therefore, as messengers of Christ and friends to your salva-
106 tion . . .

This communication — which 'few understood' — was followed, in the course of the next few days, by long conversations in the cabins of Turtle Creek. The strangers offered not only a new belief but a new life — no 'mere speculation,' as McNemar wrote, but 'things that had for many years been reduced to practice, and established by the living experience of hundreds.' Malcolm and Richard had witnessed the excesses of the revivals, the inevitable aftermath of high-pitched emotionalism, the relapses into mental confusion and indifference. The revivalist had been preaching salvation, but the Shakers had entered into 'actual possession of that salvation.' The revivalists had been foretelling the second coming of Christ; but He had already come to lead the Believers, 'step by step in a spiritual travel, and separating farther and farther from the course of a corrupt and fallen nature,' until they should arrive at 'the perfect stature and measure of the sons
107 of God.'

Conversion of the two leading 'Christian' spirits established the faith of Ann Lee on western ground. On 23 May the first 'society meeting,' for the purpose of instructing the people in Shaker customs, was held on the farm of one David Hill, a mile from Turtle Creek on what was known as the 'ministerial reserve.' John Meacham opened the occasion with a discourse on the economy, dress, and deportment of the order, the importance of union and uniformity. Then

Issachar 'pitched up a step song,' and the 'young Believers' united, awkwardly at first, in the laboring exercises led by Elders John and Benjamin. Youngs wrote in his journal,   *108*

After speaking, we sung an hymn, & while singing the following,

> With him in praises we'll advance
> And join the virgins in the dance,

Jane McN[McNemar] got exercised in dancing for some time . . . Rd [Richard] also got to dancing & P [Polly] Kimball a woman of 27 who had not opened her mind was exercised . . . and from this she went to turning which was the first regular gift of turning we had seen since we left N Lebanon — & This she said she never had before, though she had had both the Jerks & dancing — Calvin M [Morrell] was also exercised in a sort of shaking & quick stamping on the floor-Rd & he were soon clasped together and rolled on the floor . . .   *109*

At that inaugural meeting was 'one old-heaven minister, two ordained Elders, two licensed Exhorters, two practical physicians and between 20 and 30 respectable members of the great protestant community . . .'

Activity was stimulated in July by the arrival from New Lebanon of David Darrow, Daniel Moseley, and Solomon King. Conversions increased rapidly, and in September the leaders concluded it was *110* time, 'and a righteous thing,' to have a home of their own. A quarter-section of land was accordingly purchased from one Timothy Sewell, who wanted to get away from the Believers, and work began the following spring on the first Shaker house in the West.

The tireless zeal of the frontier missionaries is revealed in a letter one of them wrote home concerning this building. Addressed to New Lebanon from Lebanon, Miami Country, Ohio, 17 March 1806, it read in part:

In the first Place we have ben in a close Labor of mind to know Our duty about Building, at first a proposal was made to Build Small and Cheap for the Present, But neither our Judgment nor Feelings would admit of it on any Consideration, we have therefore Concluded and the work is on hand to Build a fraimed house 30 By 40 feet, Two Story with a Straight Roof, and two Staks of Chimneys the Inside Somthing in the form of the East house at N ——— L ——— We have Been in not a Little Tribulation Lest Because we once Lived in Large and Comfortable houses we Should appear to Carry The Same Sense with us and Reach Beyond our Measure, But we can assure our Brethern that no Selfish motives have Influenced us to Such an undertaking, But on the Contrary we are willing for our Selves to do any way so that the work of God may But go on . . .

When we are all together in these Parts our Principle and best abode is Malcoms, whose house is framed . . . Fifteen is the Number when we and his family are all together, Besides a Continual Coming and Going, all the time that we have Not Ben Ingaged in Labouring for Souls, we have through the Course of the Winter and Still are Faithfully Imployed in Getting out timber Shingles Claboards and what ever we are able to do with our own hands which may Lesen the Expenditure of Money . . . 12000 Black walnut Shingle we have already got out Our Selves . . . Part of the Claboards Riven out of white oak, About all the timber is Cut Down, and Most of it hewed . . . [Follows a bill of expenses for building materials, land, cows, wheat, corn, cloth, tools, etc., amounting to $2,525] . . . As the sittuation of the yong Beleavers In these parts now is, we do not feel it Right to Require any Contribution From them, of time or money towards these matters, for most of them are yet Living in Cabbins and unsettled, and beeing waked up to a Sence of their Loss, have as much as they can do to' get along with their own
111 Business . . .

112 Eleven brethren and eight sisters, constituting an 'elders family' or 'old believers order,' moved into the new building 22 October 1806. The group was organized as 'a kind of Church order' on 27 November, when a letter was received from Mother Lucy Wright appointing David Darrow its 'first Elder Councillor.' Because this message, written October 9 from New Lebanon, marks the official opening of western Shakerism, it is herewith given in full. It is one of the few letters by Ann Lee's successor that have been preserved:

As some of you have answered me according to my desire, in relation to your faith — I am satisfied you all may feel Elder David your first Elder Councillor & Protector there in that distant Land, which is a great comfort & satisfaction to me, & I think it may be to you all.

I am Sensible you have diversity of Gifts, but by the same Spirit: I desire you may build up & strengthen each other in the Gift of God — You may consider you could not be so complete if you was all a Head, or an Arm, or a Foot — therefore Labour to bring your gifts into Subjection to the work of God that you are called to in that Land. —

If any of you should rise too high by reason of having great Gifts of God, I Desire you would labour to creep down the best way you can: for if you should fall it might hurt you. —

I Desire you may not be deceived so as to feel your justification in making a great noise, or Sound, — Although I believe the people must have an outward work before they are able to have an inward, as a body, but the work of mortification must increase as they travel — that will be coming down into the work of God, not rising above, if they do they rise above their protection, & of consequence must suffer Loss — What I have written is my intention of doing you good. —

This From your Parent in the Gospel. *113*

Material progress was rapid in the next few years. A great deal of the land in Ohio was 'untaken up' at the time. 'It is heavily timbered,' the missionaries had written home 1 June 1805, but when cleared was 'free from stone and therefore easy to hill and brings forth in great abundance.' The best land sold for three dollars an acre, which the *114* purchaser was allowed a number of years to pay. Worley had consecrated his quarter-section to the Shaker church. On the adjoining quarter, occupied by McNemar, three hundred dollars was due; the sum was paid by the Believers. This half section, together with the Sewell property and a farm purchased in December 1806, from Abraham LeRue, gave the first western society nearly a square mile of fertile territory within two years of its establishment. Two sawmills were erected in 1807 and 1808, and a frame meeting-house in 1809. On 14 March 1810, fifteen brethren and eighteen sisters affixed their names to the first western covenant, drafted by Elder Youngs. Two *115* years later a ministry consisting of David Darrow, Solomon King, Ruth Farrington, and Hortense Goodrich was appointed from New Lebanon and confirmed by the members at Turtle Creek. In the elaborated church covenant executed on 15 January 1812, the community was renamed 'Union Village.'

Meanwhile the testimony was being preached, often in the face of stubborn resistance, through various parts of Ohio, Kentucky, Indiana, and Illinois. Bates speaks of traveling the western world — this wild wooden world' — by day and night, 'from side to side, and almost from end to end.' Little Benjamin was no less active. Sometimes the two were alone; but often they journeyed together, or in company with such stalwarts as McNemar, Worley, Dunlavy, Darrow, and later, Matthew Houston, James Hodges, and John Rankin. Swimming rivers, wading swamps, breaking trails through the woods and 'no ways,' hungering for days were common experiences. On more than one occasion their lives were threatened.

Issachar's initial jostle with the New Lights was at Cane Ridge, Kentucky, to which outpost he had returned soon after the delegation arrived at Turtle Creek. Though Stone and Marshall had previously invited him to preach, they disapproved of the doctrine of celibacy and distrusted its propagandists. On the pretext, therefore, that the people would be confused by the Shaker belief, they forbade his speaking at the meeting. The second day, however, in answer to a persistent demand for his appearance, the indomitable Bates mounted a log to deliver a fiery discourse on 'the difference between letter and spirit.' Toward the end of April 1805, a band of 'blazing New Lights' under John Thompson invaded another gathering at Turtle Creek. Centering his attack on the Believers' claim that Christ had made His second appearance, Thompson called the Shakers 'liars' and ordered Bates 'back to hell.' So forceful was his sermon that the countryside was in an uproar. 'The very air and woods,' Issachar declared, 'rung with the appalling sound of false prophets! Seducers! deceivers! liars! Wolves in sheep's clothing! parting man and wife! breaking up families and churches!' No violence occurred at this particular meeting, though the abuse the Believers had experienced in the East was soon to be repeated with all the lawless abandonment of a frontier society.

Later in the spring the missionaries gathered 'a goodly number' at Straight Creek and Eagle Creek, about sixty-five miles east of Turtle Creek. Beaver Creek to the west, where the permanent settlement of Watervliet was to be located, was the next stop. Benjamin and Richard visited Shawnee Run, Kentucky, the site of the future Pleasant Hill colony, in the summer of 1805. At Paint Lick they won the allegiance of Matthew Houston, a former slaveholder who had been one of their chief opposers. From there the Shaker brethren proceeded to Silver Creek, returning by way of Beaver, Eagle, and Cabin creeks. The next long tour took Bates, McNemar, and Houston to Gasper, in Logan County, southern Kentucky, where twenty-three adults — the nucleus of what was eventually to be the South Union society — were converted on the first visit. At Red River and Red Bank(s) more were gathered. And so it was, Bates recorded, 'every time and every where, every how, and every place.'

It was a year of unremitting effort. At camp stands and frontier churches, in log cabins and taverns, in the open fields and along the winding trails, the missionaries carried on the battle of the spirit against the 'doleful works of the flesh.' Seldom preaching in public, they preferred to labor quietly with individuals where they were free from the opposition of both New Light and Old Light 'professors,' and unhampered by the tumult characteristic of the revival meetings. Benjamin's journal tells of frequent one- and two-hour conversations on the subjects of 'the latter day,' judgment, salvation, and so forth. When anyone, whether Deist, landholder, black girl or mulatto, poor white or mere child, came 'under a measure of concern' or, being 'struck with conviction,' opened his or her mind, Youngs carefully recorded the fact. 'Non professors' he found 'tender kind and reasonable.' The Shakers paid their way wherever they went, insuring hospitable accommodations.

Religion was a serious matter in these backwoods regions — with many an outright issue of life and death. At camp meetings, opposers drowned out the Shaker sermons with boisterous singing and shouting. Stones were hurled through the windows of their lodgings. Benjamin's horse was stolen on one occasion, and on another cropped and branded; peril and deep discouragement were daily fare. The Shaker cross — the vow of celibacy — was the great 'stumbling block,' causing contention in families, arousing intense bitterness and 'darkness' of mind. Gradually, however, little coteries of Believers formed and increased at scattered outposts in the country. In the society meetings they knelt in silence or listened attentively to the new gospel. When the active part of the service began, they were greatly exercised in dancing, singing, shaking, turning, and jerking. A typical meeting, at Shawnee Run, is thus described by Youngs:

In the evening a few in number met to whom B & Jn spoke abt an hour — after this we spent 2 or 3 hours in singing — during which time several were remarkably exercised — particularly Sally Montford — who was for spells of 15 or 20 minutes each exercised in propper danceing — & some of it after singing — while thus dancing she frequently fell down & lay Straight on her back by spells from half an hour, to an hour each, in which time She would sing Solemn Songs, more distinct, & Slow than those while dancing — & very Solemn — & part of the time while laying thus — She would speak thus 'O the glory, it is the way, it is the way — O the views of heaven!' & some of the time She would clap her hands — & also play the time with her hands on her breast — & Some-times on the floor — her exercises continued near or quite 4 hours & were enough (if possible) to convert a nation . . .

116

At Turtle Creek, on 3 August, McNemar announced that that
'stand' would henceforth be for the exclusive use of the Shaker society. A special meeting was held during which one Easter Knox from
Eagle Creek

> was exercised with singing in the breast as it has been called, but it was
> a propper Solemn song as is Sung in the Church! In the meantime her
> body also would be full of signs — such as heaving her hands over her
> head intimating they shall come with songs & joy upon their heads —
> Stretching out her hands & drawing them in again, bowing to the ground
> — calling as it were the nations to come & bow down to the gospel . . .
> and with her hands & fingers playing on her breast as on an organ . . .
> it was the most striking & solemn sight of all the exercises we had yet
> seen . . . [but] the Spectators at this meeting were very uncivilized and
> 117 hard-hearted.

The diarist's account of another meeting illustrates how the Baptist and Methodist revival songs were adapted by the Shakers to their
own purposes:

> Thence to Elijah's when in the evening several families of the believers
> met who understood that we were there — the meeting was 14 in all —
> we labored 4 or 5 songs & from thence exercises began which lasted full
> 4 hours — numbers were exercised in a sort of jerking, singing, dancing,
> turning in abundance, running round, & about all manner of figures [?]
> with the most Solemn expressions — the singing of P. [Polly] Kimball
> was Solemn and Singular. While singing the tune which has been sung
> much in this country since the revival — to the words 'Children of the
> Heavenly King' — the sounds were He, he, he; He, he, he, he, He, he, he,
> hi Ho! etc. & after singing in this manner a long time, She cryed out in
> extasy of joy My Jesus Christ has learnt me to Sing so — Yea, yea, yea
> — *These dumb devils.* He himself — yea Jesus Christ, has learnt me to
> Sing without words! Yea, yea, yea.
> She had many exercises while running in circles — having Cast her
> 118 Shoes off — Sometimes backwards and Sometimes forward.

Among American religious orders the Shakers were distinctive for
their success in colonization. Amana had seven branches, all within a
circumscribed area. The followers of John Humphrey Noyes lived at
one time in three separate colonies. But most of the communistic experiments were confined to a single location or moved by circumstance
from place to place. The Society of the Believers, on the other hand,
was constantly expanding, either by adding new families within a

given community or by encouraging experiments in distant places —
colonies such as Narcoossee, Florida, and White Oak, Georgia, which
were the responsibility of communities already well established. This
flexibility of organization, wherein lay much of the strength of the
movement, is well illustrated by the spread of the faith in the West.

Every preacher, every layman, every spot where there was promise
of successful effort was tirelessly sought out. The conversion of every
man of means gave strength to the movement, and if he had landed
property, widened the opportunity for communal settlement. Since
revivalism, the tree on which the Shaker system was grafted, was a
rural phenomenon, such property, and with it the current of community interest, was dominantly agricultural. In those cases where
societies were actually started the consecrated farms were large, con-
tiguous, or so located that by relatively small outlays intervening
lands could be acquired. Once these compact areas were developed,
the Believers were in a position to offer unusual economic benefits to
prospective proselytes.   *119*

Just as the dedication of farms by Darrow, Bishop, and others at
New Lebanon, Daniel Goodrich at Hancock, Benjamin Whicher at
Canterbury, James Jewett at Enfield (N.II.), David Meacham at
Enfield (Conn.) and Elijah and Ivory Wilds, John Warren, and Nathan Willard at Shirley made possible the founding of communities
in those townships, so did the sacrificial spirit of certain pioneers in
the country north and south of the Ohio River provide the basis for
the western extension of the communal system. Malcolm Worley's
benefactions, as we have seen, gave birth to Union Village. In 1806,
Elisha Thomas consecrated a 140-acre farm at Shawnee River to the
Shaker church — the nucleus of grants which made possible the acquisition of fertile lands at near-by Pleasant Hill, in the heart of the
bluegrass country. About the same time Jesse McComb, a large landholder at Gasper Springs in Logan County, southern Kentucky,
bequeathed all his property to the united interest of 'the one true
faith.'

As in the eastern openings, the first meetings of the infant communities were held in the houses of the leading spirits. By purchase,
donation, and inspired industry the small bands of Believers collected
in those centers so improved their status that in a few years they were
prepared for 'gospel order' and the introduction of communistic
practices. The date for the founding of the Gasper Springs or South

120 Union colony is usually given as 1807; the principal gathering was in 1809; the meeting-house was built in 1810. In 1811 Benjamin Youngs, who took a personal interest in this community, was appointed to the first 'lot' in its ministry, continuing there nearly twenty-five years. Organization at Pleasant Hill, called 'the topmost bough upon the Tree' and 'the cream of Kentucky,' followed a parallel course. Believers began to collect in 1806. The first stone building was erected in 1809, the year in which the society was chiefly 'gathered.' John Meacham, one of the three missionaries, was the first elder and Lucy Smith the 'elder sister' when 128 brethren and sisters signed the Pleasant Hill covenant in June, 1814.

In Ohio, the foundation of the Union Village community had scarcely been laid when its leaders turned their attention westward. As early as May 1805, on the request of one William Stewart and others, Bates and Youngs paid a visit to the New Light preaching station at Beaver Creek, or Beulah, about six miles southeast of Dayton in Montgomery County. John Thompson, the minister there, exerted every effort to protect his 'innocent lambs' from the 'ravening wolves . . . that were going about the country in sheep's clothing.' But in the ensuing conflict Issachar Bates, Benjamin Youngs, and Richard McNemar emerged victorious. John Houston, a wheelwright, farmer, and owner of a quarter section of land, confessed his sins in October, John and William Stewart early the next year, and about the same time John Patterson, the first settler at Beaver Creek, who also owned a quarter section. Though the Beulah society did not hold its property jointly at first, a Shaker order, with John Stewart as the leading elder, was inaugurated in March 1806; and the erection of a common sawmill soon afterward indicated a dawning communal consciousness. The Turtle Creek elders made frequent visits in the next few years, and in 1810 sent twenty-seven brethren to help the Beulah people raise a log meeting-house. Two years later a gristmill was in operation, in 1813 a tannery, and in 1814 a coopers' shop, woodenware industry, and woolen mill. Wagons, brooms, and ironware were being manufactured in the course of the next ten years. In the covenant executed 7 December 1818, the Beaver Creek community was called by its new name — Watervliet — after the original

121 settlement in the East.

A curious story about this small community should be told. It seems that a member at Union Village had a vision commanding the Shakers to put a curse upon Lebanon, the source of continued persecution, and a blessing on Dayton, whose citizens had always been kind to the Believers at Watervliet. Obedient to the divine will, two chosen messengers rode through the streets of the former town, waving their broad-brimmed hats and shouting 'woe, woe, woe' on its inhabitants; then, proceeding to Dayton, they pronounced God's blessings on the people there. According to the tale, the progress of Dayton dated from this event; convinced that a community blessed by 'holy men of God' would surely prosper, farmers sold or rented their farms and moved into town. Its population rapidly increased, whereas Lebanon's remained stationary over the decades.

On a visit to Gasper Springs, Bates and Youngs had heard of a people living at Busro Creek, on the Wabash River in the Indiana Territory. The first visit to that outpost region was made in June 1808, by Bates and others. At Vincennes the party visited Governor William Henry Harrison, who promised them protection from the Indians and freedom of worship. The long, dangerous journey through the wilderness had its reward, for in three weeks seventy persons had 'opened their minds' at Busro and along the border of Illinois. Land was so cheap, water power so plentiful, and the people so enthusiastic that Elders David Darrow and Solomon King decided in 1810 to form a permanent society in Indiana. For five years the Believers at Eagle Creek (three miles from the present West Union, Ohio) and Straight Creek (now Georgetown, Ohio) had tried unsuccessfully 'to find an opening for a foundation'; and though Bates had warned the leaders that the country was 'naturally sickly and right on the very margin of a frontier,' that war with the Indians was just at hand, and that it would 'take the wisest man on earth to lead that Society,' nevertheless the plan was adopted to consolidate at one place the Believers at Busro and some of the members of the Straight Creek, Eagle Creek, and Red Bank settlements. Archibald Meacham, another son of Father Joseph, was selected to gather the Busro community into temporal and spiritual order. *122* *123*

Bates's forebodings proved true. Trouble with the Indians broke out soon after the Shakers had started fencing and tilling fields and building cabins and mills. War was in the air, 'people all forting and armies coming among us, till the greater part of our people were so filled with fear that they could not rest day nor night.' Governor Harrison offered the Believers refuge and guards in Vincennes, but they decided to leave the settlement until the danger was over. The removal was carried out late in 1812. In the summer of 1814, however, peace being restored, the Busro colony returned to its former location. Here they remained until inroads of malaria so reduced their numbers and undermined their spirit that the community was finally permanently abandoned in 1827. The remnants of the colony were gathered into Watervliet and Union Village.

Originally given as evidence of Shaker 'idolatry,' another story, also probably apocryphal, is told about the Wabash mission. On one of their journeys Youngs, Bates, and McNemar lost their way in the wilderness and, having run out of provisions, were on the point of starvation. Little Benjamin, gloomy over the prospects of survival, proposed that they all kneel down and pray. Thereupon Issachar, ignoring the tradition against vocal prayer, irreverently offered up the following: 'O Lord God, here we are, all-sufficient, self-dependent creatures, going up and down the universal world, ding-split, devil-like: — if we had our just deserts, we should not be here, nor there, nor no where else!'

124

Two more communities, those at Whitewater and North Union, were founded in Ohio in the 1820's. The origin of the Whitewater settlement goes back to 1801, when a revival at Lyndon, Vermont, gave rise to the Christian or New Light church in that part of New England. Members of this order in Connecticut and Rhode Island migrated to Ohio, settling on Darby Plains in Union County. The sect attracted the notice of the Union Village Shakers about 1818, when in the course of another revival several hundreds confessed their sins and sought to right their wrongs by a purer life. Elder Douglass Farnum was their leader.

125

Richard McNemar and Calvin Morrell visited Darby Plains in June 1820, talked with Farnum, and held a meeting. In the summer the New Light elder called at Union Village, where he impressed Father David Darrow as the 'weightiest man' who had ever come to see them. Visits were interchanged in the course of the next two or three years. Farnum died, but his successor, a young preacher named Nathan Burlingame, was converted to the Shaker cause in 1822 and so succeeded in winning over his followers, some forty in all, that it was decided to form a community at Darby Plains. The plantation of Samuel Rice was selected for the site, and with the help of brethren from Union Village a meeting-house was raised in August 1823. But

Darby did not prosper. Many cases of fever convinced the leaders
that the location was unhealthy, and military and legal claims to the
surrounding land obstructed the course of future development.
Rather than persist against obvious odds, the Shakers followed their
characteristic course of strategic removal. Fortunately, in an opening of the gospel on the dry fork of the Whitewater, in Hamilton
County, a promising site was provided where the Darby colony could
begin its development anew.

Foundations for a community already existed at Whitewater. One
Miriam Agnew, the groping subject of a Methodist revival which had
run its course in the neighborhood, had sought out and joined the
Shakers at Union Village in the spring of 1823. A mission headed by
Richard Pelham gathered in her husband, Joseph, and his brother,   *126*
Brant Agnew, and by autumn thirty young, enthusiastic persons had
started a vigorous movement in Whitewater. It was a natural spot for
the people of the Darby Plains society to transfer to, and they welcomed the suggestion; and under the guidance of Morrell and Burlingame the removal was made in the course of the year 1824. Had it
not been for the resources of the now prosperous Union Village society, however, the Whitewater community would probably not have
survived very long. The forty-acre lot on which it was settled was
mostly unproductive, uncleared land. The people were poor. Some
were faithless. Sickness persisted. Morrell records that:

. . . meat with them was scarce. Sugar they had little or none, and milk
but seldom. Bread was greatly lacking, while tea and coffee were out of
the question . . . The common manner was to buy a side of bacon and
make sop for their johnny cake. The sop was made by mixing a sufficient
quantity of milk and water with enough meat cut in small pieces to make
the composition somewhat greasy, end the whole was fried together until the meat had nearly vanished. This was used mornïng and noon. For
breakfast they had herb tea. For dinner potatoes and sauce. For supper
milk porridge, but more commonly water porridge . . .   *127*

Fortune's wheel turned with the purchase of better lands and the
construction of houses to replace the cramped huts and cabins. Crops
were abundant in the year 1826. Apples and peaches were plentiful.
Corn averaged sixty bushels to the acre. Eight acres of broomcorn
were harvested. A new spirit of industry pervaded the settlement,
which was furthered in 1827 by the arrival of the majority of the
Believers from the abandoned project at Busro. An austerely beauti-

ful brick meeting-house built in the fall of that year symbolized
Whitewater's confidence in the future.

In the origin and early progress of the community at North Union,
near Cleveland, two factors basic to the success of religious communism were present: the bequest of good land and a strong leadership.
Ralph Russell owned a farm on section twenty-two of the township.
Adjoining his property were farms owned by his brothers Elijah and
Elisha and two other settlers, Riley Honey and Chester Risley. Rod-
ney Russell had acreage in another part of the same township. Why
Ralph, in October, 1821, visited the Shakers at Union Village, is not
known; but he was so impressed by the orderly community and its
'inspired' administration that he immediately joined the sect. He
spread the doctrine so zealously that his brother, neighbors, and their
families were all confirmed to the ideal of a religious colony. Since
their fertile lands now lay at the service of the church, the elders at
Union Village, instead of accepting Ralph into that fellowship, proposed that a branch of the order be instituted in the north of the state.
In March 1822, Pelham and James Hodge were sent to Russell's
home, where they spent six weeks instructing the new Believers in the
tenets and temporal economy of the order. Another mission, headed
by Richard McNemar, organized the community the same year under
the name of North Union (being north of Union Village). An adjoining section of land was purchased by the Union Village trustees.
The order of elders was instituted in 1826, the covenant signed in
1828.

For thirty-six years North Union had the ablest type of leadership. Ashbel Kitchell, the first presiding elder, was a gifted adminis-
trator, commanding in stature, just, intelligent, iron-willed. In the
five-year period of his office the community built a frame dwelling,
meeting-house, gristmill, horse barn, cow barn, grain barn, tan house,
and office building. Land was cleared and agricultural and industrial
activities inaugurated on a progressive scale. Kitchell was succeeded
by Matthew Houston, who was followed in two years by David Spinning, one of the most talented thinkers and preachers of the order.
From 1840 to 1858 the destiny of North Union was in the hands of
Samuel Russell, like Kitchell a man of unusual executive ability.
Under the energetic management of these four men the colony continued to grow in peaceful prosperity. Three families were established
on its 1,366 acres of land.

Soon after the organization of Whitewater and North Union, still another colony was founded on the southern shore of Lake Ontario, in New York State. Sodus Bay, whose covenant was signed on 1 January 1829, was geographically a central link between the eastern and western societies and the last successful communizing venture of the Shaker order.

The establishment of Sodus was the outcome of a mission, headed by Elders Calvin Green and Jeremiah Talcott of New Lebanon, to the town of Lyons, New York, where one Joseph Pelham had sought light on the millennial faith. The journey took Green and Talcott to Sodus Bay, the location of which impressed them greatly, and when the mission succeeded in gaining a surprising number of converts in the vicinity of Lyons, the site was selected as a permanent home. In February 1826, Pelham, collaborating with Proctor Sampson, Samuel Southwick, and Jeremiah Talcott of New Lebanon, purchased nearly thirteen hundred acres of land abutting the lake, and in March moved into the new settlement. Covenants were signed by the center, or first, family in 1829 and 1832, and by a second family, the 'east,' in 1833. Soon after the first dwelling was completed in 1834, however, the newly organized Sodus Canal Company made overtures to the Believers for the property, which formed a natural terminus for their contemplated line. Apparently the offer was too attractive to be long refused, for on 21 November 1836, the tract was sold to the corporation. Negotiations were already under way for a substitute site in Groveland, or Son Yea, in Livingston County, where 1,670 acres were purchased in December. The next year the 150 believers at Sodus moved to the new settlement.

The planting of colonies in the West was carried on in the face of sickness, discouragement and persecution. 'I have thought many a time,' wrote Joseph Allen, one of the South Union brethren, in 1816, 'that it was almost impossible for any one not here to Conceive of the Sufferings and tribulation of those who left their most dear friends and Comfortable homes for the Sake of the further Increase of Gods work in this Western world — Enemies without and within Persecutions afflictions . . .' In 1813 fifty or sixty members of that colony died of the 'cold plague.' Fevers and chills, whooping cough, canker rash, influenza, measles, and mumps seriously affected the health and morale of the community. Similar epidemics, we have seen, caused the abandonment of societies at Busro and Darby Plains. Excessive toil, exhausting rituals, poor food, and inadequate shelter lowered resistance to whatever contagions prevailed.

Religious prejudice, cropping out in sporadic violence, was an even more relentless foe. The wildest stories, originated in some instances by the New Light ministers themselves, circulated about the Shakers. They were accused not only of parting husband and wife and ruining families but of deliberately planning, under the cloak of piety, to steal people's land and property. It was rumored that each Believer thought himself a Christ, that the Shakers consequently saw no need for Bibles, that they boasted they would never die. In 1810 Colonel James Smith published two scurrilous pamphlets in which he charged the leaders of the sect with inciting the Indians against the govern-
132 ment and supplying them with money for ammunition. The basis of this accusation was probably the Shaker mission, in 1807, to a tribe of Shawnees at Greenville, Ohio. Hearing of a revival that had broken out among the natives there, Darrow, Youngs, and McNemar visited them in March and again in August. About ten dollars in money, and provisions enough to require twenty-seven horses to transport, were delivered on the two trips. In May, James Patterson and his wife brought '21 Indians and 2 squaws' with them from Beulah. Toward the middle of June, 'upwards of twenty' appeared at Turtle Creek, encamped in the woods, and stayed four days, worshipping in the woods and at the Shaker meeting-house. In August, fifty more Shawnees came to Turtle Creek, where they were kindly received. No Indians were gathered into the Shaker society, though the visits gave rise to many rumors. 'Some had it,' McNemar reported, 'that a number of the Indians had joined the Shakers, and many more were coming on: Others, that an Indian had offered to confess his sins, but the Shakers could not understand him, and therefore the Indians were convinced, too, that the Shakers were deceivers. Some tried to make believe that the Shakers were encouraging them to war, or at least to
133 contend for the land on which they had settled.'

Colonel Smith declared that Darrow ruled like a pope, and controlling the treasury, autocratically dominated a state which was 'fundamentally and practically' opposed to the existing government and American liberty. Corporal punishment was common, the education of children a pretence. Natural affection was destroyed, giving place to perverted and immoral practices: the Shakers themselves,

Smith declared, had said that 'if they bore the cross, and abstained from women for some time, they would become so holy, that it would be no sin for them to connect with their most holy women.'

From tongue to tongue such stories went, elaborated upon as time went on. The practice of celibacy was a particularly fruitful source of gossip. Smith feared that Shakerism would finally depopulate America. The Shakers castrated their males, he charged, and some people swore they danced naked, after which they blew out the candles and went into a promiscuous debauch. 'The fruits of their unlawful embraces,' it was whispered about, 'they concealed by the horrid crime of murder.' The rumors that emasculation was a common practice in the society led later to the indictment, on such a charge, of five Whitewater elders, quashed only after two doctors, testifying for the defense, proved that the two boys involved 'labored under a natural deformity.'

134

The feeling aroused by such extravagant tales found frequent outlet in personal assault and the destruction of Shaker property. Fences were broken down, windows and doors shattered, apple trees felled, horses cropped or otherwise disfigured, cattle turned into the Believers' grainfields. The firing of the Union Village meeting-house was one of the first of many incendiary acts which destroyed scores of buildings, both in the eastern and western societies, throughout the first half of the century.

The culminating act of mob rule occurred at Union Village on 27 August 1810, when a body of five hundred armed men, followed by a rabble of twice as many citizens, marched on the peaceful settlement. Leaders of the militia 'insolently' demanded, first, the release of certain children, held, it was charged, against both their wishes and the law; secondly, the abandonment by the Shakers of their sectarian practices, mode of worship, and manner of living; and lastly, their immediate departure from the country. The Believers retorted that the children were there with the consent of their fathers, that they themselves were living on land they had purchased by their own industry, and that the constitution of the country guaranteed them freedom to worship as they pleased. Delegates from the crowd were invited to inspect the buildings, visit the school, and question the children. The young people answered without exception that they were well fed and cared for, that they liked the Shaker life and would not leave under any condition. Only after the outsiders had searched the premises for imprisoned children and signs of abuse and neglect, without finding either, did they unwillingly and noisily withdraw from the scene.

135

Mob violence reoccurred in 1813, 1817, 1819, and 1824. In each case the object of the invaders was the procurement of some child or young sister in the society. Once, for the sake of peace, the Shakers gave up the indenture by which a father had bound over his children. Once, when several Union Village brethren, on the authorization of his Shaker father, brought back a boy who had left the society, they were arrested and indicted. The final disturbances, agitated in part by the anti-Shaker paper *Western Star* of Lebanon, involved a number of young sisters whom the mob tried to spirit away against their will. Conflict with the law on the intricate problems of membership, property, and the bearing of arms continued until the covenant of the United Society had been strengthened and certain test cases had established precedents for legal action.

In many respects the early history of Shakerism in the West is a repetition of the rise of the eastern communities. Both sections of the society were built on revivals in older faiths, from which restless, discontented, and liberal elements alike were drawn by the appeal of 'the one true church.' Presenting a bold and definite program, inspired missions in both cases were able to proselyte with great success, not only among the poor, unlettered, and religiously bewildered classes, but among those who intelligently sought a more significant way of life. Both divisions of the United Society were born amidst scenes of persecution — a continuous oppression which served to bind the communes into a close unity and separate them from the world. Union Village became the center of western Shakerism, the home of the western ministry, holding a status similar if subordinate to the central church at New Lebanon. The other societies in Ohio, Kentucky, and Indiana received their immediate orders, their chief elders, and immeasurable temporal aid from the Warren County community, as did the eastern colonies from New Lebanon. And finally, East and West progressed materially at comparable rates. In 1823, eighteen years after the three missionaries arrived at Turtle Creek, 1700 brethren and sisters had been gathered into the millennial order.

Little Benjamin, Issachar, and their co-workers had done their work well. From the Shaker point of view, most important increments to the numbers, resources, and spiritual strength of the order were to accrue from the mission. And in the larger view the undertaking may be seen as a phase of our whole westward movement: a colorful, distinct chapter in which religious faith rather than economic opportunity played the dominant role.

CHAPTER VI

Temporal Labor — Principles and Practice

Therefore our labor is to do good, in our day and
generation, to all men, as far as we are able, by
faithfulness and frugality in the works of our hands.

— *Shaker Memorial*, 1816

AMONG THE worldly, admiration for the temporal economy of the
sect was often accompanied by criticism of fundamental doctrine.
Extravagant, even evil, principles were considered to co-exist with
sound character and good work. Religious belief was subjected to
scorn, yet its temporal manifestations were praised. Thus Dwight,
though convinced that its doctrines were so gross they could never
spread far, admitted that 'the industry, manual skill, fair dealing and
orderly behavior of the Brotherhood, render them useful members
of society.' One should distinguish carefully, Harriet Martineau
thought, between the moral and economic principles of the Shaker
(and Rappite) societies: 'whatever they have peculiarly good among
them, is owing to the soundness of their economic principles, whatever they have that excites compassion, is owing to the badness of
their moral arrangements.' In a similar vein A. J. Macdonald, the
wandering student of American socialisms, though he disapproved
of their theology, felt that 'all the other features of Shakers (as re-
gards real usefulness to mankind) sink into insignificance compared
with their economical system.'

Whether acting can be thus divorced from thinking and feeling, it
remains true, as Mary Hennell pointed out, that the foundation of
monastic or sectarian co-operative unions has usually been 'the belief
of certain religious doctrines, and an enthusiastic zeal in support of

them, not the conviction that this community of labor and property is the best means of securing the . . . well-being of all.' An interac- *136* tion of concept and accomplishment was recognized by George J. Holyoake himself, who observed that 'it is true of movements as of men,' that 'those who act and do not think, and those who think and do not act — alike perish.' The failure of the American communities es- *137* tablished by or under the influence of Owen, Fourier, Cabet, Ripley, and other reformers may be ascribed to the fact that their philosophies were not or could not be converted into practice. Though the Believers had, in the beginning, a much simpler concept of an ideal society, they had the zeal and ability to translate it into an effective program. A body of ideas, with a deep emotional content, found outlet in an efficient system of combined labor, in model farms and villages, in fine workmanship and a remarkably productive industry. To appreciate these fruits of the spirit, let us briefly examine the Shaker faith as it was eventually established, and particularly as it affected the temporalities of the order.

In 1806, the year that ushered in the second gathering of the church, attention was turned to developing the rather diffusive utterances of Ann Lee, Whittaker, and Meacham into a comprehensive system of belief. From the time the church was organized in 1792 there had been a growing need for an explicit exposition of principles as well as for uniform laws prescribing the 'relation which is of the spirit.' A new generation, unfamiliar with the personal testimony of the first witnesses, was seeking entrance into the eastern societies. In the West, Youngs and his companions had few 'way-marks' to guide new Believers in their proselyting labors: there was no official defense against the anti-Shaker professors and the attacks of the Rathbuns, Taylor, and West. Equipped only with Joseph Meacham's *138* inadequate *Statement* and McNemar's *Kentucky Revival*, the minis- *139* ters of the expanding society had but a generalized concept of the meaning of Shakerism. To give it definitive form, therefore, the zealous Youngs undertook the first authoritative work on the Millennial Church. The time was July 1806; the place of composition, a bare attic room in the recently completed Turtle Creek dwelling.

The plan of *The Testimony of Christ's Second Appearing*, the *140* title of the projected work, was submitted to New Lebanon by David Darrow and Little Benjamin in August, and approved by Mother Lucy Wright in her reply:

THE

TESTIMONY

OF

CHRIST'S

SECOND APPEARING

CONTAINING

A GENERAL STATEMENT OF ALL THINGS
PERTAINING TO THE FAITH AND PRACTICE OF
THE CHURCH OF GOD
IN THIS LATTER-DAY

PUBLISHED IN UNION.
BY ORDER OF THE MINISTRY

Now is come salvation, and strength, and the kingdom of
our God and the power of his Christ.   REVELATION.

LEBANON, STATE OF OHIO :
FROM THE PRESS OF JOHN M'CLEAN
OFFICE OF THE WESTERN STAR

1808

TITLE PAGE OF FIRST EDITION OF *The Testimony*

(Canaan) 9th 10 mo. 1806

Beloved Brethren —

. . . I am sensible that what you have written is the Gift of God . . .
I have felt & experienced considerable with Father Joseph in relation
to writing, & making more fully known to the world the foundation of our
Faith — We always felt the time was not come — But now I feel satis-

fied, the time is come & the gift is in you and with you to accomplish this work — I am sensible your Gift & calling that you are called to, in the present opening of the Gospel, brings every gift clear & plain that is necessary for the full accomplishment of this work.

I am with you, & the Church also; & can strengthen you in the work . . .

I hope & trust my Life may be spared to see this work accomplished . . .

It will not be unexpected to me if the wicked should write against the circulation of such Books

These few lines from your Parent in the Gospel

N B I trust you will labour to have it printed free from all involvements, so that it may have free circulation. I hope & trust you will consider well & not get anything printed but what you are willing to Live by & die by.   *141*

Reduced to simple terms, Youngs' argument was this: that the true spiritual life, as revealed by Jesus and Mother Ann, was superior, and by its very nature opposed to the natural life typified by Adam after the fall, and by the world in general; that spiritual life was founded on the practice of celibacy, which in its fullest sense meant abstinence from all the sins of the flesh; that this, the only road to salvation, logically demanded, after the initiatory rite of confession, a separation from the world; and that a separate way of life, to survive and succeed, required a unified organization and a close community of interests. In support of this framework of doctrine the author expanded the early Shaker ideas of a dual deity and dual messiahship (the 'joint parentage' of Jesus and Ann Lee), forming the quaternity of Father–Son–Holy Mother Wisdom–Daughter; spiritual baptism, which was the beginning of the resurrection; atonement and salvation by conduct or works, not vicariously through the blood of the crucified Lord; guidance by 'gifts' of continuous revelation; and lastly, the perfectibility of man and society. Cleansed of carnal desire by degrees, aided by divine communications, man makes his progress towards perfection through rectitude of thought and deed, first in the mundane sphere, and then on, uninterruptedly, in the heavenly world.

In Shaker thought the most nearly perfect society yet attained by man — an order which they believed could be re-established in America — was that of the primitive church at Jerusalem. The spirit of that fraternity had inspired Ann Lee, and Meacham had also held

that the government of a church society should be patterned on the
142 apostolic experience. McNemar, John Dunlavy, Seth Youngs Wells,
and Calvin Green, whose works supplemented *The Testimony*, alike
maintained it was man's duty and privilege to build on the foundations laid by Jesus and his disciples. These were specified, they insisted, in the most unequivocal language. The true believer, contended
Youngs, is called out of the world to a life of self-denial, with all its
trials and compensations:

There is no man [he quotes] that hath left house, or brethren, or
sisters, or father, or mother, or wife, or children, or lands, for my sake
and the gospel's, but he shall receive an hundred fold now in this time,
houses, and brethren, and sisters, and mothers, and children, and lands,
with persecutions; and in the world to come, eternal life.

The cross separated him from the course of the world:

If any man come to me and hate not his father, and mother, and wife,
and children, and brethren, and sisters, yea, and his own life also, he
cannot be my disciple. And whosoever doth not bear his cross, and come
after me, cannot be my disciple.

Such hatred was not of persons themselves but of those selfish dispositions and corrupt earthly ties 'which reviled God's claim to the
principle seat of man's affections.' To separate oneself from the fashions of this world was a call explicit in the letters of St. Paul:

Walk in the Spirit and ye shall not fulfil the lust of the flesh. For the
flesh lusteth against the Spirit, and the Spirit against the flesh, and these
are contrary the one to the other.
But this I say, brethren, the time is short: it remaineth, that both
they that have wives be as though they had none; and they that weep,
as though they wept not; and they that rejoice, as though they rejoiced not; and they that buy, as though they possessed not; and they
that use this world, as not abusing it: for the fashion of this world
passeth away.
He that is unmarried careth for the things that belong to the Lord,
how he may please the Lord: But he that is married careth for the things
that are of the world, how he may please his wife . . .

Not only the teaching but the way itself was made clear. Believers
in these teachings, being 'of one heart and one soul,' chose to practice
them by also uniting their temporal interests:

. . . neither said any of them that aught of the things which he possessed was his own; for they had all things common . . . Neither was
there any among them that lacked: for as many as had possessions of
lands or houses sold them — and distribution was made unto every man
according as he had need.

The importance of union, oneness, harmony, equity was emphasized. Again the example is the devoted fellowship in Jerusalem, where
all were members of Christ's body and, being actuated by one spirit,
suffered and rejoiced together. The Church of the New Jerusalem
is likewise one in faith and practice, Youngs concludes: 'one in doctrine, discipline, and government; and one in the mutual and equal
enjoyment of all things both spiritual and temporal.' Its faith was
the faith of Christ, which 'overcometh the nature and spirit of the
world.' 'It is one in doctrine, which is according to godliness, sound,
pure, wholesome, and free from error.' 'The Church hath but one
government, because all the members are governed and influenced by
one Spirit, which is the spirit of Christ, who is the head of the body,
and the centre of influence to the members.' 'It is one in practice,
which is righteousness and peace.' 'The Church is one joint-interest,
as the children of one family, enjoying equal rights and privileges in
things spiritual and temporal, because . . . love is the only bond of
their union.' The Church has 'one common cross' — 'they crucify
one root of evil, which is the flesh with all its affections and lusts; and
hence they possess one common salvation from all sin.'

With effective use of analogics, Youngs contended that the Shaker
mission was a 'completing' work. The same conditions were present
at the opening of both the Pentecostal and Shaker churches. By the
gift of tongues and other wondrous signs the apostles were commissioned to preach the Word. So it was with Ann. The first disciples
were plain, unlettered men. So were the founders of the present order.
Christianity was built on divine revelation, not on any system 'artfully formed by man's device.' So was Shakerism. Scriptural precedent was constantly in evidence. And in this relationship, as here fully
expressed, lay the rationale of the Shaker faith: for the Believers, in-
terpreting certain passages of the Bible literally and convinced that
the Christ spirit had again called men out of the world to complete
an unfinished work, could not but commit themselves to a revival of
the primitive religious commune.

Community of goods was more specifically discussed by John Dunlavy, the chief minister at Pleasant Hill, who, in *The Manifesto* *143* (1818), treated it under the term 'united inheritance,' and by Calvin Green and Seth Youngs Wells, who devoted an important section of their *Summary View of the Millennial Church* (1823) to 'The Right *144* Use of Property.' A competent Biblical scholar, Dunlavy probably had a clearer insight into the nature of religious communism than any other Shaker writer. For him it was the only logical manifestation of equality and universal love: only by sharing prosperity with others could it be shown that such love was genuine affection. Faith in the brotherhood of man was meaningless without corresponding works. The true followers of Christ were distinguished from the world not only by their denial of carnal desire but by the oneness of their spirit and possessions.

What of the world? 'All that is in the world, the lust of the flesh, the lust of the eyes, and the pride of life, is not of the Father, but is of the world.' 'From whence come wars and fighting among you? Come they not hence, even your lusts that war in your members?' 'For whereas there is among you envying, and strife, and divisions, are ye not carnal and walk as men?' The love of God unites, but the lust of the flesh separates and divides. In the world everyone finds it expedient to keep his moiety unmixed with that of his neighbor, or even his brother; everyone seeks to advance his own individual profit; sooner or later everyone finds it to his advantage to obtain his share in a property apart from other claimants.

What of the unworldly? 'The children of this world marry, and are given in marriage; But they which shall be accounted worthy to obtain . . . the resurrection from the dead, neither marry, nor are given in marriage.' 'If ye were of the world, the world would love his own; but because ye are not of the world, but I have chosen you out of the world, therefore the world hateth you.' The fact that individuals widely different in race, age, disposition, education, and wealth could form a successful community proved, Dunlavy insisted, that the union was 'according to the mind and purpose of Christ Himself.'

The Pleasant Hill minister closed his defense of the institution with a comparison between the United Society and the monastic orders, which he admitted had produced good fruits, though not in perfection. The monastics, he claimed, were 'a select number, professing greater sanctity than the church in general, and consequently greater

than was indispensably necessary to salvation.' They were a dependent branch of the church body, supported not by their own industry
but mainly by gratuities. When persons entered the cloisters they
were free from 'incumberance' of wife, husband, children, not having
to sacrifice family ties when they took up their holy orders. They were
bound by oath or vow, not by conscience alone, to lead the celibate life.
They were 'patronized by public approbation and authority,' whereas
the Shakers were marked out as enemies to mankind. In brief, the road
of the latter was harder, and their success a measure of a faith deeper
than that of the 'Roman monks and nuns.'

To Wells and Green, the virtues of simplicity, humility, and charity — three of the twelve foundations of the law of Christ — were
'fully displayed' in the common ownership and use of property. Such
a use was a 'distinguishing privilege of the gospel.' 'The true followers of Christ,' they wrote, 'are one with him, as he is one with the Father. This oneness includes all they possess: for he who has devoted
himself to Christ, soul, body and spirit, can by no means withhold his
property.'   145
Under the influence of selfishness, the authors of *The Millennial
Church* maintained, mankind is led to glorify 'dear self,' to support
and build up a separate interest in all things. 'But it is impossible to
souls who really enjoy the unity of the spirit, to feel satisfied with a
separate enjoyment which their brethren and sisters might, with equal
propriety, partake with them. Their comfort, their peace, their happiness, their enjoyment of every kind, are greatly augmented by sharing them in union with their brethren and sisters.'
Rightly employed, property should be devoted in part to charitable
uses. The improvement of time, talent, and temporal possessions —
God's gifts to man — was a sacred obligation. 'As faithful stewards
of God's heritage everyone was accountable for the use he made of his
privileges. And if others, through misfortune, lacked the good things
which the privileged enjoy, it was mandatory that the hand of charity
be held out to them. What was professed charity for a poor neighbor
when one gives him nothing?'
In conclusion, Wells and Green contended that the law of Christ
was best served, and property best used, when it was united 'in a common stock, where all belonging to the Society, can unite to make it an
increasing interest, for benevolent purposes, and at the same time, en-

joy a competency out of it, upon terms of equality.' The experience
of the Shakers had proved, they wrote, 'that a little, with union and
harmony, and under judicious management, suffices to supply many
wants.'

A discourse *On the Propriety and Necessity of a United Inheritance in All Things,* by William Leonard of the Harvard community
(1853), may make the Shaker view on property clearer. The pattern
for a perfect society, this author contended, was set by Jesus, who was
not 'settled over' the first Christian Church for so much money a
year:

He was no speculator in stocks, trade, or estates. He could not be
distinguished by the carriage he rode in, the palace he dwelt in, nor
the cloth he wore; by the multitude of his servants, golden ornaments,
nor refined literature; nor by being, in these respects, exalted in any way
above the rest . . .

Whoever reads the history of Christ and this first Christian family,
will be, I think, peculiarly struck by the perfect equality which reigned
among them. It would seem that as one labored, they all labored; as one
traveled, they all traveled; as one preached, they all preached; the cross
and chastisement laid upon one, seemed to be the common lot of all.
Upon what one subsisted, they all subsisted; whether upon Peter's fish, or
some simple substitute . . . Among them there were no Christian Kings,
Lords, Statesmen, Military Officers, or fashionable Gentlemen according to the fashion of this world. There were no high nor low among them;
for Jesus said to them, 'I call you not servants; but I have called you
friends.'

146

The unjust differences in the economic conditions of individuals in
the world afforded proof, in Leonard's mind, that those who profess
the Christian name were not of the Kingdom for which Jesus taught
his disciples to pray. 'We are prepared to expect this difference between the children of this world; but when we find these wide extremes
now existing in the (Christian) Church, we are led to inquire, "How
does this compare with the life of Jesus and his Apostles?" . . . In
these days what has the poor man to rejoice about in respect (to property), after he joins the Church, any more than he had before?' In the
'natural world,' private property may play its part. But Jesus appealed to the chosen to set about 'a higher, holier, and more heavenly
employment,' teaching them not to lay up treasures on earth but in

heaven; for man can not serve, at the same time, both God and selfish gain.

Communities of interest in the world fail, concluded the Harvard author, chiefly because they have permitted marriage, which is inextricably involved in the institution of private property. Over twenty such societies, he wrote, had arisen within a few years in the United States: four or five in New York, two in Ohio (at Zanesville and Trumbull), one in Wisconsin, one or more in New Jersey, and three in Massachusetts — Brook Farm at Roxbury, Hopedale at Mendon, and the Northampton Phalanx. These started with zeal, splendid talents, and liberal donations, 'under every combination of elements to insure success.' They were led by philosophic and philanthropic men and women who felt intensely the evils of existent social and economic conditions. They accorded to labor its proper place, with inherent rights, 'administering to the non-producer as his master, rather than his slave.' Invariably their lecturers held up the success of the Shakers as a proof that the experiment could succeed. 'But their foundation, being laid on the principle and practice of generation and the individual family, in the end their care was more for the things of this world, and they sank back into the "natural order." '   147

Far from taking the form of a barren asceticism, escapism, or mere evangelism, the Shaker doctrine thus justified was conscientiously transformed into a living system. Unlike the schools of Owen and the French utopians, who tried to apply elaborate social theories to the   148
hard facts of American life, the Believers — perhaps because they were practical-minded Yankees — faced these facts squarely, beginning at the root, growing organically, evolving a flexible economy suited to the prevailing conditions of the early republic. The convictions of Youngs and other apologists of Shakerism were based not on faith alone, but on the accumulating evidence that the principles they propounded could be, and in fact already had been, successfully realized.

'Consecrated labor' was the foundation of the New Jerusalem. In this term, as used by the Shakers, temporal and spiritual values were curiously fused. With their hands they labored to build up a temporal order which would grow in strength and wisdom. In worship, they 'labored,' or 'traveled,' to make the order a spiritual kingdom. In both cases it was an increasing work, a travel, and in a sense 'travail' — not without joy, not without the cross — and all in all a unity of seeking, with a consciousness of nearing, and often finding, the perfection and oneness with God that were the signs of a mystic faith.

Hand labor was an integral part of the process, if only to avoid
149 poverty, which was no less an evil than idleness or riches. But manual work was glorified from higher motives. It was good for both the individual soul and the collective welfare, mortifying lust, teaching humility, creating order and convenience, supplying a surplus for charity, supporting the structure of fraternity, protecting it against the world, and strengthening it for increasing service. It was significant that Jesus was a carpenter, Peter a fisherman, and Paul a sailmaker; that Ann was a common laborer, a cutter of wool and fur; that Whittaker was a weaver, and Meacham a farmer. Calvin Harlow could not take his place at the head of the Hancock bishopric until he had learned a trade. Every member of the order, from the youngest child to the elder who stood first in the ministry, worked at some useful occupation.

The idea that labor was a sacred commitment supplies a key that unlocks many a secret: the quietude of the Shaker villages, the pervasive atmosphere of order and permanence, the quality of their workmanship, the respect they won, eventually, from their neighbors and the world. In a letter to Charles Lane, Ednah Littlehale praised their sense of 'the Sacredness of labor' as no less an achievement than their elevation of women to equality with men. And Theodore Parker, writing to Robert White, a Quaker who had become interested in Shakerism, paid tribute thus to its abolition of 'menial service': 'None of your community think work is degrading while, in society at large, many men are ashamed of work, and, of course, ashamed of men (and women) who work, and make them ashamed of themselves. Now, the Shakers have completely done away with that evil . . . that is one
150 of their great merits, and it is a very great one.'

The Shaker attitude toward labor and property led to the practical application of what may be termed a philosophy of use. The true idea of a holy family, in Ann Lee's mind, was one in which the most exalted spiritual sentiments were represented by the simplest domestic labors. Father Joseph also saw, realistically, that labor was more useful than possessions, that it was by the accumulation of varied even though limited abilities, that an 'interest' would eventually be formed. From his 'way-marks' as well as from certain phrases in the covenant he drafted — 'according to their abilities,' 'according to their calling,' et cetera — it is evident that he contemplated the free utilization of all available skills. Being a farmer himself and lay preacher to common people, he appreciated the worth of manual toil. The great objective of the covenanters was 'to improve our time and Talents in this Life, in that manner in which we might be most useful.' To be most useful, the temporal interest should not be embarrassed by outside claims; labor should be tempered and functional, and all work keyed to an orderly plan.

Meacham's appointment of deacons set the stage for the organization of labor. Under them were the overseers, foremen, and caretakers whose special abilities qualified them to direct certain occupations or groups. At a later date a distinction was made between the trustees and deacons; the 'fixed property' was handled by the former, sometimes known as 'office deacons,' varying in number, who had the power to give and receive deeds of warranty, stand in law for the society, purchase and dispose of property, plan industry, and carry on transactions with those without; whereas the latter, under the titles of 'farm deacons,' 'orchard deacon,' 'garden deaconness,' et cetera, had

TRUSTEES' OFFICE AND STORE, NEW LEBANON.
BUILT IN 1827

the immediate direction of departments of labor and the responsibility of providing for the needs of the family.

Under the deacons' or trustees' supervision, goods were distributed directly through the office or common store. Articles were purchased from the world by the trustees; the products of the farms and shops were obtained directly from the heads of different departments. Thence they passed into the hands of the deacons or deaconnesses, who 'doled out equally, or, rather, proportionately, to diversity of condition and employ; and an account kept of what every individual receives.' This order of stewardship was religiously supported: even fruit of 'extra and rare properties' was divided among elders, trustees, and common members, male and female, with rigorous exactness. All surplus and goods for sale were in the hands of the deacons and trustees who, as stewards of the outer court, had exclusive charge of mercantile relationships with the world.

Though the family elders were immediately responsible for temporalities, it was the ministry which annually checked the deacons' accounts and had the power of appointment and removal. Though the 'lead' was a self-perpetuating office, vacancies were filled, in theory at least, on the basis of merit. The person 'who most willingly devotes his time and talents to the benefit of the Society,' W. S. Warder, a Philadelphia Quaker, reported to Robert Owen in 1816, 'must necessarily enjoy the highest esteem of his fellow members,' and being in the front rank of service, be in line for promotion. Besides, there was 'nothing to be gained by this appointment, except the honor of being the servants to the rest of the members; for we perceive that they all are expected to perform manual labor.'   'Their political principles are strictly republican, viewing all hereditary rank in civil or religious government, as repugnant to the spirit of Christianity.' Nevertheless, after 1792 the ministry withdrew from access to the people, no longer hearing confessions but working through the elders and deacons. Living apart in the meeting-house, working in their own shops, it was the office of the 'lead' — 'in their ways and manners . . . in their hand labor . . . in all their deportment' — to set an example for the rest of the community.

The division of each community into family units — there were eight at New Lebanon — had distinct advantages. It led to a certain flexibility of production. Each family carried on its industrial activities independently, buying from and selling to the world or other

families and societies. Each had its own store or trustees' office to serve
as a supply depot and clearing-house for outgoing or incoming goods.
Preferential discounts and exchange policies prevailed. Experience
proved that the ideal size was about fifty members: if larger, 'the energy evoked by the communal system was apt to be dissipated over so
wide an area' that the group became a 'petty municipality'; if much
smaller, the advantages of combination and division of labor were to a
degree lost. The system had an additional merit, for under it, if one   *154*
family, through such misfortune as fire, sickness, failure of crop, or
mismanagement, should suffer a reverse, it could be limited to a given
area and there repaired. Shaker history is replete with examples of
one family or community coming to the aid of another.   *155*

TRUSTEES' OFFICE, NISKEYUNA

Within this general framework of economic organization, labor itself was relatively free and plastic: combined industry did not degen-
erate into a rigidly regulated system, nor did the individual's feeling
of responsibility toward the group result in regimentation. On the
contrary, there was recognition of native ability and individual initiative, of the satisfactions that come from diversity of occupations,
and of the virtues of moderate as opposed to excessive toil. Such concepts led to a progressive economy — the introduction of new trades,

efficiency in industrial practices, and a wholesome combination of agricultural and shop activities — which may be favorably compared with that of other American religious communities.

Labor flowed naturally into those channels where it could be most effectively utilized. If a brother had experience in, or aptitude for, a certain trade, he usually devoted the major part of his time to that work; and if qualified, he assumed responsibility for its direction. At New Lebanon, for example, Henry Markham was at one time the head cooper, Benjamin Bruce and Benjamin Lyon the chief machinists, Garret Lawrence the leading herbalist, and Henry DeWitt the director of the reel business. The broom industry at Watervliet was managed by Theodore Bates. The master builder of eastern meetinghouses was Moses Johnson of Enfield (N.H.). Thomas Corbett of Canterbury, an experienced medical botanist, was placed in charge of that department in his community. Sometimes the shop would be operated by a single individual, but if there were others, the foreman worked along on the same level with his associates. If he were a 'caretaker' of boys, inducting them as apprentices into 'the art and mystery' of an occupation, supervision took a kindly paternalistic form. Each shop was an independent unit keeping its own accounts.

More often than not, however, the brethren followed two or more callings. Believing that variety in work was 'a source of pleasure,' the order encouraged its members to master several skills. Richard McNemar, for example, was a weaver, bookbinder, chairmaker, printer, editor, author, and preacher; Elder Harvey L. Eads, of South Union, was a tailor, shoemaker, teamster, seedsman, wool carder, tin and sheet-iron worker, dentist, printer, painter, and hatter — as well as author and elder; Giles Avery of New Lebanon was a joiner, cooper, wagonmaker, plumber, mason, and carpenter. In 'his history in verse' Brother Isaac Youngs recorded that

> I've always found enough to do
> Some pleasant times, some grievous too
> Of various kinds of work I've had
> Enough to make me sour or sad,
> Of tayl'ring, Join'ring, farming too,
> Almost all kinds that are to do,
> Blacksmithing, Tinkering, Mason work,
> When could I find a time to shurk?
> Clock work, Jenny work, keeping school

Enough to puzzle any fool!
An endless list of chores & notions,
To keep me in perpetual motion.   *156*

Two typical cases, that of Henry Blinn of Canterbury and Enfield, who rose to the ministry, and that of Benjamin Gates of New Lebanon, who later held a position of responsibility in that society, indicate how varied was the occupational life of the Shaker workman.

Blinn, a native of Providence, Rhode Island, entered the novitiate order at Canterbury in September 1838, when he was fourteen years old. His first occupation, under the charge of a young brother, was sawing staves for pails. Later in the fall he was transferred to the farm. In October he entered the community blacksmith shop, but when it was found he was not strong enough for this work, he was placed under the care of Brother Thomas Hoit, 'a universal chore man,' who had charge of the carding mill and the stove, tinware, and cut-nail industry. Having served his apprenticeship as a wool carder, Blinn was elevated to the management of the mill. At the age of nineteen he qualified, under the laws of the state, as an instructor of children and youth, a position which kept him busy only in the three winter months and which he held for eight years. Besides teaching, the young brother instructed his charges in the braiding of whiplashes, worked on the farm at harvest time, for ten years took his turn as a night watchman, and began the study of printing and binding. It was in the latter occupation, first as typesetter and later as a historical writer and editor, that Blinn made his most notable contribution to the welfare of the order. For nearly sixty years this was his major occupation, even while serving as a family elder and a leading member of the Canterbury-Enfield ministry. But these elevated offices did not prevent him from working, at spare times, at those tasks in which he had had some experience as a youth, or from learning dentistry and bee-keeping. Altogether he had some thirteen or fourteen occupations.   *157*

A typical month's work by Benjamin Gates, who was apprenticed to a tailor and learned the trade while still attending school, is thus recorded in his journal:

September 1832
S   1st   Helped clean out the ditches in the swamp so as to let the
           water on the meadow.

M	3d-Sa 8th	Ploughing and harrowing above the south orchard with the old horses chief part of the time, and the rest of the time drawing dung from Jones's on the flat.
W	5th	The family move in to the house! . . But me no go, that to my sorrow . . .
M	10th	I help finish sow the wheat
T	11th	Draw dung
W	12th	Help clean up the taylors shop, and geather [gather] myself in
Th	13th	Help cut onion seed; and began a blue jacket for Hiram Rude
Fr	14th	A M.go down to the grist mill and mend conductors P M cut onion seed
S	15th	Work on Hiram's jacket
M	17th	I work on Hiram's jacket
Tu	18th	I finish said jacket, & do various choars
W	19th	I began a blue jacket for Philip B.
Th	20 & 21	I help shingle the hog pen
S	22nd	I finish Philip's jacket, & do various choars
M	24th	Began a blue jacket for Benjamin Lyon
Tu	25th	I finish said jacket
W	26th	I go a butternutting with Rufus Hinkley
Th	27th	Began a jacket for Aaron Bill, thick blue
Fr	28th & 29th	I work at the north house, preparing hoof and horn for buttons

158

Gates' journal reveals his participation in many other activities: in the fall, picking apples, making cider, digging potatoes, gathering herbs, roots, and hemlock bark, cutting carpet rags, getting out seeds, printing seed bills, helping to slaughter hogs; in the winter, when not attending school, drawing and cutting wood, binding books, working at the fulling, bark, and gristmills; in the spring, cleaning up shops, working in the physic and kitchen gardens, trimming trees, preparing tin for roofing; in the summer, berrying, haying, gathering herbs again, carpentering, washing sheep, distilling spirits, getting out stone, helping at the blacksmith shop, working on the Shaker section of the public highway. All the time tailoring was Benjamin's basic occupation but, having no rigid production schedule, he was free to assist the deacons, foremen, overseers, or caretakers at any time.

The above routine, or lack of it, is characteristic. The sisters' diaries, as the following selection from that of Elizabeth Lovegrove will show, are comparable, with the difference that a more systematic rota-

KITCHEN, CHURCH FAMILY, NISKEYUNA

:ion of labor was practised. Monthly 'tours' were taken in housekeeping and in the kitchens, bakery, and wash house, every few months;
and there were similar, if more irregular turns, in the dairy, weave
shop, and herb house. Seasonal activities like preserving and maple-
sugaring drew the sisters together in bees of concentrated effort.

Sister Elizabeth left her 'habitation' at the East house in March
1837 to assist in the 'physician's lot': the early part of her journal is
a running report on influenza, lung fever, canker rash, cholic, inflam-
mation of the eye, 'quinzy' sore throat, scalding, 'fellons,' one case of
strangury, one of 'tic Dollereux,' and so on. Treatments are listed:

Betsey B. takes Phisic

Elder Sister is relieved some of her cough by the vaper bath and electric-
ty.

Lucy Bishop here to help sweat Elder Ebenezer with hemlock and hot
tones.

Commence polticeing Amy's face with camomile and Marsh mallows.

Elder Sister fell down and hurt her side — we resort to shocking rubbing
and bleeding her, likewise apply skunk cabbage leaves and make her tea
of Johnswort and pepper grass seed, all have a good effect.

Rachel Sampson severely afflicted with the sun headache, apply a blister
to the neck and arm also oint the forehead with marrow of a hogs jaw
and apply a bag of hops wet with vinagar, good effect.

SISTERS' SHOP

Though nursing is her main duty, Elizabeth takes her regular turns in the kitchen, during the summer picks medicinal herbs and makes wintergreen lozenges, and assists in such occupations as making candles, metheglin, and spring beer. In March 1838, she is transferred to the tailoring shop, starting in with cushions, and then beginning to spin in July, to make bonnets in September and to shag mats in December. Her tour at cooking continues, however, with time for other tasks. In June she turns out with the family sisters to pick up and burn brush in the orchard. The same month she spends three weeks in the office. For three weeks in September she helps package garden seeds. In the fall certain days are occupied with berrying, washing, dyeing, drying apples, painting windows, and assisting again in the care of the sick. Time goes fast. The frequent change of occupation precludes monotony. She is interested, conscientious, and wants to do more. The following entry, on 31 December 1838, 'closes her concearn' for the year: 'I must . . . consider well how I have spent it, and if I have spent it well, begin the next month with an increase.'

The Shaker idea was that in consecration, not compulsion, lay the secret of a successful economy. Age, sex, and ability were all considered in assignments to work. But once assigned, the individual became part of a co-operative in which *temperate* labor — what one writer called 'the middle way' — was a marked characteristic. 'Each member,' Silliman noticed in 1832, 'does what amount of labor he considers right and proper, without any intervention on the part of his fellow-laborers. Conscience and the examples of others are the only incitements to labor, and none are required to labor beyond their strength.' 160 Finch perceived that 'none are overworked and none ever want a day's labour.' Another English visitor, Hepworth Dixon, found life at New 161 Lebanon moving 'in an easy kind of rhythm': everyone seemed busy, but since everyone was free, no 'strain' or 'menace' was observable. 162 After a day with the Shakers, Horace Greeley also praised their 'constant, but never excessive toil.' One student of economics, in fact, suggested that the society, to maintain the balance of an 'elaborately organized division of work,' had to prevent its members from working too hard. 163

The system was also noteworthy for its many inventions and improvements: machines for turning broom handles, sizing broomcorn 164 brush, filling seed bags and herb packages, printing bags and labels, cutting leather, cutting and bending machine card teeth, twisting whip handles and lashes, splint-making, basket-making, box-cutting, fertilizing, planing and matching boards, and so on. The Shakers are credited with inventing a screw propeller, Babbitt metal, a rotary harrow, an automatic spring, a turbine water wheel, a threshing machine, the circular saw, cut nails, a pipe machine, a pea-sheller, a self-acting cheese press, a butter worker, the common clothes pin, the first one-horse wagon used in this country, a palm-leaf bonnet loom, a silk-reeling machine, a revolving oven, a machine for paring, coring, and quartering apples, and the first metal pens and flat brooms. Evidence of the satisfaction taken in improvements is seen in the considerable section devoted to that subject in Isaac Youngs's *Concise View:* he writes about 'a grindstone going by water,' a new stone bridge, the introduction of cast-iron stoves to replace fireplaces, a triphammer works, aqueducts to bring water into the kitchen, 'a proper framed wood-house,' a cast-iron bark mill, the oiling of floors, alarm clocks, a new spinning jenny, improved types of lathes, drying kilns, and wood mills, even 'exertions for improvement in our language and address.'

The Shakers were constantly bettering their systems of lighting, ventilating, heating, refrigeration, and washing. Ingenious contrivances for saving labor were 'almost endless': but with the exception of the 'wash mill,' the metallic button for the base of tilting chairs, a chimney cap, and a folding pocket stereoscope, they patented none of their inventions, believing that patent money savored of monopoly.

A MENDER OF CLOTHING   CUTTING BREAD

165   This desire to experiment — an expression, no doubt, of Yankee ingenuity — was stimulated by the fact that in the sect's communal economy the workers could reap directly the benefits of their own talent. The circular saw, for example, invented and set up at Watervliet for cutting boards for window sash, grooving floor plank, gaging clapboards, et cetera, performed, with one man and a boy to attend it, the labor of thirty men. Inventions could release labor for other tasks, but in Shaker practice they served rather to alleviate arduous

166   effort. Elisha Myrick of Harvard 'hailed with delight' his new herb-pressing machine because, as he wrote in his diary, 'every improvement relieving human toil or facilitating labor [gives] time and opportunity for moral, mechanical, scientific and intellectual improvement and the cultivation of the finer and higher qualities of the human

167   mind.' Finally, it must not be forgotten that progress, and a way of life superior to that of the world, had, in the Shaker mind, a moral

justification: 'We have a right to improve the inventions of man, so far as is useful and necessary,' Meacham had said, 'but not to vain glory, or anything superfluous . . . We are not called to labor to excell, or be like the world: but to excell them in order, union and peace, and in good works — works that are truly virtuous and useful to man, in this life.' In conformity to this precept, manufacture was confined to such branches of industry as were useful to the public, instead of those which tended to superfluity and extravagance.   *168*

Improvement in hand labor was reflected in trade. Painstakingly made, Shaker products had an intrinsic merit which was their best advertisement, and which, as time went on, gave them a premium value and price. So astute, indeed, were the Shaker salesmen that they acquired, in some quarters, a reputation for untoward shrewdness. 'Of the Shaker society,' Emerson relates, 'it was formerly a sort of proverb in the country that they always sent the devil to market.' A   *169* French writer, Mme Therese Blanc, similarly criticizes them for mingling 'a concern for material gain' with the loftiest thoughts, for too greatly emphasizing, in their revival of the practices of the primitive church, the two traits, 'they bought and sold.'   *170*

The followers of Ann, it is true, were practical merchandisers. They were strict, possibly to a fault, in their dealings with the world. As separatists, they had to survive; they were somewhat on their guard; their laws forbade indebtedness both to and from the world. That such strictness was based, however, on a severe ethical code, and outlawed misrepresentation, finds abundant illustration in Shaker practice. One story tells how several members of the family of William and Elizabeth Taylor, late of England, were attracted to the society. A Shaker brother by the name of Eli Porter owed one cent to a merchant in Hudson, New York, where the Taylors had settled, and came to pay it. William, amazed that so trifling a debt should turn a man 'out of his course,' resolved to become acquainted with a people determined 'to owe no one ought but love and good-will' and, finding them true to their principles, entered the order, where his youngest daughter, Eliza Ann, eventually became first in the ministry. In the sale of produce — to cite a more general opinion — the Believers lived up to their reputation for 'keeping the top, middle and bottom layer equally good in every basket or barrel of fruit or vegetables sent to market under their name.' Characteristic of the care that goods trade-marked   *171* with the society's name or the trustee's initials should be kept superior to, and unmixed with worldly products, was a covenant, contracted in 1819, in which the deacons and gardeners of the first bishopric — concerned 'lest there should come loss upon the joint interest, and dishonor upon the gospel' — agreed never to purchase seeds of the world and mix them with their own for sale. Such was the insistence on flawlessness that all products had to pass the inspection of the deacons before they were sent out, whatever was inferior or faulty being retained for domestic or charitable use.

With their repute for hospitality, comfortable living, and moderate toil, one would think the communities would have been overrun with what the Philistine called 'economic hoboes.' 'Wherever there are man's food and clothing, there will be man,' was Edward Everett's cynical explanation of Shaker progress. True, the law of charity forbade them to turn away from their doors anyone unfed or unhoused, with the result that beggars and tramps were in the habit of turning up after dark, secure of being fed and sheltered in the little dormitory, or tramp house, set apart for them. These 'over-ripe fruits of our labor system' went their way, often with 'tramp bags' filled with clothes or provisions, the next morning. Not so another class, the so-called 'winter Shakers' — more like the order Everett had in mind — who, showing up in the early winter with a profession of interest in the doctrine, pulled up stakes as soon as spring called them again to their wanderings. Over the years many people were drawn to the communes for material reasons; but in spite of this lure, few stayed for long if they could not accommodate themselves to the prevailing spirit. The Shakers open their doors, wrote Emerson, 'to every wayfaring man who proposes to come among them; for they say, the Spirit will presently manifest to the man himself and to the society what manner of person he is, and whether he belongs among them.' Idlers or 'slugs,' having no place in the order, were uncomfortable in its atmosphere and, not belonging, soon departed.

AGRICULTURE

As with the ancient village communities of the East and the Christian monastic orders, agriculture was the foundation of the Shaker economy. Most of the American religious associations, in fact, 'built their spiritual foundations on good tillage.' The early ones existed in a period when farming was the logical, often the only means of subsistence. Being separatists from established society, the orders fre-

quently sought out remote localities where land was cheap and life
was free. Here the communicants, assembled in a joint enterprise,
resorted to those labors in which the principle of combination could be
most effectively expressed.

The dedication of desirable tracts of land, the steady acquisition of
neighboring farms, and the assiduous cultivation of the soil turned
the Believers into large landholders at an early period. In a thinly
populated country, with 'a large, disposable body' of laborers, they
had an advantage over the individual farmer which was augmented
by a passionate urge to redeem the soil. The broad pasture lands of
the order; its finely bred livestock — horses, milch cows, 'working
oxen,' young cattle, sheep, and hogs — its apiaries; its turkeys and
poultry; its apple, pear, cherry, peach, plum, and quince orchards;
its fields of rye, oats, barley, corn, flax, turnips, and potatoes; its drying kilns and well-filled barns were all signs of a prosperity which
must have been envied by many a struggling yeoman or farmhand of
the early republic, and doubtlessly accounted for many a conversion.
In fact, the society was not above proselyting on the ground of economic benefit, as witness McNemar's letter to a group of prospective
adherents:

If ye choose to come the church can spare them . . . good land, an
apple orchard of one hundred good bearing trees and ten acres of
meadow pasture. If this is not enough we can share more farm land adjoining, until in reason ye be satisfied. This farm is located about 1½
miles from our mills, where 'little children' get all their grinding, sawing
and fulling done gratis, which may save you the mortification of being
beholden to Babylon, and also the expense and trouble of erecting those
things for yourselves.   *175*

The culture of the fields was a part of the grand scheme to deliver
the world from its evils. Waste, neglect, and misuse of God's blessings
aroused the Shaker soul. Coming from a land long cultivated, Ann's
company saw the possibilities of the Lebanon and Hancock slopes and
valleys, the flatlands of Niskeyuna, the bottom lands of the Miami
River country and the bluegrass regions of Kentucky — and longed
to make these part of the Kingdom. Planning in terms of a thousand
years, Ann had exhorted her followers to set out more apple trees,
raise more calves, till more land. Cut your grain clean, Whittaker had
taught: 'God has caused it to grow, and you ought to be careful to

save it; for you cannot make one kernel grow, if you know you must
starve for the want of it. In this country you abound in good things,
therefore you are lavish and wasteful.' In the aforementioned letter
from Father James to a Hancock farmer, appeal is made for a maximum use of the soil:

Thou art idle and slothful whereby thy Land lays unimproved and
pretty much waste; whence arises want and a great burden to the poor
man who dwells in the house not far from thee. This, Josiah, is abomina-
ble in the sight of God, and will finally bring upon thee want and poverty
. . . as the time of plowing and seeding is approaching, get thy farm
in readiness . . . And when you have done all you can towards seeding
your Land for the present Season set yourselves faithfully to put your
176 whole place in order.

In reclaiming the soil, the Believer gave it a care which was almost
affection, as if the love he withheld from the world had been diverted
to the land. To Hepworth Dixon, the English editor who visited New
Lebanon long after the letter above was written, Shaker husbandry
had a sacramental quality. He was astonished at the order and fertility of the communal land, a veritable Eden, he wrote, comparable to
his own long-cultivated English valleys. What was the secret of such
bounty and beauty? A stranger had told him the Believers 'gave their
minds' to the cultivation of the soil. But to Dixon the explanation lay
deeper:

You see that the men who till these fields, who tend these gardens, who
bind these sheaves, who train these vines, who plant these apple-trees,
have been drawn into putting their love into the daily task; and you
hear with no surprise that these toilers, ploughing and planting in their
quaint garb, consider their labor on the soil as a part of their ritual,
looking upon the earth as a stained and degraded sphere, which they
177 have been called to redeem from corruption and restore to God.

Love for garden and field took the place of the passion for money
and love for wife and children. So thought this visitor, who tells, in a
revealing passage, of an experience with Elder Evans, his host at the
North family:

This morning I have spent an hour with Frederick in the new orchard,
listening to the story of how he planted it, as to a tale by some Arabian
poet. 'A tree has its wants and wishes,' said the Elder, 'and a man should
study them as a teacher watches a child, to see what he can do. If you

love the plant, and take heed of what it likes, you will be well repaid by it. I don't know if a tree ever comes to know you; and I think it may; but I am sure it feels when you care for it and tend it, as a child does, as a woman does. Now, when we planted this orchard, we first got the very best cuttings in our reach; we then built a house for every plant to live in, that is to say, we dug a deep hole for each; we drained it well; we laid down tiles and rubble, and then filled in a bed of suitable manure and mold; we put the plant into its nest gently, and pressed up the earth about it, and protected the infant tree by this metal fence.'

'You take a world of pains,' I said.

'Ah, Brother Hepworth,' he rejoined, 'thee sees we love our garden.'

Thus, when a Shaker is put upon the soil [Dixon continues], to beautify it by his tilth, the difference between his husbandry and that of a Gentile farmer, who is thinking solely of his profits, is likely to be great. While the Gentile is watching for his returns, the Shaker is intent upon his service. One tries for large profits, the other strives for good work . . .   178

It was significant, in Dixon's mind, that the first building he came upon as he entered the village, at its very gateway so to speak, was a great stone barn. 'The granary is to a Shaker,' he felt, 'what the Temple was to a Jew.'

Similar sentiments were expressed by other English observers. A traveler 'can generally tell when he is come to their possessions,' Warder wrote, 'from the excellent improvements . . . neatness pervades every department; their fields, orchards, fences, cattle, etc. afford proof of it, and in their extensive gardens all useful plants may be found, but for weeds one might seek in vain.' When asked how the Shakers managed with their neighbors about fencing, Warder was told that little difficulty was encountered: 'we make ours good, and they generally follow the example; if they do not quite do their part, we do a little more than ours, and in time they come tolerably near to what they ought to be.' A few years later Isaac Holmes received the   179
same impression of neat orchards and an 'agricultural excellence which is scarcely equalled, and not surpassed, in the whole country.'   180
'The Shaker land is easily known by its superior cultivation, and by its substantial stone wall fences,' John Finch, the English economist, reported. The buildings are 'surrounded with beautiful and well cultivated kitchen and flower gardens, vineyards, orchards, and farms, the very best that are to be seen in the United States; their horses, their cows and their sheep, are some of the best bred and best fed that

I ever saw; their long ranges of stacks of grain, well filled barns, and
181 well filled stores, prove that they have neither want nor the fear of it.'
After a visit to a western colony, Harriet Martineau wrote, in similar
vein, that 'the land is cultivated to a perfection seen nowhere else in
the United States, except at Mr. Rapp's settlement in Ohio, where
Community of Property is also the binding principle of the Society.'

Admiration embraced both the facilities for good farming and the
manner in which they were used. One observer notices the motive
power provided by the reservoirs and dams which ran the mills and
shops. Another comments on the ingenious construction of silos and
barns and the economical methods of handling manure and releasing
yokes. A third is impressed by the quietness of all farm labor, as well
as by the admonition posted in Shaker barns:

> A man of kindness, to his beast is kind,
> Brutal actions show a brutal mind.
> Remember, He who made the brute,
> Who gave thee speech and reason, formed him mute;
> He can't complain; but God's omniscient eye
> Beholds thy cruelty. He hears his cry.
> He was destined thy servant and thy drudge,
182 > But know this: his creator is thy judge.

After a tour through the barns, storage cellars, and milk, butter,
and cheese rooms of a certain family, representatives of the magazine
The Cultivator, observing conveniences and labor-saving contrivances everywhere, did not know which most to admire: 'the skill and
ingenuity evinced in the original design, or the neatness displayed
in their use.'

That the communities, in their methods and standards, set a salutary example in the surrounding region may scarcely be doubted.
Farmers planning to buy new implements often called on the Believers
for advice. Their progressive practices were copied by the world. 'In
the absence of a rural nobility,' Emerson wrote, their service as 'model
farms' was one of the most valuable functions of the Shaker commune.

The chief occupations of the order were developed from the land.
Within ten or twelve years from the time the church was established
at New Lebanon, industries based on the soil had been inaugurated.
Seed gardens, the source of one of the most lucrative communal enter-

prises, were set apart from the crop-growing areas in the period 1789–94, and soon seeds were being put up in small paper packages and distributed over a constantly widening area. Experimenting with soils and fertilizers, selecting, testing and eliminating, the seedsmen before long had established a reputation throughout New England, the middle Atlantic and southern states, and later as far away as California, Mexico, and Europe. Another large-scale industry, the manufacture of flat brooms, was under way by 1798, when the first broom-corn was grown at Niskeyuna. The earliest gatherings of medicinal herbs, an occupation that was to develop into the most extensive enterprise of all, are traceable to 1800. During the last decade of the

HERB SHOP, NEW LEBANON

eighteenth century more and more land was acquired. Whether arable, wooded, or swamp it was utilized in some way: for pasturage and sheep walks; for seed and kitchen gardens; for vegetables and fruits; for flax, broomcorn, and other crops; for bark and therapeutic plants; for lumber and maple sugar. Resourceful in their use of abundant land and labor, the Shakers were unwittingly in the vanguard of the movement leading from a household economy to mass production.

THE MECHANICAL ARTS

The complexity of hand labor is even more in evidence when we turn from farming and semi-agricultural pursuits to the mechanical arts. From the shops of the blacksmith and tinsmith, the cooper, joiner, and wheelwright, the tailor, the tanner, the weaver and dyer, an amazing variety of products were turned out both for sale and for

domestic use. The raw materials for much of this production —
leather goods, coopers' ware, straw bonnets, woodenware, basketry,
poplar boxes, and so forth — likewise came from the joint interest.
The Believers were largely self-sufficient, though there was no objection to buying materials or consumer goods from the world if efficiency or economy was thereby better served.

Since a complete account of Shaker mechanical and domestic industries, with data on processes, prices, and the nature of the product,
183 is already available, a summary will here suffice. Among the first to be
developed, as already stated, was the preparation of garden seeds,
brooms and brushes, and medicinal herbs — taking the worker from
field to shop. Saw, grist, and fulling mills were established at the outset. Tanning was one of the first pursuits, combining with it the manufacture of saddles, saddlebags, harnesses, whiplashes, and shoes. The
early period also saw the production of spinning wheels, reels, buttons, and buckles, wagons, clocks, chairs, and miscellaneous coopery
— tubs, measures, wooden dippers, cheese hoops, and so on. 'Clother-
ing' was likewise introduced shortly after the first gathering, with
the hatcheling, carding, spinning, weaving, and dyeing done by the
sisters, and the tailoring, at first, by the brethren. The making of felt,
colt's fur, and wool hats were important branches of the clothier's
trade, as was the fulling of cloth and scouring of flannel. Hand cards
for carding wool were first made for sale in 1793. Since many incoming converts were blacksmiths or mechanics, it is not surprising that
nail-making, wire-drawing, tinkering, and the making of hollow ware,
plows, hoes, rakes, clothier's shears, et cetera, should have been initial
undertakings.

As the order grew, industry flowed into new channels, with other
colonies following the example set at New Lebanon. Most of the early
industries were first developed at this 'center of influence,' notably
those having to do with the working of wood, of which there was local
abundance. The making of baskets, oval boxes, wire and horsehair
sieves, floor mops, and wooden-stemmed pipes with clay bowls began
about 1810. Chair manufacture expanded soon after the turn of the
century, along with other forms of joinery. In response to the need
of a rapidly growing order, carpenters, masons, builders, and cabi-
netmakers were associated at this time in an extensive program of
house and furniture construction.

The 'hand-labor of females' ran parallel to that of the males but

SHAKERESSES PREPARING HERB EXTRACTS

was kept at a discreet distance by moral law. The sisters had their own workshops, or separate rooms on one side of the dwelling. All shared the domestic tasks: housekeeping and cooking, sewing and knitting, washing and ironing. But even before the communities were organized the sisters took over many shop duties: setting card teeth, braiding horsewhips, hatcheling, carding, spinning, weaving and 'coloring,' making their own clothes and all except 'the thick work' for the males. Early in the last century the sisterhood began several branches of business, preparing for sale a fine linen diaper and other kinds of cloth, poplar baskets, men's palm-leaf hats, women's bonnets, a variety of cushions, mops, brushes, paper boxes, table mats, work stands, fans, needle-books, emery balls, seed bags, stockings, footings, gloves, and so forth. With the development of the herb industry the sisters were assigned to gathering wild plants and flowers, to cleaning roots, sorting herbs, 'dressing' powders, extracts, and ointments, and printing and pasting labels. In addition, they did the milking, except in wintry weather, and made butter and cheese, apple sauce, dried apples, maple sugar, pickles, catsup, preserves, jellies, and wines, of which what could be spared went for sale. They helped in the 'nurse-shops' and schools. In the dwellings, each sister was assigned to take care of the temporal needs of a brother — making, mending, and washing his clothes.

The colonies in the East and Middle West followed, on the whole, similar programs, with the emphasis on farming, stock-raising, and the standard industries of broom-making, the growing of garden seeds, and the preparation of medicinal herbs. In Ohio and Kentucky more attention was paid, perhaps, to strictly agricultural pursuits and the breeding of fine cattle. Regional innovations sometimes occurred. The center for the manufacture of washing machines, for example, was Canterbury. Soon after the Civil War knitting machines were adopted at Canterbury and Enfield (N.H.) for making flannel shirts, drawers, and socks. A profitable industry, confined to the New Gloucester settlement in Maine, was the manufacture of oak staves for molasses hogsheads, which were exported to the West Indies. Hancock developed an industry in table swifts, and New Lebanon one in horn combs and carpet whips. Both New Lebanon and Watervliet experimented with the manufacture of metal pens. Cloak-making was a thriving undertaking at a late period, particularly at New Lebanon and Canterbury. Pleasant Hill had a linseed-oil mill, South Union a whiskey distillery. Silk worms, the source of the beautiful colored kerchiefs woven in several societies, were raised in Kentucky. North Union took advantage of its proximity to the growing city of Cleveland to develop milk routes and extensive market gardens. Raw materials, available skills, and local demands varied, but the tendency was to concentrate on trades that had been concurrently developed

SHAKER SISTERS CORKING BOTTLES, HERB INDUSTRY

within the United Society as a unit and for which a reputation had been achieved.

Sale goods were distributed by several methods. In September 1791, David Meacham, Richard Spier, and Joseph Bennett moved into an office of the New Lebanon Church family. Here accounts were kept and a center established for a retail business with other families, and with farmers and small tradesmen in the neighborhood. Sometimes goods were bartered or exchanged for commodities not produced by the society. Sometimes they were sold outright. Often they were left with small merchants in near-by villages, to be sold on commission. As industries developed, the Believers at the parent society extended their markets to such towns as Albany, Hudson, and Poughkeepsie, periodically loading their wagons with merchandise and collecting from these trade centers certain necessities, payments on their 'dubils,' and new orders. The route system, for years the standard method of distributing goods, especially in the seed business, was gradually extended until the 'shrewd, honest, sedate but kindly' Shaker peddlers, with their broad-brimmed hats, were familiar in all parts of the country. As the temporal economy expanded during the first half of the last century, as power machinery facilitated production and the railroad distribution, enterprise assumed wholesale proportions. The route system declined, and the order adopted, whenever feasible, the methods of the world.

ARCHITECTURE AND CRAFTSMANSHIP   *184*

Even as, in the superfluity and curiousness of raiment and food, the labour of nature is perverted and the matter falleth into wrong if it be without art, so also is it in the superfluity, curiousness and sumptuosity of buildings . . . this superfluity and costliness of buildings and stone walls is a cause why we have in these days less pity and alms for the poor; since we are not rich enough to feed them while we spend also upon such superfluous expenses.

The divine man has no right to waste money upon what you would call beauty, in his house or his daily life, while there are people living in misery.

In these parallel passages, the first from a twelfth-century discourse on architecture by Petrus Cantor (Peter the Precentor),* the

* Coulton, C. G. *Life in the Middle Ages,* vol. II, Cambridge, England, 1930, pp. 25–7.

second from an interview with the Shaker elder, Frederick Evans, is expressed a continuing tradition which is a key to the character of the craftsmanship of the sect. The passages suggest that display, pride, and superfluity, 'what the world called beauty,' was considered an 'absurd and abnormal' concept. If the community's buildings were to be reconstructed, Evans would concentrate on 'more light, a more equal distribution of heat, and a more general care for protection and comfort . . . but no beauty.' Order, harmony, utility — these, not 'ornamentation,' were the objectives of good workmanship.

185

The carpenters, mechanics, and joiners of the sect were nevertheless true artisans. If art is thought of in its original sense — as 'the science of the making of any things whatever for man's good use . . . a principle of manufacture [which] involves the whole of the active life, and presupposes the contemplative' * — then the weaving, basketry, coopering, gardening, chair-making and other occupations of the Shakers were as much arts as their songs, dances, and religious drawings. Architecture and craftsmanship alike reflected such principles as union (basic uniformity of design), the equality of the sexes (balance, proportion), utilitarianism (adaptation to needs, durability), honesty (mastery of techniques), humility and simplicity (absence of pretense or adornment), purity (a sense of pure form). What today might be called an 'instrumentalist' conception of aesthetics — the philosophy of Dewey or Sullivan — the 'realizable union of material and ideal' — was unwittingly practised by these functionalists of the American past. The practical arts were not deprecated as inferior to the fine. Beauty was inherent in a product fashioned to meet the needs of a life based on contemplation and dedicated to rectitude of hand and heart.

Builders and joiners, therefore, inevitably impressed their character, the Shaker character, upon their work. It has a recognizable look, — not 'factory-like,' as some described their buildings, not austere or 'grim,' as Dickens once called their furniture, but rather like its users, dispassionate, reliable, unworldly. And the things they made are not without a special charm: the kind of attractiveness they had for Isaac Holmes, who found the yellow ochre buildings, though plain, singularly 'handsome'; or for James Fenimore Cooper, who had never seen, 'in any country, villages as neat, and so perfectly

* Coomaraswamy, Ananda K. 'Am I My Brother's Keeper?' *Asia and the Americas*, March, 1943.

beautiful, as to order and arrangement, without, however, being pic-   *186*
turesque or ornamented, as those of the Shakers.' Reflecting the preference for plainness and subdued, uniform colors, the furnishings of
Shaker rooms naturally harmonized with their white plastered walls,
the reddish-yellow floors, oiled and neatly carpeted, the doors, window frames, and delicately turned wall pegs of mellow brown. No
distracting elements violated the quiet simplicity of these airy, well-
lighted interiors. The colors glowed softly. 'No image or portrait of
anything upon the earth . . . was suffered in this holy place.' A
spirit of peace, almost of sanctity, pervaded the scene.   *187*

Yet such was the urge to progress that in uniformity there was
still variety. Isaac Youngs, for instance, recorded with satisfaction
the progress made in the manner of building. Buildings at first were
'inferior, and poorly adapted to the purpose for which they were
needed ; and those who dwelt in them were very much crowded.' Having little money, inferior tools, and limited experience, the early
Shakers had to build in a 'cheap style': foundations were deficient,
halls contracted, stairs narrow and steep, eaves without jets, and
exteriors unpainted. But after 1805 all structures at New Lebanon
were remodeled or rebuilt. Story-and-a-half buildings were raised to
two or three stories. Flat roofs, usually covered with tin, replaced
the steep, hipped, shingled roofs. Natural-faced, hewn, and sawed
stone took the place of rough foundation walls. Dwellings were con-
structed, or altered, with the needs of the commune specifically in
mind ; there were gathering rooms adapted to united worship ; doors,
halls, and 'retiring rooms' arranged on a dual plan to allow for the
separation of the sexes; long dining halls and commodious kitchens,
bake rooms, and storerooms. Single strips of peg-board, on which anything from a tool to a bonnet or chair could be hung, lined every wall
in shop and dwelling. The roofs were extended, the doorways hooded.
In the meeting-house, separate apartments were provided for the
ministry.

In spite of the fact that such structures were without 'superfluities,'
there was no effect of monotony or repetition. Buildings were of all
sizes. Some were of frame construction, others of brick or stone. The
meeting-house, the only structure with gambrel roof and white paint,
had its special distinction. Varying uses determined the forms of
other buildings : the imposing stone barn at the entrance to the North
family in New Lebanon ; the round stone barn at Hancock ; the great

CHURCH FAMILY, SHIRLEY SHAKERS

granite dwelling at Enfield (N.H.) ; the brick and marble dwelling of the Hancock church; the stone shop of the Second family in New Lebanon; and many others. No buildings could have been more attractive than those of the 'Georgian-Shaker' style at Pleasant Hill, which had the good fortune of having an experienced builder among its early converts. Around these dwellings, barns, and shops were trees and shrubs. Neat stone walks led from one building to another. Trim fences bordered the roads and fields. The broad stone entrance steps and landing stages, or horse blocks, were equipped with finely wrought iron railings. Many details of construction, even in structures of minor importance, combined to give Shaker architecture a subtly distinctive quality.

The same process went on in the joiners' shops. At the outset worldly styles were copied. As the forces of separation grew stronger, however, a new school of design emerged. Such virtues as honesty, humility, temperance, and simplicity ('godly sincerity and a real singleness of heart') found expression in a furniture marked always by grace of line and purity of form. It is unpretentious, like the people who made it. It is perfectly simple, but not plain. Answering communal as well as individual needs, it was at the same time truly functional: the doctrine that all things should be made according to their order and use not only set standards of workmanship but kept the joiners' craft from becoming stereotyped. The artisan was a relatively free agent. Families were independent. Societies were scattered. Demands varied. As a result, though Shaker furniture invariably bears the stamp of its origin, each piece seems to have an identity of its own.

Experimentation had its limits nevertheless. The search for improved form, either in architecture or furniture, was in no sense a restive process, a desire for change for the mere sake of change. 'We find out by trial what is best' was the simple explanation, 'and when we have found a good thing we stick to it.' By 1805, or soon after, Shaker buildings, both within and without, exhibited the general aspect they were to retain throughout the history of the society. An atmosphere of settledness and repose pervaded the villages, as though they were part of the land itself and its inhabitants were there to stay. As F. O. Matthiessen observed, within the process of our pioneering expansion, as we proceeded 'from one rapid disequilibrium to the next,' there was a 'counter-effort . . . for communal security and permanence . . . islands of realization and fulfilment' from which have come the objects, 'the order and balance of which . . . we can recognize as among the most valuable possessions of our continent.' In architecture, the author of *American Renaissance* contended, such qualities are most manifest: 'whether in the clipper, or on the New England green, or in the Shaker communities.'   *188*

What did students of socialism think of the Shaker economy?

INTERIOR OF MEETING-HOUSE, NEW LEBANON

Many a criticism of doctrine appears in the literature on American communities; but the varied comment on the order's industrial practice is largely favorable. Dwight, Plumer, Greeley, Brisbane, Emerson, Lane, Parker, Noyes, Ely, and other Americans were impressed by the practical achievements of the sect. Emerson saw in this 'important experiment in socialism' a new form of capitalism. 'What improvement is made is made forever,' he wrote in his journal: 'this Capitalist is old and never dies, his subsistence was long ago secured, and he has gone on now for long scores of years in adding easily com-
189 pound interests to his stock.' The Shakers and Rappites, Noyes affirmed, were

. . . really the pioneers of modern Socialism, whose experiments deserve a great deal more study than all the speculations of the French schools . . . The example of the Shakers (in particular) has demonstrated, not merely that successful Communism is subjectively possible, but that this nation is free enough to let it grow. Who can doubt that this demonstration was known and watched in Germany from the beginning; and that it helped the successive experiments and emigrations of the Rappites, the Zoarites and the Ebenezers . . . Then the Shaker movement with its echoes was sounding also in England, when Robert Owen undertook to convert the world to Communism . . . France also had heard of Shakerism, before St. Simon or Fourier began to meditate and write Socialism . . . It is very doubtful whether Owenism or Fourierism would have ever existed, or if they had, whether they would have ever moved the practical American nation, if the facts of Shakerism had
190 not existed before them and gone along with them.

ENTRANCES TO BRETHREN'S AND SISTERS' ROOMS

It is not clear how French attention was drawn to the Shaker experiment; perhaps this was done by Lafayette and Marbois, who

visited the Watervliet settlement in the 1780's, or possibly by Tocque-
ville. Noyes's surmise regarding English socialism, however, is supported by documentary evidence: for Robert Owen, visualizing a
development of New Lanark in the new world, was unquestionably
encouraged in his plans by the reports Warder and others had sent
him on the Believers. Warder's foreword, stating that his narrative
conveys a simple but convincing proof of the effects of the principle
of combined labour and expenditure,' was incorporated almost ver-
batim, with other passages, in issue Number 19 of Owen's *The Economist*. Owen advances its argument by publishing the following letter
from a Mr. Courtauld, who had visited the Indiana settlement in
August 1819:

There are a few remarkable settlements [those of the Shakers] where a
rapid increase of wealth, by the judicious application of capital and
labour, arrest general attention; and which, whatever may be the im-
perfection of some of their regulations, command the admiration of all
who have witnessed their wonderful success, and can duly appreciate
habits of industry, temperance, order, and neatness, with peaceable and
unobtrusive members, apparently flowing from a state of ease and con
tentment, and a serious sense of religion.   *191*

An extract then follows from John Melish's *Travels:* 'It is impossible to convey any adequate idea of the diligent industry and perseverance of this people [the Shakers]. Wherever we went we found
them all activity and contentment. But they have every inducement
to perseverance. They are all on an equal footing. Every member is
equally interested in the good of the society.' Considering their principles and objectives, Melish believed that they would not only remain
united but would serve as a model for other societies. 'They have the
mutual aid of each other; and are free from a thousand temptations,
to which mankind in general are subjected. Having no fear of want,
they have literally no care for to-morrow . . . all the duties of life
are easy, because they go hand in hand with self-interest.'   *192*

Owen's journal also prints the comment of Morris Birkbeck, the   *193*
English reformer who had set up an agricultural colony in Edwards
County, Illinois, in 1818, for the benefit of the working classes of his
own country. Birkbeck likewise admired 'the astonishing results of
their [the Shakers'] combinations,' declaring their settlements 'worthy of general imitation except for the absurd puerilities of some of
their peculiar tenets, and the revolting and unnatural regulation

which prohibits marriage.' To this criticism, and to Birkbeck's recommendation that the Shaker system should *not* be adopted, 'the author
of a plan for forming colonies of emigrants from this country, on the
principle of combined capital and labour' (Robert Owen himself)
strongly objects — 'it would be easy [he says] to form other societies,
under all the regulations and principles of the Shakers which are
really valuable — and rejecting, of course, their idle peculiarities —
foolish prejudices — and disgusting prohibitions.' Owen was convinced that 'these very defects' were a proof that human beings might
be trained to any character which society chose to give them:

Hence it is that they may be led, by the ignorance and folly of society
to the most unnatural perversion of the commonest feelings and necessary propensities of human nature; and yet present, like these Shakers
a moral character, and kind inoffensive demeanor toward all their fellow
creatures, of which the present state of society, in its best form, with all
194 its proud distinctions and benevolent institutions, affords no parallel.

195 Years after Owen's experiment at New Harmony had failed, the
accomplishments of the United Society continued to attract English
attention. The search for solutions to the problems of the industrial
revolution, bearing fruit in the social and economic reforms of the
'thirties, extended to an interest in all attempts at a better society
The movement known as *Christian Socialism*, paralleling in many respects Shaker thought and practice, was under way by the middle of
the century. It is probable, therefore, that the not infrequent allusion
to the experience of the American sect reflected a widespread concern over the betterment of working conditions for the laboring
class.

Four commentaries, of differing substance, will serve to illustrate
that concern. James S. Buckingham, who visited Niskeyuna in 1838
was interested in the relation between common ownership of property
and material well-being. 'That the property itself is better managed
for accumulation and preservation,' when held in community, he
wrote,

. . . no one can doubt who has watched the progressive advancement
which this society has made in the augmentation, as well as improvement
of its possessions, and in the neatness, order & perfection by which every
thing they do or make is characterized; this is so much the case, that
over all the United States, the seeds, plants, fruits, grain, cattle, &

manufactures furnished by a settlement of Shakers bears a premium in the market above the ordinary price of similar articles from other establishments. There being no idleness among them, all are productive. There being no intemperance among them, none are destructive. There being no misers among them, nothing is hoarded, or made to perish from want of use ; so that while production and improvement are at their maximum, and waste and destruction at their minimum, the society must go on increasing the extent and value of its temporal possessions, and thus increase its means of doing good, first within, and then beyond its own circle.   *196*

Aware that the standard of living attained by the Shakers should properly be compared not with that of the upper strata of 'old society' but with the living conditions of average mechanics and other laborers in the city, and of farmers in the country, the 'somber pilgrim' A. J. Macdonald drafted the following rough notes during his stay at the same community (1843) :   *197*

Shaker Mechanics	*World's Mechanics*
1. No fear of want (Sincere Shakers)	General Fear of Want
2. Clean and healthy Workshops in the Country.	Dirty and unhealthy in a City
3. Regular Meals of the very best kind of wholesome food	Generally regular but not equal in quality
4. Clean and good clothing never ragged	Inferior in Cleanliness, and especially in healthiness
5. Clean beds and Bedrooms — with temperature regulated according to the weather	
6. Attention in sickness	In sickness wages stopped, cost of medical attendance & nursing

Shaker Agriculturists	*World's Agriculturists*
The same advantage as the Mechanics with the addition of:	
1. Superior Cattle of all kinds	Inferior cattle
2. Good tools always kept in repair	Inferior tools and accommodation for repairs
3. Good teams, good seeds, clean fields, and gardens, and generally superior crops	Inferior teams, unclean fields, and especially gardens

There is not so much fear of want among the World's Agriculturists as the World's Mechanics, but more than the Shakers. The Agriculturist are in every respect inferior in cleanliness, inferior clad, (especially in the backwoods) and very careless about dress, relative to the change in the Weather and consequently inducing more disease, their dwelling also are very inferior to the Shakers . . .

The Shaker Community system has now been in practical operation nearly as long as this Republic, and may be said to be as well demon strated. It matters not what the means were to produce such results, so that they were peaceable, the results have been produced and some important principles have been demonstrated. We see from 400 to 600 Men and Women living together in a community, with better physical circumstances surrounding them, and more wealth to each Individual (if divided) than any other 400 Men and Women who have to work from ten to twelve hours per day, in the outer World. We see such arrangement practically carried out every day, as provide each Member of the Community, with an abundance of all the necessaries of life, and these necessaries superior in quality to what is obtained by the great mass of people who work for their living in old Society.

Finch and Holyoake both found useful, if different, lessons in Shaker experience. The phenomenal success of the societies, rising from poverty, scorn, and persecution to positions commanding respect, proved to the former that there was no natural desire for private property. In these village families there was no want, no need for charitable institutions. All lived in peace and harmony without violence or crime of any kind — 'though there is not a single magistrate, lawyer, constable, policeman, soldier, paid priest, court of law, court of justice, jail, bridewell, or penitentiary in any of them.' The 'downward progress' of the working classes, which Finch saw increasing in the industrial society of England, could be eventually changed to a condition of 'wealth and independence,' if the elements fostering cooperation in the American communes were wisely applied else where.

The chief lesson of these societies, for Holyoake, lay in their demonstration of the fact that integrity reaps dividends. He deplored their 'social crotchets,' 'fanaticism,' and 'sexual eccentricities.' But 'their commodities can be trusted. Whether seeds of the ground or work of the loom, they are known to be honest and good products. They are the only dealers in America who have known how to make honesty pay. Some say they are the only tradesmen who have at

empted it. Utopianism makes money — a thing not believed in in
England.'   *199*

Until one faction of the society, led by Frederick Evans later in
he century, advocated some participation in the world's affairs, the
Shakers remained aloof from all speculation. Living in a world of
heir own, holding to the line of separation, they were at this time
argely unaware of what the machine was doing to the ways of men.
n that sequestered world there was equality, fraternity, and an
ncreasing prosperity; but in Shaker thought success was due, pri-
narily, to an increase of the spirit, to moral rather than economic
actors. In principle, science was a compound of religion and inspira-
ion. It was not social theory but the example of the primitive Chris-
ian Church that impelled the order onward.

CHAPTER VII

Spiritual Labor — Mode of Worship

We love to dance, we love to sing,
We love to taste the living spring,
We love to feel our union flow,
While round, and round, and round we go.

— *Millennial Praises*, 1813

WHEN MOTHER Ann told her people to put their hands to work and their hearts to God, she knew it would be from the laborings of worship that they would get the strength needed for physical labor. How true this was, is realized when we read the intimate diaries and journals of her followers. Far from being considered a religious duty, the frequent meetings, often held in the evening after a long day's work were anticipated with pleasure, and viewed, in retrospect, as a source of refreshment of spirit. Dance and song were recreations. Though these exercises were often extravagant and highly emotional, they were surely not, as sometimes charged, the illuminism of ignorant minds. Their very exuberance was evidence of an afflatus great enough to sustain and continually inspire the institution.

Comparison of the religious behavior of the Believers with that of other spiritual or primitive sects shows little essential difference in the physical phenomena of worship. The mystical experiences of all spiritual fellowships — the cases of clairvoyance and clairaudience, the speaking in unknown tongues, telepathies, prophecies, and automatisms, all the charismatic gifts associated with the primitive church — were but the signs, as Rufus Jones has suggested, of more important traits : 'a unique degree of moral earnestness and passion . . . a rare acuteness of conscience . . . a unique purity of life.'

There are many analogies. The meetings of the fifteenth-century monk, Savonarola, were marked by the frankness of his denunciations — 'you live like swine,' he told the Florentines; by his mesmeric manner of speaking, inducing in his hearers a strange sort of behavior which they termed being 'fools for the love of Christ'; and by the fantastic character of the rite called the 'burning of vanities,' or the Feast of the Higher Folly,' at which a solemn dance was performed, an exercise Savonarola defended, as did the Believers, by citing the example of David.

Nearer to the Shakers, in point of time, were the French Prophets, with their visions, ecstasies, and agitations. Revelations came to Swedenborg, the Quaker George Fox, and the Mormon Joseph Smith. The early Quakers sang and danced: 'the Devil roared in these deceived souls [one witness recalls] in a most strange and dreadful Manner, some howling, some shrieking, yelling, roaring, and some had a strange confused kind of humming, singing Noise . . . about the one Half of these miserable Creatures were terribly shaken with violent Motions.' In *Seasonable Thoughts on the State of Religion in* 201 *New England* (1743), Chauncy wrote that the fanaticism of the Great Awakening reached such extremes that parents condemned their children, 'children their parents, husbands their wives and wives their husbands.' The Methodists under Wesley and Whitefield and 202 the subjects of the famous Ulster Revival in Ireland exhibited in comparable forms the peculiar psychology attendant on excessive rapture. At the meetings of the Free Will Baptists of New England, tumult reigned and 'strong men fell as if slain in battle.' The primitive Baptists of Virginia would 'roar on the ground, ring their hands, go into ecstasies, pray and weep while others did so much outrageous cursing and swearing that it was thought that they were really possessed of the devil.' The Indian 'Shakers' of Puget Sound and the 203 English Girlingites, or 'Shakers of New Forest,' had visions and trembled, shook and danced in their meetings. In our own time we have such sects as the Negro Baptists of Florida, with their 'rocking Daniel' dance, the Penitentes of New Mexico, the 'Holy Rollers,' and the recently dispersed 'Tremolanti' of Rome.

Kinship between Kentucky Revival and Shaker worship is even closer. Several months before Benjamin Youngs and his comrades reached Kentucky, the Schismatics, as we have seen, were already using the dance to express their faith. In the spring of 1804, Mc-

Nemar relates, Brother Thompson had been constrained just at the
close of the meeting to go to dancing, and for an hour or more to
dance in a regular manner round the stand, all the while repeating
in a low tone of voice.— 'This is the Holy Ghost-Glory.' By the be
ginning of the ensuing winter the Schismatics as a body were encour
aging one another 'to praise God in the dance and unite in that exer
cise.' Like the early Shakers also, but before the Believers had made
their appearance in the West, Thompson's followers indulged in
various involuntary acts of mortification, chief among which were the
'rolling exercise,' the jerks, and the 'barks.' In the first of these, the
stricken subject would roll over and over on the ground like a log, or
like a wheel with body doubled head to feet. The jerks began in the
head, which would be suddenly jolted, or twitched backward and for
ward, or from side to side — a movement impossible to suppress. The
subject would stagger about, McNemar wrote, 'bounce from place to
place like a foot-ball, or hop round with head, limbs and trunk twitch
ing and jolting in every direction, as if they must inevitably fly asun
der.' Features became distorted and the hair wildly tangled, for
neither head-dresses or handkerchiefs tied around the head were of
any avail. The jerks were often accompanied by the barks, a 'disgrac
ing' operation in which the victim would take 'the position of a canine
beast, move about on all fours, growl, snap the teeth, and bark,' some
times at the foot of a tree in a performance called 'treeing the devil.'
The quickest method of release from such exercises was to engage in

204   the voluntary dance.

'Treeing the devil' was a form of exorcism not unlike that engaged
in by those Shakers whom Plumer saw at Canterbury stamping the
feet at an unbeliever who was defending 'propagation,' and shoutin
'Oh, that cursed lust! I am ashamed of it,' and 'Damn his devil, dam
his devil'; or by those worshippers observed by Eunice Chapman at
Watervliet 'spatting their hands, stamping and jumping and whir
ing about and saying "hiss, hiss, hiss!" and crying "hate the devi

205   hate the devil, chain the devil, chain the devil." '

In time, however, 'the increasing work of God,' attended by
greater variety of exercises and greater discipline, imbued the cer
monies of the Believers with more decorum. The tendency was awa
from disorder and extravagance — the 'back' or 'promiscuous' man
ner of worship, the censorious songs, the fantastic gifts. The Shaker
began to rehearse the songs and dances before performance, and

make ritual subservient to the larger well-being of the society. This trend was marked in spite of frequent lapses during periods of revival, or when the elders wished to stir up zeal or 'war against evil' — at which times the assembly as a whole, or individuals in the ranks, reverted to the impulsive whirlings and quakings, the discordant shouting and singing of Mother Ann's day.

SQUARE ORDER SHUFFLE

Official pronouncements in the twenty-year period following Meacham's death reflect the more rational attitude toward worship. Publication in 1813 of *Millennial Praises*, a book of religious songs without notation, marked the acceptance of the hymn as a more useful form of devotion than the early chants and wordless solemn songs. Tunes with words attached were soon appearing in manuscript: anthems, 'extra' and exercise songs, welcome songs, and funeral hymns. Even these compositions changed, new ones replacing the old in popularity and acceptability; for words, as the editor of the *Praises* declared, are but 'the signs of ideas' and change with 'the increasing work of God.' To facilitate the learning and retaining of this expanding body of song, a knowledge of the rules of music, leading to more harmonious chorals, began to be cultivated about 1815, when the first anthem with notes attached was composed. 'Practised with reserve,' it was found that such rules were 'no detriment to the Spiritual gift'; and it was not long before singing schools, a simplified letter notation, a reform of modes, and manuals on the rudiments of music made their

206   appearance.

SINGING MEETING

Parallel developments took place in the dance. We are informed by Elder Calvin Green, for many years the leading preacher at New Lebanon, that the Shakers were 'led into the practice . . . nearly from the first rise, by the operation of supernatural powers. Being frequently led by the power into the exercise of shaking and dancing, they were convinced that these exercises were acceptable worship of

207   God.' Before the close of the century, however, we find the 'lead' — aware of the usefulness of the dance as an agent of communal unity — seeking to rationalize it on the ground of scriptural precedent. As early as 1798 Brown was told that 'dancing is the gift of God to the church . . . it may be clearly proved that it was a worship among the ancient people of God; and prophesied of, that it should be again

208   restored to the people of God.' Further justification was found, by the authors of *The Testimony* and *A Summary View*, in the practices of Miriam the prophetess, Jephthah's daughter, the virgins of

Shiloh, and David, who danced to celebrate a yearly feast, a victory in the field, or deliverance from captivity. On the reasonableness of dancing, Wells and Green had this to say:

God has created man an active, intelligent being, possessing important powers and faculties, capable of serving himself according to his needs and circumstances; and he is required to devote these powers and faculties to the service of God. To devote only a part . . . is to render an imperfect service . . .

God has created nothing in vain. The faculty of dancing, as well as that of singing, was undoubtedly created for the honor and glory of the Creator. . . God has created the tongue of man . . . He has also created the hands and the feet, and enabled them to perform their functions . . . And shall these important faculties . . . be active in the service of sin, and yet be idle in the service of God? . . .

As union is the distinguishing characteristic of the true followers of Christ; so it is an essential part of the worship of God . . . To render this [unity of spirit] the more perfect, a uniformity of exercise is necessary.   *209*

There is no opposition to dancing in the Bible, argued these au thors. Disapproval came chiefly from 'formal professors of the various denominations,' who, like the elder son in the parable, had lost the power and spirit of their religion and settled down into a lifeless form adulterated by the principles of the world. But when the prodigal son came home there was great rejoicing. All were invited to share the feast of the Lamb, to strip off their garments of sin and worship God in the dance.

In conformity with the idea that worship should be a whole-hearted but uniform ritual, we find the dance undergoing a gradual change. As early as 1785 the assembly was arranged in straight ranks, the males and females facing each other, for the first regular form of exercise, the square-order shuffle. Stated hours for meetings were set at the time the church was established. Meetings became more lively about 1800, when there was also an increase in gifts, operations and signs. The opening of the gospel in the western states, resulting in spirited songs and a feeling of 'increase,' aroused the muses in the eastern societies: 'the former travel of the Church began to feel too dull and formal'; exercises increased in animation; the speed of the shuffle was increased to what was called 'the skipping manner'; and even the 'quick' or 'back' manner was encouraged for the sake 'of the younger part.' In 1815 Mother Lucy introduced motioning with the hands while singing exercise songs, and two years later marching, to the accompaniment of the so-called 'step songs.' 'To enliven the sense and make the worship feel new and interesting,' ring dances were inaugurated about 1822, with the singers standing in the center of the circle. Like the folk dances of the countryside, these could be greatly varied. The marches, too, were far from simple. To the English traveler Coke, the 'manoeuvers' — the marching and counter-marching, the advancing and retiring, the open column and closed column, the perpendicular lines and oblique lines, the slow step and quick step — were those of finely drilled soldiers, the occasion like a field day. Often the worshippers marched singing into the orchards or along the highway. All such exercises were rehearsed, in family, singing, or union gatherings, during the week before the meeting. There had to be 'much exertion to keep up the correct manner, not only in teaching new comers, but also in counteracting erroneous habits among the more experienced.'

210

The elaboration of early 'gifts' and the introduction of new ones also show an increasing interest in ceremonialism. The term itself — stemming from Paul's letter on the diversity of spiritual gifts and operations, 'but the same God which worketh all in all' — was in constant though rather indiscriminate use. Divine revelations were known as 'gifts of God.' The word might carry the implication of power or innate ability, as in the gift of leadership or seership; or of duty, as in the gift of obedience to such power. Songs received in trances were called 'gift songs.' Messages from the spirit world were gifts, as were the spiritual presents and rewards of merit bestowed on the faithful. When an enraptured 'instrument' or medium, possessed by the spirit of a departed saint, came under the influence of heavenly directives, that subject was said to be the recipient of a gift. Benjamin Youngs referred to gifts of faith, wisdom, knowledge, discerning of spirits, healing, miracles, prophecy, and tongues as special dispensations from God, signs of divine anointment to be utilized by all true Believers. Some gifts — like those of shaking, whirling, and dancing — were incorporated into the regular worship. Others, like the rites of stamping in circles around an unbeliever and chasing the devil out of the room, prepared the way for the sweeping, cleansing, and bathing gifts of the 'feast days' described in the following chapter. The operations designed to mortify pride and induce humility were similarly developed into a prescribed 'fool' rite. New gifts, like *211* those of Holy Mother Wisdom and the Father and Son, were to be devised in which all could partake of the celestial parents' blessings and travel in union heavenward. The crystalization of many gifts or acts, originally voluntary, into formalized processes, accounts for a great deal in Shaker worship.

The scene of most of these rituals was the private family worship (and later the mountain 'love feasts') as distinguished from the public meetings in the church on the Sabbath. From Shaker journals and the accounts of apostates or specially privileged visitors, we learn something of their nature. Thus, for a short period beginning about 1830, the Believers followed, on certain occasions, the example set by Jesus of washing one another's feet, and that of the Pentecostal Church of breakfasting on milk and honey.

The 'smoking gift,' described by William Haskett in 1828 and C. D. Arfwedson in 1834, seems also to have been confined to a brief interval. At this meeting, held on the sixth of August to commemorate the landing of Ann Lee in America, pipes and tobacco (herbs for the children) were distributed to every member. The ritual was held in a closed room, at two in the afternoon, with an elder initiating the proceedings; but it seems that the ceremony, scheduled to last an hour, was curtailed because of the density of the atmosphere and the inability of many of the celebrants to carry it through. Apparently some of the participants were also reluctant to take the matter seriously. One account tells how an austere elder, leading the procession into the room, could hardly refrain from smiling. And a young sister, when she heard a letter from the West read aloud, in which the writer said he 'felt as though Mother's spirit was among them,' exclaimed that 'they may well say *spirit*, for if it was her *body*, they would have smoked her to death.' *212*

The 'warring gift' was of longer duration. Plumer observed it as early as 1782. Macdonald quotes Gorrie's reference (1850) to 'a race round the Room with a sweeping motion of the Hands and Arms, intended to represent the act of sweeping the Devil out of the Room.' In the 'warring gift' as described by Lamson in the same period, a sister or brother who had given evidence of waning faith or disobedience to holy orders was deluged with imprecations of 'woe, woe, woe, accompanied with a general concert of groaning, shouting, shaking [and] stamping.' The brethren seldom participated in this curious *213* warfare. In fact, evidence substantiates Dwight's early observation that whereas the motions of the Shaker men were 'very moderate . . . the gesticulations of the women were violent.' More susceptible, perhaps, to psychic influences, the sisters were usually the first to come 'under operations' and showed more zeal in shaking, whirling, and dancing. This may be an explanation for the differences in appearance so frequently commented upon: the countenances of the sisters often seemed rapt and pallid, their eyes wild, their bodies thin, their movements nervous, whereas the brethren looked ruddy, cheerful, and healthy.

The 'gift of love,' like the warring rite a climactic and spontaneous feature of worship, also lasted for many decades. An account of how the women embraced one another, and the men likewise, at the close of a meeting at Harvard (1782) has been given. In 1827 (19 May) Elizabeth Lovegrove wrote in her journal that 'we finished our meeting in hugging in loving and blessing each other in sincerity and truth.' In another manuscript of the same period it is recorded that after the singing of several songs, 'Elder Brother said let us arise from our knees and greet each other with a kiss of charity . . . so we all went to hugging and kissing in good earnest, and loved a heap.' At a 'spiritual meeting' of the New Lebanon Second family in 1855, the elder brother enjoined the members to 'improve' in the gift of love: 'accordingly we went about exchanging it.' Boyd Houghton's engraving of a Shaker meeting in 1870 shows sisters kissing each other on the cheek during one of the typical circular dances.

As would be expected, gifts of various kinds multiplied during eras of revival, of which there have been four in the sect's history. The movement was inaugurated in America in the wake of the Great Awakening. It spread to the West as a result of the Kentucky Revival. Another awakening, of less intensity, occurred in 1827, followed ten years later by what the Shakers called 'Mother Ann's Work.' The spirit was quickened in these times, and new gifts, dances, and songs introduced.

An account of the so-called 'quick meeting,' or 'Shaker high' — characteristic of family meetings during such periods — was furnished by the apostate Haskett in 1828. The elder began a certain phase of the service by remarking that every good Believer was known by the variety of his or her gifts. Then he shouted, 'Shake off the flesh!' — and stamped violently, and shook. 'In an instant the

THE GIFT OF LOVE, EVENING MEETING

spirit seized all the members; and one continued shout, and tremendous noise of stamping was only to be heard.' After a slight pause the sisters began to talk in unknown tongues and the whole room to 'shake, jump and turn.'

Then commenced a scene of awful riot. Now was heard the loud shouts of the brethren, then the soft, but hurried note of the sisters, whose 'gifts' were the apostolic gifts of tongues. These gently gestured their language, waved themselves backward and forward like a ship on the billows of a ceased storm, shook their heads, seized their garments, and then violently stamped on the floor.   214

How the orderly course of a meeting might suddenly change is illustrated by an excerpt from Horace Greeley's narrative (1838):

At length, what was a measured dance becomes a wild, discordant frenzy; all apparent design or regulation is lost; and grave manhood and gentler girlhood are whirling round and round, two or three in company, then each for him or herself.   215

In contrast, the public assemblies on the Sabbath conformed as a rule to prescribed formulae. The same spirit was in evidence, but under control; and if individuals or groups indulged in special gifts, they were not such as to disturb the general course of the service. Sometimes the dance and song were grave, sometimes lively ; but in its conscious precision the spectacle exhibited, more perhaps than the private gatherings, those symbolic qualities expressive of the deeper meanings of the faith. Two such meetings, one in the period soon after Mother Lucy's death in 1821 and the other in 1832, may be taken as representative.

SOLEMN MARCH, THE FINAL PROCESSION

The first was observed by David Benedict in New Lebanon. 'After being seated and sitting awhile in silence,' he wrote, 'they deliberately arose and formed in rows, males and females facing each other, leaving a space between them, of about six feet at one end, and about fifteen or twenty at the other.' First they sang a hymn by heart. Then two elders in succession gave short addresses, which were followed by two more hymns. It was now their privilege, the elder told them, 'to go forth to worship God in the dance.' The benches were accordingly removed and the brethren laid off their coats. Benedict continued:

They were arranged in six rows the whole length of the house, the men at one end and the women at the other, with a small space between the two companies. A number of both sexes did not join in the dance, either from age, infirmity, indisposition, or for the want of room, as all are at liberty to unite or not, in this peculiar exercise. Facing the ranks with their backs against the opposite sides of the house stood about sixteen or twenty singers male and female, who serving as musicians for the dance, suddenly struck up a tune of a suitable description, when the dancing immediately commenced, and continued through a song of considerable length. After a short pause another song was struck up and the dancing again went on and so continued through six songs. I am informed they commonly dance not more than three or four songs, and sometimes not more than two. The singers during the time of dancing kept a continued motion with their hands as if beating the time, and at the end of each dancing song and also at the close of their hymns, when they did not dance, they all made a peculiar obeisance apparently to each other, but I am informed that instead of any compliment, this is merely a reverential manner of closing the service.

The meeting closed with an elder addressing the worshippers, the 'publick speaker' addressing the spectators, and the singing of a third hymn. 'The dancing was simple in its form,' Benedict observed, 'but it was truly and properly a dance . . . It consisted in marching quickly backwards and forwards in ranks, turning round and shuffling to the tune.'

In the family meeting which this visitor attended in the evening, the dance was a march — 'a figure of marching the heavenly road, and walking the streets of the New Jerusalem.' The party consisted of about fifty males and females, who 'moved with a quick step around the hall . . . and around a company of six or eight singers in [the] centre of it, all singing hymns . . . and gently waving their hands in a horizontal position . . . At some of the rounds they all clapped their hands while singing, as if overwhelmed with ecstacy and joy.' It was Benedict's opinion that the Shakers were the most 'musical' of all the denominations.

216

The singing at the second meeting, heard at the same community in 1832 by another visitor, Professor Benjamin Silliman, was also 'in tones by no means unharmonious.' In the family meeting the elder addressed the members 'affectionately,' remarking that notwithstanding the fatigue of the day's labor 'they would find the labor of worship refreshing to their minds and bodies.' In the meeting-house the visitor

was impressed by the extreme neatness of the building; the smooth
floor with its single seam to separate the sexes; the moveable benches;
the 'pale, sallow' countenances of the sisters, in marked contrast to
the 'healthy, ruddy' appearance of the brethren; and the presence
of several Negroes, male and female, among the worshippers.

RING DANCE, NISKEYUNA

The worship commenced by the men arranging themselves in line at
one end of the room, and the women on the other, and after a few words
were addressed to them by the Elder they all kneeled down in opposite
lines, facing each other, and after a period of profound silence, they
commenced singing hymns from a book, the words of which were unintelligible to the auditors. After this they rose and marched backwards and
forwards, facing each other, to a tune which they all sung; then they
faced the wall, with their backs to the audience, and marched in the same
manner, backwards and forwards towards the wall.

When this exercise ended they formed two circles, a smaller and larger
one, and marched to the tunes sung by the inner circle, which composed
the principal singers; their hands also keeping time, either by the alter-
nate motion of swinging backwards and forwards, or by clapping them
together as they became animated by the tunes which were sung. This
exercise continued about half an hour, when they retired to their
seats.

Silliman found the worship of the people 'singular,' sometimes an occasion for smiles, but always manifestly sincere.   *217*

These services or performances had a certain theatrical quality. Spectators came primarily out of curiosity, as they would to see a strange play. By guests at the summer hotels in the region they were considered special events, and on Sunday mornings the street in front of the meeting-house was lined with fashionable equipages. No doubt on such occasions the public preacher, always directing some of his remarks to the gallery, hoped to exert a beneficent if not conversive influence on a fallen world. The attitude of the audience was, on the surface, decorous. But the dramatic element was not lacking, and many an onlooker, watching the worshippers moving in long rows, listening to a music unlike anything heard before, experienced a feeling of enchantment, of being transported to a 'different sphere of existence.' To Benson Lossing, the sisters, clad in their Sabbath white, appeared 'ethereal'. 'Upon each face,' he wrote, 'rested the light of dignified serenity, which always gives power to the features of woman.' The dancers, on their part, must have been conscious of   *218* the visual appeal of their performance. They had practiced their intricate steps, gestures, and simple songs throughout the week. The bowing, bending, and shaking, the marches 'toward heaven,' the union and manual dances, the concentric wheel dances betokening the four dispensations, the motions of the hands signifying the giving or receiving of blessings — all had symbolic overtones. The program was carried out with the faultless precision, and doubtless with something of the assurance and pride, of skilled actors.

Though the spiritual labor of the Believers reveals, in strong contrast to their hand labor, the mystical aspects of Shaker culture, their sense of order and uniformity is apparent in both fields. In meeting, the holy laws ordained, 'the ranks should be strait, not only to the right and left, but also forward and back.' Vacancies were forbidden as tending 'to excite disunion.' Specific directions were given about behavior in the 'retiring time' before service, conduct when anyone was 'under operations,' the correct method of 'going forth in holy order,' and so on. Supervision of the meetings in the church was exercised by the ministry through apertures in the walls outside their apartments.

Attention to order was nowhere better evidenced than in the dress of Believers, not only the Sabbath costume, but that worn on weekdays or when 'going abroad.' Whatever the occasion, the time of year, or the availability of material, uniformity was the rule. For years after the community was organized, the winter Sabbath costume of the sisters consisted of butternut-dyed worsted 'long gowns,' with blue and white checked aprons, 'shoulder handkerchiefs' of blue cotton, fine lawn or linen caps, and high-heeled cloth shoes. In summer, light-colored, striped, short-sleeved gowns were worn over black or blue worsted petticoats, with kerchiefs of black silk or fine white lawn. After 1810 the sisters adoped white cotton, linen, or silk neck cloths, worn over white collars with capes attached; heels were lowered and stays discarded. For several decades after 1835, the sisters under fifty years of age appeared in the summer Sabbath meetings clad in cotton dresses of pure white, or white with a delicate blue stripe.

At first the brethren dressed, on Sunday, in coats of blue fulled cloth with capes coming up to the neck and lying down flat on the shoulders; jackets or vests of similar material; a white stock; blue sleeve strings; breeches of black or blue lasting; long hose buckled or strapped above the knee; and brass-buckled shoes. Coats were discarded before the dance. About 1810 their costume was also changed, a gray mixed material replacing the blue of the coat. Until 1820, when a blue and white striped material was adopted, their cotton trousers were dyed with nutgall. Jackets were drab until 1832, when they were made of a fine blue fulled cloth; drab returned in 1840, to be replaced in 1854 by pursley blue. Somewhat later, pantaloons of blue linen with a fine white stripe were introduced.

Uniformity in style, color, and quality of fabrics — a subject to which much serious attention was always devoted — had a spiritual and social as well as practical justification. 'Equality of furnish in 219 dress, between members,' a ministry circular reads, 'contributes to peace and union in spirit, inasmuch as the ends of justice are answered, and righteousness and justice are necessary companions.' Socially it was important, serving as a 'clue to that relation which makes Zion's children feel like Brethren and Sisters, when meeting each other, either at home or abroad.' The financial aspect was rooted in human psychology: for if certain members wore garments of different pattern, color, or quality, jealousies would be aroused, others would want them, 'wants would bear the sway over needs,' changes

would constantly be necessary, and thousands of dollars would have
to be expended to uphold the doctrine of equal rights.

'You are members of one body,' sang an early Shaker psalmist:

> 'Tis not one without the other,
> That will keep the union strong;
> O, do learn to go together!
> Then you will be join'd in one.
> Be not anxious to go forward,
> And to leave your brother dear;
> You may happen to fall backward,
> And your brother forward stear.

CHAPTER VIII

'Mother Ann's Work'

Come virgins in your marriage dress,
Your joy and gladness to express,
Come forth and dance in holiness,
On Zion's hill before him!

— *Millennial Praises*, 1813

220   ON AN AUGUST day in 1837 a class of young girls, ten to fourteen years old, was meeting for instruction at the Gathering Order in Niskeyuna. Suddenly some of them began to shake and whirl. In the evening, after they had retired, the senses of three of the children appeared withdrawn from the scenes of time, and absorbed as in a trance. They began to sing, talk about angels, and describe a journey they were making, under spiritual guidance, to heavenly places. The next morning their behavior was normal; but the experience was repeated several times, and when older classes, and finally adult members of the family were affected, it became apparent that the gifts received by Ann Maria Goff and her Shaker sisters were not an isolated phenomenon.

Thus began a remarkable period in Shaker history, a decade or more of strange manifestations known as 'the new era,' 'Mother Ann's Second Appearing,' or 'Mother Ann's Work.' The ministry pronounced the songs and revelations received at Niskeyuna as genuine signs of divine notice. An atmosphere of intense expectation was created throughout the whole society: within a few months of its generation, the current of excitement was felt in Canterbury, Enfield (N.H.), Hancock, and as far west as North Union — first, in most instances, by groups of Shaker girls in the impressionable stages of

152

early adolescence. Before a year had passed the afflatus had affected the members of every society, regardless of age — an interesting demonstration of the spiritual unity of the order.

Its appearance at New Lebanon was awaited impatiently all through the fall and early winter. Accounts were read in meeting; 'vision songs' were sung; many journeyed to Niskeyuna to witness the gifts for themselves. The approach of the spirit was heralded first by the East or Hill family, where certain sisters, in the winter of 1837-8, were inspired to sing a profusion of songs in unknown words. In other out-families, and soon in the church itself, feelings were more and more animated: new songs were sung, new forms of exercises devised. But the leaders were looking for a greater inner work to begin, some significant demonstration to come out of the surcharged temper of the time.

Finally, on a Sabbath afternoon in the early spring of 1838, the 'work' opened when Philemon Stewart, a member of the Church Order, came into meeting so agitated that he needed the support of two brethren, and delivered the first direct communication from Jesus and Mother Ann, the 'sacred parentage' of the order. Thus, wrote the Shaker historian Isaac Youngs, were 'the windows of heaven and the avenues of the spirit world set open.' The seedsman Stewart was the first, and probably the most prominent of the Shaker 'instruments,' the term applied to those visionists or seers who seemingly were possessed by, and spoke, sang, or acted in the name of discarnate personalities.

The 'great operations of divine powers' under which Brother Philemon delivered his message were characteristic. 'It was a common case,' Youngs relates, 'that those Instruments who spoke by Inspiration would be suddenly seized by that mysterious power or influence, with a trembling or shaking, and severely disciplined, apparently to compel them to yield and speak what was given by the spirit.' Often they would be struck to the floor, where they lay as dead, or struggling in distress, until someone near lifted them up, when they would begin to speak with great clearness and composure. Frequently the seizure was accompanied by a complete loss, for hours or days, of 'native speech': the subject would be able to speak only in an unknown tongue or 'mongrel English,' to sing but not be able to talk in English, or be able to talk only to the elders. The gift came unexpectedly, usually in meeting, but sometimes in the dining hall, in the shop or field, or on a journey. Suddenly, the records say, the instrument would be whirled like a top, perhaps for an hour or more, without experiencing any sensation of dizziness; or he would become a prey to the jerks or fall in a trance for hours, and occasionally for days.

THE WHIRLING GIFT

Authorship of the messages followed a definite law of development. The initial communications came from 'our Heavenly Parents' — Jesus and Mother Ann. Toward the end of the year 1838, the Shakers began to hear from their 'Spiritual Parents' — Father Joseph, Mother Lucy, and other early leaders. Then, in 1840, the 'Eternal Parents' of the order, Almighty God and Holy Mother Wisdom, in a panoply of splendor and in the most solemn utterances of all, revealed themselves to their 'chosen people.' Often the words of these divine oracles were transmitted to the instruments through the intermediary agency of angels or the spirits of departed Shakers. Appearing under such names as the Sounding Angel, the Angel of Love, the Angel Gabriel, the Angel of Consuming Fire, the Holy Witnessing Angel of God, they bore scrolls on which, in scriptural diction, heavenly thoughts were transmitted to earth. Messages also came from the Apostles: from John 'the Revelator'; from the prophets Samuel, Elijah, Jeremiah, Malachi, Ezekiel, Daniel, and Esdras; and from persons famous in history — Xerxes, Alexander the Great, Queen Esther, Napoleon, Lafayette, Washington, William Penn, and many others. In visions the mediums traveled into the vast unknown, reporting on those who had found their reward or punishment or on those who were wandering about seeking the light of truth or entrance into the Shaker heaven.

221

Underlying the peculiar surface phenomena of the messages lay, in the minds of the ministry and elders, a serious purpose. In the 1830's the Shakers had passed beyond the inspiring personal influence of Ann and her followers. Inevitable departures from the 'perfect order' in which the Church had been established were taking place. Material prosperity had introduced worldly temptations, breeding impatience with traditional disciplines, especially among the young. The line once so carefully drawn between the realm of generation and a regenerate order was becoming blurred, and dreaded signs of conflict and disunion were appearing. Sensitive to such tendencies, the instruments, speaking in Mother Ann's name, pointed out backslidings and the need of purging the order of all impurities. Declaring that Christ and Ann, the Heavenly Father, and Holy Mother Wisdom were coming to visit Zion and 'search her as with candles,' they called for honest confession and repentance, the repudiation of all sin, a 'heart-searching labor of soul.' To forward the work, 'notices' were directed to given individuals during meeting, instructing, warning, and encouraging them in their spiritual travel.

In her first message, delivered 22 April 1838, Mother Ann, speaking through the instrument Philemon Stewart, pointed out ways in which the church had deviated from the true order. It should return to its early trades, its early consecration of labor, its early plainness of speech, attire, and furnishing. When the communications began to be put in writing, in 1840, the subject of 'superfluities' was elaborated. Thus, in a typical document on 11 April of that year, testimonies were given against such articles as silver pencils, 'more than four silver pens,' long green veils, and useless journals. The brethren were called to task for borrowing tools, for not repairing damaged tools and other property, for leaving broken glass scattered around, for wasting the joint interest by neglecting to clean muddy boots.

Deacons were warned to purchase only 'that which is plain and exemplary,' nothing 'which has foolish writing or printing upon it' or is 'covered with superfluous flowers and pictures.' Similar injunctions formed a section of the 'Holy Laws of Zion,' prepared for the ministry in 1840, in which Stewart argued for a complete separation from worldliness. He advocated the abandonment of certain industries; the return to an almost exclusively agricultural economy; a stricter separation of the sexes and government of children; the prohibition of animal food and strong intoxicating liquors; plainness in personal adornment; and adherence, on the part of leaders and common members alike, to duty and doctrine. A forerunner of the Millennial Laws of 1845, which for years served as the official statutes of the society, these Holy Laws — given 'by Almighty God through Father James' — were to be read by the ministry in meeting once a year for six years, beginning with three parts on 25 December (the birthday of Christ) and ending with three parts on 29 February or 1 March (the birthday of Mother Ann).

How such communications affected the mores of the society is illustrated by the reform which took place in the funeral service. To give greater significance to this ceremony, the instruments began to testify for the deceased. Thus when Abijah Worster, the last survivor of the Harvard covenanters, died in 1839,

. . . an inspired Shaker girl stood at the door, to take down the names of those old friends from the spirit world, who were expected to attend the body to the grave, in honor of Father Abijah. This girl said there were all the first Shakers present. Father Abijah was very much gratified in seeing his old friends. The old man adjusted the head in the coffin, and asked Mother Ann if she thought he had changed much, she answered no, Abijah, it looks well. (These questions are always asked and answered by the Visionist.)

We are told that Father Abijah marched out at the head of the coffin, singing a beautiful freedom song. The Pall Bearers were the Eternal Father, the Eternal Mother, Christ and Mother Ann. The brethren marched out of the house from one door, the sisters from another, preceded by the Elders, falling back a distance from the body to give room to the heavenly guests. The spirits lingered around the grave till their brethren of earth had left the yard, — then Power and Wisdome, Christ and Mother struck up a lively dance, when all the spirits joined hands and danced right merrily around the grave. — At the close of the dance the Godhead *crossed hands forming a seat* for Father Abijah, — and giving a glad shout spread their wings and ascended, followed by the heavenly host to Mother’s mansion, where a banquet was in waiting to welcome the last of the first Fathers in Harvard to his final home.

222

As Mother Ann’s work increased, the messages contained more in the way of approbation. New evidences of supernatural power occurred in all the societies. Exhilarated by these experiences, the Shakers were swept along on an irresistible tide. ‘The spiritual-minded and lover of divine things, whose heart perhaps has been desponding, for the lack of divine manifestations . . . now felt their hopes aroused, and their anticipations of a future state brightened. Every manifestation seemed designed to inspire a love for sacred things, and a confidence in those gifts.’

‘Notices’ to individuals became more common. Rewards of merit, testimonials, and messages of love would be given, in and out of meeting, to a selected brother or sister, frequently — after they came to be written down — in the form of beautifully inscribed papers and booklets. These referred to a variety of spiritual presents: fruits and flowers of all kinds; ‘diamonds of charity,’ chrysolites, emeralds, sapphires, and other precious stones; golden censers, bowls, and chains; gold boxes filled with various treasures; cakes of love and ‘sweet-scented manna on shining plates’; silver cups ‘filled with the pure love of Christ and Mother’; plates of wisdom, baskets of simplicity, balls of promise, belts of wisdom, bands of brightness and robes of meekness; heavenly doves; leaves from the tree of life; rods of correction or comfort; sharp swords, breastplates of truth, shining armor, and so on. Later the ‘notices’ took the form of exquisitely inscribed ‘cards of love,’ ‘sacred sheets,’ and cut-outs in the form of leaves or hearts bearing a message and decorated with crowns, trumpets, harps, doves, or boxes of treasure. In the larger drawings and paintings, which made their appearance toward the end of ‘the new era,’ were ‘glimpses of the heavenly sphere,’ trees of life and light, celestial bowers, baskets of fruit, wreaths of flowers, and other symbolic designs.

223

The spiritual presents were not always in written form. Often, in meeting, a gift would be presented by the instrument — in the name of some ‘sacred parent’ or departed saint — to a favored individual or group, or to the whole assembly, who would receive it with appropriate gestures and use it as the occasion demanded. The gift of spiritual wine, for example, 'carried a great evidence of its reality, by the paroxysms of intoxication which it produced, causing those who drank it to stagger and reel, like drunken people.' Elkins tells of the Believers at Enfield (N.H.) while in a 'superior condition,' 'smoking Mother's Love from pipes of peace'; snuffing 'Mother's Love in a pulverized state'; and 'grinding to pieces . . . old nature' (i.e. 'the evil, sensual principles in man') with spiritual machines deposited in the center of the sanctuary by some of 'the aboriginal inhabitants of America.' Flags were waved, trumpets sounded, boxes opened, robes draped, balls tossed, swords brandished, and cakes eaten in the solemn or joyous pantomime attendant on the reception of these various gifts. Elkins contended that for some Shakers the gifts had visible and tangible reality, while others accepted them only in a metaphorical sense as symbols of spiritual values.

The revival approached its climax in 1841 with two visits from Holy Mother Wisdom. This mysterious Being may have been a borrowing, in name at least, from older religions, a counterpart of the Sophia, Sophia-Sapientia, or Mater Dei of certain groups of Hellenic Jews and early Christians: Bardesanes taught that the first emanation from the Supreme Being, or Father of all things, was His feminine companion Sophia, or Wisdom. The concept of a dual Deity — frequent also in occult and theosophic writings, the doctrines of the Rappites, the Ephrata Kloster, and other spiritual sects, and later accepted by the Mormons, the Unitarian Theodore Parker, and the Christian Scientist Mary Baker Eddy — may, on the other hand, have been one derived independently from the Shaker thesis of a Father-Mother God. In the first hymn of *Millennial Praises*, published in 1813, are two revealing verses:

> Long ere this fleeting world began
> Or dust was fashion'd into man,
> There *Power* and *Wisdom* we can view,
> Names of the *Everlasting Two*.

> The Father's high eternal throne
> Was never fill'd by one alone:
> There Wisdom holds the Mother's seat
> And is the Father's helper-meet.

In Philemon Stewart's strange work, *The Divine Book of Holy Wisdom*, the maternal element is explained as 'the Bearing Spirit of all the works of God.'   226

Whatever her origin, Holy and Eternal Wisdom was now for the first time hypostatized, a spirit to be held in profound if vague veneration. Her visits in April and December, announced beforehand, created, therefore, a mood of awesome expectancy. Much time was spent in kneeling, prayer, and exhortations. Once a day, for six days before her coming, the only food was bread and water. Preceding the visit on Christmas day, in obedience to a sacred writing called *The Judgment Law*, a sacrifice or general opening of the mind was held, followed by the first protracted ritual of the period, the 'cleansing gift,' a curious ceremony in which a chosen band of instruments and singers marched through the dwellings and out-buildings singing a song of vengeance 'against the abominations that rested in Zion,' and 'purifying' all habitations with spiritual brooms. Returning to the place of worship, all fell on their knees 'to scour and scrub from this floor the stains of sin.'

Youngs' account of the actual visits of Holy Mother Wisdom touches but lightly on the event. On her first appearance 'she noticed each one with a short address and set a mark upon each one.' The second time she remained several days. On Christmas day, accompanied by three instruments, she visited the ministry; in the afternoon she viewed the brethren and sisters as they sat, facing each other in straight ranks, in their apartments; then she called on the trustees. On the twenty-sixth she addressed the First Order in meeting; on the twenty-seventh she bestowed a blessing on the adult brethren; on the twenty-eighth the sisters were noticed individually; on the twenty-ninth the children were noticed one after the other, and then the members of the Second Order.

A more graphic account is found in David Lamson's *Two Years' Experience among the Shakers*. When the rite was administered to   227
this believer at Hancock, Wisdom was incarnated in one of the chief instruments of the Church family, Sister Martha Van Valen. Seated at one end of the meeting-room in front of the ministry and elders, the medium was suddenly taken under operations, nodding or jerking her head irregularly and waving her right hand in all directions. After the 'labourings' subsided, those who were to receive the gift advanced

two at a time, made seven low bows, and kneeled before the instrument. The ritual then proceeded:

> Holy Mother: Elder William, do you consider this brother a good Believer?
> Elder William: Yea, I consider that brother David has good faith, understanding faith; and is endeavoring to live up to it.
> Holy Mother: Yea truly it must be so.
> David (repeating after an Elder Sister): Holy Holy Mother Wisdom! I thank thee for thy great condescension and blessing', and for thy love and mercy to me.
> Holy Mother (kneeling): Around thy head I place a golden band. On it is written the name of me, Holy Mother Wisdom! the Great Jehovah! the Eternal God! Touch not mine anointed.

As the instrument spoke, she made the motion of placing a band around the subject's head, thus setting her mark or seal on each member of the order. After the gift, the subjects again bowed seven times and retired.

New Year's Day 1842, which ushered in the most remarkable year in Shaker history, was auspiciously observed. Holy Mother Wisdom withdrew to the meeting-house to commune with the ministry. No one was allowed to approach the building all day, and no one knew what transpired. Perhaps at this secret session were planned some of the rituals that were to be inaugurated during the year: the 'Midnight Cry,' the 'Sweeping Gift,' the mountain meetings, 'taking in the spirits' of Indians and other races, the sowing of spiritual seed, the feasting on spiritual food, and the bathing in spiritual waters. Wisdom protracted her visit for several days, during which period the heavenly and spiritual parents delivered their farewell addresses to the people.

228   In 'The Midnight Cry,' a company of six males and six female instruments, led by two mediums carrying lamps in their right hands, marched through the rooms of every building, a work which took nearly two weeks. At midnight on the third day, the family was roused by the singing of four sisters who passed through the halls and sisters' retiring rooms:

> Awake from your slumbers, for the Lord of Hosts is
>   going through the land,
> He will sweep he will clean his holy sanctuary.

Search ye your Camps, yea read and understand
For the Lord of Hosts holds the Lamps in his hand.

All then arose and joined the ranks. At two o'clock the next night
the sleepers were again aroused by a company of brethren and sisters,
and at three everyone gathered for an hour of worship. For eight
years this ritual was enacted annually at New Lebanon, where it
started, and at Canterbury and other communities.

'Mother Ann's Sweeping Gift' was probably an outgrowth of 'The
Midnight Cry' and the purification rite preparatory to Holy Mother's visits and, like the 'Cry,' was enacted once a year for eight years.
A communication from the foundress had directed that a day be set
aside for a general cleaning of houses, shops, and premises — to re-
move those 'evil spirits' which harbored themselves wherever there was
dust or dirt. Accordingly, on the appointed day, a band of visionists,
preceded by a group of singers and elders, marched throughout the
community chanting, exhorting, and wielding spiritual brooms. In
the meantime the rest of the members devoted themselves to the actual
work of sweeping floors, dusting out cobwebs, picking up bits of wood
and paper, burning rubbish, cleaning out pig pens, and placing
everything in order until the village, already 'notorious for neatness,
wore an aspect fifty per cent more tidy than usual.'

Directions were issued in the spring of 1842 for the celebration of
a holy feast or passover, to be held twice a year, in May and September, on some hill, mountain top, or secluded place within the community. Following the example set at the central church, each society
cleared half an acre of land, leveled and enclosed it, and laid out in
its center a low-fenced hexagonal plot called the 'fountain.' At one
end of the enclosure at Hancock — which was typical of the other
'sacred mounts' — a marble tablet was placed the following year,
bearing on one face the inscription:

WRITTEN AND PLACED HERE
By the command of our Lord and Savior Jesus Christ
THE LORD'S STONE.
Erected upon this Mt. Sinai, May 4th, 1843.
ENGRAVED AT HANCOCK.

On the inner face was the following legend:

THE WORD OF THE LORD.
HERE IS MY HOLY FOUNTAIN,
WHICH I HAVE PLACED HERE.
For the healing of the Nations, who shall
here seek my favor.

And I command all people who shall come to this
fountain, not to step within this enclosure, nor
place their hands upon his Stone, while they
are polluted with sin. I am God the Almighty
in whose hands are judgment and mercy. And I
will cause my judgments to fall upon the wilful
violator of my commands in my own time according
to wisdom and truth, whether in this world,
or in eternity. For I have created all souls,
and unto me they are accountable.

'FEAR YE THE LORD.'

Sinai was the spiritual name assigned to a mountain about two
miles north of the Shaker village. The 'feast-grounds' at New Lebanon were called Holy Mount; at Enfield (Conn.), the Mount of
Olives; at Tyringham, Mount Horeb; at Harvard, Holy Hill of Zion;
at Canterbury, Pleasant Grove; at Enfield (N.H.), Mount Assurance; at Union Village, Jehovah's Chosen Square; at Whitewater,
Lonely Plain (or Vale) of Tribulation; at Watervliet, Vale of Peace;
at South Union, Jasper Valley; and at Pleasant Hill, Holy Sinai
Plains. Every Shaker community also received a symbolic name —
City of Peace, City of Love, Lovely Vineyard, Pleasant Garden, et
cetera — signs of the will to discard completely all that was worldly.
The same year (1842) the Believers closed their meetings to the public, and at New Lebanon erected in front of the meeting-house wooden
229 crosses warning the world away. For three years all the services of the
sect were held in secret.

Fasting, confession, and silent prayer preceded these semi-annual
pilgrimages. On the evening before the great day, spiritual garments
were distributed to all 'purified souls.' As each brother knelt before
the presiding elder, he received, from an imaginary chest, a coat of
twelve different colors; a sky-blue, gold-buttoned jacket covered with
fine needlework in floral patterns; a pair of white trousers spangled
with stars; white shoes; a white silk handkerchief bordered with gold;

and a fur hat of a silver color. To the sisters the eldress distributed gowns of twelve beautiful colors; silver-colored shoes; muslin caps 'beautifully trimmed'; silver-colored bonnets; and blue silk gloves. Clothed in these garments emblematic of the virtues of holiness, innocence, meekness, freedom, and peace, the members of every family in the community met the next morning for their journey up the holy hill.

MOUNTAIN MEETING

The ritual at Hancock on 18 September 1842 was typical of feast-day ceremonies in all the societies. Led by the chief elders, eldresses, and instruments, the worshippers at the 'City of Peace' started out about eight o'clock, marching two abreast till they reached the walnut grove, a spot halfway up Mount Sinai. Here they gathered in the love of departed sisters and brethren, bowed low four times, clapped their hands, and then, turning around, sent three hearty shouts in the direction of their homes below. The brief service at the grove ended with the distribution of spiritual spectacles which an instrument had received from Father William Lee. Prepared thus for seeing spiritual things more clearly, the company struck up a marching song and proceeded on their way.

The ceremonies at the feast grounds opened with the anointment of the instruments. As the sexes stood in ranks on either side of the fountain, the presiding elder, Joseph Wicker, speaking in the name of the Saviour, charged these 'vessels to go forth in strength and in zeal,' to 'walk upright, in all things possessing a spirit of meekness and low humiliation,' and to give themselves up 'to act or move as the spirit directs.' 'Sweet incense' from a censer was poured over the instruments' heads and 'mantles of strength' were draped over their shoulders.

Then 'liberty was given for all to go forth in a lively dance.' An instrument announced that Father Calvin Harlow 'wants to have us go forth with as much energy as tho we were going into the hayfield, he wants to have the brethren strip off their coats and all go to work.' Soon all were in motion, not like 'hirelings on the ground of bondage' but like 'eagles upon the wing,' their spirits seeming 'to soar on high in freedom to meet the heavenly showers of love and simplicity that were falling from the windows of heaven.' Each acted for himself or herself, staggering, leaping and skipping, rolling on the ground, or 'acknowledging the mighty power of God.' During a pause an elder sister spoke 'with much tenderness of feeling' of her thankfulness for being alive, for being pure, for being clothed 'with this external power' — after which the shouting, clapping, bowing, and turning were again resumed.

Following the bestowal of various gifts — a flaming trumpet on the shoulders of each worshipper, 'anointing oil' on every head, a book from the prophet Elijah, et cetera — Elder Wicker, acting as master of ceremonies, announced that the 'Saviour' had placed a large white tub on either side of the 'fountain,' one for the brethren and one for the sisters:

He then placed two vessels at the head of the fountain for Brother Grove and Sister Dana to use and dippers to dip from the fountain and fill the tubs. This was readily done, and while they were preparing the water Brothers Joseph Patten and Chester Hulett were directed to take a large basket of sponges and place them around the fountain for the brethren and sisters, and each one was to take one from the ground and all dip them into the respective tubs of water, which was now prepared for bathing, and give each other a good scrubing, that is for brethren to assist brethren and sisters to assist sisters. He then gave Martha Van Valen and Nancy Oaks some water pots to give to the brethren and sisters to rinse each other off after scouring, in the same order they had washed. This was all performed with much simplicity and faithfulness.

Then more gifts were given. One by one the worshippers 'dipped a hearty draught of Father Job's love' from a 'basket' placed on Elder Nathaniel's spiritual staff. Quaffing spiritual wine from 'bottles' fetched by the instruments, they felt quite merry, and one medium struck up what was known as the 'fool-song,'

> Come, come, who will be a fool,
> I will be a fool —

during the singing of which, 'fool' was gathered, thrown, and caught, and all acted foolishly. 'It seemed that all partook bountifully,' the Shaker scribe wrote of this incident, 'so that old stiff self conceit was pretty well worked up. It was observed that if there was a pharisee upon the ground . . . he must die with vexation . . .'

The next ceremony was the building of an altar. The four foundation stones were laid by the ministry and head elders. From a pile prepared for the purpose, every member brought one stone apiece to the three brethren selected to erect the mound. When the 'lead' had finished the work by placing four capstones on the top, the 'Saviour' directed that all should make 'an offering of the most choice things ye have, such as love, thankfulness, meekness and obedience.' This was done according to rank, the ministry first, the elders and eldresses next, then the aged brethren and sisters, and so on, each one naming the offering as it was solemnly placed on the altar.

An intermission of fifteen minutes was terminated by the blowing of spiritual trumpets. The second half of the program opened with an invitation from the 'Saviour' 'to go forth as the spirit should direct'; for, he said, 'singing unto God in solemn praise is a sweet incense before his throne.' Again there was shouting, clapping, bending, and bowing. Some spoke in unknown tongues. Tunes and songs were improvised. A song was danced 'in the quick manner while the Virgin Mary sprinkled love over the brethren and sisters and we gathered it as we danced.'

And once again there were gifts, this time from the spirits of famous men and women. Love, acknowledged by bows, was received from Napoleon Bonaparte, George Washington, Queen Esther, and Queen Isabella. 'Queen Esther placed a wreath of roses in our hands to wind around our necks.' 'Washington' brought a box of spiritual guns for the brethren and a basket of musical instruments for the sisters. The wreath was wound, the guns were loaded and fired against an imaginary enemy, and the sisters 'played up a very lively and pleasant air.'

The sowing and watering of spiritual seed, the next gift, was a common ritual in many communities during the time of 'manifestations.' Acting the role of a holy angel, an instrument placed 'small papers of seed' all around the fountain. Then the people were bidden by the 'Saviour' to go forth sowing from 'baskets of seeds' slung over their arms, and afterward 'to reap the growth.' This done, the seed in the papers was scattered over the holy ground and watered from pots the people carried on their shoulders. 'If such precious seed is sown by honest hearts,' the 'Saviour' promised, 'it will surely come up.' 'It was a most beautiful sight,' wrote the scribe, 'to see such a devoted company all moving over the ground with such simplicity and eagerness to gather a full share of blessing.'

Here, for the first time, Indian spirits were taken into the meetings. On the present occasion, one of the inspired brethren informed Elder Grove that 'there was a large company of natives that desired liberty to come in and unite with us.'

Brother Grove rather hesitated not exactly knowing whether they had confessed their sins. They were then interrogated to know for what purpose they had come. They said they had come on purpose to go forth in union with Mothers simple children, That they had confessed all their sins and had the same Mother that we had and further more they said that they were perfectly friendly and would be very civil if we would admit them into the dance.

Then Brother Grove gave them full liberty to gather into the band, and at this there was a quick song given rather on the native order. It was sung and danced with much activity. The brethren and sisters began to feel very much pleased and united with their new visitants in so much that they desired the singers to sing another song more fully expressive of the Native Language, so that they might feel a more full enjoyment in each others company.

This was done and the Natives struck in, the whoop was sounded briskly, and for some time it appeared they rather carried the day, although the brethren and sisters played their part pretty well, both companies conversing freely together as they went. After considerable exercise such as hopping upon one foot, dancing sideways, whooping, shaking hands, bowing of the head, running to and fro, catching one another, running around one another giveing and receiveing love, and diverse other simple movements of the spirit, we were called together by the Savior.

An elaborate spiritual feast, a sort of Shaker eucharist, climaxed the meeting. The 'Saviour' directed the instruments to go forth into the vineyards, orchards, and gardens to gather fruits and various kinds of food: apples, pears, peaches, pineapples, plums, cherries, apricots, grapes, strawberries, whortleberries, pomegranates, oranges, pies, sweetcakes, bread and butter, milk and honey, locusts and wild honey, white wine and manna. A 'table' for the ministry and elders was spread with this choice food, and three sisters and three brethren were appointed to attend it. After the guests kneeled in prayer, they sat down and 'regaled themselves upon the rich dainties before them, appearing very free, cheerful and happy.' A long 'table' at the other end of the 'fountain' was set with a similar feast for the brethren and sisters, who 'put forth their hands like little simple children of Mother to partake of this banquet of holiness.' As they ate, 'a Holy Angel' passed up and down the table crying: 'Can any soul murmur at the cross since by it the glory of heaven is added unto you? More zeal, more zeal, more zeal, more life, more fervency, more energy, more love, more thankfulness, more obedience, more strength, more power.'

After a final gift of the Prophet Daniel's love — received as a ball of yarn reeled over the hands — the company marched off the ground four abreast, singing:

> I will march I will go
> In this pretty shining way
> In freedom's lovely valley
> On my organ I will play.

It was half past two in the afternoon when the worshippers returned to the 'City of Peace.'

A similar ceremony, performed at Holy Mount above New Lebanon village the same month, is recorded in the 'spiritual journal' of Sally Bushnell, a member of the Lower Canaan (N.Y.) family. Spiritual dresses had been given to her and her sisters a week before. On Friday, an angel placed 'cups of tribulation' on a 'table' in the meeting-room, with the instruction that each one place a cup 'upon their right shoulder' so that when they are called for, 'it will be known who

230

has drank their cups and whose remained filled.' On Saturday no animal food was eaten, words were few, and everyone put their 'hands to
work and their hearts to God.' Sally's family arose before four o'clock
on Sunday and were ready to start at six. After receiving preliminary
gifts and warnings at the church, where the different orders assembled, the march up the mountain began. The older people or 'ancients'
were transported by carriage.

At a narrow spot where there had been a gate or bars 'lay a great
deal of unbelief, doubts, etc. that had been tumbled down the hill by
those who had ascended the Mount before us, and it was the desire of
our Savior, that all the Prophets and Prophetesses from all the families should go ahead and take their brooms and sweep the way clean
for the people to pass.' Further along, 'cups of rejoicing' were exchanged by the holy angel for the 'cups of tribulation' previously
given. At the 'half-way place,' the company formed a ring; 'an angel'
brought 'a thread of linen twine which he desired Brother Rufus and
Sister Aseneth would take at the two ends and encircle all the ring,
and we might turn our faces outward, and help twist the twine.'

Cedar posts surrounded the 'fountain' on the mountain top. Here an
angel, speaking through an instrument, cautioned the worshippers
'to take care how we treated what we might behold this day; and if we
did not understand it, to not be a-talking about it to each other, but
go to our Elders and seek wisdom.' Prophecies of tribulation and
famine were uttered by the instruments, judgments on the wicked,
and the promise that only the Shaker lands would be exempt from the
universal drouth that would soon prevail. In describing the 'fool'
ceremony, Sally admits that 'to the natural mind these things must
have looked disgustful, but to the spiritual, it was the great the
mighty power of God, that thus brought the high and lofty down into
the valley of true simplicity and become fools in order to attain true
wisdom.'

The spiritual feast was similar to that on Mount Sinai — 'our
spirits were refreshed with Holy water, with the wine of the Kingdom,
with the foolishness which confounds the wisdom of the wise, with
grapes from the kingdom, with plumbs, with pears, peaches, strawberries, cocoanuts, pineapples, oranges, lemons, maple sugar, white
sugar and every thing that hearts could desire.' In building 'the altar
of love,' the people were promised that 'every soul that had brought a
living stone . . . should grow and increase in the good things of

God.' A 'bowl of wine' was placed on the altar, and the brethren and sisters sipped from it with 'spoons.'

After the return to the meeting-room of the family dwelling late in the afternoon, an inspirational message was read, the elders set baskets upon the floor, and 'we took our beautiful dresses and put them in the basket.' They had been 'so bountifully supplied with spiritual Food,' Sally concludes, 'that all hunger for natural food was not felt or realized.'

231

There had always been a curious affinity between the Shakers and the Indians. According to one tradition, it was a native of the forest who first recognized the saintliness of Mother Ann: 'one poor Indian saw a bright light around her, and prophesied that the Great Spirit had sent her to do much good.' In another story it is related that when Ann was returning from her eastern mission she was met at the Albany ferry by a number of Indians, who joyfully cried: 'The good woman is come! The good woman is come!' The Shakers, as we have seen, preached to the Indians in the East and undertook a mission to the Shawnees in the West. Perhaps the entrance of Indian spirits, and later those of Eskimos, Negroes, Chinese, Abyssinians, Hottentots, et cetera, into the bodies of the instruments reflected an eagerness, on the part of the Believers, to share their light with those primitive peoples to whom they were in many respects akin, as well as with the great and proud 'whose souls had been brought low.' Whatever the cause, the reception of these spirits, dominating the meetings for a while and resulting in many 'native' songs and exercises, must have been a remarkable spectacle. For once possessed by the spirits, the visionists acted in a manner characteristic of the race: dancing wildly and waving the imaginary tomahawks of Indians, making the motions of driving sledges if they were Eskimos, acting 'barbarously' if they were Turks, mimicking the 'polite' manners of the French, and so on. In the Macdonald manuscript, the presence of a tribe of Indians at Watervliet was announced by a female, who, after whirling with eyes closed for about fifteen minutes, informed the head eldress that she had a communication to make:

The first Message I heard was as follows: 'Mother Ann' has sent two Angels to inform us, that a Tribe of Indians had been round there two days, and wanted the Brothers, and Sisters, to take them in, they were

then outside the Building looking in at the Windows. I shall never forget
how I looked around at the Windows [wrote Macdonald] expecting to
see their yellow faces, when this intelligence was announced, and I believe
some of the old folks who eyed me, bit their lips and smiled; it caused
no alarm to the rest, but the first Elder exhorted the Brothers, 'to take
in the poor Spirits and assist them to get Salvation.' The first Eldress
informed us more of what the Angels had said, Viz: 'that the Indians
were a savage tribe, who had all died before Columbus discovered America; but had been wandering about ever since. Mother Ann wanted them
to be received into the meeting tomorrow night.' After this, we dispersed
to our separate Bed rooms, with the hope of having a visit from the
Indians. My friend Mr. B was much amused by my enquiries, and told
me we would yet have to give the Indians our beds.

The next Dancing night, we again assembled in the same manner as
before, and went through the marching, and dancing, as usual, after
which the Hall Doors were opened, and the Elder invited the Indians
to come in. They were soon shut again, and one of the Sisters, (the same
one who received the communication spoken of) informed us, that she
saw them all around, and amongst the Brothers and Sisters. The Elders
then urged upon the members the duty of 'taking them in,' whereupon
eight or nine of the Sisters became possessed of the Spirits of Indian
Squaws and about six of the Brothers became Indians: then ensued a
regular 'Pow Wow,' with whooping, yelling, and strange antics, such as
would require a Dickens to describe.

The Sisters and Brothers squatted down on the floor together, Indian
fashion, and the Elders and Eldresses endeavoured to keep them asunder.
At the same time, telling the Indians that they must be separated from
the Squaws, and otherwise instructing them in the rules of Shakerism.
Some of the Indians then wanted some 'Suckatosh' which was soon
brought them from the Kitchen, in two wooden Dishes, and placed on the
Floor, then they commenced eating it with their Fingers, and thus continued the performance till about ten o'clock when the Chief Elder desired the Indians to go away, and they would find some one waiting, to
conduct them to the Shakers in the Heavenly world. At this announcement every man and woman became themselves again, and all retired to
232   rest.

In later years the Indian visitations were acknowledged with some
pride. Eldresses White and Taylor, for instance, explain that

. . . these tribes came to be instructed . . . They came in work hours,
went into the shops and were instructed in the various industries and
trades followed by brethren and sisters; into the kitchens, laundries,

bake-rooms and sewing rooms, learning the arts of the housekeeper. These principles of industrial education thus applied in the early forties, by direction of spiritual teachers, under Mother Ann, to these savage tribes, antedated by a half century, modern improved methods of educating savage races.

233

Native songs and dances, vision tunes, inspirational messages, spiritual presentations, and various gifts continued with little or no abatement until 1845. The old warring ceremony was revived. In the 'laughing gift' the worshippers held their sides and reeled in their chairs till they became exhausted; and there were laughing songs so contagious that the room rocked with merriment. Spiritual birds brought instruments of music which were placed on the head or shoulders, whereupon all who 'owned the gift' would join the 'bird chorus.' Mysterious signs — 'colored sheets, cloths and girdles' — were seen in the sky. In the 'Gift of the Father and Son' at Hancock, two instruments impersonating their 'sacred parents' walked in turn up and down an aisle formed by two ranks of Believers, addressing each member individually and, by gently touching the head with their forefingers, 'crowning' each with 'the seal of approbation.'

Comparable to the feast days on the mountain were the family Christmas meetings, especially those held in 1845. At Hancock the members of each family marched into the meeting-room singing and playing on 'ancient instruments.' The story of the birth of Christ was told around an 'altar,' the speaker impressing on his listeners the necessity of becoming again as little children if they were to enter the Kingdom. Most of the gifts distributed by the instruments were from the 'Saviour': celestial wine; 'a loaf of bread, with slices for each one'; lamps for everybody, 'to be kept well trimmed and burning that the enemy may not impede our progress'; gold baskets of white roses; shields of protection; 'white robes embalmed with myrrh and aloes'; 'seeing-glasses'; silver sacks filled with the bread of life; cakes of love and boxes of songs. At one time all united in waving a banner, inscribed with the words, 'Peace, Peace to the Righteous,' which had been unfurled by the 'Saviour'; at another the worshippers 'gathered simplicity' from a little child placed in their midst. 'Father Hocknell' brought some gospel fire, whereupon all clapped their hands and blew the flames. The room was swept with spiritual brooms. Circles were formed, 'bound by the chain of love and fastened by the clasp of obedience.' One family received 'a universal gift of sweeping.' Another sang a song called 'The Sound' to the rhythmic beating of hands upon the floor. Spiritual swords were flourished during a warring song:

> We have not in this war begun
> To turn our backs as traitors,
> But we will all unite as one
> Against our carnal natures.

234

An order enjoined 'perfect reconciliation, one with another,' on Christmas day. Garments and other goods for the needy were carried to the 'poor office,' and no unnecessary work was done until sunset.

In 1845 there were evidences that the strange cycle of inspiration was nearing completion. The flow of songs and messages continued; 'The Midnight Cry' and 'Sweeping Gift' were still celebrated; Christmas was observed with 'pentecostal ardour'; prophetic utterances went on. (The Shaker instruments had allegedly foretold the death of Lafayette and the invention of the telegraph and in 1847 were to predict successive revolutions in Europe and later both the Emancipation Proclamation and the assassination of Lincoln.) The Church *235* historian notes, however, that in 1845 'the degree of devotion in meeting depended more upon our own voluntary exertions than upon the aid of the communications from the spirit.' Gifts were almost wholly confined to the place and hours of worship, and the fervor had sufficiently abated to permit the reopening of the Sabbath services to the world. As early as 1843, in fact, thoughtful members of the society, while remaining loyal, were starting to question the efficacy, if not the authenticity of many gifts. 'Intercourse with the spirits of other nations was greatly calculated,' Youngs thought, 'to lessen the value and solemnity of spiritual gifts and inspiration, in the view of such as were so minded, and to give cavillers a fair chance to quibble.' The gifts were so abundant in that year, he felt, that 'the feelings of many are more cloyed . . . and a great portion of those gifts are more calculated to try the faith, than to confirm it.' In another place he acknowledges that some gifts were dubious and foolish, but condones them on the ground that they will not 'hurt the sincere heart.'

Almost from the first, the central ministry realized the need of control if the experience through which the society was passing was to be an inspiring and unifying force. Irresponsible testimonies were

Simple Gifts.

'Tis the gift to be simple 'tis the gift to be free, 'tis the gift to come down where we ought to be. And when we find ourselves in the place just right

'Twill be in the valley of love and delight.

When true simplicity is gain'd

To bow and to bend we shan't be asham'd.

To turn, turn will be our delight

Till by turning turning we come round right

REVIVAL SONG, SHAKER NOTATION

'contrary to order.' In a letter of 12 August 1839, the 'lead' thus cautioned the South Union ministry: 'When we see believers in their gifts, soaring above the simple work of God and running over . . .

then it will be time for the true watchmen of Zion's walls to look out sharp for the enemy. Yea, and Mother has given to the Ministry and Elders here, spiritual spectacles that they may see clearly and not be deceived by false spirits.' The following year the ministry ordered all messages to be committed to writing and subjected to examination before they were given out in meeting. Apparently it was necessary to re-enforce this decision, for in 1841 a communication, obviously inspired by the 'lead,' warned 'that some souls whom I (the Eternal Two in One) have chosen to be the bearers of my word and will to my people here on earth, have not attended to the order of my Zion of God on earth, with respect to the conveyance of the heavenly treasures which were entrusted to them; but instead of carrying them safely to my Shepherds [i.e. the ministry], that they might feed the lambs of my flock, have distributed them with their own hands, and thus wolves, as well as lambs, have taken thereof . . .' And again, in April 1842, a revelation from Mother Ann directed that 'no one presume to bring forward any of the sacred and solemn gifts and orders . . . without the full union and approbation of the Lord's true anointed which consists of four in number united and agreed as one.' The sacred writings were to be gathered together and put into the ministry's hands for safekeeping: 'for I greatly fear,' the messenger said, 'the use that may hereafter be made of them; and I foresee the evil of my word being too plenty among the people.' Another effort at supervision is seen in a message, received from 'the twelve holy angels' in March 1841, which was clearly designed to allay any jealousy or inferiority on the part of members not honored by gifts: 'Some are liable to feel in this way: such a one is made more of than I am: they are not in reality any better; yet they can speak to Mother, and the good spirits; so they are thought more of, and noticed more. But now I am glad we are coming more upon a level, for I never thought any more worthy than those who were not blessed with this gift . . . Remember those blessed gifts, manifested through this one and that, are not their own.'

Finally, in a directive signed by Elders Seth Wells and Calvin Green, it was ruled that inspired writings should contain no contradiction in themselves; should not contradict each other or previously established testimony; should not contradict authentic history or the import of holy scriptures; and should not be in unknown tongues,

which would make them useless unless interpreted. 'We find no unknown words in the scriptures,' the authors remark.   *236*

As time went on, whatever skepticism may have prevailed in some
quarters about the authenticity of the gifts was swept away by the
tempo of events. The central ministry was further reassured when, in
the course of a mission to a town of German origin, the 'Community
of True Inspiration,' near Buffalo, in 1846, they learned that there,
too, the divine spirit was usually manifested to individuals from
within — not 'through an external voice into the ears'; that revelations were commonly accompanied by 'violent trembling and commo-
tions of the body' (*Bewegungen*); that messages were sometimes accompanied by 'rude rhymes' and visions of heavenly scenes; and that
false inspiration was not unknown. Before the 'era of the manifesta-   *237*
tions' closed, the 'lead' gave them its official endorsement, authorizing
the collection of the inspired writings of each community, the publi-   *238*
cation of two major works — Stewart's *The Holy Sacred and Divine
Roll and Book* and Paulina Bates's *Divine Book of Holy Wisdom* —   *239*
and the transmission of five hundred copies of the former to the world,
including 'the rulers of all nations.'

It has been said that the Shakers were the forerunners of modern
spiritualism. Certain instruments had prophesied, in fact, that similar   *240*
manifestations would soon break forth in the world. In 1848, therefore, when the mysterious rappings were reported by the Fox sisters
in Hydesville, New York, the news did not come as a surprise. As the
movement spread the Believers even sent delegates 'to try the spirits,'
and invited mediums to hold seances in their own communities. But
the mechanics of modern spiritualism — the automatic writings, table
liftings, knockings, and ectoplasmic materializations — offended the
Shaker mind: the spirit of religious exaltation and the freedom and
spontaneity of genuine inspiration were lacking in these controlled
exhibitions. They were 'very uncertain and unreliable,' Youngs wrote
in 1850, 'so that to *us* it has afforded but little benefit; and we are
satisfied that this form of communion with the spirit world is not for
Believers in our faith.'

Unique and inexplicable though it was, Shaker spiritualism was
nevertheless not a wholly isolated phenomenon. It was in the year
1827, when the Believers had a brief revival, that the angel Moroni

revealed to Joseph Smith the sacred plates of Mormon, providing him with magic spectacles that he might decipher the symbols. The years during which 'Mother Ann's Work' was most active coincided with the focal periods of both Fourierism and New Engand transcendentalism. In 1843, a year of important revelations in the United Society, the Millerite excitement reached its climax. And then came the Fox sisters. Noyes felt that these coincidences were examples of 'mysterious affinities.' Who can say whether there was any connection between them, or whether they had a common cause?

CHAPTER IX

Internal Order

Order is the creation of beauty.

Never try to run on ahead, before the main body
of good believers, and above all, never fall back;
but keep close up and be in the gift.

— *Youth's Guide in Zion*, 1842

IN MARKED contrast to the rites of worship, with its elements of mystery and unrestraint, was the common life of the people, which flowed on tranquilly from day to day. Religion in the meeting-room was a catharsis. There the Shakers could indulge their love for song and rhythmic movement, for phantasy and glorious utterance, for abandonment to the joys of a divine fellowship. Outside of meeting, in the field and shop and dwelling, religion assumed the guise of a passionless devotion to utilitarian pursuits. But there were other aspects in the life of the folk — the peculiar 'intercourse' of the sexes, the 'order of the day,' the education of children, the provision for health and comfort, the funeral rites, the 'uses of charity' — attention to which was likewise a sacrament, each in its own manner aiding the traveler along the road to salvation.

Chief among the factors affecting all Shaker life was the unique relationship existing between brethren and sisters. The application, under the same roof, of the seemingly irreconcilable theories of equality and separation set the movement apart from other communal-religious institutions and aroused, more than any other characteristic of the church, skeptical comment and barbed abuse. Every reliable source, however, indicates that the dividing line was held. One sex was always conscious of the presence and support of the other. But to pass that invisible boundary was to invite both bondage of soul and communal disfavor.

Convictions concerning a fundamental tenet of the order, of course, aided the adjustment: for the rule of celibacy was a selective agent, attracting not only those who believed in the principle on doctrinal grounds, but those others, chiefly women, who were drawn in because of their desire to escape from marital difficulties and broken homes. For persons oppressed by poverty and economic ills the Shaker community, like the cloister, offered the opportunity for a renewal of life in useful service, in which case the rule was accepted as a condition of security. Once the rule was accepted, the Shakers underwent a thorough course of instruction. The work of God, they were told, proceeded by a spiritual union and relation between male and female. If, in the course of the period of probation, the cross seemed repellent, they were free to withdraw or remain in an 'out family.' On the other hand, should they wish to travel on to the junior and senior order, they did so in full realization of what it entailed. If husband and wife entered together, they were usually assigned to separate families.

The necessity of vigilance was realized early. In one of his first by-laws Meacham ruled that 'if any one knows of actual sin, or positive disorder, and have reason to believe it is not and will not be confessed, he or she shall open it in the line of order, to the elders.' Another statute denied a member the right to worship with sin unconfessed; he was 'out of union,' and even after confession was relegated, as a backslider, to the rear ranks of the assembly. Meacham's basic law — that 'no male or female shall support, or have a private union or correspondence together, neither shall they touch each other unnecessarily' — was also supported, in time, by detailed 'separation acts' and ordinances for the 'purity of the mind.' It was 'contrary to the gift,' for instance, for a brother to pass a sister on the stairs, for a brother to go into a sister's room without knocking, for a sister to go to a brother's shop alone, for brethren to shake hands with the sisters and give them presents, and so on.

Surveillance was facilitated by the smallness of the family and the lack of privacy. From two to six individuals shared each sleeping or retiring room, the day's routine was organized, and most of the work was done in groups. In meeting, as we have seen, the ministry could supervise proceedings through shuttered apertures; and at Pleasant Hill, two watchtowers on the roof of the dwelling served a similar purpose during the day. The Millennial Laws stated that if anyone knew of any transgression, he or she was morally obligated to reveal it to the elders, 'otherwise they participate in the guilt.' Under such conditions an atmosphere of mutual suspicion was almost inevitable; the feeling that one was being spied upon during every hour of the day and night was bound to deprive the individual of dignity and self-respect.

The most noteworthy device for regulating sex relations, however, was a constructive one. As the church was being organized, Meacham realized that 'correspondence' was unavoidable, that brethren and sisters must consult on temporalities, that social solidarity could not rest on negative grounds. Since they *would* have a union together,' he testified, 'if they had not a spiritual union, they would have a carnal.' His corrective was the 'union meeting,' which for over seventy years, from 1793 on, played an important role in Shaker domestic life. These gatherings usually took place two evenings a week and twice on Sundays. A group of four to ten members of each sex met in a brethren's retiring room, where they sat facing each other in rows about five feet apart. (If girls and boys were present, they were placed beside their elders or by themselves in ranks in the rear.) Then, for a stated period, one hour on week nights and one or two on the Sabbath, each member of the group conversed freely and openly with the person opposite him on some familiar or suitable subject; or the occasion might be turned into a singing meeting. The pairs had been carefully matched, on the basis of age and 'condition of travel,' by the elders. No one was worthy to attend if he or she harbored any ill-feeling toward another. 243

The conversation — 'simple, sometimes facetious, rarely profound' — was limited, for sacred, literary, and certain secular topics were all prohibited. Some visitors, like Macdonald, found the meetings dull. Nevertheless the time seemed to have been agreeably passed; the company had their own world to talk about, with zest and unrestraint if they wished; 'gentle laughter and mild amusement' were not unknown; and in the early years smoking was customary. The union meetings, in fact, belied the common assumption that the Shakers were an austere folk, though discipline varied with the family or community and was likely to be more strict in the Church Order. Self-restraint and sobriety, however, never excluded simple joys. One observer comments on 'the amenity of their intercourse [which was]

much less restricted than is generally supposed.' Another noticed that
244   they were 'disposed to be merry and enjoy a joke.' Mary Dyer attended meetings at Enfield (N.H.) where there were pipes to smoke,
cider to drink, and melons, apples, and nuts to eat; and where the
participants sang such 'merry love songs' as

> I love the brethren the brethren love me
> Oh! how happy, how happy I be,
> I love the sisters, the sisters love me,
> Oh! how the happy, how happy I be.
> How pretty they look, how clever they feel,
> And this we will sing when we love a good deal.

A former member of a Niskeyuna family recalled that two aged
brethren, one a Whig and the other a Democrat before they joined the
order, used to argue their political principles in these meetings; and
that a young sister, on one occasion, raised the issue whether members
would not be better Shakers if they were allowed to study instrumental music, languages, and fine literature. The aristocratic Mrs. Hall
found the Believers at this community 'a very conversible set of
245   people' — a verdict later shared by Howells, who felt that the renun-
246   ciation of marriage was 'the sum of Shaker asceticism.'
These social gatherings were nevertheless misinterpreted by the
world: as Isaac Youngs put it, 'advantage was taken by some apostates and evil minded persons . . . to construe this sacred order of
union, [especially the placing of certain brethren with certain sis-
ters] into a particular union or connection, as savoring of husband
and wife.' Eunice Chapman, for one, testified to seeing 'the spiritual
husbands, each with their spiritual wife,' withdraw after meeting to
their different apartments — observing to one of the sisters that there
247   must be 'general courtship throughout the house.' Furnishing further
grounds for detraction was a custom connected with the meeting,
namely that of assigning to each sister general 'oversight over the
habits and temporal needs' of the brother sitting opposite her —
taking care of his clothes, looking after his washing and mending,
providing new garments when they were needed, and so forth — in
return for which the brethren 'did needful favors for the sisters.'
Visitors sometimes noticed the tender solicitude of a brother toward a
248   certain sister, or vice versa. Though such attention was a violation of

the letter of the Separation Acts, it seems to have been accepted, quite naturally, as a justifiable expression of spiritual union.

A combination of factors — the system of orders and surveillance, communal opinion, the rites of confession and atonement, the force of principle, the union meeting, the freedom to withdraw from the society — fostered and enforced a relationship between the two sexes which one enthusiast called 'more harmonic than anyone seriously believes attainable for the human race.' As to its effectiveness, we have the empirical judgment of the student Macdonald:

I have always found that those who spoke ill of the Shakers on this subject, to be ignorant, and low minded persons, who probably judged others by themselves, and who founded their opinion upon mere supposition. Those who have been most among them, and consequently the best Judges, have been compelled to believe, that the Shakers are generally speaking, sincere, both in the Belief and practice of abstinence from sexual coition. I have heard Individuals who have lived with them, for periods varying from thirty years, to a few months, all declare, that there was no such immorality among the Shakers, as had been attributed to them. In the vicinity of Union Village, O. I heard suspicions and suppositions, in abundance, and have no doubt the same surmises may be heard in the vicinity of any of their settlements. But I have never met with one individual who was a Witness to or could prove a Case of immoral conduct between the Sexes in any of the Shaker Communities . . .

It is quite true that sometimes, young Shakers in whom the tender passion is not entirely subdued, fall in love with each other, but these generally contrive to leave the Sect, and go to the 'World' to get married and reside.

249

The 'order of the day' left little room, indeed, for vain or idle thoughts. At the sounding of the bell or 'shell,' the Shakers arose early in the morning, between four o'clock and five in summer, between five and five-thirty in the winter. After kneeling together for a moment of quiet prayer, the occupants of each retiring room stripped the sheets and blankets from their narrow cots, laying them neatly over two chairs at the foot, on which the pillows had previously been placed. Fifteen minutes after rising, the rooms had been vacated, the brethren had gone to their morning chores, and the sisters were entering to close the windows, make the beds, and put the room in order. At breakfast time, six, six-thirty, or seven, the chamber work was fin-

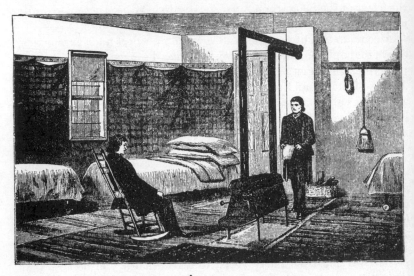

BRETHREN'S RETIRING ROOM

ished, fires had been started in the dwelling rooms and shops, the cattle
fed, the cows milked, and arrangements for the day's industry were all
complete.

Before all meals — the early breakfast, the noon dinner, the six-
o'clock supper — brethren and sisters would assemble, each group by
themselves, in appointed rooms, where for a ten or fifteen minute
pause which was a kind of 'broad grace,' they quietly awaited the bell.
Then, in two columns led by the elders and eldresses respectively, and
in the order in which they were to be seated, they proceeded to the
dining hall. Taking their places behind their chairs or benches, the
sexes at separate tables, they knelt in prayer at a sign from the lead,
and after a meal eaten in monastic silence, knelt again before departing directly to their labors. '*Ils s'agenouillent avant et apres le repas*,'
wrote Mme Blanc, '*mais sans prononcer de paroles. C'est leur avis que
l'aspiration mentale suffit et qu'il ne faut que "marcher avec Dieu"
comme avec un ami.*'

250

A series of table monitors, emphasizing economy and good manners at meals, testifies to the concern with standards of behavior. An
early monitor (undated manuscript) illustrates how detailed was the
instruction:

DINING ROOM, NORTH FAMILY, NISKEYUNA

First, All should sit upright at the table.

2d The Elder should begin first, after which all may take hold regularly.

3d When you take a piece of bread, take a whole piece (if not too large) and when you cut meat, cut it square & equal, fat & lean, & take an equal proportion of bones — take it on your plate together with the sauce, whether it be cabbage, herbs, potatoes or turnips; and not be cutting small pieces in the platter and putting directly into your mouth.

4th When you have tea or coffee, and any kind of minced victuals or meat cut into mouthfuls, it may be proper with a knife or fork to eat it directly from the platter . . .

8th Eat what you need before you rise from table, and not be picking & eating afterwards.

9th When you have done eating, clean your plate, knife & fork — lay your bones in a snug heap by the side of your plate — scrape up your crumbs — cross your knife & fork on your plate with the edge towards you.

10th When you reach a mug or pitcher to a person give the handle; and when you take hold of bread, biscuit, pies, etc. to cut or break, take hold of that part which you intend to eat yourself, and cut it square & equal — then you will not leave the print of your fingers for others to eat . . .

12th If you are obliged to sneeze or cough, don't bespatter the victuals, make use of your handkerchief.

13th Clean your knife on your bread before you cut butter, & after cutting butter before you put it into apple sauce, etc. but never clean it on the edge of the platter etc.

14th Scratching the head, picking the nose or ears, belching, snifing the nose, drinking with the mouth full of victuals, or picking the teeth, are accounted ill manners at a table & must be left off.

15th And lastly, when you drink, never extend your under lip so far down that one would think the cup was agoing to be swallowed whole. Always wipe your mouth before & after you drink your bear (beer) or water at the table.

Note — Children under the age of 12 or 14 years must have their pie cut for them & laid by their dishes — Also, when they have bread & butter, suitable pieces must be properly spread & laid by their dishes.

Another monitor, composed in 1830 for the visitors' dining room, reminded callers of Christ's injunction to 'gather up the fragments that remain, that nothing be lost':

> Here then is the pattern
> Which Jesus has set;
> And his good example
> We cannot forget:
> With thanks for his blessings
> His word we'll obey;
> But on this occasion
> We've somewhat to say.

> .   .   .

> What we deem good order,
> We're willing to state —
> Eat hearty and decent,
> And clear out our plate —
> Be thankful to Heaven
> For what we receive,
> And not make a mixture
> Or compound to leave.

> We find of those bounties
> Which heaven doth give,
> That some live to eat,
> And, that some eat to live —
> That some think of nothing
> But pleasing the taste
> And care very little
> How much they do waste . . .

The folk phrase, 'Shaker your plate,' derives from the scrupulous economy of Ann Lee and the traditions born of necessity in the early years of the order.

After the evening chores were done, at seven-thirty in summer and eight o'clock in winter, all repaired to their apartments for half an hour, known as 'retiring-time,' when, on the evenings devoted to family worship, the Shakers disposed themselves in ranks, sitting erect with hands folded 'to labor for a true sense of their privilege in the Zion of God.' If perchance one should drowse, it was the order to rise and bow four times, or shake, and then resume one's seat. At the end of the period, announced by the ringing of a small bell, brethren and sisters formed separate columns in the corridors, marched two abreast to the meeting-room, and, after bowing as they entered, formed ranks for worship.

Assemblies varied with the time and place. In the early years of the order, and often during revivals, 'labouring' meetings were held nightly, and sometimes during the day. As the society expanded, however, evenings not devoted to union meetings or the regular religious service were given over to the practice of songs and exercises. Thus, at New Lebanon in the 'seventies, singing meetings were held on Tuesday and Friday, union meetings on Sunday and Wednesday, and 'labouring' meetings on Thursday and Saturday. On Mondays, during this more liberal period, there was a general assembly in the dining hall, where the elder read letters from other communities, selections from the news of the week, or some appropriate book. At the conclusion of such gatherings, to which strangers were admitted on occasion, the family retired quietly to rest. The occupants of each room, after kneeling again in silent prayer, went to bed at a uniform hour — nine o'clock in winter and ten in summer.

Anyone watching such temperate people in the intervals between work and worship would have been impressed, above all else, by the tranquillity of their movements and behavior, as though the daily round was itself a service. No sign of tension or aggressiveness was apparent; speech was subdued; doors were opened and closed with care; all 'walked softly.' The dwelling, whose orderly, neatly furnished rooms were seldom occupied during the day, was also, in a true sense, a sanctuary. Many a visitor, like Hester Pool, was sensitive to that 'indescribable air of purity' which pervaded everything, feeling with her 'that this purity is a portion of the mental and moral as well

251 as the physical atmosphere of the Shakerian home.' Though all comings and goings followed the pattern of plainness, in the simplicity of domestic life there was an element of freedom, grace, and the contentment, or perhaps resignation, of those who had made peace with themselves and with the world.

GIRLS' CLOTHES ROOM, CHURCH FAMILY, NISKEYUNA

The Children's Order was also carefully regulated. Boys and girls lived apart from each other and the rest of the family under 'caretakers' responsible to the elders or eldresses. In the indenture agreements the trustees bound the society to provide them with 'comfortable food and clothing,' the common branches of learning, and training in such manual occupation or branch of business as shall be found best adapted to the minor's 'genius and capacity.' In return, the parent or guardian relinquished all rights over the child's upbringing. At maturity the youth was free to leave or remain.

In education emphasis was placed on character building and the useful arts. Though the early Believers, 'being chiefly of the laboring classes and generally in low circumstances of life,' were not in a condition to pay much attention to letter learning, Mother Ann strongly recommended religious and 'literary' studies. Meacham advocated the kind of learning that would lead to order, union, peace, and good work — 'works that are truly virtuous and useful to man, in this life.' The idea that instruction should concentrate on develop-   *252* ing good habits and useful talents was subsequently expanded by Seth Wells, the superintendent of the Shaker schools. Self-government, Wells believed, was the prerequisite of both moral and literary education. 'When a man is able to govern himself, and subdue his evil propensities . . . he is then in a fair way to be benefitted by moral and religious instructions.' Also, 'to give children literary instructions, without governing, and teaching them to govern the natural propensities and dispositions of their minds, and without instructing them in the principles of moral virtue, would be a ready way to lead them to ruin.' Knowledge 'sharpened' talents, making them danger-ous to society unless they had first been properly directed.   *253*

Individual aptitudes were recognized, within limits, in the Shaker system. All children were taught to read and write, while 'those who possessed the best capacities and the brightest natural talents,' Wells claimed, 'generally received a proportionate degree of literary in-struction.' Higher education, however, especially what was termed 'classical learning,' was on the whole judged purposeless, 'mere lum-ber of the brain.' The society did not wish to make great scholars of its children but rather to turn their 'rising faculties' — the 'great dis-play of sprightliness and activity' which youth always possessed — into the proper channel of usefulness for their own benefit and the benefit of their brethren and sisters.

We have seen how the principles of usefulness and self-sufficiency were converted into exact disciplines. The same care was taken to in-culcate, in children as in adults, a concern for the well-being of others. The *Juvenile Monitor*, printed at New Lebanon in 1823, described ill manners and gave detailed rules for behavior toward 'superiors, equals and inferiors,' behavior in company and toward strangers, behavior at table, and so on. By precept and example communal ethics were impressed on the young: honesty, punctuality, and up-rightness; a clear conscience, neatness, cleanliness, and industry; pru-dence, temperance, and good economy; 'the law of kindness, love and charity'; civility, decency, and good order. All were taught 'to shun contention and strife . . .   to promote the happiness of each other

. . . and to bless one another as the best means of securing the blessing of God.'

Special attention was paid to the young during the period of the
'manifestations.' One message, given by inspiration at New Lebanon
on 5 January 1842, and printed at Canterbury under the title of *The
Youth's Guide in Zion,* contains many homilies for use in spiritual instruction. For example:

Gold is valuable, when well refined at the mine; and much is thought
thereof. Souls are valuable, bright and glorious, when well refined and
tried in time.

Many words are not profitable, for leanness cometh thereby, and the
spirit is made faint.

Tribulation is sweet to the seeker after righteousness. It is the staff of
humility, and a hand-rail to honesty.

Sincerity of soul in the work of redemption is worth mountains of gold.
The offerings of the sincere are sweet smelling favors to the Father of
Heaven.

Praise thyself by good works only.

Prudence provides stores for charity to give to the poor; clothes to cover
them, and food to sustain them.

Contentment is a sign of resignation to the cross, with which all faithful
souls are marked. Let contentment dwell within thy breast. Be subject
thereunto; for it is a lovely guest.

Thou sowest thy grain, but reapest it not, nor enjoyest the increase
thereof, until the stalk is dead; the kernel still liveth. Thy body is a
stalk which dieth; but the spirit liveth.

If a tree leaneth over the water the fruit will drop therein. Bend thy
spirit heavenward, that thy fruit may fall therein, and be for thy comfort hereafter.

Love meekness, for this is a strong virtue. Pride will make no tarry with
meekness: but flee away to the high minded zeal. Zion's children are
called to speak with a new tongue. Simplicity is in the voice, and in wisdom it giveth form to its words.

Education was largely neglected until 1808, soon after the 'second
gathering,' when provision was made at New Lebanon for intermittent
instruction in spelling, the correct use of language, and the proper
manner of address, in which the Biblical 'yea' and 'nay' were retained.
In the winter of 1813–14, evening schools, soon to be followed by afternoon classes, were established. Spelling, reading, writing, and arithmetic were taught at these first regular sessions, with 'good manners'

added in 1816. The following year a 'public school,' applying the then popular Lancasterian or monitor mode of teaching, was established at the Church Order, with geography, grammar, and 'miscellaneous' subjects included in the curriculum. This was a day school, open for boys for four months in the winter, November to March, and to girls for a similar period in the spring and summer. Social meetings for the cultivation of Scriptural knowledge, tried out in 1830, were discontinued when it was found they tended to 'unprofitable discussion' and 'display' rather than to real usefulness. Family schools displaced the public school in 1835; but four years later a schoolhouse was built to serve the whole community.

Improved methods and textbooks reflected the willingness to learn from the world. When, in 1821, Seth Y. Wells, formerly an instructor in the public schools of Albany and at Hudson (N.Y.) Academy, was appointed superintendent of the Believers' schools in the first bishopric, he introduced music into the curriculum and proposed that all Shaker schools be freely opened to the inspection of strangers. Limited instruction in algebra, astronomy, and agricultural chemistry was provided about 1840 — though practical training in farming and trades, under caretakers and the quasi-guild system previously explained, continued to form the basis of educational experience. The Believers selected their best qualified members as teachers; and with the emphasis on character training and the practical arts, the Shaker schools developed a deserved repute. They were visited regularly by inspectors from their respective school districts, received their share of the public money, and were often attended by the world's children. In the educational field at least, the barriers against the 'generative plane' were lowered.

Nor was innocent recreation considered superfluous. The girls at Canterbury had gymnastic exercises and a flower garden; the boys played ball and marbles, went fishing, and had a small farm of their own. Picnics, sleigh rides, and nutting and berrying parties lent diversion to the ordinary routine. Elkins' frank account of his boyhood at Enfield is the record of a not uncolorful life, with interesting companions, mild paternal control, and normal healthful experiences in a beautiful countryside. Elder Briggs recalls that wood-chopping and maple-sugaring were gala times, like picnics, and mentions the diversions of fishing, swimming, and playing ball, the half-holidays once a

SCHOOLROOM, NISKEYUNA COMMUNITY

week during warm weather, the refreshments during haying, which consisted of sweet buttermilk; lemon, peppermint, checkerberry, raspberry, and currant shrub; cake, cheese, and smoked herring. One who had been a young Shakeress at Niskeyuna remembers many happy days in the Children's Order there:

Hiding beneath an arcade of the bridge which spanned the dear old creek, we would pull off shoes and stockings, and wade knee-deep in the cool, bright water. Then, loading our long palm-leaf Shaker bonnets with dandelions, which, grown to seed, looked like little white-capped Shakeresses, we would float them down the stream in a race, the boat which won being decorated with buttercups and violets. What mud-pies we made and baked in the sun! What fun we had secreting golden kernels of corn in clam-shells, and peeping from our hiding-place to see the chickens find them and peck them up, firmly believing that they 'gave thanks' when they turned their bills up to heaven after sipping water . . . We had no world's toys, but were just as contented with our corn-cob dolls, clam-shell plates, acorn-top cups, and chicken-coops for baby houses.

255

From sources such as the above we suspect that Shaker life was not always as austere as its principles would have had it be; that the Believers, in their effort to extinguish natural affections, tried to do the impossible — particularly where children were concerned. We read of candy-making parties, culinary favors tendered by the 'kitchen-sisters,' humorous tolerance when children behaved 'contrary to order,' the attachments for favorite children, close friendships within the Children's Order. Human nature was constantly breaking up the artificial restrictions designed to subdue 'carnal desire.' It seems that the lot of Shaker youth compared favorably with that of the sons and daughters of farmers in the rural America of the period.

What appeared to be a reasonably liberal practice was subjected, nevertheless, to acute criticism. The Shakers were charged with neglecting education, prohibiting secular reading, denying 'the right of private judgment,' and upholding the virtues, in school and out, of 'implicit faith and passive obedience.' At Niskeyuna, where the children had 'the same air of resignation and freedom from excitement which characterizes their elders,' Charles Dudley Warner found 'no evidence of superior intellectual and moral and spiritual growth in consequence of the pietism which bids us to forget the body.' The community exemplified, he felt, the faith concept or medieval type of Christianity.

Problems of indoctrination were greater when children left their own order, the girls at fourteen and the boys at sixteen, to take their places as responsible members of the society. Adolescence was a period when Shaker youth often grew resentful of authority and impatient under the many orders restricting freedom. For the more intelligent individuals, the conflict between faith and reason sometimes became acute. A case in point was Thomas Brown of Niskeyuna, who openly questioned the infallibility of the ministry and was thereupon called before the elders:

Elder John: Thomas, you are deceived by your own wisdom, self-will and evil nature. The day will come when creatures will not dare to stand against the gift of God as you do.

Brown: Elder John, it is you who have deceived me. When I first came to Niskeyuna, I heard nothing of a ministration doctrine, or obedience as the only way of salvation . . . The word of God, you told me, was in my own heart, not in what the elders said. Your gospel seems like a tunnel: the farther I travel in, the narrower it grows.

Elder John: We bear the same testimony as at first. We still tell you not to violate your conscience; but we never told you that a person who had only a measure of the true spirit would finally be redeemed, sanctified, or saved from all sin.

Brown: But you told me in the beginning that I would always have the privilege of opening my mind. The gospel, you said, don't bind creatures, but gives liberty to act our faith, feelings and mind in matters that are not sinful. Now it is not my faith, but your faith; not as I feel, but as you feel for me.

Elder John: A learned man, it is true, is worth a thousand ignorant persons; and that is one cause why we have labored so much with you. But the difficulty that attends human learning is, that it hinders people from receiving faith.

256

An obviously important function of education was to keep Shaker youth 'close up' and 'in the gift.' If any one 'broke union,' as Brown did, by an act of disobedience, he was called to confess and make atonement for the fault. Moral suasion — prayer, supplication, and 'keen admonition' — was the usual expedient. Stringent orders prohibited corporal punishment, Elkins recalled, 'except the use of small twigs applied to extremely contumacious children a dozen years of age.' Moral force, however, could in itself be severe. To prevent children from returning to the world, the lead labored earnestly to extol the advantages of Shakerism, its comforts, security, and rewards. But sometimes, especially under the extreme ardors of a revival, fear was the weapon employed. In 1840, for example, a message from Mother Lucy informed the children that 'if you ever get tired of being reproved and instructed by your Elders, and turn to the world for rest, you will have to go to hell, never to be redeemed; for the privilege which you now have is great, and will prove a savor of life unto life, or of death unto death.' Another communication for the protection of youth forbade caretakers from admonishing their charges thus:

If you are not obedient, you shall go to the world, where you can have your own ways, and do as you have a mind to, live in sin, and dress in the gaities of babylon, to the sad ruination of the soul. —

lest such expressions cause the young to gaze upon pleasure with longing eyes.

Fear of what would happen if they seceded, Macdonald thought, was one of the binding forces holding the community together. When anyone left, or a couple eloped, they did it secretly, dreading the disapproval of their associates. To the faithful, such departures were tragedies. In the Shaker mind the world was a 'beggarly element,' the road to disaster and damnation. The departure was recorded in the journals in terms of pity and horror — and sometimes in code. When the apostasy was announced in family meeting, a dolorous knell was sometimes chanted, one verse of which was as follows:

> I'll sense the awful situation
> Of the souls that turn away;
> They lose all hopes of their salvation,
> For them Believers cannot pray.

That the interests of growth, if not survival itself, demanded firm and wise control, was recognized by the leaders. Officially, however, the defense of authoritarianism was on other grounds. Subscribing to government by revelation, and eventually to the tenet that only the Deity was absolutely perfect, they held that, in spiritual matters at least, the less perfect should submit to the more perfect, the less capable to the more capable. The ministry had been chosen, in a pure line of apostolic succession from Ann Lee, on the standard of spirituality. The members were heirs to a tradition of deference to ecclesiastical rules. It was not strange, therefore, that the government of the Believers resembled, in many respects, the oligarchic Puritan state.

In the attempt to clarify the society's position, we have suggested that such principles of order did not completely outlaw democratic procedures. The Shakers lauded the republicanism of the American government but felt that, being man-made, it was supported too much — 'particularly at electioneering times' — by pride and contention. Believing in the separation of church and state and in the bill of rights, they nevertheless favored introducing into political action a 'sense of the spirit of Christ'; for without religion and the fear of God, they argued, neither wisdom, freedom, or liberty could save a nation. In regard to their own institution, union worked from the top down, as well as from the bottom up, all being responsible for the common welfare. Nor did the limitations on freedom imposed by the communal conscience necessarily restrict individualism. For as Elder Eads of South Union put it, individuality, 'though cemented in the body, was left intact as well *in* obedience as *out* of it, as well in employing one's faculties, judgment, reason, art, ingenuity and skill . . . in doing what some one lays out for them as in doing what they

257 lay out for themselves.' Moreover, in external matters — scientific, mechanical, even intellectual — 'the ministry may not be qualified to lead.' It will be recalled that temporal responsibilities were delegated to those thought best qualified to assume them, and that initiative, if used for communal ends, was deliberately encouraged.

In conclusion, we may say that the educational system was proficient, perhaps above the average for its time and place, in moral training and such sciences as were immediately applicable, but deficient in its neglect of 'useless' cultural studies. The school prepared the pupil for life — the Shaker life. That it could do little to counteract the growing tendency toward disunion is evidenced by the small proportion of young people, about one in ten, who resisted the call to the world after the Civil War. As the society grew in experience, it became increasingly cautious in its policy of adoption, seldom accepting children without their parents or careful investigation of parental background. At New Lebanon, the point was reached, soon after the Civil War, where almost all applications were declined. Here, as in other communities, preference had come to be given to young men and women in their early twenties, at which period, it was felt, their best energies were available and they had had 'enough of the world to satisfy their curiosity and make them restful.' Only at South Union did Nordhoff find the fondness for children so strong that the society 'would rather have bad ones than none.'

The belief in progress, or 'travel,' found expression in the field of medicine as in education. Ann Lee's bias against physicians was shared by Joseph Meacham, who assured a doubter that 'they that have my spirit have no occasion to go to world's doctors.' In the early 258 years Shakers were healed by faith or the laying on of hands. The 'gift' against professionals was still held in 1813, when Mother Lucy's attitude to that effect was recorded; but Father Job Bishop, speaking 'beautifully' on the same subject, qualified his stand by asserting that a surgeon might be called 'in case of a broken bone or any very bad wound.' About this time greater reliance was placed on regimen and simple medicines, with resort to shocking, bleeding, sweating, poulticing, and blistering. With the development of the herb industry in the 1820's, the Thomsonian medical practice, which relied on steam baths and herbal remedies and required little academic knowledge, came into increasing favor. Another step was taken in 1840, when messages prohibiting the use of strong drink, swine's flesh, and tobacco ushered in a reform which was more than temporary. In mid-century, largely through the influence of Elder Frederick Evans of New Lebanon, Grahamism and vegetarianism won converts in certain families. Proper diet, supplemented by the water treatment, simple massage, and hot herbal drinks in case of sickness, was the prevalent prescription late in the century. Faith in the 'healing gift,' however, persisted all this time, with many a cure allegedly effected by spirit touch and mental control.

As interpreted by Elder Evans, the science of health had a theological basis. To provide better food, clothing, and housing, a better distribution of heat, improved lighting, ventilation, and sanitation was the proper field of science. In the 'new earth' the human body should be 'the central object of influence and attraction,' whose 'salvation' was no less important than the 'health' of the soul. Evans suggested eight main principles of dietetics:

1. Supply the family with at least one kind of course grain flour. Avoid cathartics.
2. Have the 'sickly and weakly' cease using animal food, especially fats.
3. Keep the skin clean by regular bathing, with the water at such a temperature as to cause a warm, glowing reaction.
4. Keep room at a temperature not exceeding 60°.
5. Clothing — 'regulated on the same principles as water and fire' — should be light, 'a little less than you could possibly bear.' The young should dispense with underclothes. 'Sleep under as little clothing as possible.'
6. Breathe pure air. Every room of the home should be of equal temperature. Ventilation of bedrooms important.
7. Thorough ventilation of beds and bedding.
8. 'Be comfortable in mind and body.'   *259*

While these views were the opinion of one person, a natural reformer, they were not unrepresentative of Shaker practice. The vent pipes over the lamps, the slots placed between the two sashes of every window, and the holes in the baseboards in the halls and under the radiators in the gathering rooms were additional evidences of a concern for fresh air. Baths, sinks, and water closets were well ventilated. Pure spring water was ingeniously piped for refrigeration. Temperate outdoor labor, regular hours, wholesome food, good clothing, comfort of mind, and the utmost cleanliness everywhere combined to promote the health of all. On the latter characteristic in particular, often contrasting favorably with conditions elsewhere, strangers were wont to remark from the earliest times. 'Great importance is attached to cleanliness,' Blackwood's correspondent reported in 1823; 'this

260 luxury they appear to enjoy in a truly enviable degree.' 'Visit them upon any day in the week,' the historian of the town of Shirley wrote, 'at any hour of the day, and when they are engaged in almost any employment, and you will scarcely ever find them in dirty dishabille. The shirts and pants and frocks of the men are rarely soiled, and the

261 plain linen caps and kerchiefs of the women never.' 'Everything is . . . kept so delicately clean,' remarked an English visitor in 1884, 'that an air of refinement, not to say luxury, seems to pervade [the]

262 bedchambers, in spite of their absolute simplicity.'

Testimonies on the health of the Shakers are nevertheless conflicting. The contrast in the effect of worship on the two sexes has been mentioned. With allowances made for prejudice, it is a matter of wonder, from the phrases used about the sisters, whether they were in health or out. They were called 'a wretched-looking lot of creatures' (Fountain); 'their pale faces . . . and flabby condition indicated . . . a low state of health' (George Combe); 'the females and sedentary people . . . were occasionally indisposed' (*Blackwood's* correspondent); 'the females . . . look remarkably pale and sallow (Silliman); the women were 'pallid, thin and withered' (Martineau); the sisters, with few exceptions, were 'old, wizened, ascetic — perfect specimens of old maids' (Colonel A. M. Maxwell). The difference in the physical appearance of males and females was due, according to one mid-century author, to the 'unaspiring, earthly' quality of the former, and the effect on such natures of a comfortable life, outdoor work, plenty of food, and an absence of anxieties. 'The Shaker woman, by contrast, has a more melancholy lot. Love — "the first necessity of woman's nature" — is dwarfed, in her case, to most un-

263 natural ugliness. She must renounce the natural affections.' On the other hand, Finch was struck with 'the cheerfulness and contented looks' of the people in all the communities; Dixon remarked on 'the rosy flesh' of the people of New Lebanon — 'a tint but rarely seen in the United States'; and the usually reliable Nordhoff spoke of the fresh fine complexion [which] most of the Shaker men and women

264 have — particularly the latter.'

If the Shaker way of life was detrimental in any way to physical

well-being, certainly life was not shortened. The longevity of members of the sect has often been reported. In 1875 Nordhoff, making the first fact-finding tour of the communities, was impressed by the low rate of mortality: at Harvard, where the average age at death for a number of years was 60 to 68; at Union Village, where a large proportion of the members were over 70, and many over 90; at North Union, where many were past 80; at Pleasant Hill, where a considerable number lived past 90; and at Enfield (N.H.), Watervliet (N.Y.), and South Union, where the brethren and sisters often lived well over 75 years.

To support an argument on the 'Longevity of Virgin Celibates,' Elder Giles Avery advanced facts [selected?] that in five families at New Lebanon, during the period 1848–50, the average age of 29 members at death was 70½ years; at Alfred, during an unspecified period, the average age of 200 members at death was 62¾ years (with 100 over 70, 37 between 80 and 90, and 13 between 90 and 97); at Watervliet (N.Y.), in the decade 1870–80, the average age of 39 members at death was 73 years; and at New Gloucester there were 'at the present time' (c. 1880) 14 persons over 70 years of age, of whom seven were between 79 and 89 years old. Elder Evans estimated that life expectancy among the Believers was over a decade more than that of the world.

265

The vital statistics of two communities in the east, Harvard and Enfield (N.H.), available for over a century, afford more reliable data, showing a relatively high and constantly advancing average age at death. See tables on p. 198.

Granting some validity to these figures and therefore to the existence of a supranormal life-span, we are curious to know the cause. The Believers gave most of the credit to the condition of sexual purity — for life, they claimed, was vastly shortened by the 'abnormal development of the passional nature.' Many factors may have contributed: regular routine, wholesome diet, the care given the aged, a scientific domestic economy, freedom from worry. There was security, physical as well as spiritual, in the Shaker life.

When death occurred, complete simplicity marked the funeral. The coffin was pine, plainly lined, unpainted and unadorned. In the mind of the Believer, the life of the spirit was so real that death was but a way-mark in 'travel,' and the 'trappings of grief' superfluous. Following the Quaker custom, the Shakers, led by the elders and

TABLE I

AVERAGE AGE AT DEATH BY DECADES

Harvard (from 3 Nov. 1784 to 10 July 1889)			Enfield (from 21 July 1793 to May 1895)		
	No. of Deaths	Average Age		No. of Deaths	Average Age
1784–1790	9	42.3	1793–1800	7	34.7
1791–1800	15	51.1	1801–1810	11	33.9
1801–1810	14	60.6	1811–1820	21	52.8
1811–1820	41	55.5	1821–1830	38	50.7
1821–1830	33	59.3	1831–1840	39	50.7
1831–1840	34	58.8	1841–1850	51	56.9
1841–1850	31	61.1	1851–1860	41	54.9
1851–1860	44	55.0	1861–1870	31	60.0
1861–1870	30	66.4	1871–1880	13	60.9
1871–1880	32	67.4	1881–1890	18	66.9
1881–1889	18	71.3	1891–1895	5	82.0

TABLE II

AVERAGE AGE AT DEATH FOR DECREASING PERIODS, EACH PERIOD ENDING
WITH THE SAME FINAL DATE

Harvard (from 3 Nov. 1784 to 10 July 1889)			Enfield (from 21 July 1793 to May 1895)		
	No. of Deaths	Average Age		No. of Deaths	Average Age
1784–1889	301	59.73	1793–1895	275	54.8
1791–1889	292	60.2	1801–1895	268	55.3
1801–1889	277	60.8	1811–1895	257	57.7
1811–1889	263	60.8			
1821–1889	222	61.7	1821–1895	236	56.5
1831–1889	189	62.1	1831–1895	198	57.7
1841–1889	155	62.9	1841–1895	159	59.3
1851–1889	124	63.3	1851–1895	108	60.5
1861–1889	80	67.9	1861–1895	67	63.9
1871–1889	50	68.8	1871–1895	36	66.8
1881–1889	18	71.3	1881–1895	23	70.1
			1891–1895	5	82.0

eldresses of the family, devoted the main part of the service to personal tributes and memories. Songs were sung, and during one period of Shaker history, messages from the spirit were communicated by the instruments. The procession to the grave was not unlike the heavenly march of worship. Throughout the ritual the tone was one of reverence, strength, and inspiration.

Since followers of Mother Ann did not believe in physical resurrection, they thought of the living soul and not of the dead body. 'He is not here,' they testified at the burial service. Appropriate, therefore, were the simple slabs of stone, all alike and engraved only with initials, age, and date, which marked the resting place. Many advocated that even these be replaced by a mound of earth, or perhaps a shrub or tree, not as a memorial but rather as a contribution to earth's fertility and beauty.

Comparison of the living conditions of the early Shaker colonists with those prevailing a century or so later furnishes an index to the temporal progress of the society. In 1780 its possessions were limited to a few unpromising acres, a single cabin, the slim resources of John Hocknell. Eight years later the Believers at Niskeyuna were still poor. Money was scarce, and the community was not allowed to run into debt. According to the account of Jonathan Clark of Hancock:

Our principle food was rice and milk, sometimes we went to the river to procure fish. . . We had little, and sometimes no bread, butter or cheese, but upon this simple fare, we all subsisted during the Spring and Summer . . . All our work was very laborious, and at the end, we looked more like skeletons, than working men . . . Our breakfast consisted of a small bowl of porridge. Supper the same. Dinner, a small bit of cake about 2½ inches square which Aaron Wood cut up, and gave to us. One day Joseph Preston and another brother went to the River to catch Herring; and Joseph stated that he was so hungry, that he ate two *raw*, as soon as they came out of the water . . . We had but little house room, and of course were obliged to lie upon the floor . . . Fifteen of us lay upon the floor in one room; some had one blanket to cover them, while others had none . . . [266]

When Rebecca Clark came to live at Hancock in 1791, fourteen slept in one room. She wrote:

When we arose some packed the beds one on another; some swept the room; others got water to wash in. After our morning meeting we went to our several employments, some to getting breakfast for the brethren, as they ate first. Our buildings were small, and we had to eat and live accordingly . . . We had but few feather beds, our beds were mostly of straw; and we made them on the floor. Many of us slept three on one bed; and when we washed our bedding we had to dry it the same day, and put it on at night . . . For breakfast and supper we lived mostly upon bean porridge and water porridge. Monday morning we had a little weak tea, and once in a week a small piece of cheese. Wheat bread was very scarce; and when we had butter it was spread on our [rye and Indian meal] bread before we came to the table. Our dinners were generally boiled. Once in a while we had a little milk, but this was a great rarity . . . [267]

For a time the diet at New Lebanon consisted wholly of broth and bread. Bread was 'allowanced' for three years, a small piece by each

one's dish, with a piece of pie on special occasions. After a while potatoes and bean porridge became the staple food, and a typical breakfast consisted of bread, sometimes with a little butter, fried potatoes,
fried gammon, and sage, celandine, or root tea. For coffee the root of
water avens was used, or burnt rye or barley. When pork, beef, mutton, eggs, turnip, and cabbage appeared about 1800, they were considered luxuries.

The 'manner of dress and building' was in the same inferior state.
'Those who first believed, in America,' Youngs wrote, 'adopted such
dress as seemed the most suitable, of the common plain forms that prevailed among people at the time they lived in England'; and the
form, fashion, and quality of garments were 'extremely various.' In
form and manner of construction, buildings also were of poor quality
268 and ill-adapted to the purpose for which they were needed.

SISTERS' EVERYDAY COSTUME

In all departments, however, the Shakers, by the will to make
everything uniform with the best, steadily raised their standard of

living. During the nineteenth century the preparation of wholesome food was considered more and more important, and as a result the Shakers achieved a considerable reputation for their recipes and public meals. As for clothing, painstaking care came to be paid to the needs of age groups and occasions, to uniformity of color and material, to the marking and laundering of garments. Buildings, too, were constantly improved and their numbers increased to meet the expanding needs of the colony. In New Lebanon, for instance, from the few small farmhouses which the Shakers took over in the 1780's, the community grew until it had 125 buildings in 1839, and property, including 2,292 acres of land, valued at $68,225. Within the same period the original colony at Watervliet had grown to a community of over 2,500 acres, valued, with buildings, at $46,900. When Nordhoff made his survey in 1875, the home farms of the eighteen societies, taken by themselves, amounted to nearly 50,000 acres, to which figure must be added extensive outside holdings in mills, wood lots, and 'outfarms' — one in Kentucky, owned by the Watervliet (N.Y.) society, as large as 30,000 acres — which were often operated by tenants.

Following the eight immigrants from England some seventeen thousand persons, at one time or another, were gathered into the society. To the Shakers this was a 'great harvest' — the 'blessed binders' had followed closely on the reapers, 'severing all the worthless cockle till the work was done complete.'

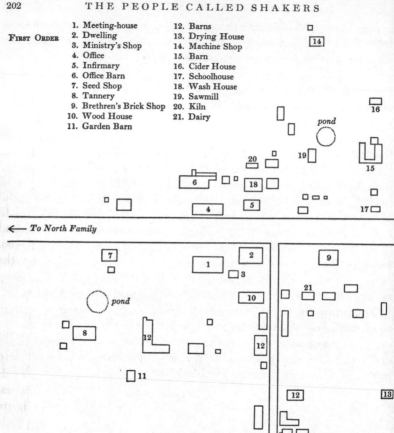

FIRST ORDER

1. Meeting-house
2. Dwelling
3. Ministry's Shop
4. Office
5. Infirmary
6. Office Barn
7. Seed Shop
8. Tannery
9. Brethren's Brick Shop
10. Wood House
11. Garden Barn
12. Barns
13. Drying House
14. Machine Shop
15. Barn
16. Cider House
17. Schoolhouse
18. Wash House
19. Sawmill
20. Kiln
21. Dairy

⟵ *To North Family*

The accompanying diagram, from Isaac Youngs's manuscript history, charts one of the larger Shaker families, that of the New Lebanon Church. It is informative because it shows the general plan, as well as the diversified purposes, of building. Youngs did not identify each structure but wrote a summary of buildings which provides a commentary on yearly 'increase' and 'improvements.'

The 'first class' of buildings, he noted, belonged to the period before 1805. In 1790 the community had a gambrel-roofed meeting-house (later converted into a seed shop — No. 7) ; its first 'great house' or unitary dwelling (No. 2) ; a small brick shop and a fulling mill; a 'tan house,' hatters' shop, blacksmith shop, two 'spin-shops,' a 'bake-shop'

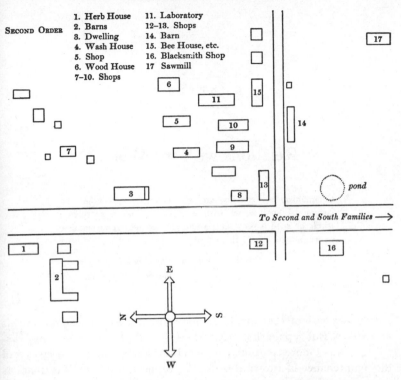

SECOND ORDER

1. Herb House   11. Laboratory
2. Barns   12–13. Shops
3. Dwelling   14. Barn
4. Wash House   15. Bee House, etc.
5. Shop   16. Blacksmith Shop
6. Wood House   17 Sawmill
7–10. Shops

pond

To Second and South Families →

E

N ⟵ ⟶ S

W

CHURCH FAMILY, NEW LEBANON SHAKERS, 1856

and a 'cook-shop.' In the next five years another dwelling, called the
'East house,' was erected; also a home for the aged people, a youth's
house, a small building and store for the trustees, a 'wash house,' a coal
house, another blacksmith's shop, another 'spin-shop.' Construction in
the period between 1796 and 1805 included a saw mill, a trip-hammer
works (No. 16, Second Order), a cider mill, and a water-powered 'wash-
mill' and grindstone, besides barns and additions to houses. At this time
the Shakers were active in laying out stone paths and walls, building
stone bridges and dams, and laying wooden aqueducts to carry water
into their kitchens.

———•◆•———

CHAPTER X

Relations with the World

Communism is a mutiny against society. Only, whether the
communist shall rebel with a bludgeon and a petroleum
torch, or with a plow and a church, depends upon whether
he has not or has faith in God.

— Charles Nordhoff: *The Communistic Societies*
of the United States, 1875

'YE ARE NOT of the world,' Dunlavy reminded the Shakers in his
Manifesto. But separation from 'the fashions of the world,' they discovered, was a more complex problem than separation of the sexes and
the maintenance of internal order. In repudiating such 'fashions' as
marriage and private property, politics and the bearing of arms, they
exposed themselves to attack, and therefore to contact with the world.
To spread their faith, they chose to keep their meeting-houses open to
the public. In education, they found it expedient to form ties with
neighboring townships. The uses of charity bade them welcome any
who came for food, clothes, or lodging. Indeed, they aspired always
'to use this world, as not abusing it.'

Property was the crux of the problem. In this regard the position
of the order was an anomalous one — for though it engaged in industry and trade, and owned and increased its personal property and
real estate, its property was dedicated to religious purposes. And
though its covenant gave each member 'one joint interest,' this interest was not equivalent to ownership, like the possession of one share
of stock; it merely entitled the holders to 'Just and Equal rights and
Privileges, according to their needs, in the use of all things in the
Church.' It was a religious, not a property right. Legally, therefore,

the total property could be considered neither a joint tenancy or a tenancy in common, but rather 'a consecrated whole.' Though the *273* property was dedicated to sacred or charitable uses, the Shakers never petitioned for exemption from taxation. The problem centered in the conflicting rights of the order and seceders from the order to properties that had been consecrated to the cause.

A number of court cases — among the earliest in America in which the laws of contract and the First Amendment were invoked — clarified the issue. The first test of the validity of the covenant was an action of assumpsit, for work, labor, and services, brought by Benjamin Goodrich against Jonathan Walker, deacon of the New Lebanon Church Order, in January 1799. Heard before the Supreme Court of *274* Judicature of New York State, meeting in Albany, the case revolved on the question whether duress had been employed by the society to get Goodrich to sign a discharge. The overseers of the church, David Meacham and David Osborne, had paid him, according to Shaker custom, discharge money, in this case forty pounds, whereupon the plaintiff, who had been a member about eight years, had signed papers releasing the trustees and community from any further charges. Witnesses testified that Goodrich had proclaimed himself satisfied, at the time, with the settlement and, since no sound evidence of intimidation was produced, the jury found for the defendant. Though the covenant thus successfully withstood the test of a court case, we have seen it was later revised into a stronger instrument.

Subsequent decisions recognized the fact that the covenant was a binding contract. Thus, in the case of John Heath, an apostate, *v.* Nathaniel Draper, deacon of the Enfield (N.H.) community, in 1810, Chief Justice Livermore of the Superior Court summed up the proceedings in favor of the Shakers, and the jury found accordingly, on the following grounds: that no coercion or misrepresentation was used when the plaintiff, on reaching his majority, signed the covenant; that there was no stated or implied promise to pay wages; that the money given to the society represented a 'complete and effectual' gift which could not be retracted; and that 'labor gratuitously performed gives no cause for action.' Since it was a matter of belief with the society that each member should freely give of his time and talents, for the mutual good, the suit was a breach of faith as well as of contract. Finally, as for the suggestion that the dedication of property and labor was to 'superstitious uses,' and therefore not binding, the court remarked: 'No one can see the improvements made in husbandry and manufactures by this sect, and at the same time believe the existence of the sect to be against the policy of the law. Whatever we may think of their faith, their works are good, and charity bids us think well of the tree when the fruits are salutary. We cannot try the question which religion, theirs or ours, is the better one . . . Theirs is equally under the protection of the law, as ours . . . There certainly are some reasons for saying that the religion of this sect of Christians bears a greater resemblance to that of the primitive church than ours does . . .'

275

When relatives of Malcolm Worley contested his grant of property to Union Village on the grounds that the donor was insane, the celebrated lawyer, Tom Corwin, appearing for the Shakers, is said to have remonstrated that 'George Fox wore leather breeches and did many eccentric things; Martin Luther threw his inkstand at the devil; but the Quakers will not admit that George Fox was crazy, and Protestants will not admit that Martin Luther was crazy; neither can it be allowed that Malcolm Worley was crazy, because by a deed drawn by himself he chose to give his property to this peculiar people!'

The most explicit decision rendered on the issue was that of the Court of Appeals in Kentucky, in May 1834. About twenty years earlier that 'war-like state' had taken a liberal position on the question of whether the Shakers should bear arms or render an equivalent service to the state, declaring such requirements unconstitutional; but in 1828, under the influence of 'reactionary' elements, the Legislature had passed a 'prejudicial' act making it lawful to prosecute suits against the Shaker communities without designating individuals, or serving processes otherwise than by attaching a subpoena on the door of their meeting-house. Six years later, however, in the case of Gass and Banta v. Wilhite et al., Judge Nicholas delivered an opinion that renewed the standing of the covenant. As seceders from the Pleasant Hill society, Gass and Banta were seeking a division of the property belonging to the community and 'having their shares allotted to them, either upon the principle of equality as two of its covenant members, or according to the amount of property each carried with him into the society.' It was the court's opinion, however, that the covenant precluded any claim to a division: that, according to its article three, the property brought in became the property of the whole society — as a *society*, and not as 'a community of goods among individuals . . . with a several right of use conferred on each member as a member, and by consequence only whilst or so long as he remained a member'; that the covenant conveyed explicitly the idea 'of an absolute divestiture of all individual interest in the property, otherwise than as members of the society'; and that it was expressly agreed, in that instrument, that no demand should ever be made against the church for services rendered or property consecrated. To the objection that members were 'constrained to a continuance in this particular faith for fear of a forfeiture of their interest in the joint property,' Judge Nicholas declared that the donation was one thing, the becoming a member another: 'property may be donated without becoming a member, and membership may be acquired without donation of property.' Acts of mortmain, he reminded the court, were confined exclusively to corporations. Nor could 'the use created by the trust for this society' be deemed a 'superstitious' one: 'we have no established religion . . . by our constitution, all religions are viewed as equally orthodox. . . It is neither for the legislature nor the judiciary in this state, to discriminate and say, what is a pious and what a superstitious use.' The final decision was to declare the purposes of the trust under which the Shaker property was held legitimate and valid.   276

None of the suits instigated by apostates for property or services proved successful. But complications arose from two other sources: first, the custom of receiving children into the society accompanied by one parent, usually the father, who had 'deserted' the other, and secondly, the refusal of the Shakers to bear arms. The charges of abandonment and secretion were particularly troublesome, for though it was against Shaker statutes knowingly to aid any man or woman in deserting wife or husband, or to receive children against the will of either parent, cases did occur when children were brought in under fraudulent conditions. The investigations that followed furnished pungent and uncomplimentary material for the newspapers, as well as for several books 'unmasking' Shakerism.

Ohio was the first state to indict the society on the desertion count. On 11 January 1811, in a law aimed directly at the sect, the legislature empowered the courts to issue a summons against husbands who had 'violated' the marriage covenant; to ascertain what property they possessed; to deprive them of authority over their children; to declare void any grants of money or property which would 'deprive the wife or children of that support to which they are entitled'; to award such part of the husband's property as seemed right to the use and support of the children; and to make it a punishable offense for any person intentionally to entice a married man or woman to join a sect advocating celibacy.

277   In the East, the first case of the kind was that of Mary Dyer, who had joined the Enfield (N.H.) community with her husband Joseph and their three children in 1811. Mary left the society four years later, and to recover the children, instituted several suits, accompanied over the years by books and pamphlets 'documenting' with sworn affidavits the 'misconduct' of the Shakers, their 'debaucheries' and 'obscenities,' their 'deceptions' and 'cruelties,' and so on. Refutation of the charges was given in *A Compendious Narrative*, by Joseph Dyer, the whole body of testimony, pro and con, constituting an early type of realism or yellow journalism which apparently found avid readers.

Mary Dyer damaged the Shaker name more than anyone had since Valentine Rathbun's time. If the depositions she assembled in her *Portraiture of Shakerism* (1822) were to be accepted as true, the movement would go down as one of the greatest hoaxes in American history. Ann is represented as a hypocrite, a fortune teller, a wine bibber and 'rummer,' a sadist, a prostitute. She was charged with ordering that children be stripped naked and whipped, strung up by their wrists, left alone all night in the woods, and even beaten to death. Ann and Father William were alleged to have fought bloody exhausting battles with each other over Whittaker's succession to the lead. Cases of perversion were detailed. The malicious Mary, like a Greek fury, continued on her career of revenge — peddling the *Portraiture* all over New England and reprinting the material, under the title of *The Rise and Progress of the Serpent from the Garden of Eden*, as late as 1847. Many people were doubtlessly willing to believe the worst, and seeds of suspicion about the sect were planted that continued to germinate long after her death.

The following excerpts are typical:

We, the undersigners, do testify that between 47 and 49 years ago, a number of people, four or five strangers and outlandish, came to Concord, New-Hampshire — made tarry of a number of months — the names of those who appeared to be the head ones, were Ann Lee and

Wm. Lee — their singularity caused many people to call and see them. . . They pretended to telling fortunes — also, where stolen or lost goods were. They used ardent spirits to excess — they frequented Samuel Farnum's house, a near neighbor, and at times stayed all night — the family, united with them in drinking, and the report from the family, was that Ann Lee lodged with Farnum, and Wm. Lee with Farnum's wife. . . They practised singing, dancing, gambling with cards, gaming and lounging about — Ann told Samuel Farnum he had a pot of money hid under the earth, if he would give her and William each a suit of good clothes, she would tell where the money was. Farnum believed it, and got the clothes for them — Ann then pretended to tell where the money was — Farnum with others, went to digging for the money, but found none. . .

A sister of mine by the name of Hannah Beck, who lived in the same family with me, was very industrious, became sick, and was some deranged, but was gentle; she being ill, refused to work, as they said. They [the Shakers] ordered me to make a chain, that they could confine her to a spinning wheel; and of sufficient length to spin on the great wheel; also to reach her couch which lay upon the floor, for her to sleep on. This was in cold weather, and the place she was confined in was a wash-shop, in a chamber, over the wash-room, and had a single floor with open cracks, which made her uncomfortable. There was a small stove in the room, but she was chained so far from it, that she could not reach it, and was depending on others for wood and fire — it was an apartment separate from the men's concerns. However, as I was passing there, I heard her crying and lamenting. I went to the shop, and looked through the cracks; she saw me and said, 'do make me some fire and light my pipe.' She begged again and again; my feelings were sensibly struck and I attempted to go in, but saw two of the sisters coming; and knew I was out of my order, I stept a little aside, and heard her continue in supplication, and think she got no relief. Again I was passing there, heard contention and heard talk; went to Hannah's room, and there saw one of the leading sisters with a large stick in her hand, threatening Hannah to make her work. My sister said, 'I am sick and cannot spin.' I saw the woman strike her three times with the stick. It would not do for me to interfere; I could not bear it, and went away . . .

A young woman, by the name of Elizabeth Cook, was stripped and whipped by Noah Wheaton, for her thoughts. Her father prosecuted Wheaton for whipping his daughter naked. Her sister, who was present, was called as a witness. She went to Elder Whitaker, and asked him what

she should say. He answered, 'I cannot tell you what you must say, for I don't know what question will be asked you; but,' says he, 'speak the truth, and spare the truth, and take care not to bring the gospel into disrepute.' She accordingly testified before the court that her sister was not naked. Thus she observed Whitaker's orders; for, strictly speaking,
278 she was not naked; she had a fillet on her head.

Mary Dyer lost her case. Following her initial hearing in 1816 before the New Hampshire Legislature, an act was introduced, one provision of which made six-months residence among the Believers a cause for divorce. The bill was defeated for several reasons, one being the argument that its operation would 'cast a stigma on the Shakers which they did not deserve, and abridge the right of conscience.'

Eunice Chapman, in a somewhat parallel case, was more successful in New York State. With her husband James and three children, she had entered the Watervliet society in 1811, later seceding and bringing suit, aided by public sympathy and legislative 'prejudice,' for the custody of her children. Eunice's methods were indirect. In March 1816, a bill had been passed exempting the Shakers from military service and fines. In January 1817, largely, it seems, through her influence, the act was nearly repealed, the action being averted by a Shaker *Remonstrance* (20 March) and a *Memorial* by James Chapman refuting his wife's arguments (24 March). But Eunice was not discouraged. Her first step was to publicize the 'conduct' of the Be-
279 lievers. Then, with the collaboration of a legislative group, an act was drawn up specifically designed for her relief. Introduced in the assembly on 10 February 1818, it provided, first, that her marriage be dissolved; secondly, that in the case of any minors received into the society accompanied by a parent who was separated from the other, the chancellor or Supreme Court judge be empowered to allow a habeas corpus to bring the children before him, and if they had been 'concealed,' to issue search warrants; and thirdly, that the chancellor or judge might award custody of the child to the parent who was not a Believer. Should the child or children be secreted or removed to another state, all persons concerned were to be deemed guilty of a great
280 misdemeanor.
281   Interest in the above act, which was passed on 7 March 1818, centers in the objections raised to its passage. In a letter to Albert Gallatin on 16 June 1817, Thomas Jefferson wrote:

Three of our papers have presented us the copy of an act of the legislature of New York, which, if it has really passed, will carry us back to the times of the darkest bigotry and barbarism, to find a parallel. Its purport is, that all those who shall hereafter join in communion with the religious sect of Shaking Quakers, shall be deemed civilly dead, their marriages dissolved, and all their children and property taken out of their hands. This act being published nakedly in the papers, without the usual signatures, or any history of the circumstances of its passage, I am not without a hope it may have been a mere abortive attempt . . .   *282*

The 'other side of the question' was also presented, ably though unsuccessfully, by an eminent Council of Revision composed of Governor De Witt Clinton, Chancellor Kent, Chief Justice Smith Thompson, Judges Ambrose Spencer, W. W. Van Hess, Joseph C. Yates, Jonas Pratt, and Attorney General Martin Van Buren. Re   *283* porting on 27 February, the Council objected to the bill on three counts affecting 'the fundamental principles of civil society.' First, the marital tie should be indissoluble, except on the grounds of adultery — remedies for abandonment, neglect, and abuse of parental authority being already provided for by law; furthermore, the law conferred on fathers exclusive guardianship and control of minor children. Secondly, the bill set an unsound and dangerous precedent by dissolving the marriage contract 'by statute authority, without any previous judicial inquiry and trial by jury.' Thirdly, it violated that article of the state constitution which ordained 'that free exercise and enjoyment of religious profession and worship, without discrimination or preference, shall forever hereafter be allowed within this state to all mankind: Provided, That the liberty of conscience shall not be so construed, as to excuse acts of licentiousness, or justify practices inconsistent with the peace and safety of the state.' Applying as it did to a particular sect, the Council felt that the regulation was essentially a penalty, making a discrimination whereby 'the equality of civil rights [as between persons or different religious professions] is essentially impaired':

If the Legislature can constitutionally deprive a man of his parental rights, merely because he is a Shaker, they have an equal right, for the same cause, to disfranchise him of every other privilege, or to banish him, or even put him to death.

No evidence, the Council concluded, existed of 'acts of licentiousness' or 'practices inconsistent with the peace and safety of this

state'; such dangers must be 'imminent' and 'certain,' not 'merely
speculative.' To condemn a religious tenet, by legislative authority,
is 'to assume a power . . . that would be not only unprecedented in
the annals of our state, but highly dangerous and alarming in its
consequences.' Freedom of the press was also involved: for Mr. Stone,
editor of the *Albany Daily Advertiser*, who had denounced the final
decision on the bill and printed the names of the opposition in conspicuous letters, was notified that he would no longer 'be indulged
284 with a seat' on the floor of the Assembly to report its proceedings.

A month and a half later, probably because of Mrs. Chapman's
activities, the Legislature went on to revoke its military exemption
bill of 1816, substituting an act requiring every able-bodied Shaker
between the ages of 18 and 45 to pay a $4 annual fine in lieu of mili-
285 tary services.

During the Revolutionary War the pacific principles of the Shakers were violently resented. After the conflict, when the church was
being organized, Joseph Meacham prepared the following 'way-
mark':

As we have received the grace of God in Christ, by the gospel, and are
called to follow peace with all men, we cannot, consistent with our faith
and conscience, bear the arms of war, for the purpose of shedding the
blood of any, or do anything to justify or encourage it in others. But if
they require, by fines or taxes of us, on that account, according to their
laws, we may, *for peace sake*, answer their demands in that respect, and
be innocent so far as we know at present. . . We believe that we are
free by the gospel, and that the time is near when others will be so far
286 enlightened that they will be willing to exempt us.

In accordance with this instruction, the Believers regularly paid
their muster fines — some $2000 at New Lebanon alone — until
February 1815, when the conclusion was reached that such payments,
or the hiring of substitutes for those drafted for the War of 1812,
indirectly supported the cause of bloodshed. Accordingly, on the second of that month, the New Lebanon society published a declaration
showing its reasons for refusing to aid or abet warfare in any way.
Basing their objections on a sense of duty to God, to themselves, and
to their fellow creatures, the Shakers found support in divine revelation, the natural rights of man, and the state and national constitu-
tions.

Duty to God, the *Declaration* stated, was paramount. Made known by the revelation of divine light only, it established the principle of conscience, 'the throne of God in the heart of man':

That God has required of us to abstain from all acts of violence against the lives of our fellow-creatures, is a truth in which we are as firmly established as we are that there is a God. . . And being called into the Kingdom of Christ now established on earth, it is required of us to be faithful soldiers in his cause, even at the expense of our lives. We cannot therefore render service to any authority which stands in competition with His will. He has expressly declared that, 'The Son of man came not to destroy lives, but to save them.' . . . We are firmly persuaded that those who subject themselves to the cross of Christ, and after his example, subdue those evil propensities which lead to war and strife, render more essential service to their country than they possibly could do by bearing arms and aiding war.   *287*

Universal peace will prevail only when a people set a conspicuous example and maintain it at all hazards.

Alluding to the principle of unalienable rights, as set forth in the Declaration of Independence, the Shakers cited their own covenant, where persons and property, being wholly consecrated to God, were 'irredeemable'; to devote them to other uses was to commit 'the crime of sacrilege.' The Believers had therefore abstained from politics and all 'the honours and emoluments' of office, in the meanwhile serving their country by maintaining their own poor, making public and private donations for the relief of suffering, expending money and labor on roads and bridges, paying taxes, and so on. As to paying a tax as an equivalent for military service, it would require them 'to purchase of government liberty to serve God with our persons, at the expense of sinning against him with our property.'

On the third point the framers of the *Declaration* used substantially the same arguments that the Council of Revision was to employ three years later. The free exercise of religion was guaranteed by both state and federal fundamental law. If it were abridged in one thing, then it might be in another, until no barrier existed 'to prevent as complete tyranny as ever existed.'

Similar reasons were offered in a *Memorial* dated 19 February 1816, which was the Shakers' first address to the New York Legislature, and in a pamphlet entitled *Observations on the Natural and Constitutional Rights of Conscience*, published the following day by   *288* the Watervliet community. The former document is interesting for its definition of the purpose of the order: 'Our labor is to do good in our day and generation, to all men, as far as we are able, by faithfulness and frugality in the works of our hands; by relieving the necessitous; by setting examples of virtue, humanity and charity; by works of public convenience and utility, and by promotion of good order in society.' The *Observations* argued the cause of separation of church and state; declared that a government which must coerce conscience must stand on a 'very precarious foundation'; protested that a fine is a punishment presupposing a crime; and pointed out the injustice of taxing or claiming property held in trust for a continuing community, donated in large part by those who were now dead, and never possessed by the 'delinquents' who were the subjects of the fine.

Presumably as a result of these protests, the New York Legislature passed an act on 29 March 1816 exempting the Shakers from military service and fines. But their triumph, we have seen, was short-lived, and from 1818 on, particularly in the 1820's, they were engaged in a continuous legal struggle for their constitutional rights. In Massachusetts, New Hampshire, and Kentucky such rights had earlier been recognized, and Maine had later followed suit. The obvious step, therefore, taken by the New Lebanon-Watervliet bishopric in 1823–4, was to transfer all the young brethren liable to duty over the state line to the Hancock settlement.

289

The Civil War again involved the Shakers with the world. From the first they had opposed the institution of chattel slavery and welcomed Negroes, as well as former slaveowners, into the society. There were a few colored members in the northern communities soon after they were organized. In 1813 a Negro family, with its own elder, existed at South Union, Kentucky; and for a number of years a Negro 'out-family' held meetings in Philadelphia, later moving to Watervliet.

To pursue a consistent policy, however, presented difficulties, especially in the South; and the central ministry at New Lebanon was evasive on such challenging questions as those put forth by Elder John Rankin of South Union:

1. Shall money or property which has been obtained by the sale of Negro slaves be refused or accepted by the Church of Christ?
2. If refused, how far removed from the sweat and blood of the slave must money or property be, in order to render such money or property

acceptable to the Church? Our sugar and coffee come directly from the toiling slave thro his master, and is acceptable. Should money be equally so?

3. There is a sister of 25 years standing in the society and 15 years in the church, whose father, in Tennessee, being the owner of some slaves, died intestate. By the laws of that state, 'Made and provided' the court has to sell the property, slaves included. The proceeds of this sale brings to the heirs, $2000.00 each. We have received for the heir who is with us, $1600.00 & soon will have the balance — When question No. 1 is answered we will know what to do.   *290*

Then to complicate the problem the writer adds: 'If the slaves are brought to Kentucky they cannot, by the laws here, be freed, and be allowed to remain the slaves of Jency and Judith or those to whom they may sell or give them.'

Bishop Harvey Eads, the foremost spokesman of the sect in Kentucky, opposed the practice of freeing the slave by hiring him from his master and paying the latter for the sweat of the former. Eads's solution, put into operation in the Blue Grass State, was to place the slave, after receiving him on agreement from his legal owner, on 'decent' Shaker wages so that the Negro himself could 'buy his body and soul.' The liberal attitude of the Kentucky Believers toward the racial question doubtlessly complicated their relations with the world: the Kentuckians 'speak evil of them without cause,' Finch noticed in 1844, for 'the Shakers in their midst, all free, wealthy and happy, are an everlasting reproach upon them and their accursed slavery system.'

In its early years the community at South Union suffered from the inroads of both the Confederate and Union forces, maintaining its faith by impartial ministrations to the sick, wounded, and hungry of both sides. But the draft law of March 1863, re-opened the issue of   *291* military service. Before its passage the central ministry had advised the brethren at Union Village 'to give freely to the Sanitary Committee for the benefit of the suffering soldiers [but] not to take hold of a gun or do anything as a soldier, not pay a fine, hire a substitute, or pay instead, that the government may hire one in the room of a Shaker.' Immediately afterward, Benjamin Gates and Frederick   *292* Evans interviewed Lincoln and presented Secretary of War Stanton with a memorial requesting exemption on the grounds of the religious character of the institution, the constitutional rights of conscience, the precedent set by the states, and the 'radical nature of their doctrinal and conscientious scruples, vital to their faith, against taking up arms or taking part in controversies and business affairs of the world.' Added to the petition was a wholly new claim for exemption, namely, that there was a sum of money, amounting (with interest) to $439,733, in the national treasury that legally belonged to the society through those who had served in the wars of the Revolution and 1812 but had not been permitted by Shaker regulations to draw their pensions or bounty lands. Since only about seventy Shakers were liable to Civil War service, the petitioners argued, the government would receive in fines an amount equivalent to but 4½ per cent of the unclaimed money. After listening to the Shakers, Evans later recalled, Lincoln leaned back in his chair and asked:

'Well, what am I to do?'
'It is not for me,' Elder Frederick replied, 'to advise the President of the United States.'
'You ought to be made to fight,' Lincoln said. 'We need regiments of just such men as you.'

Nevertheless, the petition was granted and the draftees given an indefinite furlough.

Commitment to the principles of peace followed constructive as well as defensive lines. Earlier, after the troubles with the New York Legislature had subsided, certain Shakers, concerned with the problem of the causes of war, prepared articles which represent the sect's first active participation in world affairs. In 1831 the American Peace Society published *Remarks on the Militia System*, by 'A poor man's son,' — Garret Lawrence, the New Lebanon herbalist. The same year Seth Y. Wells of Watervliet, under the pseudonym of 'Philanthropos,' composed an historical argument against war as an instrument of national policy. Subsequently, at the request of *The Harbinger of Peace* (which had asked for dissertations on a congress of nations for the prevention of war), Wells expanded his thesis, including suggestions on enforcement curiously anticipatory of modern proposals and sanctions. Matters of dispute between two nations, he asserted, should be submitted to arbiters previously appointed by all the other contracting powers; these arbiters, acting as advocates rather than as judges, would constitute a 'court of Nations'; and a 'non complying party should pay a heavy forfeit' or 'not be allowed commercial intercourse with the other confederate Powers till the required terms shall be fulfilled . . .'   297

Interest in the peace movement lasted throughout the century, culminating in a convention, held by the Shakers at Mount Lebanon on 31 August 1905, which was attended by a number of publicists and scholars. Eldress Leila Taylor offered various resolutions bearing on the reduction of armaments to limits necessary for an international police force; the consequent diminution of taxes for the producing classes, which would serve as a remedy for industrial disturbances; 'the establishment of the great waterways of commerce as neutral zones'; and the interdiction, by neutral powers, 'of the public issue of war loans in their territories, thereby making continued hostilities on a large scale impossible.' In the relations among nations, the resolutions insisted, a moral element must be recognized.

In New York State, neither the Goodrich and Chapman cases nor the proceedings relating to exemption from military requirements greatly clarified the legal status of the order. Fearing lest the revised statutes of 1829 invalidate their right to hold property — a revision apostates were preparing to take advantage of — the Shakers sent delegates to Albany to work for an act that would confirm their title deeds. The result was the Trust Act of 1839, passed over the determined opposition of Samuel J. Tilden, which entitled the order to hold real or personal property with an annual income of not over $5,000. Deeds of trust executed before 1 January 1830 were declared valid, and the act stated that the legal estates could be continued 'so long as may be required for the purposes of the trust.'   298

Reflecting the growing concern that the United Society was expanding its holdings to a dangerous degree, Tilden had remonstrated on the grounds that the act tendered a special privilege; that it would enable the society 'to hold in perpetuity the aggregate of the individual property of all its members, and to an unlimited amount'; and that it involved the 'odious principle' of entailment of private property, rather than the holding of property for religious purposes or as a public utility. With his charges of 'arbitrary government,' 'irresponsible ministry,' 'internal police,' 'unqualified submission,' 'ignorance,' 'delusions of judgment,' 'destruction of natural affections,' et cetera — principles which would 'uproot our whole social system'

— the future governor sought to support his argument with the traditional indictment of the sect. A movement to repeal the act was
started in 1848. Tilden's *Considerations* were reprinted, with a foreword claiming that the Shakers already had 'a very large real and
personal estate, estimated at over one million of dollars,' and that
they were 'increasing it very fast; encroaching in their purchases
upon other denominations, and threatening in time to embrace whole
towns, and perhaps counties, in their possession.' Confirming this
early fear of big business was the report by James Johnston, an English traveler, of a prevalent jealousy of Shaker 'independence': it
was felt that the Believers were 'increasing, prospering, and buying
land so fast, that they were forming a dangerous monopoly of the
land of the State.'

An investigating committee appointed by the Assembly submitted
a sympathetic report on the principles and practices of the sect (including a statement that the 3 communities in the state owned about
10,000 acres, a fraction of over 10 acres to each person), and recommended that the matter be dropped. But the Senate, unconvinced, resolved on 8 February 1850 that the Shaker trustees be required to
report on all real estate owned in 1839, property acquired since, the
exact nature and value of all parcels, property sold (with prices),
the aggregate value of personal property, monies on hand, and money
or property received in trust since February, 1839. Complying as
faithfully as possible with the difficult demands, the trustees made a
report the following month which apparently dispelled the fear that
the order was becoming a 'dangerous money power.' Since speculation was forbidden, and only industries useful to the public tolerated
(instead of the more profitable ones tending to superfluity and extravagance), the excess of sales over expenditures at New Lebanon
was less than $600 for the year preceding the report. Charities and
maintenance of the poor absorbed more than $2,000 a year. In 11
years additions to real estate had amounted to about 3,000 acres
(equivalent to 28 acres for each world's family of 5 persons) and an
annual gain to each member of about four dollars — 'a sum that
might have been absorbed by a single useless article of dress.'
The upshot of the whole matter was that in 1852, though its enemies still sought to dissolve the order as an illegal institution, the
Legislature extended the charter to allow an annual income of
$25,000.

Appealing for the right to exist as a free community, the Shakers often cited the expenditures made for the relief of the needy. That these statements were more than lip service to a principle of the covenant is shown by works already mentioned: the kindness of the Shakers to beggars, the Christmas donations, the reception into the society of the orphaned and destitute. The right use of property brought the Believers, as it did the monastics, into almost daily contact with the unfortunate, helping in no small way to leaven 'the lump of pioneer civilization.' The bestowal of goods to such charitable uses is illustrated by the following excerpts from the records of the 'poor office' at New Lebanon for the year 1807–8:

4 Indians, each of them a pair of shoes
1 Black woman and 2 white women from Canaan, 3 small pails, 1 pr. Shoes, 1 Shift, handkerchief, 1 cap, 1 apron, 1 short gown, cloth for a small petticoat
A poor woman by the name Allen had 1 pr. shoes, 1 pr. stockings 1 Jacket for her grandson
Sam Hike, a Black man from Chatham, 1 strait-bodied coat, 1 Jacket, 1 pr. trousers.
2 Squaws from New York, shoes, stockings, mittens, etc.
A traviler, 1 pr. footings
A lame man from Stillwater, 1 Bed Quilt
Gillet, the Lame man, 1 tub, 1 pail, 1 piece of Deer's leather
A man and his family moving to the westward, some bread and cheese, apples and garden seeds
A traveling woman, 1 woolen frock
George Williams, a man that had the dropsy, 1 dollar.
A poor traveler, one shirt
Henry Wheeler, a Blind man from Schodack, a shirt, pr. trousers, 1 Jacket, 1 pr. shoes, 1 pr. footings.
A Frenchman from Petersburg said his Brother had his house and barn burnt and he received 1 strait bodied coat, 4 Shirts 4 pr. Trousers, 2 shifts, 2 Jackets and 25 cents money
Broughton of Stephentown with a recommend to ask alms and received 10 lbs. mutton, 10 lbs. pork, 1 bushel of corn and clothing
Widow Wait of Stephentown said her husband had been dead about one year, and received ½ bushel of rye, some small pieces of beef and pork, 2 quarts fat, a piece of cheese, etc.   *304*

Besides doing their share in maintaining the county poor, and sending clothing, foodstuffs, tools, industrial products, money, and labor to needy branches of the United Society itself, the order made public donations to outside communities which had been stricken by sickness or other disaster. Thus, on 7 November 1798, during a severe epidemic in New York, the New Lebanon, Hancock, Watervliet, and Tyringham colonies dispatched 27 wagons to that city loaded with provisions, together with $300 in money. At the time of the outbreak of yellow fever in the same city five years later, the first two communities repeated their benevolence, consigning $326, 853 pounds of pork, 1,951 pounds of beef, 1,744 pounds of mutton, 1,685 pounds of rye flour, 52 bushels of rye, 24 bushels of beans, 179 bushels of potatoes, 34 bushels of carrots, 2 bushels of dried apples, and 2 bushels of beets — a gift acknowledged by Mayor De Witt Clinton in the following letter:

To employ so large a proportion of the fruits of your meritorious Industry in relieving the helpless children of poverty must Entitle you to the esteem of your fellow men and that you may reap your reward in the Smiles of the great dispenser of all good is the sincere prayer of your friend Dewitt Clinton.

305   [Letter of 2 December 1803]

306   The Youngs manuscript cites other cases:

March 28, 1803. The Chh [at New Lebanon] sent 150 and Hancock 100 dollars to the inhabitants of Portsmouth who had suffered from fire.

August 10, 1815. A donation [of $400] was sent to Petersburg in Virginia, for the relief of sufferers by fire.

December 7, 1819. A donation of three wagon loads was sent to Schenectady, to sufferers by fire.

1826. To the Greeks in Hudson, three barrels of pork, two barrels of beef, and five dollars.

November 23, 1832. A donation of eight waggon loads was sent to New York, to go to the Cape de verd Islands, for the relief of the inhabitants, suffering from famine.

August 30, 1838. A number of waggons loaded with articles of provision, clothing, etc. were this day forwarded as a donation to the city of Hudson, for the relief of sufferers there by a late fire.

March 16, 1847. It being a time of much suffering in Ireland, a donation [of clothing and provision] was made by the Church, for the relief of the sufferers by famine, and conveyed to Albany, thence to be shipped.

The Shaker way of life was publicized by a stream of inquirers from America and abroad. Many have been mentioned. President James Monroe was at Enfield, New Hampshire, in 1817, and two years later, accompanied by Andrew Jackson, visited South Union. In the period 1830–35, a Mexican, don Lorenzo de Zavala, and a Spaniard, Dr. don Ramon de la Sagra, reported on the customs of the New Lebanon community. Dickens included this society in his *307* American tour. Secretary Stanton went to New Lebanon to repay *308* the visit of Gates and Evans to Washington, and Robert Dale Owen to study the social and educational practices of the order. One of the standard expositions of Shakerism, *The Millennial Church* (1823), had been written, it was said, at the request of a Russian consul in New York for publication in his homeland. In 1888, a shorter exposition was translated into German at Union Village. Interested in how *309* the Shakers, as non-resistants, managed to hold communal property, Leo Tolstoy carried on a late-century correspondence with Frederick Evans. *310*

Not negligible was the effect on American literature. In the field of humor the order furnished a subject for Artemas Ward. Howells' *The Undiscovered Country, A Parting and a Meeting,* and *The Day of Their Wedding* were based on Shaker materials, as were Hawthorne's *Shaker Bridal* and *The Canterbury Pilgrims,* Catherine Sedgwick's *Redwood,* and Kate Douglas Wiggins' *Susanna and Sue.* The archangel Gabriel, in Melville's *Moby Dick,* came from the 'crazy society of Neskyeuna Shakers.' *In doctum Parliamentum,* a play based on the Chapman case, and Samuel Johnson's *The Shaker Lovers,* a one-act comedy first performed in Boston in 1849, were early representations in the field of drama.

There were frequent contacts with other cultures. The relations with early revivalist sects, the missions to the Shawnee Indians, and the delegation to the Community of True Inspiration have been mentioned. The 'Halcyons,' a mid-western sect embracing certain Mil- *311* lerite and Mormon doctrines, also seemed to have been influenced by the Shakers, with whom they first came in contact about 1815. The 'Mummyjums,' another unorthodox cult, 'exhibited' at Union Village in 1817. There were visits to Rapp's Harmony society and the community at Zoar, Ohio, and correspondence with Noyes' society at Oneida.

The Transcendentalists at Fruitlands, particularly Charles Lane

and Bronson Alcott, were greatly interested in the Shaker experiment, often visiting the Harvard community to discuss, among other matters, the secrets of its material success; and when the Con-Sociate family at Fruitlands broke up, Lane and his son joined the society. The philosophers and educators at Brook Farm, on the other hand, seem to have been little influenced by the neighboring example of religious communism: George Ripley's comment (in a letter of 1842 to Charles A. Dana) — 'It is a detestable, miserly, barren aristocracy, without a grain of humanity about it. Enormous wealth is made at
312 the expense of all manly pursuits and attainments' — summarizes the official attitude of the West Roxbury community. Later in the century Frederick Evans proposed, without success, a union of the
313 Shakers and the Koreshan Unity. It is possible, though not demonstrable, that Mary Baker Eddy, who at one time lived near Canterbury, was influenced by the Shakers, especially in regard to the con-
314 cept of the motherhood in deity.

More important were the relations with the Mormons and Millerites. Though documentation is absent, and Joseph Smith himself disclaimed any inspiration from the Shakers, rumor had it that in his schemes for a religious community he was indebted to the section on united inheritance in Dunlavy's *Manifesto*. Others said Smith was influenced by a sect near Kirkland, Ohio, called 'The Family,' who, before their conversion to Mormonism, had been affected by the doctrines preached at the neighboring Shaker settlement of North Union. Be that as it may, after two years of friendly trade between the groups, Smith received a revelation in March 1831 to send three delegates to North Union on a proselyting mission. The inevitable issues regarding marriage, 'lust,' and the nature of the messiahship precipitated a stormy debate, ending with Elder Ashbel Kitchell angrily expelling the equally excited Mormons from the community. Later Kitchell went to the Mormon farm to 'labor' with a certain
315 Elder Knight, with results that are undisclosed. In a manuscript entitled *The Early Shakers*, Daryl Chase, without pressing the issue that Mormon doctrine was influenced by Shakerism, noted the following similarities: the reception of revelations on a gold plate; the belief by both faiths that time was divided into long 'dispensations,' and that theirs was the last and greatest; the claim by both that their church was 'a divine restoration of the primitive Christian church'; and acceptance of the doctrine of a dual Deity.

It is unlikely, however, that many Mormons adopted Shakerism. After the Millerite fiasco, however, disillusioned members of that sect joined the order in considerable numbers. Comparable principles made the transfer a natural one, many, like Enoch Jacobs, editor of the Second Adventist *Day-Star*, preferring 'knowledge and sight' to 'faith and hope.' In 1846 about two hundred Millerites joined the western communities, Whitewater in particular. In the East, Harvard, Canterbury, and Enfield (N.H.) were the chief beneficiaries. At the invitation of the Millerite society in Philadelphia, Mount Lebanon sent missionaries who organized a Shaker family there, including a Negro contingent led by Mother Rebecca Jackson. This group, as we have mentioned, moved to Watervliet but later returned to Philadelphia, where it existed for several years. *316*

These successful in-gatherings encouraged spasmodic missionary efforts which continued for about twenty-five years. A communication from Union Village to the central ministry, on 6 November 1866, refers to a revival in Sweden and a letter signed by one Olaf Olson, Elfdarlen, Rot (22 August 1866), listing fifty-three Swedes who had accepted the Shaker doctrine. This letter — written to Elder Andrew Bloomburg and Lars Ericson, two brothers at the 'West lot' in Pleasant Hill who had joined the Shakers after the break-up of the Bishop Hill colony — prompted the ministry to commission Bloomburg to visit his homeland to preach the gospel and, if possible, to bring the Believers to America. The result of the mission, the first foreign enterprise in the history of the society, was the eventual transfer, in 1869, of some fifty-four Swedish brothers and sisters to Pleasant Hill. Though part of this group stayed on, others left within a few years, and the society never considered the experiment a success. Its outcome nevertheless did not dissuade Elder Frederick Evans from a similar trip to England in 1871, a mission which publicized the beliefs of the order and added a few members to its rolls.

In its welcome to people of diverse races and religions, Negroes as well as whites, Catholics and Jews as well as Protestants, the United Society, in contrast with the foreign-origin communities, was characteristically American. Though their relations with the world were often strained, the record is one of increasing adjustment; of growing confidence and even pride, on the part of the Believers, in American institutions; and, conversely, of a greater awareness, by those 'without,' of the true merits of the Shaker order.

CHAPTER XI

Decline of the Order

The fiery reformer embodies his aspiration in some rite or
covenant, and he and his friends cleave to the form and lost
the aspiration. The Quaker has established Quakerism, the
Shaker has established his monastery and his dance; and although each prates of spirit, there is no spirit, but repetition,
which is anti-spiritual.

— Emerson: 'Goethe; or, The Writer'

A CURVE plotting the growth and decline of the Shaker movement
would be an almost symmetrical one. In point of numbers the United
Society reached its zenith in the decade before the Civil War, when
there were some six thousand members in its eighteen branches and
fifty-eight families. Fifty years before that time the church had had
about a thousand adherents; fifty years later, after a gradual retro-
gession, the number was back to a thousand. Today, as in those years
when Mother Ann's pioneer commune was struggling to survive, only
a few espouse the faith.

Why this curve? Why did the order, drawing vitality from so
many sources, not keep on progressing, in numbers and all good
works? Was it true, as some Shakers have said, that the cycle of
growth and decay is the destiny of all human institutions? The cen-
tripetal forces were strong — the curve spans a century and three-
quarters. What were the centrifugal forces that irresistibly weakened
the movement?

There is no simple answer. It is possible, however, to summarize
the basic factors in the ascendency of the order, and then suggest
why, or to what extent, they ceased to be effective. Success may be
attributed to:

1. The religious principles which inspired adherents
2. Religious revivals, in the world and in the society itself
3. The cohesive forces of communal organization
4. Control over the sexual relation
5. The economic well-being of the society
6. Its function as a sanctuary

These agents are clearly interrelated. It was a matter of conviction, to hundreds of seekers, that the 'family of Christ' was a form of association superior to that of marriage familism. They came into the order in the wake of revivals, and once there, were absorbed into a compact social system where certain beliefs regarding sex were reenforced by controls over sex relations. Removed from the world, they were protected from many of its temptations. Inspired by an ideal, they created, over the years, a sound expanding economy. Success was cumulative; and as time went on the order attracted people from the world for other than strictly religious reasons. Women in particular responded to its offer of a refuge from unhappy marriages, releasing them 'from sexual maladjustments without their running away from their partners or attempting freedom through the agency of the severe divorce laws of that period.' For children, in lieu of other institutions, it served as an orphanage. Foundlings were willingly taken in. Frequently whole families joined. To hundreds of 'the friendless and deserted' the United Society was a place of security and of opportunity to begin life anew. Though many had little of this world's goods to offer, they added increments of labor, at least, to the expanding church. Out of these elements — economic, social, and religious — a program took form with more promise of permanence than any of those based on the family relation or pure social theory. All signs pointed toward growth.

Then momentum slackened. Signs of discontent, particularly among the younger members, were seen in Ohio and Kentucky as early as the 1820's; but it was not until the 'forties that failure of the appeal of principle became seriously disturbing. Deterioration was at first almost imperceptible: the change that came over the fortunes of the society, first in the western and eventually in the eastern communities, was measurable only by the decrease in accessions and slow shrinkage of membership. The decade before the Civil War, however, revealed an unmistakable trend. 'Much depression of spirit has been felt, and struggling thro' dark and gloomy prospects,' Isaac Youngs wrote in his journal for 1856, 'on account of apostacies, lifelessness and backslidings of unfaithful members, and the scanty ingathering from without.' Though attempts had been made to reopen the testimony, 'there is such a stupidity of soul, and absence of conviction for sin in the world, that there is rarely one to be found who is willing to submit to the mortifying terms of the gospel.' By the end of the War of the Rebellion it was clear that there were increasingly fewer people who preferred the cross to 'the flowery path of nature.'

Economic factors, which played an important role in the success of the movement, were involved in its decline. Outstanding were (1) the expense of maintaining the order, (2) the Shaker policy regarding land ownership, (3) the mismanagement which followed in the wake of prosperity, and (4) the impact of the industrial age.

318   1. In the middle of the last century Calvin Green, the New Lebanon elder, summarized the reasons why the society never became wealthy: the first Shakers were 'mostly poor and in debt'; those who joined afterward were likewise destitute or persons of small property; the trustees were not allowed to speculate; the labors of the ministry were supported by 'their own group,' not by the public; the order was under heavy expense in educating children, many of whom left before they gave any material returns in labor; there were expenses in getting favorable legislation passed, and in contesting law suits by apostates; a great deal of property went in settling with those who withdrew; and finally, though the Shakers never received any public money, they were 'generous to the poor' and paid their share of public expenses. The small excess of income over expenditure — in one of the largest communities in the period of greatest prosperity — bears out Green's contention. Much of the money earned, after taxes were paid, went into maintenance and internal improvements, which of course added to the total value of the society's estate.

2. Earnings were also spent on the expansion of property. Though speculation in stocks and bonds was prohibited, it was the policy of the Shakers to invest a considerable percentage of surplus capital in land. Planning was sound in the era of steady growth and rising revenues; and since the land repaid the Shakers handsomely for the labor expended on it, they felt that progress lay in the direction of larger farms. But the time came when additional acreage was no longer required and could no longer be cultivated by the Believers themselves

Still they bought — out-farms, wood lots, lands, and mills in distant states — and, to make such property productive, resorted to the hiring of world's labor and the renting of lands on the Metayer system, both practices a violation of the basic principle of separation.

With membership decreasing and taxes rising, the Shakers eventually came to realize that the returns on land increase were not commensurate with the cost, that management and labor might better be concentrated on home industry and the family domains. Frederick Evans told Nordhoff in 1875 that in spite of the prosperous look of their extensive, well-improved lands, they were of no real or pecuniary advantage. 'We ought to get on,' he said, 'without the use of   *319* outside labor. Then we should be confined to such enterprises as are best for us.' That simple manufacturing, employing only a few hands, would yield more satisfactory returns than 'large acreage carried on with hireling labor' was the corroborating opinion expressed a few years later to Hinds. It was Noyes's view, and the Shakers would probably have agreed, that the 'lust for land' — which involved the owners in the uncertainties of agriculture, kept them from the more lucrative business of manufacturing, and tended to isolate them from the centers of modern progress — had much to do with the failure of American communities. As the average holdings of each of the Shaker societies amounted, in 1875, to about 2700 acres, the issue of limitation became increasingly acute. Indeed, land limitation, as applied to the world, was one of Evans's pet theories; the rights to life and land were inseparable, he held, but land monopoly was the primary cause of poverty, and poverty of war. In one treatise he advocated the limitation of individual holdings to a hundred acres — on the death of large landholders each heir could take up this limit but would be required to sell the surplus within a year. In another treatise, somewhat inconsistently, he came out strongly for the nationalization of land, limiting rights to usufruct.   *320*

3. When investment took other forms, however, further troubles beset the unworldly Shakers. Prosperity — which many members, in retrospect, felt was the chief cause of their undoing — came at a time when there were fewer and fewer officials capable of managing the increasingly complex affairs. Ministerial supervision slackened. Appointments to trusteeships were unwisely made. The ban on speculation and indebtedness was relaxed or disregarded, and certain trustees became involved in transactions detrimental to the good name

and welfare of the society. According to Nordhoff, New Gloucester suffered 'several severe losses by unfaithful and imprudent agents,' incurring an indebtedness which had to be paid off by other societies; Canterbury, he reported, experienced similar defalcations in 1848–9, with less serious cases at the two Enfields, Harvard, and North Union; at Groveland one family fell in debt through an 'imprudent purchase of land' without the society's knowledge; and at Pleasant Hill the 'carelessness' of an aged trustee resulted in the loss of $10,-000. Other losses, perhaps more crippling, were due to a certain naïveté on the part of the order's representatives. In certain cases, when dwindling communities placed large properties on the market, unscrupulous lawyers or agents took advantage of the situation. North Union was thus 'fleeced' out of $12,000, and Union Village of $40,000. In violation of the order regarding usury, the latter community in 1885 allegedly lost about $16,000 in loans to the Dayton Furnace Company. About $20,000 was squandered by the Enfield (N.H.) society when a trustee became involved with a company producing 'Shaker flannel.' To such misfortunes should be added those incurred by the frequent fires, incendiary or accidental, which constantly plagued the order. The Kentucky communities suffered greatly from the Civil War, and even the northern communities were affected, particularly Enfield (Conn.), whose lucrative seed trade with the South was ruined.

321

4. More far-reaching in their effect were the economic enticements and industrial competition of the world. Largely self-sufficient, abjuring the profit motive, dependent on a handicraft economy, the sect was the product of an age that was passing. A new America was growing up around the isolated Shaker domains, luring forth its members, keeping for itself many who might, under other circumstances, have joined the order. Such principles as submission to authority, the abnegation of self, and communal ownership had diminishing appeal in a country glorifying liberty and the individual or corporate acquisition of property. Under the impact of an expanding democracy, the westward movement, and the industrial revolution, people were on the march, restless and full of ebullient energy, striving toward new achievements and material rewards. Not in personal salvation and perfection was utopia to be sought, but in personal advancement and the opportunities presented by cheap western lands, rich natural resources, the railroads, factories, and beckoning machines. A common

attitude toward the Shaker utopia was encountered by Finch in 1844. 'We Americans,' he was told,

love liberty too well to join such Societies as these. What are they but pure despotisms, where all are subject to the will of one man, a few leaders, or even a woman? Are not these places opposed to science and all improvements? We Americans are a go-ahead people, not to be confined anywhere or stopped by anything.

322

There was still a place, however, in the restive American scene, for security, discipline, and selflessness. Against the evils of enslavement and war, of poverty and industrial turmoil, of social unrest and economic greed, the religious orders offered the blessings of stability and spiritual consummation. Indeed, Catholic monasticism in the United States has exhibited, since the 1840's, a constant growth. The Shaker order, however, with its unorthodox doctrines, with no connection with lay organizations or a mother church, with no systematic scheme for recruitment, waited, with what it had to give, and found that each year fewer knocked at its gates.

That the society was not submerged by these forces of worldliness, that it was indeed destined to continue into the middle of another century, was due to many factors; these were the protective status of isolation, its extensive properties, its still vigorous industrial plant, the uncorrupted faith of all 'true Believers,' and lastly, the society's ability to adjust itself to changing conditions. The Shakers still had something to contribute to the new age. Adhering sometimes to old handicraft techniques but often introducing improved methods, the shops continued to provide a substantial revenue. Their output served basic, not transient needs, and the reputation of their goods remained high. Though some obsolete employments were dropped, the demand continued for garden seeds, medicinal herbs, brooms, chairs, and other products. The dried sweet-corn industry was developed into a major enterprise; the tanneries continued to function; small shop work such as oval boxes found a ready market. As the number of brethren decreased, upsetting a desirable balance in membership, the sisters took their places in key industries and expanded the output of their own shops. Fancy work, poplar basketry, the lining and 'furnishing' of boxes, the making of chair mats, court plaster, small brushes, leather pocketbooks, spool stands, blankets, cushions, and so forth, kept the community stores well supplied. The 'kitchen industries' flourished. Knitting machines were introduced, and new industries inaugurated, such as the manufacture of cloaks, coonskin gloves, carpet whips, shirts, and rugs. Reviving the early practices of the brethren, Shaker sisters made regular tours to distant marts, this time the mountain and seaside resorts, to peddle their wares. That these enterprises eventually languished was due, not to a failing market, but to the numerical decline of the sisterhood itself.

Paralleling the shift of occupations from the male to the female line was the change from stock-raising to small farming — a move, the Shakers explained, that was 'in the line of physical and moral evolution,' the outcome of convictions on vegetarianism. More attention was paid to poultry and bee-keeping; some stock was kept, as the dairy market was a lucrative one; but increasing emphasis was placed on fruit and berry culture, on kitchen and market gardens. Little recession occurred in the herb and seed business. Retrenchment was most apparent in the shrinkage of herds and lands, and in the hiring of Adam's sons to till the fields.

Though these four factors, in varying degrees, weakened the structure of the society, they do not, in themselves, sufficiently account for its steady decline. Just as the order, in its rise, had drawn continuous nourishment from an afflatus, so its decline must be ascribed, in the main, to a loss of such spiritual support.

What caused that loss? Too rigid adherence to the tenets of celibacy and common property? Disagreements on the principle, or extent, of separation from the world? The Shakers would say no, that in their doctrine was their strength. The weakness lay, first, in the 'apostacies, lifelessness and blacksliding of unfaithful members,' and secondly, in the 'scanty ingathering from without,' for which they blamed the increasing 'stupidity of soul, and absence of conviction for sin in the world.'

It is clear, however, that the doctrine of celibacy not only precluded natural growth but, with other 'eccentricities of belief opposed to human nature,' severely limited accessions. Over and over again, in his work in the field, the author has encountered the question: 'What would become of the world if all became Shakers?' How can one justify a way of life, these people ask, if in its logical developments it leads toward the extinction of the race? It is not, they contend, a universal ethos.

Though it frequently fails to satisfy the inquirer, the best answer is that given by the Shakers themselves, in a pamphlet first published in 1868 and often reprinted to meet renewed questioning. The spokes- 323 man of the sect, in this case Richard Pelham of Union Village, opened his argument by reminding his readers that the Shakers never condemned marriage in toto, nor did they consider procreation a great wrong. But 'the great Architect,' he explained, 'has divers grades of workmen, all necessary in their places . . . to complete the building.' In the moral world 'there be eunuchs who have made themselves eunuchs for the kingdom of heaven's sake.' Even in the world of nature there was no law requiring that the powers of reproduction should be used absolutely. Every vegetable seed has such organs. Do birds and animals eating seeds, or people eating bread, therefore violate nature's laws? The millions of eggs in a single codfish are not all fertilized. 'The sacrifice of these organs to a higher and nobler purpose,' Pelham contended, 'is Nature's general law . . . Nature evidently designed vastly the greater proportion of vegetable seeds for the support of animal life, and thus to pass into a higher grade of being, at the expense and destruction of their use for reproduction.'

Proceeding from this analogy, the author buttressed his argument by an appeal to Malthus. Abstinence from marriage, he claimed, also subserves the best interests and ultimate existence of the race, for 'unrestrained generation' would overpopulate the earth. Powerful checks were needed, including the elements of continence and celibacy based on religious conviction. Nature's, or God's, great law of progress, he concluded, involves a system of checks and balances, of supply and demand and compensation, 'sublimating each lower grade of being to subserve the grade above,' and ultimately, 'the sublime mentality of the human intellect.' In building the temple of God, the Believers were not the brickmakers; that was the work of generation. But as 'master-builders' they wanted the best bricks the world could make.

The second article in their creed, the commitment to separation from the world, also placed the Shakers on the defensive, and even induced, perhaps, an unhealthy feeling of inferiority. Having repudiated the world, they were in a position of being themselves criticized, or at least regarded with curiosity as a class apart. It was difficult, in any case, to hold the separating line. The third principle, that of community of goods, was unpopular in a country devoted to private enterprise and property. The fourth, confession of sins, made them suspect in predominantly Protestant communities. There was an exclusive quality to the Shaker tenets that was bound to relegate the society to a minority status.

Disagreement over the interpretation of such doctrines, especially that of separation, did in time generate internal strains which weakened the order. Evidences of disunity were intermittent at first, but eventually rough groupings emerged: a liberal school favoring closer relations with the world and active social reform, and a conservative wing favoring strict adherence to traditional principles. Though there was never an open breach, each group had its spokesmen, and the elements for a dangerous schism existed.

The outstanding representative of the former view was Elder Frederick Evans of New Lebanon, who had come to America from

SHAKER EVANS AT HOME

England in 1820 and, after a search for the ideal community, had thrown in his lot with the Shakers in 1830. A radical, and at first a materialist, deist, and free-thinker, he had been for several years associated with his brother, George Henry Evans, in the publication of

The Workingman's Advocate, *The Daily Sentinel*, *The Bible of Reason*, and *Young America*, papers of Jacksonian complexion expounding such principles as the right of man to the soil ('vote yourself a farm'), freedom of public lands, inalienable homesteads, land limitation, a general bankruptcy law, equal rights for women, and abolition of the United States Bank, chattelism, wage slavery, and imprisonment for debt. As a vigorous pamphleteer Evans continued to promulgate these and other reforms, relating them to Shakerism after he joined the society. We have already spoken of his interest in arbitration, sanitation, dietary reform, and scientific agriculture. Attacking class education as discriminatory and aristocratic, he suggested that industrial, self-supporting public schools be established for everyone up to the age of twenty-one, with mandatory instruction in chemistry, hygiene, and physiology. In the field of government he wanted to apply Shaker ideas by making the presidency and governorship dual offices, limiting the national and state senates to women and the lower houses to men, and confining leadership to a class of 'intellectual celibates,' male and female, who would be married only to the state. 'Spiritual granaries' — orders like the Shaker communities — would provide inspiration for the leaders of this 'new earth.' Other manifestoes protested against war, restrictive Sabbath-day laws, cruelty to animals, Mormon persecution, the banking system, and the whole system of credit — which Evans considered unnecessary, together with the lawyers and brokers who supported it, on the principle that every man should trust another at his own risk. The elder corresponded with Henry George on the single tax; with Tolstoy on co-operation and non-resistance; and with Edward Bok on a memorial to Henry Ward Beecher. He lectured, wrote for the press, and invited the world to come to Mount Lebanon. The society, he felt, should break with its tradition of isolation to join the forces of humanitarianism working for a better social order.

Despite the fact that his dogmatism, self-assurance, and personalized interpretation of Shakerism alienated many Believers, Evans was a natural leader whose word carried great weight in the movement. In the world he was considered its official spokesman, a role strengthened by his writings, his strategic position as public speaker in the central community, his keen interest in people and ideas, and his bent toward science as well as mystical religion. In his attempt to harmonize science and mysticism he epitomized Shaker thought. Liberal tendencies creeping into the monastic culture — the acceptance of flowers, pictures, newspapers and magazines, books on travel, history, and science, organ music, reading meetings, and in one society a lyceum or debating club — were proof that the trend of the times, on the whole, favored a rapport with the world. Evans was constantly working toward the realization of this trend. His argument took the line that saints were as deserving of the good things of this world as sinners.

324

Two other leaders interested in developing the movement into an instrument of reform should be mentioned. One, Daniel Fraser, the son of a silk weaver in Paisley, Scotland, immigrated to America in 1834 with the object of establishing a workers' community and found in the New Lebanon society an organization already fulfilling his ideal. Here he spent the rest of his long life, in the course of which he wrote trenchantly on many subjects, among them hygiene and dietetics, his particular interests. The other, James S. Prescott, a relative of the historian William Prescott, joined the North Union society in 1826 and was soon elevated to the eldership. Prescott was an early advocate of eugenics. Just as Shakerism hoped to select, in a spiritual sense, the 'best bricks' made by man, so did he anticipate, 'by scientific selection and combination in obedience to certain given laws of reproduction,' the physical improvement of the human race. 'As things are,' Prescott wrote in a letter to the *American Socialist*, 'multitudes of persons of both sexes are no more suitable to reproduce human beings in the image of God than the roach-backed, crooked-legged, spindle-shanked, slab-sided, Indian ponies are suitable for generating the best types of the noble horse!'

325

In sharp and sometimes outspoken opposition to Evans's position stood Elder Harvey Eads of South Union, the ablest representative of the conservative ideal. This remarkable man had had the unusual experience of being born among the Shakers, for his parents were converted shortly after their marriage. He was placed in the children's order at South Union before he was a year old, and spent his whole life, eighty-four years, in the Kentucky societies, the last twenty as presiding bishop of the two communities in that state. Eads argued for the principle of rigorous separation, maintaining that by setting an example of pure and righteous living the Shakers could best serve the world. Contamination was inevitable, he believed, if they became concerned, even as reformers, with outside political or

326

social institutions. The whole interest of the church should be the spiritual welfare of its members, the building of an order of increasing virtue which would attract men *from* the world. A believer in self-improvement and self-sufficiency, he staunchly defended Shaker discipline and government — 'the true-souled and obedient Shaker,' he wrote, 'is the freest person on the foot-stool of God, because all his bonds are self-imposed.' Only by the path which Mother Ann had blazed could the church fulfil its appointed destiny.   327

The difficulty faced by this group, and a problem inherent in the whole concept of separation, was where to draw the line between worldliness and sainthood. What was intrinsically or potentially good in the world was often appropriated for the holy cause. If certain conveniences were condoned, who could say what ones should be denied? If beauty were resident in utility and order, was it wrong eventually to accept it for its own sake? Committed to the principle of scientific progress, how could the order totally insulate itself from the materialism of the industrial age? In short, how was the lead to know at just what point compromises with pure Shakerism might be made? The framers of the original covenant, like those of the American constitution, indulged in generalities which were susceptible to loose or strict construction. The covenant of the Church Order at New Lebanon was repeatedly revised and implemented by circulars.   328 Society and family covenants, though patterned on the first constitution, contained such divergencies that in 1829 the Shakers tried to make them all uniform, a move complicated by the separate social character and relative independence of each of the communities. The western bloc of colonies, furthermore, was too far removed from the eastern for an efficient, unified administration; certain weak or ambitious leaders sent to the West by the central ministry were resented; and a difference in regional outlook, impalpable but real, further separated the sections. In the federated Shaker system, the balance of powers between the central and local authority was never clearly defined or attained.

A middle stand between the positions of Evans and Eads was taken by Eldresses White and Taylor of Mount Lebanon. Students of the sect's history and heirs to the best in its thought, they advocated the retention of covenantal principles but pleaded for a 'more radical application' of the doctrine of united interest, broadened to meet the spirit of the time, its 'growing intellectuality,' and the 'self-governing

329   power of the individual.' These leaders of latter-day Shakerism would
try to abolish the competition and 'distinctive interests' which they
saw increasing between societies and families, regulate finances more
stringently, and reawaken the spiritual gift which had depreciated
since money matters had assumed too great an import and the ministry had been called upon to take over too much of the temporal care.
They were convinced that the society could be an instrument of reform in the world without sacrificing a single element of its fundamental faith. But even as they spoke, with confidence in the future,
the structure they would save was collapsing about them.

Another source of disunity, doubtless inevitable in a theocracy,
was the tendency of the system to produce two classes, those who governed and consequently had opportunities for individual initiative
and development, and those who were governed and lacked the same
facilities for self-expression. All were subjected to the same religious
discipline. In theory the leaders were the greatest servants. But in
practice it must be admitted that the assumption of responsibilities
carried with it privileges, powers, and freedoms denied to the com-
monalty. Signs of discontent among the governed, particularly the
youthful members, first appeared in the western communities. Surrender of property and 'confinement to small areas of land,' one observer wrote, were not western ideals; irritation was felt over the rule
of strict obedience, especially to eastern leaders. At Union Village,
about 1825, a faction proposed that appointments be made on the
democratic basis of majority vote of members instead of by the min-
330   istry. At Pleasant Hill, demands for change in the method of selecting officers, and even for a division of property, were being put forth
about 1827; one proposal was to divide the church into two governments, one spiritual, one temporal, each with its own officials. All such
suggestions, however, were overruled by the central ministry, who
took the position that 'if we let the people govern by vote . . . we
should soon fall to pieces, for the order and government of Christ's
Kingdom was not in that line . . .'

Elder Briggs of the Enfield (N.H.) society, whose forty-year devotion to the cause had not obscured his critical faculties, was convinced that both the leadership and indenture practices of the sect
were gravely deficient. In contrast to the monastic system, where
'girls must return to homes to gain a knowledge of life, duties and
pleasures, to become old enough to decide intelligently,' the leaders

of the United Society, he wrote, were 'educated to be children, usually remain children, and the product of their teaching is again children.' With many others, this elder had often revolted at being 'subject to the dictation of others no wiser than himself in matters of slight importance,' of 'giving up his own way to come or be sent.' In another connection, speaking for the male members, he deplored 'our deprivation of female association,' which served 'to distort us into unevenly developed beings and worked an almost irreparable injury.' Close friendship, either among members of one sex or between the sexes, was frowned upon as 'marriage.' After a lifetime of experience, Briggs concluded that the society was more of an institution than a home, 'like boarding school with no vacations . . . no ending of the term.'   *331*

The leadership principle was indeed a complicated one. It may have been true that brains came to the top naturally, and that leaders were appointed with the mutual approbation of the whole body. But with no provision for actual voting, and with the appointing body (the ministry) a self-contained office, there was no guarantee against undemocratic choices or outright favoritism. Once in power an incompetent officeholder could, and sometimes did, use the position unwisely, even dictatorially, until perchance he or she was removed.

Nor was a leader's judgment infallible just because it rested on revelation. False inspiration was not unknown. Besides, since 'gifts'   *332* were the prerogative of any member, they could be contradictory. An illustration of the conflict between obedience to an inner gift and the rule of obedience to the elders is given in a story related by Edward Everett:

A youth in one of the Shaker settlements . . . was once asked whether he had his liberty and could do as he pleased. 'Certainly,' said the youth, 'we do whatever we have a gift to.' On being asked what he should do, if he wanted on a fine winter's morning to go and skate on Enfield pond, he replied, 'I would tell the elder that I had a gift to go down and skate.' Being asked further, whether the elder would probably permit him, he answered, 'Certainly, unless the elder had a gift that I should not go.' 'But if you still told the elder, that you had a gift to go down and skate, and go you must?' 'Why then the elder would tell me, that I had a "lying gift" and he had a gift to beat me, if I did not go about my work immediately.'   *333*

Strong spiritual guidance was needed to sustain the afflatus. This the order had in its first four leaders: Mother Ann was followed in turn by the dynamic Whittaker, the competent Meacham, and the beloved Lucy Wright. But when Mother Lucy died in 1821, no highly respected single authority remained. The four-fold ministry at New Lebanon continued to direct. The branch ministries continued to function, with many capable elder brothers and elder sisters in these offices. Such distribution of power, however, with no outstanding personality at the top, was not conducive to unity. Furthermore, in the 1820's there were few witnesses left who had participated in the inspiring experience that brought the church into being. The revivals of 1827 and 1837 re-animated the movement. The Shakers continued to look for another revival that would awaken the old spirit and replenish their communities. But more and more, after mid-century, did service become a repetition of the old forms — which, in essence, was 'anti-spiritual.'

That the course led downward in the end is no reflection on the people who traveled the road. The conviction that man, through labor that was worship and through worship that was a 'labouring for a sense of God,' could progressively elevate himself, here and in the hereafter, to the plane of pure spirituality — above sensuality and material concerns — was an inspiring ideal which gave meaning to the great adventure. Many must have questioned at times the means of attainment, wondering to themselves whether character might not best be formed by direct combat with evil *in* the world; whether the marital vow, honorably pledged, might not be as pure and sacred as the vow of chastity; whether man could best perfect himself by separation *from* the world. Doubts may have obscured the vision of a heaven on earth, but that there was such a vision, 'bright and glorious,' we may be sure.

Whatever may have been the limitations in the strange personality and simple teachings of Ann Lee, it is certain that her testimony attracted individuals of integrity and native ability. Their names crowd the rolls — the Meachams, Lucy Wright, David Darrow, David Osborne, Ruth Farrington, Eleazer Rand, Ruth Landon, Rachel Spencer, Hannah Kendal, the Goodriches, the Tallcotts, the Bishops, the Wells family, the Youngs family, Eliab Harlow, Sarah Harrison, Ebenezer Cooley, Issachar Bates, Betsy Bates, Richard McNemar, John Dunlavy, David Spinning, James Jewett, Henry Blinn, Abraham Perkins, Richard Pelham, John Vance, William

Leonard, Grove Blanchard, John Whiteley, Eunice Bathrick, Calvin Green, Antoinette Doolittle, George Lomas, Harvey Eads, James Prescott, David Parker, Daniel Hawkins, Aurelia Mace, Otis Sawyer, Mary Hazzard, Polly Reed, Harriet Bullard, the Knights and Whites, Elijah and Elisha Myrick, Martha Anderson, Dorothy Durgin, Daniel Fraser, Frederick Evans, Richard Bushnell, Catherine Allen, Leila Taylor, Anna Case, Amos Stewart, George Wickersham, Giles Avery, and hundreds more — men and women of personality, intelligence, and virtue. As we study their lives or read what they wrote, so often the product of vigorous minds, it is difficult to believe such people could have been deluded followers of a false prophet. In an age of seeking, Shakerism was a clear answer to the question: What shall I do to be saved? It offered a discipline and a means of service. And in the end it bore fruit in abundance.

Indeterminate values lay in sheer character itself, in individual power augmented by consciousness of common purpose. If the Believers are to be judged by their works, as they would wish, emphasis must be placed on the influence, over the years, of what one member has termed 'consolidated goodness.' In a close union, the bonds of fellowship were so re-enforced as to transmute good will into an agency of progress. Who can measure how greatly this society affected the forces working for equalitarianism in America? As examples of the extent to which man can subordinate self to the common good, who can say what contribution Shakerism made to a restless age of competitive individualism? Its aims were doubtless beyond its reach, but the spectacle of a devoted company daily committed to certain fundamentals of Christian living must have raised challenges and established standards of widespread import.   *334*

Qualities of heart and mind found expression in many ways to form a more tangible heritage. The songs and dances and rituals; the inspirational drawings and paintings; the craftsmanship which so truly exemplifies principle; the buildings bespeaking integrity and purpose; the surviving products, stamped with the seal of a uniform excellence, of a progressive industry; the labor of hands in every sphere — products (in Thoreau's words) of 'some unconscious truthfulness, and nobleness, without even a thought for the appearance' — remain to tell us of the character of the 'indweller.' The Shakers loved order and peace, simplicity and humility, the fertility of the field, and the sanctity of the communal home. The forces which operated within and upon the church evolved forms by which it is not unjust to judge the cause. And as the world slowly absorbs another dissident faith, much remains to record the seeking, and in some measure the finding, of truth, and beauty, and light.

Appendices

The Millennial Laws

THE so-called Millennial Laws of the Shakers, never printed or not even widely circulated in written form, implemented the doctrines of the order and thus, in effect, greatly illuminate not only its government but the intimate habits and customs of the people.

The history of the statutes is interesting. They stem partly from the first covenant but chiefly from the verbal instructions and 'waymarks' of Joseph Meacham, who was of course influenced by the testimonies of Ann. According to Isaac Youngs, Meacham established a number of 'bye-laws,' 'forbidding what was wrong and enjoining what was right,' to promote the protection and harmony of the order and 'secure equal rights according to the needs of each one.' These were subject to modification or alteration, and no penalties other than 'a gentle admonition' was 'annexed' to their violation. The Shaker historian gives the following samples:

There shall no one come to worship God, with sin unconfessed.

If any one knows of actual sin, or positive disorder, and have reason to believe it is not and will not be confessed, he or she, shall open it in the line of order, to the Elders.

No male and female shall support, or have a private union or correspondence together, neither shall they touch each other unnecessarilly.

No one shall buy, or sell, in the Church, nor trade with those without, but by union with the Deacons: — neither shall they hold private property.

Such laws were expanded, 'as circumstances suggested,' by Mother Lucy Wright, who was averse to having them published, believing that conditions would necessitate a constant change of content. Sometime before her death, Freegift Wells of Watervliet collected the orders, arranged them under headings, and suggested to her that the compilation be read in meeting. But Mother Lucy objected, remarking that 'if the family found that the Elders had a book of orders others would want a book of orders too. And some that had good memories would be able to provide themselves with books . . . causing them to be esteemed less sacred. And besides, there would be danger of their being taken out among the world.'

What the orders were during her regime we have no way of knowing. The apostate Brown, however, writing in 1812, mentions a few which were obviously operative in the first decade of the century. It was 'contrary to order,' he wrote, for a man or woman to sleep alone; for a man to be alone with a woman; for a man to touch a woman (especially when presents were given); for a woman to walk out alone, or be alone; for men and women to converse together, except in the presence of some of the brethren and sisters; and for a man (when on the road in a carriage) to admit a woman to ride with him. These were later known as 'Separation Acts.' Brown includes certain supplementary statutes on order and cleanliness: it was contrary to order, for instance, to leave bars down, gates open, or anything out of proper place; to spit on the floor; or to talk loudly, shut doors hard, rap hard on the door for admittance, or walk noisily upon the floor.

On 17 August 1821, about six months after Mother Lucy's death, some of these orders were recorded, though apparently only a few copies were made for distribution. In *Shakerism Unmasked*, published in 1828, Haskett lists eighty-one 'contrary to order' acts which he recalled from his recent membership, and which may well have been based on the code of 1821. Roughly divided here into nine categories, they shed so much light on the communal mind during the early period that they are given in their entirety:

I. Separation of the Sexes.

Contrary to order

to give the cooks any directions;
for brethren and sisters to milk together;
for a brother and sister to eat at one table, unless there is some company;
for men and women to sleep together;
for a brother and sister to be in a room together without company;
for a brother to pass a sister on the stairs;
to go into the sisters' rooms without knocking;
for a sister to go to the brothers' shop alone;

for a sister to go to the barn, wood-house or road alone;

for the brethren and sisters to go into each other's rooms
after evening meeting;

for brethren and sisters to talk together in the halls;

for brethren to sing or smoke in the sisters' shop;

for brethren to shake hands or touch the sisters, and vice
versa;

to shake hands with a 'world's woman' without confessing it;

for the brethren to make any presents to the sisters;

for the brethren to go into the room when the sisters are
making the beds.

II. Separation from the World.

Contrary to order

to have right and left shoes;

to pare the heels of the shoes under;

to borrow money among the world;

to go without money among the world;

for a person to go out of the door-yard after evening meeting;

to go out among the world or among other families;

to employ a 'world's' doctor;

to leave a span of horses untied among the world;

to shake hands with the 'world,' unless they first tender their
hand;

to read newspapers in the dwelling house at any time without
the Elder's permission;

to receive or write a letter without the Elder's perusal of it;

to write a letter without retaining a copy;

to take a book without liberty;

to drink any spirituous liquor among the world;

to take your place in meeting after you have been out among
the world.

III. Orders pertaining to the Sabbath.

Contrary to order

to stay from meeting on the Sabbath without liberty;

to go to meeting with sin unconfessed;

to cut hair, pare nails, wash feet, clean shoes, or shave on the
Sabbath;

to walk in the garden on the Sabbath;

to pick fruit on the Sabbath;

to read worldly books or newspapers on the Sabbath;

to go into meeting with boots on;
to go into meeting without sleeve strings.

IV. Orders on uniformity in certain acts of behavior.

Contrary to order

to wear hats above the height given by the Elders;
to fold the left thumb over the right, in prayer, or when standing up in worship;
to kneel with the left knee first;
to put the boot or shoe on the left foot first;
to kneel with handkerchief in hand;
to put the left foot on the stairs first when ascending.

V. Orders regarding 'dumb beasts.'

Contrary to order

to wear spurs;
to kick a beast.

VI. Orders regarding health.

Contrary to order

to eat any fruit after supper;
to eat bread until it is out of the oven 24 hours;
to lie on the ground;
to leave the lower sash of the window up at night.

VII. Orders regarding cleanliness.

Contrary to order

to spit out of the window;
to throw water out of the window;
to spit on the floor.

VIII. Orders on prudence, especially to avoid fires.

Contrary to order

to lean against the wall or bed with a chair;
to carry fire without a fire-box;
to take a lamp or candle without a lanthorn into the clothes room, barn, or wood-house;
to go to the drawers of clothes with a candle;
to smoke in the wood-house, barn, or carding machine factory;
to empty a pipe into the spit-box;
to empty a pipe out of the window;

> to empty ashes into the ash-house until they have stood 24 hours in a tin bucket;
>
> to leave the stove door open, either small or large, and go out of the room;
>
> to leave wood on the stove or under it;
>
> to leave the spit-box near the stove and go out of the room.

IX. Miscellaneous orders

> Contrary to order
>
>> for anyone to write the orders;
>>
>> to allow any copulation productive of mongrelism;
>>
>> to look at beasts when they copulate;
>>
>> to turn hogs and sheep together;
>>
>> to have watches and umbrellas;
>>
>> to inquire into the orders of other families;
>>
>> to tell he or she lieth;
>>
>> to play with dogs and cats;
>>
>> to go into another union meeting without liberty;
>>
>> to stay out of meeting in the evening without liberty;
>>
>> to open your mind out of the line of order;
>>
>> to expose counsel, or tell what the Elders say;
>>
>> to have any money privately;
>>
>> to play in the halls;
>>
>> to give nicknames;
>>
>> to reprove each other before the Elders.

'By the revelation of God thro' Father Joseph,' four brethren at New Lebanon — Eliab Harlow, Henry Markham, Daniel Mosely, and Jethro Turner — were commissioned in 1839 to commit to writing, 'for the benefit of the rising generation, as well as generations to come,' the most important orders and rules. The result was the 'Orders of the Church as Established by Father Joseph (New Lebanon, 1839),' drawn up under the 'three Clusters' of (1) regulations for office deacons, (2) regulations for family deacons, and (3) the duties of the elders in a temporal line. But this book, like the preceding one, was probably not widely circulated. The following year, in May, the New Lebanon instrument Philemon Stewart presented to the society 'A General Statement of the Holy Laws of Zion,' received by inspiration from, and with an introduction by, 'Father James.' There are several copies of this curious document, which reflects to some degree an acquaintance with the earlier laws, and was influential for a brief period. On 18 February 1841, the statutes were again codified, in the form of a revelation from Father Joseph, and copied by the community scribes under varying titles: 'The Holy Orders of the Church,' 'Orders Rules and Counsels for the People of God,' et cetera. In revised form and in phrasing better adapted to practical usage, the orders of February 1841 were 're-established' by the Ministry and Elders in October 1845, and transmitted, with suggestions for their use, to the eighteen societies. Though they were issued again later, the 1845 laws seem to have been the standard version. In conformity with the injunction of their gospel parents, the lead withheld these books from common perusal, preferring to read and re-read sections in meeting until the substance was thoroughly familiar to all. The student of monasticism may notice in how many instances the Laws prescribe practices similar to those enjoined centuries earlier in the famous Rule of St. Benedict.

Millennial Laws,

or

Gospel Statutes and Ordinances

adapted to the Day

of

Christ's Second Appearing.

Given and established in the Church

for the protection thereof

by

Father Joseph Meacham

and

Mother Lucy Wright

The presiding Ministry

and by their Successors

The Ministry and Elders.

Recorded at New Lebanon

Augst 7th 1821.

Revised and re-established by the

Ministry and Elders

Octr. 1845.

TITLE PAGE OF MILLENNIAL LAWS

Preface.

Believers in Christ's Second Appearing, who are united in one body, possess one united and consecrated interest, and therefore, must, in all things, and under all circumstances, be influenced, led, and governed, by one spirit, which is the spirit of God, and be subject to one general law, which is the law of Christ, in this day of his Second Appearing.

But as this general law, comprehends all that is necessary, for the moral and religious government of Believers, so it is divided into a variety of statutes and ordinances, which will apply to all general cases, and teach us our duty, in the various situations and relations, to which we may be called.

The first and great command enjoined upon all Believers, is, that we love the Lord our God with all our heart, might, mind and strength, and the second is like unto it, that we love our brethren and sisters as ourselves.

Under the influence of the first, we shall always be obedient to our Parents and Elders, in the gospel, and under the influence of the second, we shall do to others, as we wish them to do to us in like circumstances.

On these two important points, depend all the statutes and ordinances, contained in the following pages, — and many other orders and rules, relative to different lots of care, and different branches of business, carried on by brethren and sisters separately, not written in this book, which were given by the same authority, and are still considered equally binding on Believers.

For a few years past, there have been, many times, shown unto the Children of Zion, thro' the medium of divine revelation, the various orders and regulations, that were established by the revelation of God, for this holy temple, even the Church of God upon earth.

It is manifestly the will and word of the Heavenly Father, revealed through Mother Ann, Father William, Father James, Father Joseph, and Mother Lucy, (our first gospel parentage) that these holy orders be written for the more safe keeping, and the accommodation of those who do, or may hereafter, stand as Elders in the Church.

And furthermore, that these Holy Laws, and statutes of Zion, should henceforth be kept sacred, throughout all generations, in the hands of those chosen as Elders in the Church.

251

For the sake of perspicuity, this book of orders, is divided into four parts, — The first containing the rules necessary to the general organization of society, the office and calling of those in lots of care therein, and the duties of members thereunto. The second, contains more particular orders for justification and protection. The third contains orders concerning temporal economy, neatness, etc. And the fourth contains Counsels and Rules for guidance and protection in many respects. Each part is divided into sections which contains rules relative to one order of things, etc.

It may not be improper here to remark, that the orders or Laws of Zion, relative to her separation from the spirit of the world, within and without, and relative to confession and repentance of sin, and reconciliation between dissenting parties, also to self-denial, purity, and proper intercourse between the sexes — and the order of the anointing of God, and the transmission of the same to successors, etc. are unchangeable. But those rules and regulations, relative to health, economy, and such as are the necessary attendants of local circumstances, in the social connection of society, are subject to such modifications, amendments, or repeals, as circumstances require, for the union and protection of the various societies and families, throughout Zion, and it is consequently the duty and privilege of the Ministry in each Society, to add or diminish the number of such in this book, as their situation and circumstances require, for the safety, union and protection, of the people under their charge.

Part I.

The General Organization of Society.

The
Order and calling of those in Lots of Care,
with the duties of Members thereunto.

Section I.
The General Organization of Society.

In societies of Believers which are sufficiently large to admit of it,
the order of God requires a regular organization of families in order
to accommodate and provide for the different circumstances of indi-
viduals in temporal things, and also for the advancement of spiritual
travel in the work of regeneration, and the universal good of all the
members, composing such society.

2. The orders, rules and regulations in each family, concerning things
spiritual and temporal, should be such as are adapted to the protection,
benefit and increase, of the numbers gathered therein.

3. The families should be of different classes, or grades, as to order,
government and arrangement in things spiritual and temporal, adapted
to the different situations and circumstances of members in society, and
should be denominated — 1st or center family, generally called the
Church of the society, — 2nd. Family. 3rd., 4th, etc. — or the name of
each, may be such as is adapted to local circumstances, but their respec-
tive places in point of order, should be gradual and progressive.

4. The different orders and families, should in no wise have uncontrolled
access to each other, by their communications either verbal or written,
but all written communications and visits with each other, should be by
the liberty of the Elders therein; and without such liberty, members
should never go from one, to the other of said families.

5. The Church or center family, and as far as is practicable, each family
that is gathered into order, should have a lot of Elders & Eldresses and

253

a lot of Deacons and Deaconesses or Trustees, each lot of which should contain four or more persons, two of each sex.

6. The Church or center family, should be composed of such members, as are free from any involvements with those without, and such as are prepared by a previous privilege in families that are back, (where those who come in, over the age of thirteen, should be first proved), to advance into a further degree of gospel order, in a forward family, and a closer spiritual work of purification, and it would be well, if all could come in at the gathering order, and be measurably proved, before they advance further.

7. None should be gathered into the Church or first family, who cleave unto their natural kindred of Fathers, Mothers, brothers, sisters, husbands, or wives, houses or land; none should be gathered into this order, but such as may by obedience stand spotless before the Lord.

8. There should be a presiding Ministry in each society who should have the general superintendence of all things of importance therein, both spiritual and temporal, and to whom the Elders and Trustees, (and through them the body of the people therein,) are accountable for all their transactions. But two or more societies may compose one Bishopric, as circumstances render it most proper.

9. Circumstances sometimes render it difficult to establish four persons in lots of Elders and Deacons, of course no obligation to fill the number, will apply in such cases, but four is considered the true number, and it should never be neglected, unless driven thereto by necessity.

Section II.

The Order Office and Calling
of
The Ministry.

The Holy Anointed at Holy Mount, (or New Lebanon,) are called and chosen to stand as the first and leading Ministry, in the Zion of God upon earth; unto whom all other orders of the Ministry, in all other societies of Believers are accountable for all their transactions of an official nature.

2. It is the right and duty of the Ministry if found necessary, to alter or repeal certain orders, rules and regulations that may have been established, or that may be established in the vineyard of Christ and Mother upon earth. It is also their right to establish new orders and regulations as far as they find it necessary.

3. It is the right and duty of the Ministry, in each society of Believers, to establish such rules and regulations for the society over which they preside as circumstances render necessary for the protection and benefit of the members thereof.

4. It is the right and duty of the Ministry to hold the Keys of the Heavenly Kingdom of God upon earth, and to let nothing pass the doors of the House of God, or enter the gates of the Holy Vineyard below, that will in any wise, undermine the holy foundation on which it is built.

5. It is the privilege and duty of the Ministry at Holy Mount, (or center society,) to keep open the door of communication with other societies, in as much as it is their duty to link the golden chain of love and union, strength and blessing, throughout the Heavenly Vineyard of God, on earth, by such means as they in their wisdom see fit; — Therefore all visiting from place to place, must be done by their direction.

6. It is the privilege of the Ministry, to give to, or receive from other Believers, such gifts and presents, either spiritual or temporal, as they think will be a strength and benefit to them.

7. The Ministry may in no wise blend in common with the rest of the people; they may not work under the same roof, live in the same house, nor eat at the same table. But their dwelling place shall be in the meeting house, even in the most holy Sanctuary.

8. It is the right and duty of the Ministry in the center society, to go to other societies of Believers, in the land, as often as circumstances shall render it necessary, and they, in their wisdom, may deem it proper; for in their hands are placed the keys of the Holy and Heavenly Kingdom of God on earth.

9. And it is also the right of the Ministry in each Bishopric, in union with the Ministry at the center society, to make such visits there, as they find necessary from time to time, in order to keep unbroken the heavenly bond of union by which the Church of God is united in one.

Section III.

The Office and Calling of Elders, and The Duty of Members thereunto.

Those who are called as Elders, (in union with the Ministry,) are the head of the body, that constitutes the Church of God, they stand in their order, next to the Ministry.

2. It is the duty of the Elders to look to the Ministry for strength, counsel and wisdom, wherewith to guide and direct, the body of the Church of God; — Therefore it becomes necessary for them, from time to time, to make known unto the Ministry, the standing, state and situation of the family, over which they preside, in all things both spiritual and temporal, which according to the order established, must come to the knowledge of the Elders.

3. It is the duty of the Elders strictly to oversee the family placed under their care, and to gather the family to them by the arm of love and rod of correction; to teach them their duty and lead them in the path wherein they should go; to direct all moves and changes in the family, and to take counsel together, in union with the Ministry, to do that which will tend to the general good of each and every individual. To see that good order is kept and supported, in all things, and that disorder is checked. To give and establish from time to time, in union with the Ministry, such needful orders, rules and regulations, as circumstances, in their several families require, for the safety and protection thereof.

4. It is the right of the Elders to know at all times the state and standing of every individual, and to know everything owned and possessed by everyone under their charge.

5. The Elders must never be so engaged in hand labor, as to neglect their duty, which is to stand as witnesses between the Throne of God and the souls of the people. And their duty as it respects the confession of sin, is it not written in the Holy Laws sent forth by the will and hand of Almighty God.

6. It is the duty of every one, to acknowledge and look to their Elders as their lead and protection, in all things.

7. It is the solemn and sacred requirement of God, that every member should keep the door open to his or her Elders, by a free and honest confession of every ignorant and willful transgression, of the holy and sacred orders of the Church, or family in which they reside. And all are required to lay open to them, the true state and situation of their minds.

8. As it is the duty of the Ministry to judge of the doings of the Elders, no common member may judge them, unless they teach that which they know is sinful, or contrary to the gospel; but should consider them as mediators standing between their souls and the Throne of God. And every one should at all times consider it the duty of the Elders to check, reprove or admonish them if they be in any wise out of the way; and of this, it is not the place of members alone to decide.

9. Members may not plead and reason with the Elders, the necessity of their own way and will, as pleading justification when admonished for a fault, as striving against order and government, or for the purpose of obtaining indulgences; but are required to yield reconciliation, and a

*willing obedience to their word, and reverence and respect them. But all
are privileged to suggest such things as they deem an improvement, and
offer the same for consideration, showing the propriety thereof, according to their understanding.*

*10. Persons occupying any place of care, in the family, either spiritual
or temporal, are responsible to the Elders for all their official transactions; and such transactions should be done by their general approbation.*

Section IV.

The Order of Deacons or Trustees,
and
The Duties of Members thereunto.

*Those called as Deacons or Trustees, shall stand as stewards in the
house of God, and their dwelling place should be at the outer court.*

*2. It is the duty of the Deacons and Deaconesses, or Trustees, to see to
the domestic concerns of the family in which they reside, and to perform
all business transactions, either with the world, or with believers in other
families or societies. All trade and traffic, buying and selling, changing
and swapping, must be done by them or by their immediate knowledge
and consent.*

*3. No new fashions, in manufacture, clothing, or wares of any kind, may
be introduced into the Church of God, without the sanction of the Ministry, thro the medium of the Elders of each family thereof.*

*4. All monies, book accounts, deeds, bonds, notes, etc. which belong to
the Church or family must be kept at the Office, unless some other suitable place be provided therefor, by the proper authorities. Exceptions
with regard to spending money are sometimes necessary, which must
always be directed by the Elders in union with the Ministry.*

*5. The Deacons or Trustees should keep all their accounts booked down,
regular and exact, and as far as possible avoid controversies with the
world.*

6. Believers must not run in debt to the world.

*7. The purchase of needful articles that appear substantial and good,
and are suitable for believers to use, should not be neglected, to purchase those which are needlessly adorned because they are a little
cheaper.*

8. Neither Trustees nor any one in their employ should be gone from home among the world, on trading business, more than four weeks at one and the same time.

9. Three brethren who shall be appointed by the Ministry, two of which if consistent, should be Deacons or Trustees, are sufficient to go to the great and wicked cities to trade for any one family.

10. Believers should have no connection in trade or barter with those who have turned their backs to the way of God. Neither should they sojourn with them at night, nor keep company with them in the day, if possibly consistent to avoid it. But if it be necessary to hold conversation with them, do it in such a manner, that when you return home, you can give a correct account of it to your Elders, which should always be done.

11. When you resort to taverns, and public places, you shall not in any wise blend and gather with the wicked, by uniting in unnecessary conversation, jesting and joking, talking upon politics with them, or disputing or enquiring into things which will serve to draw your sense from the pure way of God.

12. All who go out among the world, should observe as far as possible, the order of kneeling, and should always kneel in prayer twice each day, if they have to do it by the road-side, or in the waggon while driving along.

13. Trustees desiring the help of members, not in the Trustees order, to do business for them, or to perform any of their official duties, at home, or abroad, must apply to the Elders for the same.

14. Members employed by the Deacons or Trustees to do business at home or abroad, must render a full and explicit account to them, of all their transactions and expenditures, when such duties are performed, specifying particularly every article for which such expenses were made.

15. Those who reside at the Office, should not, in any wise, all leave home at once and be absent more than eight or ten hours, if consistent to avoid it.

16. When two or more are out together, they should as far as possibly consistent, all eat at one tavern, and lodge in one room, and when you walk in the streets, you should keep so close together that there would not be room for even as much as a dog to run between you and your companion.

17. Those who go out on business for the Deacons or Trustees, have no more right to buy, sell, barter or trade in any way, than any other member in the family, save by the authority of those who send them.

18. It is contrary to good church order for any persons except the Ministry and Elders, to have correspondence with the Deacons or Trustees, relative to their official lot and calling, such as their bargains, and con-

tracts in general, except in cases wherein they are by them employed to do business, in union with the Elders, and in such a manner as the nature of the case may require. But it is reasonable and consistent for members to know the market prices of articles bought or sold, as groceries, dry goods, provisions, hard ware, and other wares if they desire to. But it should be understood that the Deacons are under no obligation to tell common members just what they paid for articles bought, or what they received for articles sold; but they should be free to tell the market prices.

19. *The order of God forbids that Believers should lend money upon usury (or interest) to their brethren of the household of faith, neither should Believers accept interest (or usury) from their brethren, should it be offered.*

20. *As the Deacons or Trustees are called to be examples of godliness, gospel plainness, prudence and good economy in temporal things, they may not purchase for themselves, or receive as a gift, to be kept by them, or at their place of residence, any article or articles, that are superfluous, unnecessary, or such as are disowned in the Church or family in which they reside.*

21. *The Trustees are required to keep all their transactions plain and open to their visible Lead, and when they sustain losses, whether in money or other things, to lay it open before the Lead in its true light. They are also required before making any heavy purchases, to ask counsel and obtain union of the leading influence of the Church or family in which they reside.*

22. *The Trustees are required to attend meetings with the family, as far as their circumstances will possibly admit, as they need the union and strength of the body of the family. They should also attend meals with the family as much as possible, that they may know how to feel for their temporal needs and circumstances, in the line of provisions.*

23. *When brethren and sisters want anything bought, or brought in from among the world, or from other families of Believers, or wish for any article or articles which it is the duty of the Deacons and Deaconesses to provide, they must apply to them for whatever they desire, those of each sex in their own order.*

24. *A supply of such small tools and articles as sisters need, which brethren make, should be made by order of the Deacons, and delivered to the Deaconesses, to whom the sisters should apply for the same, when desired.*

25. *If sisters desire tools, conveniences, or articles of manufacture which come in the brethren's line of business, and which it would require much time to make, they must apply to the Deaconesses, — but if it be*

small chores, they may apply to either Deacons or Deaconesses for the same.

26. When brethren need help of the sisters in their line of business, that will require much time, they must make application to the Deacons, but if it be small chores, they may apply to either Deacons or Deaconesses, as the case may require.

27. No work done in the family for sale, shall go out of the family, save by the knowledge and direction of the Deacons and Deaconesses, except in some uncommon emergency, and then a correct account should be rendered as soon as may be.

28. The Deacons and Deaconesses or Trustees are required by the orders of the gospels, to give to the Elders from time to time a correct account of all matters of importance that have come within their knowledge, concerning the temporal business of the family, and of things that have given out.

29. It is the duty of the Deacons and Deaconesses, to see that suitable furniture for rooms, and suitable food for the family are provided, (as far as lies in their power,) and to see that the food is cooked with good economy.

30. Brethren and sisters have no liberty to make for themselves or for others, accommodations, or conveniences without the union and consent of the Deacons and Deaconesses, each sex in their own order.

31. It is the duty of members to render due respect to the Trustees, Deacons and Deaconesses.

Section V.

Respecting Physicians or Nurses, and the Obligations of Members thereunto.

As the natural body is prone to sickness and disease, it is proper that there should be suitable persons appointed to attend to necessary duties in administering medical aid to those in need.

2. When a brother is so unwell as to be necessitated to resort to the place of the sick, the physicians or nurses, (as the case may be) should make the circumstance known to the Elder brethren, and the Eldresses in union with the Deaconesses should provide a suitable person to attend the sick.

3. Brethren may not apply medical aid to sisters who are sick, without the knowledge and union of the sisters who officiate as nurses in the fam-

ily. Neither should they administer any medicines to the sisters, without telling the sisters in care, what it is made of; — and sisters should do the same in these respects to the brethren.
4. Those appointed as physicians or nurses, should give to the Elders from time to time, a full account of their proceedings with the family in regard to the administration of medicine.
5. If any of the brethren or sisters need assistance in the medical line, they should apply to the physicians or nurses in their own family, and of their own sex, (if there be such) and if not, to such as are appointed, and give themselves up to their direction as it respects their medical treatment. But all have liberty to request such medicines as they desire, but should abide the judgment of their medical advisers, whether it be suitable for them to have it, or not.
6. The order of God forbids that Believers should employ Doctors of the world, except in some extreme cases, or the case of a sick child, whose parents are among the world, and desire such aid; and in such cases, the Ministry or Elders should decide whether it be proper or not.

Part II.

More Particular Orders
for
Justification and Protection.

Section I.

Orders concerning the Confession
of Sin, and Opening the Mind.

No Believers can be justified in keeping any sin covered, under any pretence whatever, but all are required to make confession thereof to those who are appointed in the order of God to hear them.
2. If any member should know of any sin or actual transgression of the Law of Christ, in any one of the family or society, and have reason to believe the same is not known, or has not been confessed in order, the member to whom the matter is known is bound to reveal it to the Elders, so that sin may be put away, otherwise they participate in the guilt and condemnation thereof.

3. *All who ignorantly, carelessly, or willfully break the sacred orders of the gospel, are required to confess the same in the line of order, and this should be done, before such one or ones, as transgress, assemble to worship God.*

4. *If any member or members not appointed to hear openings, shall attentively hear disorderly persons disclose their trials, or their disaffected and unreconciled feelings concerning others, whether in relation to Ministry, Elders, Deacons, brethren or sisters, — it is solemnly enjoined on such member or members, to make confession of the matter to their Elders, as a transgression of the orders of God, in hearing such openings.*

5. *All trials must be opened according to the order of God, and Believers are strictly forbidden to open their trials or their minds, only to those set in order to hear them.*

6. *Believers are forbidden to open the gifts, orders, or regulations of, or pertaining to, their own family or order, to persons in other orders, or to unbelievers.*

7. *If brethren have aught to open concerning any sister or sisters, they must open it to their Elder brethren, — and if sisters have aught to open concerning any brother or brethren, they must open it to their Elder sisters.*

8. *No member or members in the family, who may be admonished or reproved by the Elders, for any fault whatever, are allowed to make any inquiry or take pains to find out, by whom the matter was opened to the Elders.*

9. *No member or members should ever go to the Ministry to open their minds, without the knowledge and approbation of their Elders, unless the Ministry call upon them, for that purpose, in which case it is their duty to be free.*

10. *If any members or member, should discover any violation of the Law of Christ, or any thing contrary to the known doctrines of the gospel, in any person or persons entrusted in any lot of care, either spiritual or temporal, however high or important their calling may be, the person making the discovery is bound to make it known to the Ministry, or to some one, in whom he, or she can place the greatest confidence for salvation.*

11. *If any person should be overcome with anger, so as to lay a brother or sister in a lie, or speak or act contrary to the gospel of Christ, or by any means try to irritate or wound the feelings of a brother or sister, the person so offending, is thereby debarred from any place in our ranks in meeting, and must stand behind all in the worship of God, until restored by confession.*

Section II.

Orders concerning the Spiritual
Worship of God,
Attending to Meetings &c.

Believers are required by the orders of God, to retire to their rooms in silence, for the space of half an hour, and labor for a sense of the gospel, before attending meeting.

2. All should sit erect in straight ranks in retiring time, or if infirmity render it necessary, they may stand erect *or walk the floor in the fear of God, and attend to the reading of the hymn or anthem, to be sung in meeting, which should be read in retiring time; and none should have any conversation upon anything whatever, neither should they sleep nor idly lounge away the time, or leave the room except it be very necessary.*

3. No member is allowed by the orders of God to present himself to worship him, when under the condemnation of sin unconfessed. But all are required to present themselves to worship, with clean hands, pure hearts and justified consciences.

4. All should go into meeting in the fear of God walking on their toes, and two abreast if the passage way be sufficiently wide to admit of it, keeping step together, and none should have any talking, laughing, or hanging on the railing, while going to, or coming from meeting.

5. When brethren and sisters place themselves in a body in meeting, for the worship of God, the ranks should be straight, not only to the right and left, but also forward and back; forward ranks should always be as long as the rest, and by no means should there be vacancies in the ranks, it has a tendency to excite disunion.

6. Brethren and sisters should not allow themselves to be gaping or yawning in meeting.

7. No one may be absent from meeting, without liberty from the Elders, or some other person authorised by them to give permission, and none should go out of meeting if consistent to avoid it.

8. When any person is under the operation of the power of God, or on their knees in devoted prayer, whether in meeting or elsewhere, all who are present, should attend carefully, and not be otherwise engaged.

9. Brethren and sisters may not go to each other's shops to learn songs, it has a tendency to naturalize them.

10. When Believers go forth in holy order, they must take three steps forward of an equal length, setting the feet straight forward at the turn if possible; and brethren should set off with the left foot and sisters with the right; brethren turn to the right and sisters to the left. But in the march all should set off with the right foot.

Section III.

Orders of the Sabbath.

The gospel strictly forbids that there should be any hand labor performed on the Sabbath, which can consistently be avoided; but all must keep it holy and sacred unto the Lord.

2. There must be no baking of bread, pies or cakes, no frying of cakes, and no cooking of meat, or fish in any way, and no preparing the same in any way to cook, or eat, except by liberty from the Elders. No paring, cutting or stewing of any kind of fruits, for kitchen use. Neither may pumpkins or potatoes be pared on the Sabbath, on any occasion whatever; and no beans or rice may be picked over.

3. Fruit and vegetables must not be gathered on the Sabbath, unless in case of great necessity.

4. All cutting of the hair, paring of the nails, blacking or greasing of the shoes, and boots, and such like things, are forbidden to be done on the Sabbath, and shaving the beard should never be done on the Sabbath except in case of great necessity, when it would be quite inconsistent to avoid it.

5. No one may walk in the fields, gardens, or orchards, on the Sabbath day, unless duty requires; Nor is it allowable to go to shops unless it be of a very short and necessary errand, without liberty from the Elders, but all must keep in the dwelling house, and in their own rooms as much as they consistently can.

6. There should be no riding out, or visiting done on the Sabbath, unless duty requires. When visitors are with us from a distance, they may be visited on the Sabbath.

7. Shop windows fronting the street, should not be left open on the Sabbath, except by special liberty, and on some needful occasion.

8. Brethren and sisters are not allowed to carry their dirty clothes to the wash house, after sun rise, before sun set, on the Sabbath, and the sisters may not go to sort or pick them over, before that time.

9. No bathing, or showering the body in water should be done on the

Sabbath, unless it be very early in the morning, except in case of sickness, and by order of the Physicians.

10. All Believers are required to abstain from the use of cider or other spirituous or fermented liquors on Saturday and Sabbath. And it would be much better not to use such liquors at all.

11. None should converse unnecessarily upon what is going on among the world, upon the Sabbath, nor tell stories that ye may have heard, or collected from the wicked and unclean.

12. No loud or boisterous talking or laughing, should be done on the Sabbath, but ye should keep the fear of God, in all your goings forth, remembering it is a holy day unto the Lord.

13. It is the order of the Church (or centre family,) to have a general singing meeting, the first Sabbath afternoon or evening in each month; and for all the middle aged and young to attend; and as many others as feel to.

14. No books, pamphlets, advertisements, almanacs, newspapers, or publications of any kind, save the Bible and such publications upon religious subjects, as have been or may be published by the United Society called Shakers, may be read on the Sabbath, without the union of the Spiritual Lead, *with which union such other publications as are suitable, may be read. But it is not compatible with gospel to study the arts or sciences of human invention, on the Sabbath.*

15. No kind of meat or fish may be eaten on the Sabbath by Believers, except in case of ill health and by direction of the Physicians or Nurses.

Section IV.

The Order of Christmas, Thanksgiving and Fast Days.

As the signal by which all true followers of Christ are known, is unfeigned and unalloyed love to each other, the order of God requires that on Christmas day Believers should make perfect reconciliation, one with an other; and leave all grudges, hard feelings, and disaffection one towards an other, externally behind on this day; and to forgive, as we would be forgiven; and nothing which is this day settled, or which has been settled previous to this, may hereafter be brought forward against an other.

2. It is the order to attend one general meeting, and one union meeting on this day.

3. It is order to remember the poor of this world on this day, and to carry to the place of deposit, at the Trustees Office, such garments and goods, as are designed for them.

4. This day must be kept sacredly, and no work, except such necessary chores as are allowable on the Sabbath, may be done on this day, or until sunset.

5. Days appointed by the Government, for Thanksgiving and Fast, are also required to be kept and regarded, — and Believers should attend one meeting, and devote the remainder of such days in cleaning, and putting things and apartments in order.

Section V.

Orders concerning Intercourse between the Sexes.

The gospel of Christ's Second Appearing, strictly forbids all private union between the two sexes, in any case, place, or under any circumstances, in doors or out.

2. One brother and one sister, must not be together, alone, at any time, longer than to do a short and necessary duty or errand; and must not have private talk together at all, which they desire to have unknown to the Elders. Neither should brethren and sisters touch each other unnecessarily.

3. Brethren and sisters must not work together, except on special occasions, and then by liberty from the Elders.

4. Brethren and sisters may not make presents to each other in a private manner.

5. Brethren and sisters may not write for each other nor to each other, without liberty from the Elders.

6. If brethren and sisters need instruction in reading, writing, or music, or any other branch of literature or science, they must receive it from those of their own sex, or by such persons as the Elders may appoint.

7. Brethren and sisters may not pass each other on the stairs.

8. Brethren and sisters may not shake hands together.

9. It is contrary to order for Believers to offer to shake hands with apostates; and if brethren shake hands with women of the world, or if sisters shake hands with men of the world, they must open it to their Elders before attending meeting.

10. Brethren and sisters may not go to each other's apartments, with-

*out a just and lawful occasion; but when they do go, they should rap at
the door, and go in by liberty.*

*11. When brethren go to brethren's rooms, or sisters to sisters' rooms,
they should ask if they may come in, but this is not the order or duty of
Ministry or Elders.*

*12. There must not be any sitting or standing on the outside steps, rail-
ings or platforms, nor in the doors, or halls to hold lengthy conversations, either of brethren with brethren, sisters with sisters, or of brethren
and sisters together.*

*13. Brethren and sisters must not go into each other's apartments, after
evening meeting at night, except on some very needful occasion.*

*14. The brethren must all leave their rooms, while the sisters are doing
the necessary chores therein; unless prevented by sickness or infirmity.*

*15. Sisters must not mend, nor set buttons on brethren's clothes, while
they have them on.*

*16. Sisters should not use cloths that have their own initials on to do up
brethren's clothes in, nor keep the brethren's clothes with their's, neither
hang them side by side, nor together.*

*17. Brethren and sisters must not wear each other's clothes, nor be try-
ing them on, on any occasion whatever.*

*18. When brethren and sisters come together to support union, their
conversation should be open and general, and no whispering or blinking
may be done at such times; and blinking should never be practised.*

*19. None should sit crosslegged nor in any awkward posture, in the time
of any meeting for worship; and in union, or singing meeting there
should be at least five feet distance, between the seats of brethren and
sisters, when there is sufficient room to admit of it.*

*20. No fans, cologne water, or any kind of perfumery, may be used in
time of union meetings, or any other meeting, neither should any one or
ones, scent themselves with perfumes, immediately before attending such
meetings.*

*21. All are required to attend union meetings at the appointed times,
unless special duty requires them to be absent; and such absence should
be by liberty of the Elders. Real flesh hunters, are generally willing to
be absent from an orderly union meeting, and to meet their peculiar fa-
vorites in private.*

*22. None should leave union meetings, or any meetings for worship, only
on necessary duties, which should seldom occur, requiring such absence.*

*23. Brethren's and sister's shops, should not be under one and the same
roof, except those of the Ministry.*

*24. When sisters walk out into the fields, to the barns, or out buildings,
or even to the brethren's shops, there should be at least two in company,*

*for it is considered improper for one sister to go alone on such occasions,
unless by special liberty of their Elder sisters.*

*25. Brethren and sisters must not take opportunities to come together
to settle difficulties or make reconciliation with each other, without liberty from the Elders; neither should they accept for company at such
times, a youth under eighteen years of age.*

*26. It is not allowable for brethren to go to sisters' shops, to partake
of melons, fruits, or nuts; neither should they go to the kitchen for that
purpose, except at meal times. Neither may sisters go to brethren's shops
for a like purpose.*

*27. Brethren and sisters may not lend things to each other; intending
never to take them back, without the liberty of the Deacons and Deaconesses, each sex in their own order.*

*28. Sisters must not take a girl that lives in the children's order, to be
their only companion, when they go to brethren's shops on errands.*

*29. It is disorderly for brethren and sisters to spend much time in mak-
ing conveniences or articles of manufacture for each other, save such as
come within the regular line of business, done by brethren and sisters in
general, except by the direction of the Deacons and Deaconesses, each
sex in their own order.*

Section VI.

Orders concerning the Language of Believers.

*Believers are not allowed to call nicknames, or use bywords, nor to call
each other by the last name, adding the title of doctor, friend, etc.*

*2. No Believer should ever repeat the cursing and swearing of the world,
when relating any circumstance, or telling stories.*

*3. Believers should never use vulgar expressions, like the following, viz.
I wish I was dead! I wish I could die! I wish I had never been born! My
Stars! Good heavens! My gracious! etc. or any thing of the like nature,
it is wicked.*

*4. Believers should not use rough, vulgar words, nor tell light, vain, non-
sensical stories which are known to be untrue.*

*5. All filthy stories, and all conversation which tends to excite lustful
sensations, are directly contrary to the purity of the gospel, and utterly
forbidden. And whoever offends in this manner, must make confession
before meeting, or stand behind all in the ranks, when assembled for wor-*

ship. All who hear or listen to any such story or conversation, are required to open it before meeting.

6. It is contrary to order, for any Believer to blend with the world in conversation upon politics, jesting, joking or talking upon any thing that will serve to draw the sense from the pure way of God.

7. All telling of falsehood, evil speaking one of an other, backbiting or tattling, are utterly forbidden by the gospel.

8. No one should carry news, from one to an other, that will stir up and make mischief; or bring up faults and failings that have been confessed and put away. Neither should the mistakes and missteps of any one, either those in the body or out, be handed down from generation to generation.

9. It is ungodly for brethren and sisters to talk of rejecting their privilege among Believers, or in the way of God, and of falling back to the world.

Section VII.

Orders concerning rising in the Morning and retiring to Rest at Night.

All are required to rise in the morning at the signal given for that purpose; and when any rise before the usual time they must not be noisy.

2. Brethren should leave their rooms, within fifteen minutes after the signal time of rising in the morning, unless prevented by sickness or infirmity.

3. Sisters must not go to brethren's rooms, to do chores, until twenty minutes after the signal time of rising in the morning.

4. There must be no unnecessary conversation after evening meeting, and none at all in bed, unless absolutely necessary.

5. All who sleep in a room must go to bed at the same time, and together, *if not prevented by other duties.*

6. All who lodge in one room, must kneel down together as much as they consistently can, both evening and morning, but none are required to lie in bed, until the signal time for rising, unless they desire to.

7. No one may sit up after the usual time of retiring to rest, to work, read, write, or any thing of the kind, without liberty from the Elders, and the knowledge of those who have the care of the room where they lodge.

8. All should retire to rest in the fear of God, without any playing, or boisterous laughing, and lie straight.

Section VIII.

Orders concerning Attending to Meals, Eating, &c. &c.

It is an established order, for Believers to kneel, before and after eating, when at home and among themselves, and when among the world, as far as is consistent.

2. All should leave their work, when the signal is given for them to gather in at meal time, and be in their rooms, or the sitting-room in readiness to repair to the dining room, in order and in the fear of God, keeping step together.

3. No talking, laughing or playing is allowed of when going to, coming from, or at the table.

4. When kneeling, none should hold their handkerchiefs in their hands, but they should close their eyes, and devote their spirits in prayer and thanksgiving to God, without leaning or lotching [sic] on any thing, unless infirmity require it.

5. All not engaged in duty in the kitchens, are forbidden to throng them at meal time, or at any time, unnecessarily, or to hold unnecessary conversation in them at any time.

6. Brethren and sisters may not go to the kitchens to wash, unless duties relative to the kitchen call them there.

7. If any are unwell, and have need of a diet different from the family for a few meals, they may go to the cooks, and ask for it freely, and it is their duty to prepare it for them. But none should expect to be urged to have something different from common, while they are able to ask for themselves.

8. No one or ones, except those set in order for that purpose, may instruct the cooks in their duty, or undertake to represent to them.

9. It is the duty of the Deacons and Deaconesses to dictate [to] the cooks; and the duty of the Elders and Eldresses to see that good order is attended to concerning the same.

10. No unripe fruit is allowed to be eaten in its natural state.

11. No one or ones, may eat any kind of raw fruit, or nuts, before breakfast, or after six o'clock at night.

12. No one may be absent from meals, unless duty requires, or in case of ill health.

13. No one should talk while eating, and no one present should talk to any person that is eating, unless it be very necessary.

14. If any go on errands to other families, they should avoid being there at meal time, as far as is possibly consistent.

15. All who do not reside in the gathering order, that have occasion to go there of errands etc. are counselled not to be there at meal time, and to have a meal got for them there, as they are unequally burthened with getting meals for visitors.

16. It is not allowable to eat wheat bread the same day it is baked; for it is considered very unwholesome.

Section IX.

Concerning Caretakers of Dwelling Rooms.

It is the duty of those who are placed as caretakers in the rooms, to see that the furniture is used carefully, the room kept clean and decent, and to know that good order is maintained therein; And if the inmates deviate therefrom it is their duty to kindly admonish them, and if they do not receive the admonition, they should make the case known to the Elders, and there leave it.

2. It is the duty of those who have care in the rooms, to make known to the Elders, from time to time, the situation of the room, and the general conduct of those therein, where they have placed them to take charge.

3. If a brother or sister desires to make any change of furniture, in the room, it must be done by the union and consent of those who have the charge therein.

Section X.

Orders concerning Furniture in Retiring Rooms.

The following is the order in which retiring rooms should be furnished, the number of articles may be more, or less, according to the size of the room, and the number of inmates therein.

2. Bedsteads should be painted green, — Comfortables should be of a modest color, not checked, striped or flowered. Blankets or Comfortables

*for out side spreads, should be blue and white, but not checked or striped;
other kinds now in use may be worn out.*

*3. One rocking chair in a room is sufficient, except where the aged reside.
One table, one or two stands, a lamp stand may be attached to the wood-
work, if desired. One good looking glass, which ought not to exceed
eighteen inches in length, and twelve in width, with a plain frame. A looking glass larger than this, ought never to be purchased by Believers. If
necessary a small glass may hang in the closet, and a very small one may
be kept in the public cupboard of the room.*

*4. Window curtains should be white, or of a blue or green shade, or some
very modest color, and not red, checked, striped or flowered.*

*5. The carpets in one room, should be as near alike as can consistently
be provided, and these the Deaconesses should provide.*

*6. The following books may be used, and kept in retiring rooms, viz.
Bibles, Testaments, Concordances, such religious books as have been or
may be published by Believers, Dictionaries, Grammars, Spelling books,
and such other books as the Leading Influence deem profitable for such
purposes. But works on the sciences, (except it be moral science) such as
Natural Philosophy, Natural, Civil or Profane History, Biography,
Miscellany in general, Allegory etc. are not suitable to be kept in retiring
rooms, where souls meet to labor for the gifts of God.*

*7. No maps, Charts, and no pictures or paintings, shall ever be hung
up in your dwelling-rooms, shops, or Office. And no pictures or paintings
set in frames, with glass before them shall ever be among you. But modest advertisements may be put up in the Trustees Office when necessary.*

8. Newspapers may not be read in your retiring rooms on any condition.

*9. Each room should be provided with a tin, earthen, or other safe ves-
sel, to keep friction matches in.*

*10. If any person, or persons, mar, break or destroy, any article or ar-
ticles of furniture in the retiring rooms, it is such an one's duty, to acknowledge the same, to the Deacons or Deaconesses, as the case may be,
and if possible to repair the injury.*

Section XI.

Orders concerning Books, Pamphlets,
and Writings in General.

*Believers are allowed to make plain bound books for writing hymns,
anthems, etc. or for Journals, Records, etc. But very superfluously marbled books, or paper, are not allowed to be used or made among Believers.*

2. Brethren and sisters are not allowed to purchase, or borrow books, of the world, or other families of Believers, without permission of the Elders of the family wherein they live.

3. No one should read books, when out among the world, that are not allowed of among Believers. If the world should offer any Believer a book which would be allowed of, though they might not have had liberty to get such a book, it would be better to receive it, than to give offence, but it should be shown to the Elders before it is read or circulated.

4. No books, or pamphlets of any kind, are allowed to be brought into the family, without the knowledge and approbation of the Elders, except on conditions as before shown.

5. Almanacs of every kind, must be inspected by the Elders, before they are used in the family.

6. If any member of the family should receive a letter from any person, or persons, such person receiving the letter, must show it to the Elders before it is opened, and it should be opened and read in their presence.

7. If any member should write a letter to send abroad, it must be shown to the Elders, before it is sealed, or sent away. But the Office Deacons are allowed to write or receive letters on temporal business, without showing them to the Elders.

8. No hymns, anthems, or songs of any kind, or any other writings, may be carried out of the family, or brought or received into the family without the knowledge and approbation of the Elders thereof.

9. Newspapers, shall be received alone by those at the Office, or outer court, and should there be returned and kept, when they have been perused in the family; and none should come into the family except by the knowledge of the Elders.

10. Two family Journals should be kept by, or by the order of the Deacons and Deaconesses, in which all important occurrences, or business transactions should be registered.

11. One or two Journals of spiritual things, may be kept, by order of the Elders in each family.

Section XII.

Concerning Marking Tools and Conveniences.

The initials of a person's name, are sufficient mark to put upon any tool, or garment, for the purpose of distinction.

2. Blue and white thread should generally be used for marking garments.

3. It is considered unnecessary to put more than two figures for a date, on our clothes, or tools, and it is strictly forbidden unnecessarily to embellish any mark.

4. No one should write or print his name on any article of manufacture, that others may hereafter know the work of his hands.

5. It is not allowable for the brethren to stamp, write or mark their own names, upon any thing which they make for the sisters, nor for sisters to do in like manner, upon articles made for the brethren.

6. No writing with red ink, may be done for ornament, and none at all without liberty from the Elders.

7. No gilding or lettering may be put upon books, manufactured among Believers, except printed books.

8. No names of individuals may be put upon the out side of the covers of books, of any kind.

Section XIII.

Orders concerning Intercourse between Families.

No member may go out of the family wherein they live, to any other family, on an errand, or on a visit, without liberty of the Elders.

2. Visiting between parents and children, or with relatives from other families, or from among the world, should be done at the Office as a general rule; and wherein it is proper to deviate from this rule, the Elders must direct according to circumstances.

3. Brethren and sisters may not go to the Office to see visitors, without liberty from the Elders for the same.

4. Common members are forbidden by the orders of God, to make known the orders, rules, regulations or gifts of the family wherein they reside, to persons residing in other orders, or families, except by liberty, or direction of the Elders.

Section XIV.

Orders concerning Hunting and Wandering Away.

Boys under fifteen years of age, may not go a hunting with guns, and the longer they let guns alone the better.

2. Brethren and sisters are not allowed to wander away from their companions in employ, without giving them information where they are going, if to be absent over half an hour.

Section XV.

Orders concerning going Abroad, and Intercourse with the World.

No members except those in the Deacon's or Trustee's order, may go from home, even off the farm, without liberty from the Elders.

2. When any of the family go abroad, they must apply to the Deacons or Trustees for spending money, and when returned home, a correct and explicit account of all such expenditures, as have been made while absent, should be rendered unto that order and office, wherefrom the money was received, specifying all, and singular, the articles and purposes for which it was expended.

3. When any of the family go from home on business or for a ride, on their return home, they must give the Elders an account of their proceedings and their attending circumstances which have occurred in their absence.

4. When any of the family go out and stay over night, or longer, on their return home, and before they take their places in the family, they must give the Elders an account of their journey, as it respects protection, success, etc. etc. while absent. And they must take their places behind all, in the spiritual worship of God, if they assemble on the evening of their return; but are not required to continue in that place, longer than through one meeting, unless they have been absent a number of days; in which case, the Elders should direct them, when to return to the ranks.

5. Persons employed on journeys, which require them to be absent at meals, (or on long journeys) have liberty to purchase such drinks and eatables, as are allowed of at home, for their present comfort, but none such are allowed to buy fruits, nuts, confectionery, etc. etc. to bring home with them, unless employed by the proper authorities so to do.

6. None who go out, may buy for themselves, articles of any kind, without liberty from the Deacons or Trustees.

7. When two are out together among the world, and duty calls them to be separated, when they meet again, they are required to give to each other, a correct account of what their duty and business was, in their absence.

8. *No one should call into merchant's stores and enquire the price of articles that they have no business with, and that they do not expect to buy.*

9. *It is not allowable for any to loiter around, and blend with the world, in unnecessary conversation either in public or private.*

10. *It is forbidden for Believers to go into Museums, Theatres, or to attend Caravans or shows, to gratify curiosity; and none should go on board of Steam Boats or Vessels, or into prisons or jails, unless duty requires.*

11. *If any have conversation with backsliders, or reprobates, whether at home or abroad, they must open it to the Elders; but such conversation should always be avoided, if consistent with propriety.*

12. *When brethren and sisters ride out they must clear the horses from the waggon, when they stop to bait, to prevent accidents.*

13. *One brother, and one sister, must not walk out, or ride out, together, alone; nor take with them for company, a child under ten years of age, for their only companion.*

14. *As opportunities for riding out are unavoidably unequally offered to all, owing to their situation and circumstances, it is considered good order and equality to have such articles as would be liable to be purchased by those who ride out, and such as are allowable at home, as melons, choice fruits, nuts, sweetmeats, raisins, figs, confectionery, etc. purchased by the Deacons or Trustees, if purchased at all, and equally divided among all, that none may be slighted. It is therefore improper for those who ride out, freely to indulge in the purchase of such things; but the sick and feeble, may at all times be provided for comfortably.*

Section XVI.

Orders concerning Literary Education and the Schooling of Children.

Children of different families among Believers gathered into order, should not be schooled together, if it can reasonably be avoided.

2. *Girls school should be kept in the summer, and boys school in the winter, and they should never be schooled together.*

3. *Spelling, Reading, Writing, Composition, English Grammar, Arithmetic, Mensuration, The Science of Agriculture, Agricultural Chemistry, a small portion of History and Geography, Architecture, Moral*

Science, Good Manners, and True Religion, are sufficient as general studies for children among Believers.

4. No member but those appointed by the Ministry may study Physic, Pharmacy, Anatomy, Surgery, Law, Chemistry, etc. etc. And Phrenology, Mythology, Mesmerism, and such sciences as are foreign from Believers duty, may not be studied at all by Believers. The Ministry and Elders must be the proper judges, how far any of the studies allowable, may be prosecuted.

5. Those who teach school, shall devote their time to teaching their scholars, and not to studying themselves, further than is necessary to enable them to do their duty in teaching; but they should have a good understanding of all the branches they are required to teach.

6. The Bible should be read in schools, and the New Testament made use of as one of the general reading books. Children should be taught the History of the Rise and Progress of Believers, and the names of the founders of our society.

7. Picture books, with large flourished and extravagant pictures in them may not be used by Believers.

8. In connection with other school studies the children should be taught to sing.

9. Children should be kept in an order by themselves, where it can be done consistently. And as a general rule, boys should remain in the children's order, until sixteen years of age, and girls until fourteen.

10. No one but such caretakers as are appointed, should interfere in the dictation of children.

11. Children should never be made equals and playmates of, by those who are older. All should be sociable with children, but not familiar.

Section XVII.

Orders concerning the Dead.

When the spirit is departing and a person is breathing the last, all present should kneel in prayer.

2. In an hour after the breath has left the body, the corpse may be laid out in the fear of God.

3. A corpse should be dressed in a shirt and winding sheet, a handkerchief, and a muffler if necessary, — and for a female add thereto a cap and collar.

4. The laying out, dressing and burial of a corpse is the duty of the

Deacons and Deaconesses to direct, and the Elders may not take any part therein, unless necessity require. It is their duty to lead and direct the funeral.

5. Children under twelve years of age, are not allowed to attend any funerals, save in the family where they live, except on some special occasion, and by liberty of the Elders.

6. Children under twelve years of age, are not allowed to join in the procession to the grave.

Section XVIII.

Miscellaneous Orders.

All wrestling, scuffling, beating, striking, or fighting, is utterly forbidden by the gospel.

2. Lengthy conversation should not be held in the street, if it can consistently be avoided.

3. No person or persons in covenant relation, may work as hirelings, gaining time, and counting it their own, to spend and use as they please.

4. No person or persons may have privacies in communications, written, spoken, or in action, intentionally secreted from their Elders.

5. No one may mock, ridicule or treat with disrespect, the aged, infirm, and decrepit.

6. Sisters may not go to washing in the morning, until the signal time of rising, in the summer, and not until they can see to wash without candles in the winter.

7. The miller and boiler, may go to washing half an hour before the signal time of rising in the summer, and at the time of rising in the winter.

8. Sisters may not go to ironing until they can see without a candle in the room.

9. Ye shall not turn away the poor who ask alms of you, knowing that your Heavenly Father will provide for you.

10. It is not allowable to redrill a hole in a rock while it is charged for blasting.

11. No kind of ardent spirits may be used among Believers, as a beverage, nor on any occasion except by order of the Physicians.

12. No one should take tools, belonging in charge of others, without obtaining liberty for the same, if the person can consistently be found who takes charge of them.

13. When any one borrows a tool, it should be immediately returned, without injury, if possible, and if injured, should be made known by the borrower to the lender; — 'The wicked borrow and never return.'

14. No one should lean back against the wall, bed, or ceiling of dwelling rooms. It is also wrong to sit with the feet on the rounds of chairs.

15. Melons, & choice or uncommon fruits, should be equally divided to the family, as far as consistent; and no member should raise or gather them, neither should they gather nuts, to give to particular individuals to court favor or affection.

16. It is manifestly the will and gift of God, that the use of very exciting, stimulating, or stupefying drinks or food, should be discontinued by his people, except for physic or medicine. As health is the next blessing to the gospel, and as the whole power and strength of our bodies should be devoted to the service of God, and not to serve our own appetites and passions, and should be excited not to drunkenness and gluttony, by the stimulating beverages of man's compounding, but to love and good works by the spirit and power of God. Therefore, agreeable to the covenant of 1841, concerning these things, none of the middle ages and rising generation, under the ages therein mentioned at the date of 1841, may henceforth make any use of cider, strong beer, foreign tea or coffee, neither of tobacco or opium, unless it is taken as a medicine, by order of the Physicians, in union with the Elders.

Part III.

Concerning Temporal Economy.

Section I.

Of Prudence Neatness and Good Economy.

No private interest or property is, or can be allowed of in families that have come into the covenant relation of a full dedication; but each and every one of the brethren and sisters, are under special injunction to take good care of all things, with which they are entrusted, and to see that no loss comes through their neglect.

2. It is considered good order, to lay out, and fence all kinds of lots, fields and gardens, in a square form, where it is practicable.

3. Buildings which get out of repair, should be repaired soon, or taken away, as is most proper.

4. No kind of filthy rubbish, may be left to remain around the dwelling houses or shops, nor in the dooryards, or streets in front of the dwelling houses or shops.

5. Every Saturday night, and Monday morning, the street opposite the meeting house, should be cleaned of rubbish and litter.

6. All of the gates should be closed on Saturday night and work rooms should be swept; the work and tools should be in order, and safely secured from thieves and fire.

7. When a pane of glass gets broken in a front window, it must be mended before the Sabbath.

8. Doors and gates must not be left swinging, but should be kept either shut, or fastened open.

9. No kind of liquid matter, no apple parings, nor the refuse of any kind of fruit, may be thrown out at the windows of the dwelling houses; neither should curtains be left in such a manner as to be blown out at the windows of dwelling houses, or shops.

10. No garments of any kind, or carpets, rubbers, nor anything of the kind, may be hung, or shook out at the windows of the dwelling houses.

11. No garments of any kind, may be hung on the fence next to the road.

12. No kind of garments may be left spread or hung out over night.

13. Brethren and sisters must not spit out at the windows, on the floors, walks, cellar bottoms, nor in sinks.

14. Brethren and sisters may not throw away their old shoes, boots, socks, or garments; but they should be carried to those who have the care of such things to be disposed of as they deem proper.

15. Brethren and sisters are not allowed to give away any of their garments, or tools, without the union of the Deacons, or Deaconesses, or Tailors or Tailoresses, who have charge of providing such things.

16. It is not allowable for Brethren or sisters, to give to, or swap with each other, any tools, garments, or books of any kind, without the knowledge of those who have charge of such things.

Section II.

Orders to Prevent Loss by Fire.

No one is allowed to carry fire about the dooryards, or among the buildings, unless safely secured in a lantern, fire-box, or other safe vessel.

2. No one may enter a closet, garret, or clothes room, or other places not frequented, with a lighted lamp or candle, unless it be enclosed in a lantern.

3. Lighted lamps or candles must not be carried to the barns, or out buildings unless inclosed in a lantern, and no lanterns are allowed to be carried into hay mows, nor to be opened in the barns, in any place, where sparks would be liable to set anything on fire.

4. No lighted lamps or candles may be held over chests, drawers, shaving baskets, or wood boxes.

5. No one may go to chests of clothing, drawers, shaving baskets, wood boxes, closets or back and bye places, with a lighted candle, or pipe.

6. No one may smoke in their rooms or shops, under an hour previous to leaving them for the night, neither may they empty their pipes in spit boxes, nor go to smoke in uninhabited rooms.

7. It is not allowable to go out of doors anywhere, among the buildings with lighted pipes.

8. It is not allowable to boil oil, or varnish in our buildings anywhere.

9. Chimneys should be burned out once a year, and at a time when the roofs are sufficiently wet to prevent taking fire.

10. No ashes may be emptied into their place of deposit in the afternoon; neither may any ever be taken up in a wooden vessel, — and no ash vessel, should be set, or hung on wood-boxes, or near shaving baskets.

11. The snuff of a lamp or candle should never be dropped into spit boxes, nor on the floor, nor in any place where there is saw dust, or any combustible matter.

12. When a room is left for the night, or much length of time, the stove doors should always be shut, and the place secured from fire.

13. No shooting with guns is allowed to be done near the barns, unless the wadding consists of leather shavings, or something not liable to take fire.

14. Spit boxes may not be left under the stove hearth, at any time.

15. No smoking or taking snuff, may be done in the kitchens, and no one may smoke and work at the same time.

Section III.

Orders concerning Clothing.

If brethren desire any garments or fixtures to garments, as pockets, etc. etc. or new articles of manufacture, that come in the sisters line of business, which are not common to the brethren in general, they must apply to the Elders.

2. Silk hat bands, may not be worn, save on fur hats, for nice use.

3. Dark colored hat bands may not be worn, on summer hats.

4. All should remember that these are not the true heirs of the Kingdom of Heaven, who multiply to themselves, needless treasures of this world's goods.

Section IV.

Concerning Superfluities not Owned.

Fancy articles of any kind, or articles which are superfluously finished, trimmed or ornamented, are not suitable for Believers, and may not be used or purchased; among which are the following; also some other articles which are deemed improper, to be in the Church, and may not be brought in, except by special liberty of the Ministry.

2. Silver pencils, silver tooth picks, gold pencils, or pens, silver spoons, silver thimbles, (but thimbles may be lined with silver,) gold or silver watches, brass knobs or handles of any size or kind. Three bladed knives, knife handles with writing or picturing on them, bone or horn handled knives, except for pocket knives, bone or horn spools, superfluous whips, marbled tin ware, superfluous paper boxes of any kind, gay silk handkerchiefs, green veils, bought dark colored cotton handkerchiefs, for sisters use: — Checked handkerchiefs made by the world, may not be bought for sisters use, except head handkerchiefs. Lace for cap borders, superfluous suspenders of any kind. Writing desks may not be used by common members, unless they have much public writing to do. But writing desks may be used as far as it is thought proper by the Lead.

3. The following articles are also deemed improper, viz. Superfluously finished, or flowery painted clocks, Bureaus, and Looking glasses, also superfluously painted or fancy shaped sleighs, or carriages, superfluously trimmed Harness, and many other articles too numerous to mention.

4. The forementioned things are at present, utterly forbidden, but if the Ministry see fit to bring in any among the forementioned articles, which are not superfluously wrought, the order prohibiting the use of such article or articles is thereby repealed.

5. Believers may not in any case or circumstances, manufacture for sale, any article or articles, which are superfluously wrought, and which would have a tendency to feed the pride and vanity of man, or such as would not be admissible to use among themselves, on account of their superfluity.

Section V.

Orders concerning Locks & Keys.

Where public stores are kept, the place of storage should be secured by locks and keys.

2. Cider if it is kept at all, should be secured by locks; and kept under the charge of the Deacon, or some trusty person appointed for that purpose.

3. No private possession should be kept under lock and key security, without liberty from the Elders.

4. Locks and keys should not be used in the dwelling house, except where public stores are to be kept, and no false locks may be used in the dwelling house, on any private possession.

5. It is desirable to have all so trustworthy, that locks and keys will be needless.

Section VI.

Concerning Dooryards, Farms, &c.

Brethren and sisters should turn out in the spring, and clean the dooryards and street.

2. Ye shall throw no dirty rubbish into the dooryards, or highways, as apple cores, or parings, broken glass or earthen[ware], etc. etc.

3. Cattle or sheep should never be allowed to feed in the dooryards, nor be driven carelessly through them, and dooryards should be mowed twice a year.

4. It is not orderly to cut up the dooryards into little cross paths, and by roads, but when consistent, all should keep on the walks.

5. In the spring of the year, the fences about the farm should be mended; for Zion is called to be a pattern of economy and order in all things.

6. Dooryard gates should be kept closed except in the winter, when they should be taken from their hinges, or otherwise properly secured.

7. *When brethren and sisters are about the farm, and pass through bars, or gates, they should always have them closed, unless they find them evidently left open on purpose. And when brethren are about the farm, and find gates open, bars down, or fences broken down, they should put them in order, if consistent, if not, inform those set in order to take care on their return home.*

8. *All implements of labor, carts, waggons, sleighs, sleds, etc. should be put in their proper places, on Saturday night, and as far as consistent every night; and all of these things should be done in season to retire at the time appointed, if possible.*

Section VII.

Order concerning Beasts, &c.

No Believer is allowed to play with cats or dogs, nor to make unnecessary freedom with any of the beasts of the field, or with any kind of fowl or bird.

2. *No cats may be kept in the shops, without permission, and none at all in dwelling-rooms.*

3. *No dogs may be kept in any family gathered into order.*

4. *No beasts belonging to the people of God, may be left to suffer with hunger, thirst or cold, in consequence of neglect, on the part of those who have the care of them. But all should be kept in their proper places, and properly attended to according to their needs.*

5. *Beasts may not be called by the given or christen names of persons.*

6. *No kinds of beasts, birds, fowls, or fishes, may be kept merely for the sake of show, or fancy.*

7. *No beasts or any living thing, may be wantonly pained, injured, or tortured. And no living thing may be chastened or corrected in a passion.*

Section VIII.

Concerning the Order of the Natural Creation.

Believers may not spend their time cultivating fruits and plants, not adapted to the climate in which they live.

2. *Different species of trees, or plants may not be engrafted or budded*

upon each other, as apples upon pears, quince, etc. peaches upon cherries, or contrary wise.
3. The different species of animals should also be kept distinct, each in their own order.
4. No fowls, may be set on the eggs of fowls of different kinds.

Section IX.

Concerning Building, Painting, Varnishing and the Manufacture of Articles for Sale, &c. &c.

Beadings, mouldings and cornices, which are merely for fancy *may not be made by Believers.*
2. Odd or fanciful styles of architecture, may not be used among Believers, neither should any deviate widely from the common styles of building among Believers, without the union of the Ministry.
3. The meeting house should be painted white without, and of a blueish shade within. Houses and shops, should be as near uniform in color, as consistent; but it is advisable to have shops of a little darker shade than dwelling houses.
4. Floors in dwelling houses, if stained at all, should be of a reddish yellow, and shop floors should be of a yellowish red.
5. It is unadvisable for wooden buildings, fronting the street, to be painted red, brown, or black, but they should be of a lightish hue.
6. No buildings may be painted white, save meeting houses.
7. Barns and back buildings, as wood houses, etc. if painted at all, should be of a dark hue, either red, or brown, lead color, or something of the kind, unless they front the road, or command a sightly aspect, and then they should not be of a very light color.
8. It is considered imprudent and is therefore not allowable, to paint or oil such articles as the following, viz. Cart and ox waggon bodies, or any kind of lumber waggon or sleigh boxes, sleds or sleighs, except those kept at the office for journeying; wheelbarrows, and hand cart bodies, or hand sleds for rough use, hoe handles, or fork stales, rake stales, broom or mop handles, for home use, plough beams, milking stools, and all such articles as are exposed to very ready wear, whether for in doors or out.
9. The following articles may be painted, viz. All kinds of cart and waggon wheels and gearing. All kinds of carriages and sleighs for nice use, wheelbarrows, hand carts, and hand sleds, kept exclusively for nice use.

Ox yokes and snow shovels, may be stained or oiled. The frames of cart and waggon bodies, also gates may be put together with paint, but not painted.

10. Varnish, if used in dwelling houses, may be applied only to the moveables therein, as the following, viz., Tables, stands, bureaus, cases of drawers, writing desks, or boxes, drawer faces, chests, chairs, etc. etc. Carriages kept exclusively for riding or nice use may be varnished. No ceilings, casings or mouldings, may be varnished. Oval or nice boxes may be stained reddish or yellow, but not varnished. Bannisters or hand rails in dwelling houses may be varnished.

Part IV.

Miscellaneous Rules & Counsels.

It is the duty of Believers to render due respect to each other, according to the lot, station or place in which they stand, and always to respect the Lord's Anointed, let the disposition of the person, or persons upon whom such anointing rests, be what it may.

2. No one should suffer himself to speak against his Elders in the gospel; but all trials may be freely opened to the Elders, or with their union to the Ministry.

3. Believers should not compare their brethren and sisters to filthy vagabonds of the world.

4. When Believers salute their brethren and sisters they should simply salute them by the title of brother or sister as the case may be, or each individual who bears an official title, should be addressed by such title, and no false titles or appellations should be used, such as Judge, Major, Deacon, Mister or Miss, etc.

5. When our gospel friends have been absent from home, much length of time, they should always be welcomed on their return.

6. Believers when journeying among the world, should as far as possible, keep together, and let no unclean creature pass between them, if they can consistently avoid it. Father Joseph was very particular in this respect, he would while riding along on the road, turn his horse to the opposite side of the way, to prevent either man or beast, from passing between him and his companion.

7. When we wish for a favor we should always ask, 'will you be so kind as to do me this or that favor,' and when we have received a favor, we should say, 'I kindly thank you,' and the person thus complimented, should respond by saying, 'You are kindly welcome.'

8. It is very unadvisable for individuals to send presents to other societies, or other families of the same society, as no property belongs to individuals; but all should as far as possible, share equally according to their needs.

9. When brethren and sisters enter the dwelling house on Saturday nights and Sabbath days, they should walk very softly and in the fear of God, and it is good to practise it at all times.

10. Slamming doors or gates, loud talking and heavy walking in the dwelling house, should not be practised by Believers.

11. It does not look well to see people sleeping in the windows, or leaning down on the window stools as if they were asleep; or to stand very near to windows when looking out, or to gaze out of the windows at the world, on the Sabbath.

12. When brethren and sisters go up and down stairs, they should not slip their feet on the carpet, or floor but lift them up and set them down plumb, so as not to wear out the carpets or floor unnecessarily. Also when they turn at the head or foot of the stairs, they should not turn their feet on the floor, lest they wear holes in it.

13. Drones, sluggards, thieves and liars, or deceivers, do not belong among the people of God, and all such, together with the mocker and scoffer, will in no wise pass unpunished, in the final settlement with souls.

14. Believers should not go to excess in eating, drinking, sleeping, or in anything else; nor by unwise ambition in anyway expose their health, at any time or place.

15. When we rise from the dining table, we must rise and stand erect, before we kneel; and when we kneel, all should kneel on their right knee first.

16. When we clasp our hands, our right thumbs and fingers should be above our left, as uniformity is comely.

17. All should improve their mornings and evenings, in something useful and proper for Believers.

18. Stiff will, pride or bondage, have no lot or part in the worship of God, neither hath the soul that possesses them, and indulges therein.

19. We ought not to call our own, a brute, bird, tree, or plant, that God has created; for he never intended his creation should be devoted to selfish & mean purposes.

20. No one should carelessly pass over small things, as a pin, a kernel of grain, etc. thinking it too small to pick up, for if we do, our Heavenly Father will consider us too small for him to bestow his blessing upon.

21. Believers should not work as hirelings, gaining time to do as they

*please, but every one should work diligently with their hands, according
to their strength, for the public good of the society.*

*22. Father Joseph always taught Believers not to raise buildings, or
commence heavy jobs on Friday, or the latter part of the week.*

*23. All should be dressed in uniform, as near as consistent, when assem-
bled to worship God.*

*24. When brethren and sisters are assembled to sing, or support union,
no one should read aloud, without the request of the company, lest some
greater gift should be obstructed.*

*25. When any are out of health, they should not defer applying for med-
ical assistance until Saturday night, or Sabbath day, for the purpose of
saving time for temporal employment.*

*26. No one should wear very ragged clothes, even about their work, if it
can consistently be avoided.*

*27. Brethren should not present themselves to support union with the
sisters, when they have aught one against the other. And sisters should
not present themselves to support union with the brethren, when they have
aught one against another.*

*28. It is advisable for the center families in each bishopric, to avoid hir-
ing the world to make household furniture, except for the outer court.
And the word concerning hiring the world to work around and among
Believers, is it not written in the Holy Laws sent forth by the hand of
Almighty God, whereby all of Zion's children must be directed.*

*29. All should be careful not to mar or destroy the furniture in their
shops or rooms.*

*30. Believers should not keep any beast that needs an extravagant por-
tion of whipping or beating, but such had better be sold to the children
of this world, or killed.*

Conclusion.

---

*Whoever shall knowingly or willfully, violate or break any of the or-
ders contained in this book, it shall be accounted as sin unto them, until
it is honestly confessed, and put away in the line of order.*

*2. The Elders of every family throughout Zion, should keep a record
of the orders which are adapted to the state and condition of the family
over which they are called to preside, and the same should be read or
spoken, at least annually, and as much oftener, as found necessary; that
all may get an understanding of the orders of the house of God, which
they are required to keep.*

3. Perhaps a better way of securing these orders in the minds of all, would be to read but one or two sections at a time, and read often.

The Laws close with a collection of 'Mother Lucy's Sayings Spoken at different times and under Various Circumstances.' About fifteen days before her death she said:

To my sense, believers are held together in union, by a golden chain. This chain is composed of the gifts & orders of God, & every order is a link in this chain ; & if you break any of these orders, you break this chain, & are exposed to be led astray. But while you are careful, to keep the gifts & orders of God, you are surrounded by this golden chain, & are secure from all evil.

The 1845 version of the Laws was signed and sealed on 20 March 1846, by the central ministry at New Lebanon, composed of Ebenezer Bishop, Rufus Bishop, Ruth Landon, and Asenath Clark. Their statement reads:

We the present Ministry of the Church of Christ in New-Lebanon & Watervliet, do solemnly and conscientiously own and acknowledge our full faith in, and approbation of, the foregoing Orders, Rules & Counsels, which have been given and established by our Gospel Parents, and their successors the Ministry and Elders.
And we do solemnly promise in the presence of God & our Heavenly Parents, faithfully to support & maintain the same, from this time, henceforth and forever, (as far as wisdom will admit).

Statistical View of Shaker Communities

Location	Date of Organization [1]	Number of Families	Maximum Membership (approx.)	Total Membership [2] (approx.)	Outcome
Watervliet, N.Y.[3]	1787	4	350	2,668	Dissolved in 1938. Remaining members moved to New Lebanon.
New Lebanon, N.Y.	1787	8 [4]	600	3,202	Remaining members of last family (the North) moved to Hancock in 1947.
Hancock, Mass.[5]	1790	6	300	548	One family still in existence.
Enfield, Conn.	1790–92	5	200	739	Dissolved in 1917.
Canterbury, N.H.	1792	3	300	746	One family still in existence.
Tyringham, Mass.	1792f.	2	100	241	Dissolved in 1875. Remaining members moved to Hancock and Enfield, Conn.
Alfred, Maine	1793	3	200	241	Dissolved in 1932. Remaining members moved to New Gloucester.
Enfield, N.H.	1793	3	330	511	Seven remaining members moved to Canterbury in 1923.
Harvard, Mass.	1793	4	200 ⎫	869	Dissolved in 1918.
Shirley, Mass.	1793	3	150 ⎭		Dissolved in 1908.
New Gloucester (Sabbathday Lake), Maine [6]	1794	3	150	202	One family still in existence.
Union Village, Ohio	1806	6	600 290	3,873	Sold in 1912.

Location	Date of Organization [1]	Number of Families	Maximum Membership (approx.)	Total Membership [2] (approx.)	Outcome
Watervliet (Beulah), Ohio	1806	2	100	127	Sold in 1910, members moving to Union Village.
Pleasant Hill, Ky.	1806–9	8(?)	500	?	Dissolved in 1910.
South Union, Ky.	1807–10	4	400	676	Sold in 1922.
West Union (Busro), Ind.	1810–11	2	300	?	Abandoned in 1827.
North Union, Ohio	1822	3	300	407	Dissolved in 1889, members moving to Union Village and Watervliet, Ohio.
Whitewater, Ohio	1824–5 [7]	3	150	491	Dissolved in 1907.
Sodus Bay and Groveland, N.Y.	1826 [8]	2	200	793	Groveland sold in 1895, remaining members moving to Watervliet, N.Y.

[1] Organization usually implied the establishment of a family, with elders, eldresses, etc. The building of the family dwelling, meeting-house, shops, and so on proceeded as rapidly as conditions allowed. Oral covenants sometimes preceded written covenants. The first 'gatherings,' joining together in communal order, often took place *before* actual organization of the society.

[2] Figures compiled from various records by the Western Reserve Historical Society.

[3] The original Niskeyuna community.

[4] Including the Upper Canaan and Lower Canaan (N.Y.) families.

[5] Including two families (the Second and the East) in West Pittsfield, Mass.

[6] Including the family at Poland Hill.

[7] Date of union with the Darby community.

[8] Date of organization of the Sodus Bay society. The removal to Groveland took place in 1836–8.

MISSIONS, BRANCHES, 'OUT-FAMILIES,' AND SHORT-LIVED COMMUNITIES

Gorham, Maine	One family gathered in 1808. Moved to New Gloucester in 1819.
Savoy, Mass.	A community of about eighty members existed in Savoy between 1817 and 1825. When the community was abandoned because of a severe drought, the members moved to New Lebanon, Canaan, and Watervliet, N.Y.
Cheshire, Richmond, and Ashfield, Mass.	In the 1780's groups meeting together as 'out-families' existed at Ashfield, Cheshire, Richmond, and other towns in Massachusetts as well as in other parts of New England. These were soon absorbed into the organized communities.

Canaan, N.Y.	The Lower and Upper Canaan families, branches of the New Lebanon society, were started in 1813 and fully organized by 1821. The former family was dissolved in 1884, the latter in 1897.
Philadelphia, Pa.	This family, many members of which were Negroes, had its origin in a Millerite society to which a Shaker mission was sent in 1846. Organized that same year, 'the colored contingent,' under the leadership of 'Mother Rebecca' Jackson, later moved to Watervliet, N.Y. About 1860, a few of the Negro members (twelve women, according to Nordhoff) temporarily revived the Philadelphia community.
Darby, Ohio	Organized in 1822–23, this community was soon abandoned because the location was thought to be unhealthy.
Straight Creek, Ohio	Mission undertaken in 1808, but soon abandoned. Short-lived settlements also existed at Eagle Creek, Ohio, and Red Bank, Ky.
Sodus Bay, Sodus Point, or Port Bay, N.Y.	About 1300 acres were purchased here on 23 Feb. 1826. Covenant signed 1 Jan. 1829. Property sold to Sodus Canal Co. on 21 Nov. 1836.
White Oak, Ga.	Branch of society started in 1898 but soon abandoned.
Narcoossee, Fla.	A family branch of New Lebanon, with about seven members, started in 1894 and existed for several years.

The total recorded membership of the United Society, according to figures assembled by the Western Reserve Historical Society, was 16,828, with some 300 names still to be catalogued at the time of classification. Neither the exact number of covenant members nor the exact number at any given date can be known. According to various estimates there were 1,632 Believers in the East in 1803; 1,417 in the West in 1852; and 2,415 members in the whole society in 1874. The U.S. Census Bulletin for 1891 lists 15 communities with 1,728 members. The western societies reached the zenith of membership earlier than those in the East. Thus, Union Village's 600 in 1823 had declined to 502 in 1830, to 380 in 1852, and to 100 in 1862. Pleasant Hill had 500 members in 1830, only 345 in 1852, and about 250 in 1862. The eastern communities continued to expand, or at least held their own, until the middle of the century and in some cases until the period of the Civil War.

A Note on Sources

A SHAKER BIBLIOGRAPHY, exclusive of manuscripts, would run close to a thousand items. Records of the movement by outsiders appeared as early as 1781, continuing in an unending stream to the present. The Shakers themselves began to publish expositions and defenses of their faith in 1790, with more attention paid to the printed word after the establishment of the western societies. Publication was encouraged by the ministry, and eventually several communities possessed presses which turned out a quantity of material pertaining to both the temporal and religious life of the order. How extensive such imprints, worldly and Shaker, had become fifty years ago may be seen by consulting J. P. MacLean's *Bibliography of Shaker Literature* (Columbus, Ohio, 1905). When we add to this the materials published since 1905 and the thousands of items of manuscript still surviving in public or private hands, it is manifest that the historian has abundant data for documenting the movement. The Shakers were an expressive people, and the records they kept are often ample in scope and rich in content.

The listing of all such sources lies beyond the scope of the present work. It may be of interest, however, to cite, by short title and chapter, some of the writings that were found most helpful. Additional references may be found in MacLean and the selective bibliographies in the books on Shaker industries, craftsmanship, and the religious arts published by the author and his wife during the last twenty years. It seemed unnecessary, in the following lists, to repeat a once-cited title, even though the sources may have been consulted in succeeding chapters.

Chapter I

The Constables Accounts of the Manor of Manchester, Manchester, 1892.
Tylor, Charles. *The Camisards,* London, 1893.
The Testimony of Christ's Second Appearing, Lebanon, Ohio, 1808.
*Testimonies of the life, character, revelations and doctrines of our ever blessed
Mother Ann Lee,* Hancock, 1816.
Brown, Thomas. *An Account of the People called Shakers,* Troy, 1812.

Chapter II

Evans, Frederick W. *Shaker Communism,* London, 1871.
'Sketch of the Life and Experience of Issachar Bates' (manuscript).

Rathbun, Valentine. *Some Brief Hints, of a Religious Scheme,* Norwich, 1781;
    reprinted: Salem, 1782.

Taylor, Amos. *A Narrative of the Strange Principles, Conduct and Character
    of the People Known by the Name of Shakers,* Worcester, 1782.

Plumer, William. 'The Original Shaker Communities in New England,' *The
    New England Magazine,* Boston, 1900.

'The Letters of François, Marquis de Barbe-Marbois . . . 1779–1785,' pub-
    lished under title of *Our Revolutionary Forefathers,* New York, 1929.

Dwight, Timothy. *Travels: in New-England and New-York,* New Haven,
    1822, vol. III.

Lamson, David R. *Two Years' Experience among the Shakers,* West Boylston,
    1848.

*Minutes of the Commissioners for detecting and defeating Conspiracies in the
    State of New York,* Albany County Sessions, 1778–81, Albany, 1909.

Public Papers of George Clinton, First Governor of New York, Albany, 1902.

Chapter III

Stewart, Rev. I. D. *The History of the Free Will Baptists, for half a century*
    (1780–1830), Dover, 1862.

The Shaker (monthly periodical of the society appearing under that title in
    1871–2, and later as *Shaker and Shakeress, The Shaker Manifesto,* and *The
    Manifesto*), published at Shakers, N.Y., and Shaker Village, N.H., through
    December, 1899.

Smith, J. E. A. *The History of Pittsfield, Massachusetts* (1800–1876),
    Springfield, 1876.

West, Benjamin. *Scriptural Cautions against embracing a Religious Scheme,*
    Hartford, 1783.

Rathbun, Daniel. *A Letter, from Daniel Rathbun . . . to James Whittacor,*
    Springfield, 1785.

Testimonies concerning the character and ministry of Mother Ann Lee . . . ,
    Albany, 1827.

Rathbun, Reuben. *Reasons offered for leaving the Shakers,* Pittsfield, 1800.

White, Anna and Taylor, Leila. *Shakerism: Its Meaning and Message,* Colum-
    bus, Ohio, 1905.

'Covenant of the Church of Christ, in New Lebanon' (manuscript), 1795.

Rufus Bishop, comp. 'A Collection of the Writings of Father Joseph Meacham
    Respecting Church Order and Government' (manuscript), New Lebanon,
    1850.

Chapter IV

Grosvenor, Roxalana L. *The Shakers' Covenant,* Boston, 1873.

A Concise Statement of the Principles of the Only True Church, Bennington,
    Vermont, 1790.

'A Short Account of the People known by the name of Shakers, or Shaking
    Quakers,' *The Theological Magazine,* New York, 1796.

'A Concise Statement of the Faith and principles . . . of Believers: Second family covenant' (manuscript), New Lebanon, 1815.

A Brief Exposition of the Established Principles and Regulations of the United Society called Shakers, Albany, 1830.

Chapter V

Chase, Daryl. "The Early Shakers. An Experiment in Religious Communism' (manuscript), Chicago, 1936.

McNemar, Richard. *The Kentucky Revival*, Cincinnati, 1807.

——. *A review of the most important events relating to . . . Believers in the West*, Union Village, Ohio, 1831.

MacLean, J. P. *Shakers of Ohio*, Columbus, Ohio, 1907.

The Constitution of the United Societies, of Believers, Watervliet, Ohio, 1833.

Smith, James. *Remarkable Occurrences lately discovered among the people called Shakers . . .* , Carthage, Tenn., 1810.

Youngs, Benjamin S. 'Journal of One Year': 1 Jan. 1805 to 31 Dec. 1805 (manuscript).

——. 'A Journey to the Indians, Miami near Lebanon, Ohio, 3d month' (manuscript), 1807.

——. *Transactions of the Ohio mob . . . Miami Country, State of Ohio*, Aug. 31, 1810.

Chapter VI

Hennell, Mary. *An Outline of the various Social Systems and Communities which have been Founded on the Principle of Cooperation*, London, 1844.

Dunlavy, John. *The Manifesto*, Pleasant Hill, Ky., 1818.

A Summary View of the Millennial Church, Albany, 1823.

Leonard, William. *A discourse on the order and propriety of divine inspiration . . .* , Harvard, Mass., 1853.

Weiss, John. *Life and Correspondence of Theodore Parker*, New York, 1864.

Lane, Charles. 'A Day with the Shakers,' *The Dial*, Boston, 1843.

Elkins, Hervey. *Fifteen years in the Senior Order of Shakers*, Hanover, 1853.

Peculiarities of the Shakers . . . By a visitor (Benjamin Silliman?), New York, 1832.

Baker, Arthur. *Shakers and Shakerism*, London, 1896.

Blinn, Henry C. *In Memoriam*, Concord, N.H., 1905.

Gates, Benjamin. 'A Day Book . . . Beginning October 1, 1827' (manuscript), New Lebanon.

Warder, W. S. *A Brief Sketch of the Religious Society of People Called Shakers*, London, 1818.

Hodgson, Stuart. 'An American Communist Experiment,' *The Contemporary Review*, London, 1933.

Howells, William Dean. 'A Shaker Village,' *The Atlantic Monthly*, Boston, June 1876.

Report of the trustees of the United Society of Shakers in . . . *New Lebanon,* Albany, 1850.

The Complete Writings of Ralph Waldo Emerson, New York, 1929.

Blanc, Mme. Therese. *Choses et Gens d' Amerique,* Paris, 1898.

Dixon, W. Hepworth. *New America,* Philadelphia, 1867.

Holmes, Isaac. *An Account of the United States of America,* London, 1823.

Finch, John. *The New Moral World; and Gazette of the Rational Society,* London, 1844.

Martineau, Harriet. 'The Shakers,' *The Penny Magazine,* London, 1837.

Nordhoff, Charles. *The Communistic Societies of the United States,* New York, 1875.

Noyes, John Humphrey. *History of American Socialisms,* Philadelphia, 1870.

Cooper, James Fenimore. *Notions of the Americans: Picked up by a Travelling Bachelor,* Philadelphia, 1828.

Owen, Robert. *New View of Society,* London, 1818.

——. *The Economist,* No. 19, London, 2 June 1821.

Buckingham, James Silk. *America, Historical. Statistic and Descriptive,* New York, 1841.

'Journal of A. J. Macdonald' (manuscript).

Holyoake, George Jacob. *The History of Co-operation in England,* London, 1879.

Chapter VII

Davenport, Frederick Morgan. *Primitive Traits in Religious Revivals,* New York, 1905.

The Wonderful Narrative: Or, a Faithful Account of the French Prophets . . . , Glasgow, 1742.

Sweet, William Warren. *Religion on the American Frontier. The Baptists,* 1783–1830, New York, 1931.

Chapman, Eunice. *Account of the conduct of the people called Shakers,* Albany, 1817.

——. *Being an additional account* . . . , Albany, 1818.

Youngs, Isaac N. 'A Concise View of the Church of God and of Christ, on Earth . . .' (manuscript), New Lebanon, 1856.

Greeley, Horace. 'A Sabbath with the Shakers,' *The Knickerbocker,* or *New-York Monthly Magazine,* New York, 1838.

Benedict, David. *A History of All Religions,* Providence, 1824.

Chapter VIII

A Return of Departed Spirits . . . *into the Bodies of the 'Shakers'* . . . , Philadelphia, 1843.

A Revelation of the Extraordinary Visitation of Departed Spirits . . . *Through the Living Bodies of the 'Shakers'* . . . , Philadelphia, 1869.

Avery, Giles B. 'Miscellaneous Writings' (manuscript).

'A True Record of Sacred Communications . . .' (manuscripts), New Lebanon.

Warner, Charles Dudley. 'Out of the World,' *Scribner's Monthly*, August 1879.

Chapter IX

Maxwell, Col. A. M. *A Run through the United States*, London, 1841.

Abdy, E. S. *Journal of a Residence and Tour in the United States of North America*, London, 1835.

Hall, Mrs. Basil. *The Aristocratic Journey*, New York, 1831.

Dyer, Mary. *A Portraiture of Shakerism*, Concord, N.H., 1822.

Pool, Hester A. 'Among the Shakers,' *The Manifesto*, 18 November 1888.

Lyell, Sir Charles. *A Second Visit to the United States of North America*, New York, 1850.

Eads, Harvey L. *Expression of Faith*, Orange, N.J., 1875.

Evans, Frederick W. *Essays.*

'A Visit to the Shakers,' *Blackwood's Edinburgh Magazine*, April 1823.

Chandler, Seth. *History of the Town of Shirley, Mass.*, Shirley, 1883.

Pidgeon, Daniel. *Old-World Questions and New-World Answers*, London, 1884.

Chapter X

Johnson, William. *Reports of cases adjudged in the supreme court of . . . New York (1799–1803)*, New York, 1846.

Investigator . . . , Lexington, Ky., 1828.

A Memorial . . . , Harrodsburg, Ky., 1828.

The Decision of the Court of Appeals (In Kentucky), Dayton, Ohio, 1834.

The Other Side of the Question, Cincinnati, 1819.

Revised Statutes of the State of New York, Albany, 1836.

A Declaration of The Society of People (Commonly called Shakers), Albany, 1815.

'Union Village Church Record Books' (manuscript).

A Brief Illustration of the Principles of War and Peace, Albany, 1831.

Wells, S. Y. 'Proposition for all peace societies . . .' (manuscript).

An Act in Relation to Certain Trusts, Albany, 1839.

The Writings and Speeches of Samuel J. Tilden, New York, 1885.

Johnston, James F. W. *Notes of North America*, Boston, 1851.

Ferguson, Charles W. *The Confusion of Tongues*, New York, 1928.

Wilson, James Harrison. *The Life of Charles A. Dana*, New York, 1907.

Chapter XI

Robinson, C. E. *The Shakers and their Homes*, East Canterbury, N.H., 1893.

Notes

Chapter I

1. J. P. Earwaker (ed.), *The Constables Accounts of the Manor of Manchester. From the Year 1612 to the Year 1647, and from the Year 1743 to the Year 1776* (Manchester: 1892), Vol. CXI.

2. The word 'Shakers,' applied to some other sect—perhaps the Ranters—was in use as early as 1648.—*New English Dictionary* (Oxford: 1888–1933), VII, ii, 605.

3. Betty Lees was the widow of Charles Lees, a brother or cousin óf John Lees. After the Shakers came to America, James Whittaker tried vainly to induce John Jackson and Betty Lees to 'forsake their native country for Christ's sake.'

4. The cathedral registry also records the baptisms of Nancy (1734), Joseph (1741), William (1743), and George (1749)—all as children of 'john Lees, blacksmith.' James' and Daniel's names do not appear, and the Mary Lees baptized on 13 February 1742 is listed as the daughter of 'John Lees, taylor.'

5. Charles Tylor, *The Camisards* (London: 1893), pp. 329–30.

6. *The Testimony of Christ's Second Appearing* (2nd ed.; Albany: 1810), p. xxv.

7. The death of Elizabeth is recorded in the cathedral registry on 7 October 1766.

One of Ann Lee's children may have survived for a few years. In a letter from Seth Youngs Wells to the ministry at Watervliet, New York, dated 25 April 1822, Wells tells of his 'many conversations' with Molly (Mary) Hocknell, who at one time 'lived' with Mother Ann: 'We have also ascertained [Wells writes] that Mother was once confined in Bedlam or the Mad-house so called, and have concluded from several circumstances that this was her *first* imprisonment. She was doubtless supposed to be deranged, or at least that was the pretence, otherwise she would not have been sent to a place designed only for insane people - How long she was kept there is uncertain - indeed we can learn but little about it - Molly has often heard of it, but says it must have been some time before she went to live with Mother. One thing appears evident - it was while one of her children was living - for this child was frequently carried by Nancy Lee where Mother could see it thro' the window . . .'

8. Mother Ann's testimonies regarding her marital troubles, her persecutions and miraculous escapes, her visions, etc., are taken from a rare volume, *Testimonies of the life, character, revelations and doctrines of our ever blessed Mother Ann Lee* (Hancock: 1816), the testimonies having been 'collected by living witnesses.' The book was used solely by the elders and was sometimes called the 'Secret book of the Elders.'

9. Thomas Brown, *An Account of the People called Shakers* (Troy: 1812). In this history of the Shakers, the author claimed that both Hocknell and Partington had formerly been 'noted men' among the French Prophets. According to Hocknell's daughter Mary, however, he belonged to the Church of England until he left to join the Methodists. His wife Hannah at first disapproved of his Shaker sympathies, and it is recorded that her three brothers were so enraged that, on some pretext, they had him committed to prison at Middlewich. She joined her husband, however, after the Shaker society had become established in America.

10. *Testimonies of the life* . . . , pp. 53–4.

11. *Ibid.*, pp. 50–52.

12. William E. A. Axon, 'Biographical Notice of Ann Lee, a Manchester Prophetess and Foundress of the American Sect of the Shakers,' *Transactions of the Historic Society of Lancashire and Cheshire* (Liverpool: 1875), p. 57.

Chapter II

13. Frederick W. Evans, *Shaker Communism: or, Tests of Divine Inspiration* (London: 1871), p. v.

14. The district was later known as Water Vliet and Watervliet, and is now called Colonie or West Albany. The earliest spellings (from conveyances of 1669) were Canastagioene, Canestegeone and Canestagione. In 1770 it was Canastageone. In the records of the common council of Albany for 1773, the name was Nestigeunoe or Nestigooune, and in 1781 Nisteguane or Nisqueunia. Later it was called Niskayuna or Niskeyuna.

15. It was one of the natives of the forest, according to Shaker tradition, who first discovered anything peculiar about the society; 'one "poor Indian" saw a "bright light" around Mother, and prophesied in true native simplicity, that the "Great Spirit had sent her to do much good." '— Roxalana L. Grosvenor, *The Shakers' Covenant* (Boston: 1873), p. 10. The Shakers later preached to the natives in New Lebanon, and when Ann was returning from her eastern journey, she was met at the Albany ferry by a number of Indians who joyfully cried: 'The good woman is come!

The good woman is come!'—*Testimonies of the life* . . . , p. 202. No Indians, however, ever joined the society.

16. Ann Lee had heard Whitefield preach in England. At the beginning, she said, 'he had great power and gifts of God,' but after his persecution in America he 'took protection under the King,' and thereby lost his power and 'became formal, like other professors.' Perhaps the help which Whitefield received from the Countess of Huntingdon, as well as his advocacy of the Calvinist doctrine of unconditional election and reprobation, represented in Ann's eyes a retreat from his early heretical liberalism.

17. The township of Canaan was later divided, and the name New Lebanon given to that part which included the Shaker settlement. Since the latter appellation was the common one for the Shaker village itself, even before the division was made, it is used throughout this history. When a post office was installed in the society in 1861, the community was referred to as Mount Lebanon to distinguish it from the main postal district of the town.

18. *Testimonies of the life* . . . , p. 21.

19. *Ibid.*, p. 21.

20. 'Sketch of the Life and Experience of Issachar Bates' (manuscript).

21. *Testimonies of the life* . . . , p. 296.

22. One morning, at Niskeyuna, Mother said: 'Last night I was under great sufferings, and a great number of the dead came to me, and some of them embraced the gospel; but others chose rather to go to hell than confess their sins.'—*Testimonies of the life* . . . (Testimony of Lucy Prescott). Mother Ann often testified to seeing particular persons in the world of spirits laboring, dancing, or preaching to the other dead. Sometimes she would speak to them in unknown tongues.

23. The apostate Valentine Rathbun was told by the Shakers that they were the first fruits of the tribe of Benjamin, 'the youngest tribe, and last in the account, yet first in the order, of being sealed.'—Valentine Rathbun, *Some Brief Hints, of a Religious Scheme* (Norwich: 1781), p. 10.

24. *Testimonies concerning the character and ministry of Mother Ann Lee and the first witnesses of the gospel of Christ's Second Appearing; given by some of the aged brethren and sisters of the United Society* (Albany: 1827), pp. 40, 51, 92–3.

25. *The Testimony of Christ's Second Appearing* (1st ed.; Lebanon, Ohio: 1808), pp. 470–71.

26. *Ibid.*, p. 472.

27. Valentine Rathbun, *Some Brief Hints, of a Religious Scheme* (Salem:

1782). Of this company, three males and two females 'profess to be perfect ... the other seven not perfect yet, but very far advanced.'

28. *Ibid.*, pp. 7–8.

29. *Ibid.*, p. 12.

30. Amos Taylor, *A Narrative of the Strange Principles, Conduct and Character of the People Known by the Name of Shakers* (Worcester: 1782), pp. 15–16.

31. William Plumer, 'The Original Shaker Communities in New England,' *The New England Magazine* (Boston: May, 1900), pp. 305–6.

32. He was Secretary of the French Legation in the United States, 1779–85. His letters, edited by Eugene Parker Chase, were published under the title *Our Revolutionary Forefathers* (New York: 1929).

33. *Our Revolutionary Forefathers*, pp. 182–3. Valentine Rathbun had given a similar account in 1781: 'a strange power begins to come on, and takes place in the body, or human frame, which sets the person agaping and stretching; and soon sets him a twitching, as though his nerves were all in a convulsion. I can compare it to nothing nearer in its feelings, than the operation of an electerising machine; the person believes it is the power of God, and therefore dare not resist, but wholly gives way to it. . . . This power, as it increases, it brings on, many times, extreme weakness of body, so that their limbs fail, other times, it brings on great shakings,—and shrugging of the shoulders,—and tramping about with the feet,—dismal groans and out cries,—and perhaps, may issue, for that time, in great laughter and lightness. . . .'—Valentine Rathbun, *op. cit.*, pp. 11–12.

34. Valentine Rathbun, *op. cit.*, pp. 11–12. 'They meet together in the night [Rathbun wrote] and have been heard two miles by people, in the dead of the night. . . . They run about in the woods and elsewhere, hooting and tooting like owls; some of them have stripped naked in the woods, and thought they were angels, and invisible. . . .'—*Ibid.*, p. 14.

35. Brown, *op. cit.*, p. 83.

36. Timothy Dwight, *Travels: In New-England and New-York* (New Haven: 1822), III, 157. Of the 'gift of shaking' the Believers were also proud. 'Love that power,' Ann once told Elizabeth Johnson, who had been seized with trembling, 'for it is the shaking of dry bones, to bring bone to its bone.'—*Testimonies of the life* . . . , p. 312.

37. Compare an early Quaker method of proselytism, as described in Cotton Mather's *Magnalia Christi Americana:* 'The Quakers proselyte People merely by stroaking or by breathing on them; they had no sooner used some such Action towards such as they had a Design upon, but the bewitched People would behave themselves just as if a Philtre had been given them, and would follow their Converters in every Thing, without being able to render any Reason for it.'

38. Valentine Rathbun, *op. cit.* The 'warring gift,' persisting for a long time in Shaker practice, was described by Lamson as late as 1848. See David R. Lamson, *Two Years' Experience among the Shakers* (West Boylston: 1848), pp. 90–91.

39. Victor Hugo Paltsits (ed.). *Minutes of the Commissioners for detecting and defeating Conspiracies in the State of New York, Albany County Sessions, 1778–81* (Albany: 1909), II, entry of 7 July 1780, p. 452. The commissioners were John M. Beeckman, Jeremiah Van Rensselaer, Mathew Visscher, and Isaac D. Fonda. Samuel Stringer sat on the board in other deliberations affecting the Shakers.

40. Mary Partington accompanied 'the grand actress' to the Pough-keepsie jail, though she was not considered a prisoner and apparently was allowed to come and go as she pleased, and to bring 'groceries,' et cetera, for the comfort of the accused. After a few weeks the pair were removed to the house of James Boyd and his wife, whom Mother had converted, where they were later joined by Mary Hocknell. Religious meetings were held in Boyd's house until Ann's release.

41. *Public Papers of George Clinton, First Governor of New York* (Albany: 1902), VI, 420.

42. Paltsits, *op. cit.*, p. 592. Apparently no action was taken on two later charges against the sect: one, on 27 February 1781, accused Jabez Spencer of publicly reading, in Rensselaerwyck, the amnesty proclamation of the British commander, Sir Henry Clinton; the other, on 30 May 1781, informed the board 'that a Number of the People called Shaking Quakers had lately purchased Arms & Ammunition . . . to assist the Enemy.'

Chapter III

43. Benjamin Osborne was one of the original grantees of Mount Washington, then known as Tucconock Mountain, a wilderness district adjacent to Livingston's Manor in New York State, whence proceeded many curious people to attend Ann's mission.

44. Jemima Wilkinson, influenced perhaps by the messianic example of Ann Lee and the success of the Shakers, established her religious community in the Genesee country in western New York State in the period 1790–1819. Although Jemima turned out to be somewhat of a charlatan, the community enjoyed a brief period of prosperity. Its leader died in 1819.

45. The Square House was 'a retreat or hiding place for him [Shadrack Ireland] as he was persecuted for his testimony, which was for a season, sharp and powerful against the flesh, root and branch. It was raised in the night.... The proprietors ... were David Hoar, Malabar Bean, Isaac Willard, Abel Jewet, Samuel and Jonathan Cooper, Ethan Phillips, John Manor and Zacheus Stephens. . . . The House was built with a Square roof, and a Cupola, where he could look out and see when strangers approached, and from thence there was a secret trap door, and a stair case or ladder, that went down by the side of the chimney to the cellar.'—'Circumstances, relative to the building of the Square House at Harvard. Related by Jonathan Clark Junr, Abel Jewet and others' (manuscript in author's library). The deed of the house and farm was given to 'the man,' as Ireland was called, 'in confidence to hold as consecrated property.' The Shakers purchased the property from his son-in-law Thomas Robbins, Mother Ann personally contributing $144; but because the property had been so consecrated, Ireland's 'heirs' and his successor, David Hoar, were prejudiced against its occupation by the Believers. Mother Ann later converted Ireland's spiritual wife to Shakerism.

46. Elder Benjamin Randall (1749–1808), who had come under the influence of the Rev. George Whitefield in 1770, settled in New Durham in 1778. He was ordained 'to the work of an evangelist' in 1780; one account of his life implies that he drew up a covenant that year, but in Stewart's history the original draft is dated 13 April 1791. See Rev. I. D. Stewart, *The History of the Free Will Baptists* (Dover: 1862), pp. 110–11.

47. According to Stewart, Ebenezer Cooley 'made high pretensions to spiritual life and practical piety, shrewdly keeping in reserve, for a time, most of the objectionable features of his religion.'—Stewart, *op. cit.*

48. Zadock Wright was one of Ann's first converts at Niskeyuna, and was imprisoned for dissuading people from taking up arms against Britain. When the Canterbury community was organized, he became its first deacon.

49. Otis Sawyer, 'Origin of the Shakers in Maine,' *The Manifesto*, XV (January, 1885), No. 1, pp. 11–12.

50. *The Manifesto*, XV, No. 4, p. 80.

51. Stewart, *op. cit.*, pp. 67–8.

52. As early as March 1781, Rathbun had moved and carried a resolution appointing a committee in Pittsfield to devise 'some measures to take with those people known as Shakers.' The report, signed by Thomas Allen on 2 April, charged that the Shakers in Richmond, Hancock, and New Lebanon were 'irregular and disorderly in their conduct and conversation, if not guilty of some high crimes and misdemeanors.' Insinuating that there was evidence of 'blasphemies, adulteries, fornications, breaches of sabbath,' et cetera, the committee recommended that steps be taken to suppress 'all disorders and breaches of the peace,' and that intercourse be checked between the Shakers at Niskeyuna and their adherents in western Massachusetts.—J. E. A. Smith, *The History of Pittsfield . . . Massachusetts, from the year 1734 to the year 1800* (Boston: 1869), p. 454.

53. *Testimonies of the life . . .* , pp. 115–16; quotations in the following pages are from the same source. It should be borne in mind that these accounts of persecution, as recalled by the participants, may understandably have been exaggerated and highly colored.

54. The gathering in this orchard had assumed a legendary character as early as 1816, when the first 'testimonies' were recorded. On Saturday, forty horses were turned into Bishop's eight- or ten-acre pasture; but on Monday afternoon, when they were taken out, 'it was more fresh and green than . . . if there had not been the hoof of a creature in it for a whole week.' Numbers of pails of milk were also used by the visitors, but more butter was made by the family that week than in any week of the entire season. The power that fed five thousand with five barley loaves and two small fishes manifested itself again and again. At Ashfield an assembly was fed on a small amount of bread and cheese, broken into small pieces. Abigail Talcott served forty unexpected visitors from a small pot of meat and vegetables.

55. Another was Benjamin West, in his *Scriptural Cautions against embracing a Religious Scheme* (Hartford: 1783).

56. The title page of this pamphlet, bound in with a revised version of Rathbun's *Some Brief Hints, of a Religious Scheme*, reads: *A Dialogue, Between George the Third of Great-Britain, and his Ministers; giving an Account of the Late Mob in London, And the original of the Sect called Shakers. Who lately went from England to North-America.* Supposedly it was first printed in London, then reprinted in Worcester in 1782; no trace of the London edition has been found, however—perhaps it never existed. The 'Late Mob' evidently referred to the Gordon riots of 1780.

57. Taylor, *op. cit.*, p. 3.

58. Daniel Rathbun, *A Letter, from Daniel Rathbun, of Richmond, in the County of Berkshire, to James Whittacor, Chief Elder of the Church, called Shakers* (Springfield: 1785).

59. The apostate Thomas Brown, in a mood of honest inquiry, once questioned the aged Mary Hocknell concerning the report that 'in Mothers day, by her gift,' men and women danced naked together. Her answer was: 'Because the brethren pulled off their coats, or outside garments, to labour, or as the world call it, dancing; and in warm weather the sisters being lightly clothed, they would report we danced naked. And you know how apt the ignorant and vulgar part of mankind, are to misrepresent what they see. If one told they danced part naked, or with but few clothes on, another in telling the story, would leave out the part, or few, and so it was reported that we danced naked.'—Brown, *op. cit.*, p. 47.

60. Daniel Rathbun, *op. cit.*, pp. 37, 114, 118. Rathbun charged the prophetess with greed and an illegitimate use of consecrated property. He claimed that because his own gift was confined to 'victuals and cloathing' he was publicly criticized by Elder Partington.

The *Testimonies concerning the character* . . . were primarily intended to contradict such 'base and unjust slanders' against the ministry and moral character of the first founders. The following statements are typical:

'Can any man or woman of common sense suppose that thousands of rational beings, born in a land of liberty and civilization, and brought up in the midst of moral and religious principles and instructions, and in pursuit of a pure and undefiled religion, and who possessed all the propensities of human nature common to other people, would deny themselves of all worldly pleasures and enjoyments, and subject themselves to the dictates of a woman of base character, who lived in direct opposition to those principles which she daily preached to others?'—(Testimony of John Farrington), pp. 14–15.

'Strife and contention, tyranny and oppression, bondage and slavery, lewdness and intemperance, dishonesty and fraud, hypocrisy and deceit, are all in direct opposition to the fundamental principles of the Society. . . . Can any rational person believe, that an institution to prevent drunkenness, could be established and maintained by drunkards, and even flourish and prosper under their protection?'—(Testimony of Job Bishop), p. 165.

61. This letter is dated 'Ashfield ye 29th of ye 2^d month 1782' (manuscript in author's library).

62. Reuben Rathbun, *Reasons offered for leaving the Shakers* (Pittsfield: 1800), p. 7. He states that the order was later 'taken off—they were told the time had not come, but that it was a gift to try their faith—so that they which had sold, had to buy again, and so the matter rested.'

63. Plumer, *op. cit.*, pp. 307–8. The reference is to Acts II, 44; V, 2.

64. The phrase 'Joint Interest' in the Harlow manuscript was probably coined by Elder Joseph Meacham, who used it in the first Shaker covenant (1795). This and the terms 'united interest' and 'united inheritance' appeared in Shaker literature decades before the word 'communism.'

65. This document was included in 'A Collection of the Writings of Father Joseph Meacham Respecting Church Order and Government; Evidently intended for way-marks, for all who were or should be called in spiritual or temporal care, In the Church' (manuscript in the library of the Western Reserve Historical Society), pp. 97–9. Between 1791 and 1796, the year he died, Meacham wrote many papers as guides to the policy and government of an ideal Christian community. These roughly drafted instructions were collected by Elder Rufus Bishop of New Lebanon in 1850. Harlow's account was printed in somewhat altered form in Anna White and Leila Taylor, *Shakerism: Its Meaning and Message* (Columbus: 1905), p. 301.

66. Father James Whittaker, 'Copy of a Letter, written by Father James, while on Earth. Parts, near Albany, Feby 20th 1784' (manuscript in author's library). Whittaker sent this letter to his parents, Jonathan and Ann Whittaker, in England.

67. 'Father' William Lee is important in Shaker history chiefly for the physical and moral support which he rendered his sister and the pioneer Believers. He was four years younger than Ann, light-haired, blue-eyed, with a tall, 'commanding' figure and a powerful voice. As a youth William had been apprenticed to his father, but he left the blacksmith shop to become an 'officer of horse' in a regiment of the King's guard. He married, had a son, and was leading a carefree life when he came under the chastening influence of the Wardley society.

68. *Testimonies of the life* . . . (Testimony of Mehetabel Farrington), p. 352.

69. Ann never claimed that the body was immortal. Discussing the subject with certain followers of Shadrack Ireland, she emphasized the fact that the evidence of the senses made such a doctrine ridiculous. Neither did she prophesy the end of the world, as it was asserted, but only, for Believers, the end of *worldliness*.

70. Whittaker, *op. cit.*

71. The last two chapters in *Testimonies of the life* . . . were devoted to 'Remarkable Instances of the Judgments of God upon Reprobates and Persecutors.' Thomas Law of the New Lebanon mob lived as a vagabond, poor and despised, and died 'without warning.' Selah Abbott, Jr., of the same mob, died in an 'awful manner,' and his father 'unexpectedly.' Eleazer Grant was taken with 'a strange disorder and died under great horror of mind'; Daniel Rathbun died of lockjaw, Reuben Rathbun was crushed to death by a falling tree, et cetera. The chief persecutors at Harvard suffered extreme poverty, while the whole town of Petersham, for some years after the outrages there, seemed to be under a curse—a wave of suicides and other misfortunes.

72. See Brown, *op. cit.*, pp. 325–6.

73. 'A Transcript of the Dedication of the first Meeting house built by the United Society at New Lebanon, or Holy Mount, which was built in the year 1785' (manuscript in 'A Collection of the Writings of Father Joseph Meacham . . .'), pp. 94–5.

74. *Testimonies of the life* . . . , p. 379. Elder John Hocknell, a heroic figure who was well over seventy when he came to America, died at Watervliet on 27 February 1779, about two years after the decease of his wife Hannah. Though Partington left the society, allegedly in protest over Whittaker's elevation to leadership, his daughter Mary remained in the order.

Chapter IV

75. David Meacham, the first deacon or trustee of the Church family in New Lebanon, was born in Enfield in 1743 and died at New Lebanon in 1826. His initials, D.M., stamped on many goods produced by that family, were its trade-mark.

76. From an early manuscript we learn that Joseph Meacham was at this time 'about five feet ten inches tall, slim and straight built,' with a 'fair complexion, hazel colored eyes—high forehead, dark brown hair, large nose, pale countenance; A countenance that commanded respect.'— 'A Description of Father Joseph Meacham' (manuscript copied by N. E Moore of South Union, Kentucky, August 1864). Elsewhere he is called 'a straight trim walking man.' All accounts agree on the power of his testimony, his ability as a public speaker, and his deeply religious yet practical turn of mind.

77. It was common talk among the 'worldly' at the time that, were it not for the 'wilful' Meachams, the Shaker 'delusion' would have ended with Whittaker's death.

78. The Shakeresses White and Taylor claimed that Lucy Wright' qualifications were first suggested to Meacham by Childs Hamlin, one of his young ministerial assistants.—See White and Taylor, *op. cit.*, p. 74 Hamlin was born in Alford, Massachusetts, on 23 January 1760, and died at New Lebanon on 4 May 1790.

79. 'A Collection of the Writings of Father Joseph Meacham . . . , pp. 26–7. 'The first gathering of the Church and establishment of Church order [Meacham wrote] is the foundation for all others in this day; in relation to gathering and building according to their order; it was therefor necessary that the greatest faith and abilities of all that were prepared both old and young, should be gathered into the first building, that it may be in the order of the Temple of the Lord.'

80. *Ibid.*, pp. 26–7. The third court was sometimes known as the 'third' or 'elderly people's' family. Later it became known as the office family.

In the 'death book' of the New Lebanon church it is recorded that 105 persons (fifty-seven brethren and forty-eight sisters) came into the church in 1787. The next year eighty-nine were gathered, and in 1789 forty-six more. During the following decade, when the testimony was closed to the world, the total 'income' was only twenty-seven. The 'death book' gives the names of 229 members who joined the church from 1787 to 1805 inclusive.—'Names and Ages of those who have been gathered into the Church; With the place of their Birth, and time of coming; Departure, Deaths, . . .' (n.d. Manuscript written by Isaac N. Youngs).

81. *The Testimony of Christ's Second Appearing* (1st ed.), p. 495.

82. Thus, when Peter Ayers came to the Church at New Lebanon on 10 May 1787, he made out the following bill of goods dedicated to that society: 'One horse, One wagon, One lot of tackling, Two cows, One two year old heifer, 27 sheep, 25 pounds of wool, One chaise, 60 lbs. of flax, 130 lbs. of tobacco, One axe, One saddle, One sleigh, One pad-lock, One pound worth of pork, 14 bushels of potatoes, One bed and bedding, 65 bushels of wheat, 16 bushels of rye, 4 bushels of corn, Two sickles, 4 turkeys, 11 hens, One pair of plow irons, 2 chains, Four dollars worth of fur, And 16 dollars in money.'—*The Manifesto* (October, 1882), p. 219. See also Edward D. Andrews, *The Community Industries of the Shakers* (Albany: 1933), pp. 29–30.

83. Jonathan Walker was selected as second deacon, and Richard Spier and Joseph Bennett as assistants. These officials were stationed in the third or outward court.

84. For a description of the early 'families' at New Lebanon, see Andrews, *op. cit.*, pp. 54–7.

85. David Darrow was appointed as the first elder of the Church family, his official title being 'Elder brother of the first family.' Ruth Farrington, who later was to become a member of the first Ohio-Kentucky ministry, was selected as 'Elder sister.' At the same time, the ministry appointed Rufus Clark as elder brother of the Order of families, and his wife Jeruah Clark as elder sister. The Clarks had 'immediate care, charge and oversight' of these families, though each group had its own lead and managed its own temporal affairs.

86. 'A Collection of the Writings of Father Joseph Meacham . . . ,' p. 19–20. 'The first lot' was the position held by Meacham, appointment to which, to use his own words, was 'by the prophecy of God' in Mother Ann. The 'second lot' in the first ministry (or 'first building') was the first in the office of deaconship, viz., David Meacham, his brother. Father Joseph states in these writings that 'the order and manner of the gathering and building of the Church' was given to him by revelation.—*Ibid.*, pp. 58–63. 'The revelation and gift of God,' reads the Shaker testimony, 'is given to the Ministry, as the head of the body, in relation to lots of office and trust, and other matters of importance; and through these, communicated to the other members. Yet nothing is considered as established in the Church until it receives the free and mutual consent, and united approbation of the whole body . . .'—*The Testimony of Christ's Second Appearing* (2nd ed.), pp. 513–15. This 'approbation' was recorded not by vote, but rather vaguely, it seems, by 'the spirit of union.'

87. 'The Millennial Laws' are given as an appendix to this volume, pp. 243–89.

88. Father Calvin Harlow, first in the ministry of the Hancock-Enfield-Tyringham bishopric, was born on 11 June 1753 in Hamburg, Sussex County, New Jersey. He took his place in the ministry on 17 December 1790, after a probationary period at hand labor which Mother Ann had required of him. He died at Hancock on 20 December 1795.

Elder Henry Clough, assistant to Harlow in the organization of the Hancock bishopric and to Eleazer Rand in that of the societies at Harvard and Shirley, was an important figure in the organization of Shakerism. Born on 6 February 1751 in Canterbury, New Hampshire, he became a prosperous farmer and eventually a preacher of the New Light Baptist faith. In 1788 he was called by Father Joseph to be his assistant and, until his death in 1799, was considered a member of the central ministry. Throughout the preliminary work of bringing the various societies into order, he shared with David Meacham, Harlow, David Darrow, Job Bishop, Rand, Elizur Goodrich, Ebenezer Cooley, Israel Chauncey, and John Farrington the responsible posts of itinerant ministers. For a biographical sketch of Clough, see *The Manifesto* (October–November, 1883).

89. A complete Shaker ministry consisted of two elders and two eldresses. On 19 April 1794, when Sabbathday Lake (West Gloucester, New Gloucester, or Thompson's Pond Plantation) community was organized, the Maine ministry included, besides Barnes and Kendal, Elder Robert McFarland of Gorham and Eldress Lucy Prescott of Harvard. Edmund Lougee held 'the second Lot' in the New Hampshire ministry, and Anna Burdick assisted Hannah Goodrich. The ranking members of each foundation ministry were affectionately known as 'Father' and 'Mother.' All the New England and New York societies had orders of elders by 1794.

In 1808 a Shaker colony was organized at Gorham, Maine, but the location proved unfavorable for economic development and the group was moved in 1819 to Poland Hill, the novitiate order of the New Gloucester community.

90. For the complete text of the document, from the original manuscript, see Edward D. Andrews, *The First Covenant of the Church of Christ (Shaker) in New Lebanon, New York 1795* (Pittsfield: 1935). In 1796 a copy of the same covenant was signed by forty members (nineteen brethren and twenty-one sisters) of the New Lebanon church. The first covenant of the Free Will Baptists had been signed at New Durham, New Hampshire, on 13 April 1791; it contains Shaker-like articles on 'non-conformity to the world,' avoidance of lawsuits with the world, the bearing of arms ('carnal weapons'), the wearing of 'superfluous apparel,' et cetera.—Stewart, *op. cit.*, pp. 110–11.

91. On 21 August 1792 (some records say May) a house for the children and youths who had been in the second court was erected north of the meeting house, and separate orders established for the two groups. After the period of apostasy the orders were combined, and in 1796 dissolved altogether, the young being transferred to the Church or First family. According to Isaac N. Youngs' family record (manuscript), 1796 was the year of the greatest number of apostasies, twenty in all. In 1790 sixteen 'went out,' in 1791 fifteen, in 1792 twelve, in 1793 five, in 1794 one, in 1795 four, in 1797 none, in 1798 five, and in 1799 eight.

92. 'A Collection of the Writings of Father Joseph Meacham . . . ,' pp. 91–2.

93. *A Concise Statement of the Principles of the Only True Church, According to the Gospel of the Present Appearance of Christ. As held to and practised upon by the true followers of the Living Saviour, at Newlebanon* (Bennington: 1790).

94. 'A Short Account of the People known by the name of Shakers, or Shaking Quakers,' *The Theological Magazine, or Synopsis of Modern Religious Sentiment*, I (New York: 1796), 232–3. The letter was signed 'Philo, Jan. 13, 1796.—A Traveller, Cambridge, New England.'

95. Manuscript in author's library. The phrases 'freely contributed' and 'as a suitable gift,' or their equivalent, were inserted in the discharge because the church had taken the firm position that 'what had been freely given, could not be remanded, or diverted from the purpose for which it was given, without the free will and consent of the person or persons to whom it had been voluntarily resigned.' Brown claimed that ten dollars a year was all that was allowed for labor, whereas the 'discharges' indicate that the recompense was often much more than that.—Brown, *op. cit.*, p. 299.

96. For an account of this test case, see p. 205 of this volume.

97. *The Testimony of Christ's Second Appearing* (2nd ed.), p. 508. In revising its covenant, the church may have been influenced by the example of the order of (six) families. This order, under the leadership of Rufus Clark, renewed and confirmed its covenant in 1799 'so that neither we ourselves or heirs or assigns ever here after can make any claim charge or demand upon the said Rufus or any member of the said family on account of the above said services.'—'Copy of a Covenant for the Families' (manuscript). In the document quoted, 1790 and not 1791 is given as the date when the 'families' were first organized. The covenant was again revised in 1815. See 'A Concise Statement of the Faith and principles upon which the joint Union & Covenant Relation of Believers are formed, the nature of that Relation and the Order and Manner of attaining and entering into it. Second family covenant' (New Lebanon: 1815. Manuscript).

Chapter V

98. Benjamin Seth Youngs was born in Schenectady, New York, on 17 September 1774. He was the eldest son of Seth Youngs and Martha Farley, both of whom, together with her family, joined the Watervliet colony about 1794. Although he later wrote the standard work—and one of the most scholarly—on Shaker doctrine, Benjamin had only a common school education. After a remarkable career in opening the testimony in the west, he was appointed first elder in the South Union (Ky.) society, a position which he held from 1811 until 1835. Recalled to the east in the latter year, he died at Watervliet in 1855.

99. Issachar Bates, one of the strongest forces in early Shakerism, was born in Hingham, Massachusetts, on 29 January 1758. After several years of farming and trading, Bates entered the Baptist denomination and later became a preacher. He joined the Shaker movement in 1801. In 1835, after a long period of arduous devotion to western Shakerism, Bates was called back to New Lebanon, where he died on 17 March 1837.

100. 'Sketch of the Life and Experience of Issachar Bates.'

101. John Meacham (1770–1854) became a Shaker soon after Ann began to preach at Niskeyuna; Timothy Dwight refers to a discussion with him at an inn in Chicopee, Massachusetts. For a while he was first in the ministry at Pleasant Hill, Kentucky, but was recalled to the east in 1818. Two other sons of Father Joseph also held responsible posts in the west: Archibald (1774–1844), who held the lead at Busro, Indiana, during the existence of that society, and David, Jr., who was first in the central ministry at Union Village, Ohio, from 1835 to 1836.

102. In 1800, Ohio had a total population of only 45,000; Cincinnati, the largest settlement, had only 500. Kentucky had increased its population from 73,000 to about 220,000 in 1800.

103. Late in 1804 there were regular societies of Schismatics at Turtle Creek, Eagle Creek, Springfield, Orangedale, Salem, Beaver Creek, and Clear Creek in Ohio; Cabin Creek, Flemingsburgh, Concord, Cane Ridge, Indian Creek, Bethel, Paint Lick, and Shawnee River in Kentucky—besides 'an innumerable multitude' dispersed through Tennessee, North Carolina, Virginia, and western Pennsylvania. All were exercised with the same spirit: 'praying, shouting, jerking, barking, or rolling; dreaming, prophesying, and looking as through a glass, at the infinite glories of mount Zion, just about to break open upon the world.'—Richard McNemar, *The Kentucky Revival* (Albany: 1808), p. 69.

104. Since no previous mention of Turtle Creek occurs in the journals of the missionaries, it is unlikely that they had planned to make this place their final destination. They had constantly sought a favorable chance to speak, and at two churches had even read the pastoral letter which they carried from New Lebanon, but the strange doctrine of celibacy had always been received with perplexity or indifference. The itinerary was dictated wholly by the location of the New Light preaching stations, of which McNemar's at Turtle Creek offered the most promising opening.

That the Shakers believed their course to be guided by a higher power, however, is indicated by Bates' poem celebrating their arrival:

> In confidence and patience,
> With weary limbs we went;
> The spirit of Elijah
> We sought whom God had sent;
> And there behold we found it,
> When on the spot we came,
> In one whom God had chosen
> And Malcolm was his name.

105. Richard McNemar, *A Review of the Most Important Events Relating to the Rise and Progress of the United Society of Believers in the West* (Union Village: 1831), p. 10. McNemar was given the name Eleazur Wright by Lucy Wright who, in a personal interview with 'the lion-hearted hero of the west,' exclaimed: 'Brother Richard, I name you Eleazur, for you are right!' Whereupon McNemar replied: 'Mother Lucy, I will accept the name, if you will permit me to spell "right" with a W.'

106. *Ibid.*, pp. 6–9. The letter was written on 31 December 1804.

107. McNemar, *The Kentucky Revival*, p. 76.

108. McNemar, *A Review . . .* , pp. 15–16.

109. Benjamin Seth Youngs, 'Journal of One Year, Tues. Jan'y 1st 1805 to Dec. 31, 1805' (manuscript in author's library).

110. MacLean states that sixty families, besides 'many married persons of both sexes and all ages,' joined the Shakers in 1805 or 'shortly thereafter.' —J. P. MacLean, *Shakers of Ohio* (Columbus: 1907), p. 63.

111. Unsigned letter in author's library. 'To the new Shakers or young Believers, the manner in which the dwelling was "laid off"' was new and singular . . . being equally divided into separate apartments opposite each other, for the equal accommodation of brethren and sisters.'

112. The family included nine new recruits who had arrived from New Lebanon the preceding June: Peter Pease, Samuel Turner, Constant Moseley, Eldress Ruth Farrington, Lucy Smith, Molly Goodrich, Ruth Darrow (David's daughter), Martha Sanford, and Prudence Farrington. The arrival of the newcomers 'made us feel strong [Bates wrote], yea, and it made our persecutors feel strong also. But we kept the ground by battles of shaking.'

113. Manuscript in the library of the Western Reserve Historical Society. The letter was received at Turtle Creek '5.27.11. 1806' (Thursday, 27 November 1806).

114. Letter written from Turtle Creek, Warren County, Ohio, on 1 June 1805, probably by John Meacham (manuscript in author's library).

115. For the full text, see *The Constitution of the United Societies, of Believers (Called Shakers) containing sundry Covenants and Articles of Agreement, definitive of the legal grounds of the Institution* (Watervliet, Ohio: 1833). In this first Ohio covenant, the subscribers agreed never to bring debt, blame, or demand on Elder David or others for labor or service. It was specified, however, that 'when any one or more of us shall see cause to move from this family to any other family of the community or to withdraw from the community, we shall be at full liberty so to do, and to take with us our property, if any we have brought in.'

116. Youngs, 'Journal of One Year . . .'

117. *Ibid.*

118. *Ibid.*

119. See McNemar's letter, quoted in Chapter VI, p. 117 of this volume. In the offer and acceptance of economic advantage as a substitute for salvation, or additional lure, we glimpse even at this date a weakness in the Shaker rampart—small fissures for the seepage of worldliness.

120. White and Taylor, *op. cit.*, give the date as 1810. Eldress Molly

Goodrich served with Youngs at the head of the first Kentucky ministry, and for about the same period, 1811 to 1835.

121. James Patterson and Nathaniel Taylor, acting in union with David Darrow and Ruth Farrington at Union Village, were the first official elders of the Watervliet (O.) society.

122. The settlement, variously spelled Busro, Busroe, Buserow, Bussrow, and Bosserun, was located in Busseron Township, in the northwestern part of Knox County. The Shaker society there was first called West Union (being west of Union Village) in 1816.

123. Brother Archibald was described as a 'wise, far-sighted man' by Father David, who wrote in 1814 acknowledging a gift of money from New Lebanon. 'What he undertakes generally prospers, and he would half starve rather than be in debt to the world.' MacLean, however, believed that all the sons of Joseph Meacham—Archibald, John, and David, Jr.— were weak men, and that their advancement to positions of trust was pure favoritism.

124. Manuscript in author's library.

125. Calvin Morrell was a physician and one of the first converts to Shakerism in the west. He was born on 29 April 1765 and died on 3 September 1833.

126. Richard W. Pelham (1797–1873) was the author of the famous pamphlet *The Shaker's answer to a letter, from an inquirer* (Union Village: 1868), an answer to the question, 'What would become of the world, if all should become Shakers?' (See p. 231 of this volume.) As a classical scholar, critic, writer, preacher, and organizer, he must be ranked among the most useful leaders of western Shakerism. Drawn, after long searching, into 'the true apostolic church,' he was largely instrumental in the foundation of two of its branches, North Union and Whitewater.

127. MacLean, *op. cit.*, p. 236.

128. Elder Archibald Meacham was placed in charge of the Whitewater colony in 1827 or 1828. Serving with him were Elder Calvin Morrell, Eldress Eunice Sering, Mary Hopkins, Susannah Stout, and Joanna Wallace. A large frame dwelling was erected for the first Whitewater family in 1828. In 1830 the church covenant was signed.

129. Matthew Houston (1764–1848) was born in Virginia and educated for the Presbyterian ministry. MacLean writes that 'he was a man of high standing in society, of great influence, possessed a classical education, which aided his naturally superior intellectual endowment. He had been a slaveholder, but subsequently manumitted them. . . . He was a great and good man. His greatness consisted in his humility, self-denial and

childlike simplicity and obedience to that order with which he had covenanted.'—MacLean, *op. cit.*, p. 172.

130. David Spinning (1779–1841) also took part in the Kentucky Revival
as a Presbyterian layman.

131. The colony was also called Sodus Point, Big Sodus, Sodus, and Port
Bay. Part of the colony lay in Port Bay, part in Sodus.

132. Col. James Smith, *Remarkable Occurrences lately discovered among
the people called Shakers; of a treasonous and barbarous nature, or, Shakerism
developed* (Paris, Kentucky: [1810?]) and *Shakerism detected. Their erroneous and treasonous proceedings, and false publications* (Paris, Kentucky:
1810).

133. Three years before Colonel Smith published his diatribes, the Shakers
were 'threatened with being put to the sword's point for showing charity
to the poor Indians;—this threat is by one Samuel Trousdale a militia
captain.'—McNemar, *A Review* . . . , pp. 111–19; also MacLean, *op. cit.*,
pp. 347–61.

134. These references are extracted from a republication of Colonel
Smith's charges in Mary Dyer's *A Portraiture of Shakerism* (Concord:
1822), pp. 284–6, 308–27. The aged Archibald Meacham was one of the
five elders who, as late as 1840, were arrested and jailed at Cincinnati on
the charge of one Mary Black that her two boys, aged nine and fourteen,
had been emasculated by the Shakers. Two examiners testified to the
truth of the charge, and it was only after belated permission was given to
two other doctors, acting for the defense, that it was proven that the boys
'labored under a natural deformity.'—See J. P. MacLean, 'Origin, Rise,
Progress and Decline of the Whitewater Community of Shakers,' *Ohio
Archaeological and Historical Quarterly* (October, 1904), pp. 420–23.

Commenting on the 'infinite variety' of these anti-Shaker charges,
McNemar had this to say: 'Such reports and conjectures . . . were generally
taken upon the authority that Mr. *Such-a-one* heard a man say, that he
saw a woman, who had it from a very respectable man, who saw the
person who saw it.'—McNemar, *The Kentucky Revival*, p. 95. See Note 59
above.

135. Benjamin Seth Youngs, *Transactions of the Ohio mob, called in the
public papers 'An Expedition against the Shakers.' Miami Country, State
of Ohio, August 31, 1810.* The attempt to coerce the Shakers—called by
Youngs 'one of the most extraordinary instances of unconstitutional
proceedings, and the most formidable appearance of the infringement on
the rights of conscience that ever was witnessed in this country'—was
instigated principally by Colonel Smith and three apostates. Smith's

son James, Jr., had taken his children into the society against the wishes of his wife Polly, who had urged her father-in-law to get them back.

Chapter VI

136. Mary Hennell, *An Outline of the various Social Systems and Communities which have been Founded on the Principle of Cooperation* (London: 1844), p. 30.

137. George Jacob Holyoake, *The History of Cooperation in England* (London: 1879).

138. On 1 June 1805, Youngs, Bates, and John Meacham wrote home: 'As some Books are found to be in circulation that prove hurtful to the mind of many—we have felt as though a Coppy of R. Rathbun's letter would be profitable to some individuals, particularly to Such as labour with us in the word' (manuscript). This letter to his father, c. 1790, was a reaffirmation of Rathbun's (then) firm faith in the doctrine of celibacy.

139. *A Concise Statement of the Principles of the Only True Church . . .* The Shaker theory of progressive revelation was first committed to print in this interesting pamphlet. In the history of man, Meacham wrote, there have been four 'dispensations' of grace. (1) The first light of salvation was made known to the patriarchs, typified by Abraham, who, being perfect only in his own generation and according to his light, was not completely generated from a 'fleshly or fallen nature.' (2) The law given to Israel by Moses was a further manifestation of salvation, but made nothing perfect or completely pure, as the dispensation was short, and the people returned to sin. (3) The Christ spirit first appeared in Jesus, the 'author of eternal salvation.' Those who were obedient to his doctrine, 'by denying all ungodliness and worldly lusts . . . became entirely dead to the law by the body of Christ . . . [and] were in the travel of the resurrection from the dead.' But before the mystery of God could be finished there must be a falling away from faith and a reign of anti-Christ. (4) The fourth dispensation began with the second appearance of Christ (i.e., in Ann Lee). Foretold by Daniel and St. John as beginning in 1747, it was to be introduced by visions, prophecies, and such spiritual gifts as were received by the apostles at Pentecost. These four steps to complete regeneration were symbolized by Ezekiel's figure of waters rising first to the ankles, then to the knees, then to the loins, and finally submersion (complete baptism) into the life of the spirit. For the 'calculation' of the prophecy of Daniel, see *The Testimony of Christ's Second Appearing* (1st ed.), pp. 518–20.

140. *The Testimony of Christ's Second Appearing* (1st ed.). The preface to the book, a duodecimo volume of 600 pages, was signed by David Darrow, John Meacham, and Youngs. It is doubtful whether the first two elders collaborated in the work, although Youngs may have consulted with McNemar, Worley, and Matthew Houston, all of whom were versed in church history and the classical languages. Seth Youngs Wells edited the second edition (Albany, 1810), McNemar collaborated with Youngs on the third (Union Village, 1823), and Calvin Green and Youngs revised the book before its last printing in Albany in 1856.

The publisher of the original edition was John MacLean, owner of *The Western Star* in Lebanon, and later a justice of the United States Supreme Court. After a 'repeated reading,' Jefferson was said to have pronounced it 'the best ecclesiastical history' that had yet been written. 'If the principles contained in that book were maintained and carried out,' he was quoted as saying, 'it would overthrow all false religions.'

It is instructive to compare the Shakers with other groups of 'spiritual reformers' and mystics, beginning with the second-century Montanists and ending with the Quakers, to all of whom Youngs paid tribute in *The Testimony of Christ's Second Appearing*. Among them, according to Rufus M. Jones, we find a common belief in progressive revelation and 'sporadic visitations,' often accompanied by 'charismatic manifestations'; in a gospel of love, brotherhood, and humanitarianism untrammeled by a strict Catholic or Protestant theology; in heaven as a 'condition of complete adjustment to the holy will of God,' and not as a terminal place of reward; in salvation as an 'inner process of moral transformation,' a traveling towards 'complete spiritual health and wholeness of life'; and in the Church as a Fellowship or Society—'the continued embodiment and revelation of Christ, the communion of saints past and present who live or have lived in the spirit.' For these 'spirituals,' the visible pattern to be followed was the apostolic church, to be preserved in its purity by rigorous church discipline. Its true mission being prophetic, it was a 'growing, changing, ever-adjusting body,' dependent on revelation and the interpretation thereof. And lastly, in line with the principles of the Spiritual Reformers, the Shakers, accepting those 'august ethical aspects which must attach to any religion adequate for the growing race,' attempted to widen its scope and 'carry it into the whole of life.'—See Rufus M. Jones, *Spiritual Reformers in the Sixteenth and Seventeenth Centuries* (London: 1914) and *New Studies in Mystical Religion* (New York: 1927).

141. Manuscript in the library of the Western Reserve Historical Society.

142. McNemar, *The Kentucky Revival* (Cincinnati: 1807).

143. John Dunlavy, *The Manifesto, or a Declaration of the Doctrines and*

Practice of the Church of Christ (Pleasant Hill: 1818). Dunlavy, formerly a Presbyterian, was a New Light Preacher in charge of a congregation at Eagle Creek, in Adams County, southern Ohio, at the time of the Shaker mission. Confessing his sins on 29 July 1805, he was one of the earliest western converts to the faith of Ann Lee. Soon after the Pleasant Hill colony was organized, Dunlavy became its chief minister, a role in which he exercised a great, if quiet, influence until his death on 16 September 1826 at West Union.

The Manifesto . . . was probably the only Shaker book printed on paper made by the Believers themselves. Excerpts were published under the titles *Plain Evidences* (Albany: 1834) and *The Nature and Character of the True Church of Christ proved by Plain Evidences* (New York: 1850). A second edition of *The Manifesto* . . . was issued in New York in 1847.

144. Seth Youngs Wells and Calvin Green, *A Summary View of the Millennial Church, or United Society of Believers* (Albany: 1823).

145. *Ibid.*, p. 269. Cf. Tolstoy, in a letter written to the Doukhobors: 'The Christian teaching cannot be taken piecemeal: one bit taken and another left. If people, accepting Christ's teaching, have repudiated violence, law-courts, and wars, then they must also repudiate property. For violence and law-courts are only wanted to retain property. If people are to retain property, then they need violence and law-courts, and all the arrangements of this world.'—Aylmer Maude, *A Peculiar People, The Doukhobors* (London: 1905), p. 274. Elder Frederick W. Evans later corresponded with Tolstoy on the problem of reconciling the holding of common property with the belief in non-resistance.

146. William Leonard, *A discourse on the order and propriety of divine inspiration* . . . (Harvard: 1853), pp. 66–7.

147. *Ibid.*, pp. 84–5.

148. Saint Simonism 'electrified the world with its vivid representations of universal order and harmony, but it was not adapted for taking root in the earth. . . . it is a law of nature . . . that a house shall not be built by beginning at the chimney tops.'—Rev. J. E. Smith, quoted in Hennell, *op. cit.*, pp. 178–9.

149. Often quoted in Shaker literature is St. Paul's exhortation to the primitive church: 'Study to be quiet and to work with your own hands, as we commanded you, that ye walk honestly toward them that are without, that ye lack nothing.'

150. John Weiss, *Life and Correspondence of Theodore Parker* (New York: 1864), I, 384 (letter from West Roxbury, 31 July 1848).

151. See Hervey Elkins, *Fifteen years in the Senior Order of Shakers*

(Hanover: 1853), pp. 28–9. For a detailed account of the regulations governing the trustees' office, see 'The Millennial Laws,' appendix, pp. 243–9 of this volume.

152. Barnabus Bates, *Peculiarities of the Shakers* (New York: 1832), p. 39. The author was not, as is usually supposed, Benjamin Silliman.

153. W. S. Warder, *A Brief Sketch of the Religious Society of People Called Shakers* (London: 1818), pp. 8–9.

154. Arthur Baker, *Shakers and Shakerism* (London: 1896), p. 15. At times, certain families numbered over a hundred persons and others not more than twenty-five.

155. Many examples of mutual aid may be cited. Isaac N. Youngs wrote in 1858 that the Church at New Lebanon had given 'upwards of sixteen thousand dollars for the establishing and support of the gospel in the western states,' and the 'out families' at New Lebanon about ten thousand and more, exclusive of 'private donations,' gifts of food, clothing, and articles of use. Public gifts from this society alone to brethren of families in distress in various parts of the order—chiefly because of losses by fire— had amounted, when Youngs wrote, to about five thousand dollars. Often, when misfortune occurred, wagonloads of supplies were sent to the afflicted family, and brethren from other orders assembled to rebuild and restore the community.

156. Manuscript in author's library.

157. Henry C. Blinn, *In Memoriam . . . 1824–1905* (Concord: 1905. Autobiographical notes).

158. Benjamin Gates, 'A Day Book or Journal of Work and Various things. . . . Beginning October 1, 1827' (manuscript).

159. 'Journal kept by Elizabeth Lovegrove' (New Lebanon. Manuscript).

160. Barnabus Bates, *op. cit.*, p. 40. For Silliman, read Bates—see Note 152 above.

161. John Finch, in *The New Moral World; and Gazette of the Rational Society*, V (London: 3 February 1844), 3rd Series, No. 32, quoted in Baker, *op. cit.*, p. 22.

162. William Hepworth Dixon, *New America* (3rd ed.; Philadelphia: 1867), p. 306.

163. Stuart Hodgson, 'An American Communist Experiment,' *The Contemporary Review*, CXLIV (London: September, 1933), No. 813, p. 321.

164. For a detailed list of inventions, see Andrews, *The Community Industries of the Shakers*, pp. 40–45.

165. William Dean Howells tells of an experience at Shirley which serves to illustrate this characteristic trait. 'We were asked down to the village,' he relates, 'to see the first harvest of their new Wachuset blackberry, a recent discovery by Brother Leander, who noticed a vine one day by the wayside on which the berries hung ripe, while those on neighboring bushes were yet two weeks from their maturity. He observed also that the cane was almost free from thorns; he marked the vine, and when the leaves fell, transplanted it.'—William Dean Howells, 'A Shaker Village,' *The Atlantic Monthly* (Boston: June, 1876), p. 702.

166. Baker, *op. cit.*, p. 13. In contrast, the English socialist wrote, 'the competitive system exacts from all its victims the maximum of labour, whatever be the quality or condition of their work.'

167. Elisha Myrick, 'A Diary Kept for the use and convenience of the Herb Department' (Harvard: 1853), entry of 31 December 1855 (manuscript).

168. *Report of the trustees of the United Society of Shakers in the town of New Lebanon, Columbia Co., N.Y. (Document) No. 89. In Senate, Mar. 19, 1850* (Albany: 1850), p. 8.

169. Ralph Waldo Emerson, 'Essay on Power,' in *Complete Writings* (New York: 1929), p. 540.

170. Mme. Therese Blanc (Th. Bentzon), *Choses et Gens d'Amérique* (Paris: 1898), pp. 67–8, 104–5.

171. White and Taylor, *op. cit.*, p. 310.

172. Edward Everett, in *North American Review* (Boston: January, 1823).

173. Howells, *op. cit.*, p. 701.

174. Emerson, 'Essay on Worship,' in *Complete Writings*. 'Not in vain,' Emerson continues, 'have they [the Shakers] worn their clay coat, and drudged in their fields, and shuffled in their Bruin dance, from year to year, if they have truly learned this much wisdom.'

175. Manuscript, dated 15 February 1819, in the library of the Western Reserve Historical Society.

176. Letter from Elder James Whittaker to Josiah Tallcot. See Note 61 above.

177. Dixon, *op. cit.*, p. 303.

178. *Ibid.*, pp. 322–3.

179. Warder, *op. cit.*, pp. 8, 12.

180. Isaac Holmes, *An Account of the United States of America* (London: 1823), p. 393.

181. Finch, *op. cit.*, quoted in Baker, *op. cit.*, p. 22.

182. At the suggestion of the Quaker Robert White (father of Eldress Anna White), who had united with the Shaker society at Hancock in 1846, this writing—which Robert had posted in his farm buildings in New Jersey —was printed and displayed in many Shaker barns.

183. See Andrews, *The Community Industries of the Shakers*.

184. For a fuller treatment, see Edward D. Andrews and Faith Andrews, *Shaker Furniture; the Craftsmanship of an American Communal Sect* (New Haven: 1937—also Dover reprint), and Edward D. Andrews, 'The Shaker Manner of Building,' *Art in America*, XLVIII (1960), No. 3.

185. Charles Nordhoff, *The Communistic Societies of the United States* (New York: 1875), pp. 164–5.

186. [James Fenimore Cooper], *Notions of the Americans: Picked up by a Travelling Bachelor* (Philadelphia: 1828), XI, 248.

187. For a description of retiring-rooms at Enfield, New Hampshire, about the middle of the last century, see Elkins, *op. cit.*, pp. 25–6, 39–40.

188. F. O. Matthiessen, *American Renaissance. Art and Expression in the Age of Emerson and Whitman* (New York: 1941), p. 172.

189. Ralph Waldo Emerson, *Journals* (Boston: 1909–14), VI, 261–4. Emerson visited the Harvard community in company with Hawthorne.

190. John Humphrey Noyes, *History of American Socialisms* (Philadelphia: 1870), pp. 141, 669–70.

191. Robert Owen, *The Economist* (London: 2 June 1821), No. 19, p. 291.

192. *Ibid.*, p. 293.

193. Morris Birkbeck (1763–1825), the author of *Notes on a Journey in America* and *Letters from Illinois*, visited Robert Owen in New Harmony in 1825. The agricultural colony he had set up, on a tract of some 16,000 acres, was known as 'the English settlement.'

194. Owen, *op. cit.*, pp. 294–6. Though not quoted or credited, this paragraph was extracted from the foreword of Warder's *A Brief Sketch . . .* and may originally have been either Owen's or Warder's statement.

195. George Finney lists over thirty English travelers—including those mentioned by Jane L. Mesick in *The English Traveler in America, 1785–1835* (New York: 1922)—who commented on the Shakers.—George Finney, 'The Shakers in American Life and Literature' (unpublished thesis; Williams College, Williamstown, Massachusetts: 1938).

196. James Silk Buckingham, *America, Historical. Statistic and Descriptive* (New York: 1841), XI, 75.

197. Macdonald's valuable notes, lost for some time, were recovered by

John Humphrey Noyes, who used selections in his *History of American Socialisms*. The manuscript is now in the Yale University Library.

198. John Finch, in *The New Moral World; and Gazette of the Rational Society*, V (London: 3 February 1844), 3rd Series, No. 32. The four articles on the Shakers, by the ironmaster John Finch, President of the Rational Society, represent one of the first studies of American communitarianism, reflecting a growing European interest in socialism prior to the revolutions of 1848.

In an appraisal of an economic system founded on useful labor and combined industry, a brief view of Shaker principles and practices in the light of two early treatises on the subject may be suggestive. In Sir Thomas More's *Utopia* (1516), it is deplored that little work was done by women ('the half of mankind') or by priests, the rich, or beggars, and that 'we give occasion to many trades that are both vain and superfluous.' If all worked at useful trades, More claimed, 'a small proportion of time would serve for doing all that is either necessary, profitable, or pleasant to mankind.' In the *College of Industry* conceived by John Bellers in 1696, the Quaker writer, proposing that the common people be trained 'in the art of taking care of themselves,' advocated ideas of economy which were largely realized by the Shakers: no useless trades; no bad debts, 'dear bargains,' credit, or lawsuits; no 'loss of time for want of work'; the 'saving the labour of many women and children'; 'saving by abolishing beggary'; 'saving much fetching and carrying of work and provisions'; 'saving clothing hurt in the making and not fit for sale'; 'securing that the land should be better tilled by the labourers being owners'; 'securing that waste land should receive attention'; and 'providing mechanics to help in the harvest.'

199. Holyoake, *op. cit.*, XI, 293.

Chapter VII

200. See Frederick Morgan Davenport, *Primitive Traits in Religious Revivals* (New York: 1905).

201. *The Wonderful Narrative: Or, a Faithful Account of the French Prophets, their agitations, ecstasies, and Inspirations. To which are added, Several other remarkable Instances of Persons under the Influence of the like Spirit, in various Parts of the World, particularly in New-England.* In a letter to a Friend (Glasgow: 1742), p. 76.

202. Chauncy's report found an echo in Daniel Rathbun's accusations against the Shakers; an early song from one of them ended with the verse:

> Of all the relation that ever I see
> My old fleshly kindred are furthest from me,
> So bad and so ugly, so hateful they·feel,
> To see them and hate them increases my zeal.

203. This quotation has been adapted from Morgan Edwards, 'History of the Baptists in Virginia' (manuscript). See William Warren Sweet, *Religion on the American Frontier. The Baptists, 1783–1830* (New York: 1931), p. 10.

204. McNemar, *The Kentucky Revival* (Albany: 1808), pp. 60–61. McNemar's reference to the 'holy laugh' and 'singing ecstasy' recalls Valentine Rathbun's account of the early Niskeyuna meetings.

205. Eunice Chapman, *Being an additional account of the conduct of the Shakers, in the case of Eunice Chapman and her children . . . written by herself* (Albany: 1818), p. 17.

206. For an explanation of Shaker musical notation, see Edward D. Andrews, *The Gift to be Simple* (New York, 1940—also Dover reprint). A full account is here available of the songs, dances and rituals of the order.

207. Manuscript in the library of the Western Reserve Historical Society.

208. Brown, *op. cit.*, p. 20. The elders referred Brown to the passage in Jeremiah in which the prophet says: 'Then shall the virgins rejoice in the dance, both young men and old together.'

209. Wells and Green, *op. cit.*, pp. 84–5.

210. Isaac N. Youngs, 'A Concise View of the Church of God and of Christ, on Earth' (New Lebanon: 1856. Manuscript).

211. Lamson, *op. cit.*, pp. 93–107.

212. William J. Haskett, *Shakerism Unmasked* (Pittsfield: 1828), pp. 144–6.

213. Lamson, *op. cit.*, pp. 90–91.

214. Haskett, *op. cit.*, pp. 189–91.

215. Horace Greeley, 'A Sabbath with the Shakers,' *The Knickerbocker, or New-York Monthly Magazine*, XI (New York: June, 1838), 537.

216. David Benedict, *A History of All Religions* (Providence: 1824), pp. 259–61.

217. Barnabus Bates, *op. cit.*, pp. 56–9. For Silliman, read Bates—see Note 152 above.

218. Benson Lossing, 'The Shakers,' *Harper's New Monthly Magazine* (July, 1857).

219. *Circular Concerning the Dress of Believers* (n.d.), p. 1. For a fuller account of Shaker costume, both Sabbath and weekday, see Edward D. Andrews, *The Community Industries of the Shakers*, pp. 175–9, 197–202, and 'The Dance in Shaker Ritual,' *Dance Index*, I, no. 4, p. 66.

Chapter VIII

220. The material for the present chapter is based almost entirely on original manuscripts, chiefly of Shaker authorship. Isaac N. Youngs' 'A Concise View . . .' was a valuable source, as were the records in the author's library of spiritual messages, mountain and Christmas meetings, and diverse gifts. The Shakers have been understandably reticent about the period, and reluctant to discuss certain of their own contemporary publications. One of the few printed accounts published by the society itself is a small pamphlet: Elder Henry Blinn, *The Manifestation of Spiritualism among the Shakers* (East Canterbury: 1899).

221. Two Philadelphia publications give extended accounts of these visitations: *A Return of Departed Spirits of the Highest Characters of Distinction into the Bodies of the 'Shakers.' By an Associate of the Society* (Philadelphia: 1843) and *A Revelation of the Extraordinary Visitation of Departed Spirits of Distinguished Men and Women of all Nations Through the Living Bodies of the 'Shakers.' By a Guest of the 'Community' near Watervliet, New York* (Philadelphia: 1869).

222. *Extract from an Unpublished Manuscript on Shaker History* (Boston: 1850), pp. 12–13.

At Watervliet the deceased, through a female instrument, thanked those who had attended her in her last illness, told of her meeting with Mother Ann and many brothers and sisters in heaven, and 'gave a flattering account of the happiness enjoyed in the other world.'—Macdonald manuscript; see Note 197 above.

223. See Edward D. Andrews, 'Shaker Inspirational Drawings,' *Antiques* (December, 1945), pp. 338–41.

224. Elkins, *op. cit.*, p. 114.

225. In the dual Shaker deity, Holy Mother Wisdom represented the female, maternal, or 'bearing' spirit, forming with the Eternal Father a unity of 'Incomprehensibles.' As the work of the Father was manifested in the Power to create, so that of Wisdom was devoted to bringing this creation into its proper order.

The concept of a Father-Mother God is an ancient one. According to Cabalistic doctrine, which affected Jewish thought a hundred years before Christ, the Wisdom of the Eternal was a feminine deity whom the Hellenistic Jews called Sophia. Certain early Christians conceived of the Holy Ghost as the Mater Dei, a maternal being whom they called Sophia-Sapientia. In the early eighteenth century, Conrad Beissel, founder of the Ephrata Kloster in Pennsylvania, taught that it is 'the very foundation of your vows of celibacy that man was first a spirit containing both the elements of man and woman; that this spiritual virgin, the Sophia, left him.'—Ulysses S. Koons, *A Tale of the Kloster* (Philadelphia: 1904), pp. 218–19.

226. *The Divine Book of Holy Wisdom* (Canterbury: 1849) was written by Paulina Bates, *not* by Philemon Stewart.

227. Lamson, *op. cit.*, pp. 93–7.

228. One wonders whether the Millerites got the name of their influential periodical, first published in 1843, from this Shaker ritual.

229. Printed on the bars of one cross were the words:

> Enter not within these gates, for this is
> my Holy Sanctuary saith the Lord.
> But pass ye by, and disturb not the peace of
> the quiet, upon my Holy Sabbath.

The other, in front of the trustees' office across the road, read:

> This is a place of trade and public business,
> therefore we open it not on the Sabbath,
> So let none contrive evil against my people
> saith the Lord, lest with my hand I
> Bring evil upon them.

230. 'A record kept of the several meetings held upon Mount Sinai by the Family Orders on Days of the Feasts, Hancock, 1842–1845' (manuscript in author's library).

231. Sally Bushnell, 'A Spiritual Journal Commenced June 1st, 1841. Canaan, New York, Lower Family' (manuscript).

232. See Note 197 above.

233. White and Taylor, *op. cit.*, pp. 236–7.

234. 'An account of the meetings held in the City of Peace [Hancock], City of Union [Enfield, Connecticut], and City of Love [Tyringham, Massachusetts] on 25 December 1845' (manuscript in author's library).

235. Isaac N. Youngs, in *op. cit.*

236. Seth Youngs Wells and Calvin Green, 'Remarks upon inspired writings' (n.d. Manuscript), in Giles B. Avery, 'Miscellaneous Writings' (manuscript).

237. 'A brief account of the society of Germans, called the True Inspirationists, residing seven miles south East of Buffalo. Written by Elisha Blakeman from recollections of Peter H. Long and himself after visiting them in the month of August, 1846' (manuscript in the library of the

Western Reserve Historical Society). Another similarity to 'Mother Ann's Work' was reported: a great number of the Inspirationist communications at Eben-Ezer were to individuals; the person was called by name—'then the word is delivered to them, sometimes it is mortifying and at other times pleasing and comforting.'

238. The official transcript, in eleven volumes, was called 'A True Record of Sacred Communications; Written by Divine Inspiration; By the Mortal hands of Chosen Instruments; in the church at New Lebanon.' This collection, together with compilations from other communications, is in the library of the Western Reserve Historical Society. Separate books of messages are numerous.

239. Paulina Bates was an instrument at Watervliet. Her book received less notice than Stewart's, also published at Canterbury, undoubtedly because the afflatus had by that time spent its force.

240. For an account of the era of spiritualism in the western communities, see MacLean, *op. cit.*, pp. 388–415.

241. Noyes, *op. cit.*, p. 613.

Chapter IX

242. This was not always true, however, as the case of John Mantle indicates. Mantle, a cooper at New Lebanon, told Colonel Maxwell that during the four years of his probation he had dwelt in the same house with his wife, and that for thirty years after they had lived in the same family, loving each other 'with pure and unadulterated affection, being the greatest of friends, and meeting daily.' Their two children, also placed in the same family, remained with the Shakers after they had reached maturity.—Col. A. M. Maxwell, *A Run through the United States* (London: 1841). It was customary, when a brother who had been married was sick, to allow his former wife to nurse him.

243. In 1841 an inspirational message directed a rotation in the seating for the better distribution of conversation, but frequent admissions and withdrawals, mixed ages and conditions, and different degrees of spiritual travel made increasingly difficult 'the right use of a near connection with the opposite sex.'—Isaac N. Youngs, *op. cit.*

244. E. S. Abdy, *Journal of a Residence and Tour in the United States of North America* (London: 1835), I, 256.

245. Mrs. Basil Hall, *The Aristocratic Journey* (New York: 1831)—letters of Mrs. Hall, 1827–8.

246. William Dean Howells, *Three Villages* (Boston: 1884), p. 108. 'I should be sorry [Howells wrote] to give the notion of a gloomy asceticism in the Shaker life. I saw nothing of this, though I saw self-restraint, discipline, quiet, and heard sober, considered, conscientious speech. They had their jesting, also; and those brothers and sisters who were of a humorous mind seemed all the better liked for their gift of laughing and making laugh.'

It will be recalled that the Shakers did not condemn marriage: it was a normal institution of the earthly or human plane from which they had been regenerated. They did distinguish, however, between 'promiscuous' intercourse and coition for the purpose of begetting offspring.

247. Dyer, *op. cit.*, p. 236.

248. Isaac N. Youngs, *op. cit.* Warner, at Watervliet, noticed 'a most tender solicitude on the part of the sisters for the comfort of the brothers. In the care of their rooms and their clothes, and in the consultation of their tastes at table, all the otherwise repressed womanly tenderness seemed to come out.'—Charles Dudley Warner, 'Out of the World,' *Scribner's Monthly*, XVIII (1879), No. 4, p. 553.

249. Macdonald manuscript; see Note 197 above.

250. Blanc, *op. cit.*, pp. 82–3.

251. Hester A. Pool, 'Among the Shakers,' *The Manifesto* (November, 1888), p. 251.

252. 'Instructions concerning the education of youth and Children,' et cetera, in 'A Collection of the Writings of Father Joseph Meacham . . . ,' pp. 44–6.

253. Wells and Green, *op. cit.*, pp. 63–4. Wells was chiefly responsible for the philosophy and content of Shaker education.

254. See also 'A Book of Orders, Given by Mother Lucy for all that belongs to the Children's Order. Copied August 21st, 1840; Written by Daniel Crosman Jan'y 1842' (manuscript).

255. Anonymous, 'Fifteen years a Shakeress,' *The Galaxy*, XIII (New York: January, 1872), no. 1, p. 36.

256. Brown, *op. cit.*, p. 208 ff.

257. Harvey L. Eads, *Expression of Faith. A Discursive Letter* (Orange: 1875), p. 13.

258. *The Testimony of Christ's Second Appearing* (2nd ed.), pp. 476–89. See also White and Taylor, *op. cit.*, pp. 353–60—'Gift of Healing'; and *Our Revolutionary Forefathers*, pp. 180–84.

259. Frederick W. Evans, 'Shaker Travail,' in *Essays* (Mount Lebanon: 1891)—an essay written 27 February 1858.

260. 'A Visit to the Shakers' (signed 'S'), *Blackwood's Edinburgh Magazine*, XIII (April, 1823), p. 466.

261. Seth Chandler, *History of the Town of Shirley, Massachusetts* (Shirley: 1883), p. 257.

262. Daniel Pidgeon, *Old-World Questions and New-World Answers* (London: 1884), p. 121.

263. Godfrey Greylock (J. E. A. Smith), *Taghconic* (Boston: 1852), p. 132.

264. Nordhoff, *op. cit.*, p. 152.

265. Giles B. Avery, *Longevity of Virgin Celibates* (Mount Lebanon: n.d.).

266. 'Collection of manuscripts found among the writings of Deacon Daniel Goodrich, Sr., after his decease' (Hancock. Manuscript).

267. *Ibid.*

268. Isaac N. Youngs, *op. cit.*

269. See Mary Whitcher, *Family Cook Book*; Martha Anderson, *Social Life and Vegetarianism*; and numerous herbal almanacs. Here one finds the Shaker method of preparing raised and unleavened graham bread, graham gems, pie crust, and gruel; vegetable, potato, onion, and bean soups; cookies and 'superior' doughnuts; the famous Shaker dried sweet corn; and various sauces, salads, pies, cakes and puddings.

270. (*Document*) *No. 89. State of New York. In Senate, 19 March 1850*, pp. 1–12.

271. The total acreage and properties of the Shakers are difficult to compute, as the records of 'out-farms,' wood-lots, mills, and other holdings lying outside the home domain are not available. Local histories and traditions make mention of some of these interests: the Shaker grist-mill and pond at West Stockbridge, Massachusetts, for instance, and 'The Shaker Mills' at Windsor, New York, operated for a while by Levi Shaw, trustee of the North family at New Lebanon.

272. A few years ago the Western Reserve Historical Society had checked well over 16,000 members, about sixty-five per cent of whom were estimated to have remained in the order. The distribution:

Alfred, Maine	271	Pleasant Hill, Kentucky	494
Canterbury, New Hampshire	746	Shirley and Harvard,	
Enfield, Connecticut	739	Massachusetts	869
New Gloucester, Maine		South Union, Kentucky	676
(including Poland)	202	Tyringham, Massachusetts	241
New Lebanon, New York		Union Village, Ohio	3873
(including Canaan)	3202	Watervliet, New York	
Enfield, New Hampshire	511	(Niskeyuna)	2668
Groveland, New York		Watervliet, Ohio	126
(including Sodus or Port Bay)	793	Whitewater, Ohio	491
North Union, Ohio	407		

Chapter X

273. *The Shaker Manifesto* (December, 1882), p. 266.

274. William Johnson, *Reports of cases adjudged in the supreme court of judicature of the state of New York; from January term 1799, to January term 1803* (2nd ed.; New York: 1846). The case of Goodrich *v.* Walker is given in some detail.

275. *Investigator: or a Defence of the Order, Government and Economy of The United Society called Shakers; against Sundry Charges and Legislative Proceedings* (Lexington: 1828), p. 51. See also, in the same document, an account of the case of Wait *v.* Merril *et al.*, tried in the Supreme Court of the State of Maine in May 1826.

276. *The Decision of the Court of Appeals (In Kentucky). In a case of much interest to religious communities in general, and to the Shakers in particular. To which is prefixed A brief illustration of the ground of action* (Dayton: 1834), pp. 53–60, 61 ff. When the case was subsequently appealed to a higher court, the verdict was sustained.

In defending the Pleasant Hill covenant, Charles Cunningham pointed out the constitutional right of every man 'to possess his estate as he shall choose' and the fact that the complainants, being neither corporators nor joint-tenants, could not be governed by the rules regulating such interests. In his opinion, the Shaker covenant was a 'peculiar kind' of instrument of co-partnership in which the partners could legitimately rule against the withdrawal, by any departing members, of invested capital or profits.

277. *Laws of Ohio* (1811), IX, 13–16.

278. Dyer, *op. cit.*, pp. 36–7, 106, 180–81. Although present-day Shakers may be understandably sensitive regarding these false accusations, one cannot convey their insidious influence without citing examples as they came from Mary Dyer's pen.

279. Eunice Chapman, *Account of the conduct of the people called Shakers in the case of Eunice Chapman and her children* (Albany: 1817).

280. 'An Act for the relief of Eunice Chapman, and for other purposes,' in *The Other Side of the Question* (Cincinnati: 1819), pp. 5–6.

281. *Revised Statutes of the State of New York* (Albany: 1836), XI, 82–3; also *Laws of 1909*, Chapter 19 (as amended to 1 June 1938), Domestic relations law, Article 5, Section 71. Shaker rules, of course, forbade one parent from bringing children into the community against the will of the other parent; but presumably this sometimes happened without the knowledge of the order. In such cases the law tended to support the regulations of the society. It was probably the successful outcome of Mrs. Chapman's suit which encouraged Mary Dyer to renew hers. Backed by a public petition dated 28 May 1818, she applied in June for 'legislative interference, on account of the mal-conduct of the Shakers, and their unjust detention of her children in their custody.'

282. *Writings of Thomas Jefferson* (Monticello edition), XVI, 281–2.

283. *The Other Side of the Question*, pp. 7–12. When the Assembly, in 1849, deliberated on the propriety of rescinding the Shaker Trust Act of 1839 (see p. 217 of this volume), the Shakers, in a remonstrance addressed to that body, quoted passages from the Council's report.

284. *Ibid.*, pp. 13–14. On 27 March *The Albany Gazette* rebuked the action in an editorial entitled 'Liberty of the Press,' and *The Lansingburgh Gazette* referred to it as 'legislative intolerance.'

285. See the letter written by Eunice Chapman on 20 March 1818, on 'your boasted Military law,' to Seth Youngs Wells, Joseph Hodgson and Peter Dodge, in *The Other Side of the Question*, pp. 19–20.

This source also includes the revealing letters exchanged between Mrs. Chapman and Mother Lucy Wright before the bill for the former's 'relief' was passed. On 4 December 1817, Eunice had written to Mrs. Lucy Goodrich (Mother Lucy) in part as follows: 'I now call upon you to take the matter [of restoring my children to me] into serious consideration, and judge whether you had not better hastily restore them, and grant me some compensation for all my trouble on account of your society's abuse of me and my children, and thereby prevent your complete overthrow. . . . Remember that a woman can be as mighty to pull you down, as a woman [Ann Lee] was to build you up. If you think it is for REVENGE, *remember that a woman can dive deep in THAT art, even to exceed an army.*' Mother Lucy replied from New Lebanon on 12 December: 'I can wash my hands in innocence before God and all men, respecting any abuse to thee or thy children. . . . I have neither the will nor the power, either to hold the children or give them up to thee. . . . Their father . . . took them under his own care. . . . Thou must, therefore, look to him for thy children. . . . I think it would be inconsistent with law and gospel for me to try to wrest them from under the government of their father. . . .'

286. 'A Collection of the Writings of Father Joseph Meacham . . .'

287. *A Declaration of The Society of People* (*Commonly called Shakers*) (Albany: 1815). An almost identical declaration was drawn up the same year by the Enfield (Conn.) society.

288. *The Memorial of the Society of People of New-Lebanon, in the county of Columbia, and Watervliet, in the county of Albany, commonly called*

Shakers. In Senate, Feb. 19, 1816 (Albany), p. 2. The memorial was supported by a petition from 120 inhabitants of the towns of Canaan and Watervliet.

289. On 24 February 1823, another memorial was presented to the State Legislature; on 8 January 1824, twelve Niskeyuna Shakers were jailed but released the following day; in March an appeal was made to the representative in Congress; and on 10 January 1826, a third statement was sent to Albany.—See MacLean, *op. cit.*, pp. 15–17.

In its militia laws passed on 27 January 1818, Ohio had made the trustees of all common-stock societies responsible for fines imposed by the act. The Union Village community, in an 'address' dated 30 March protesting against the clause, included Jefferson's saying—that 'the sum of government is to restrain men from injuring one another, and leave them otherwise free to regulate their own pursuits of industry and improvement . . .'—and the following verse, probably by McNemar:

RIGHTS, CIVIL AND SACRED, CONTRASTED

To this grand truth we all agree,
That ev'ry nat'ral man is free,
When he has serv'd his parentage
Until he is of lawful age.

He has a right to choose his mate,
and his own species propagate;
and gather all the wealth he can,
Upon a Just and lawful plan.

He has a right (in common sense)
For what he claims to make defence;
And with his own he truly may
Do what he pleases, ev'ry way.

But subjects of the second birth
Who are redeemed from the earth;
While in this body they remain,
Their *sacred* rights are just as plain.

With kindred souls they may unite
And bear their cross, by day and night;
And all their int'rest, here below,
To *sacred* ends they may bestow.

To counteract their pious plan,
There is no right in mortal man;
This is the work of fiends below,
The work of God to overthrow.

> But the *free woman* and her seed
> For equal rights of freedome plead
> And while the constitutions stand,
> Our *sacred rights* we will demand.

> As freedome is the Corner Stone
> Which all Republicans must own:
> Then let the *Masons* all take care
> To keep the building plum and square.

290. Manuscript (1860) in the library of the Western Reserve Historical Society.

291. For an interesting account of the South Union society's experience in wartime, based on the diary of Eldress Nancy Moore of the South Union ministry, see White and Taylor, *op. cit.*, pp. 180–95. See also Nancy Lewis Greene, *Ye Olde Shaker Bells* (Lexington: 1930), which includes Civil War records of the Pleasant Hill community.

292. 'Union Village Church Record Books' (1862), Vol. XI (manuscript in the library of the Western Reserve Historical Society).

293. *Memorial regarding 'An act for enrolling and calling out the national forces, and for other purposes'* (1863). See also White and Taylor, *op. cit.*, pp. 182–3.

294. White and Taylor, *op. cit.*, p. 182.

295. In August 1863, John N. Rankin and Harvey L. Eads, of the South Union (Ky.) society, wrote to President Lincoln regarding the troubles the society had experienced as a result of inroads by both the Confederate and Union armies. They reaffirmed their objections to war and pleaded for the release of the 'few young persons' at South Union threatened with enrollment and draft, persons 'on whom so much depends, seeing especially each one has more to do for the support of others, than the only son of a widow, now by law exempt.'

In December several brethren were drafted, but the Provost Marshal at Bowling Green informed them that he had received a letter, dated 30 December, from Secretary of War Stanton, stating: 'If there is any religious Community within your district, whose conscientious scruples abjure war, or the payment of commutation fee, you will parole them indefinitely . . .'—White and Taylor, *op. cit.*, pp. 197–9.

296. Seth Youngs Wells (as Philanthropos), *A brief illustration of the principles of war and peace, showing the ruinous policy of the former and the superior efficacy of the latter for national protection and defense; clearly manifested by their practical operations and opposite effects upon nations, kingdoms and peoples* (Albany: 1831).

297. Seth Youngs Wells (as Philo Pacis), 'Proposition for all peace societies to unite in calling for a congress of national delegates to agree upon some method of settling national differences by mutual agreement in lieu of war' (n. d. Manuscript).

298. *An Act in Relation to Certain Trusts. (Document) No. 35. State of New York. In Senate, 11 January 1839* (passed 15 April 1839).

299. Samuel J. Tilden, 'Considerations in Regard to the Application of the Shakers for Certain Special Privileges,' in *The Writings and Speeches of Samuel J. Tilden*, edited by John Bigelow (New York: 1885), I, 88–100. The 'Considerations' were originally published in Albany, in 1839, as a separate pamphlet.

300. James F. W. Johnston, *Notes of North America. Agricultural, Economical, and Social* (Boston: 1851), II, 266.

301. *Report of the select committee on the subject of the Shakers. (Document) No. 198. State of New York. In Assembly, 2 April 1849.*

302. *(Document) State of New York. In Senate, 8 February 1850.*

303. *(Document) No. 89. State of New York. In Senate, 19 March 1850.*

304. Manuscript in author's library.

305. Manuscript in author's library.

306. Isaac N. Youngs, *op. cit.*

307. Watt Stewart, 'A Mexican and a Spaniard Observe the Shakers, 1830–35,' in *New York History* (Cooperstown: January, 1941), Vol. XXII.

308. Charles Dickens, *American Notes in General Circulation* (London: 1855).

309. *Eine kurze Beschreibung des Glaubens und praktischen Lebens der verein. Gesellschaft Gläubiger in Christi zweiter Erscheinung, gewöhnlich genannt 'Shakers'* (Union Village: 1888).

310. Manuscript in author's library. See also *Shaker-Russian Correspondence* (Mount Lebanon: 1891). 'Not until the separation of church and state . . . could communal property be held by non resistants [Evans wrote to Tolstoy]. We . . . hold and defend our communal property under the civil laws of "The new earth" . . . the American secular government.'

311. A close sympathy, strengthened by the mutual belief in inspiration, existed between the two orders. The Inspirationists had written: 'If it please the Lord our only guide, we would cheerfully enter into a nearer acquaintance and connexion between us.' To a query about Mother Ann, Benjamin Seth Youngs replied: 'That we have a Mother, we readily own, seeing that we ourselves are children!—and that this Mother, whose abode when on earth, dwelt in the earthly tabernacle or person that was known in the world as *Ann Lee*, we as readily own.—But that we ascribe more to her own personal self the grace which she possessed & which was administered through her, than to the fountain from which we must all receive grace, this we do not own; as it is not only contrary to our faith & understanding, but contrary to all her teaching & example when on earth.' —'Letter addressed to the True Inspirationists near Buffalo, embracing a treatise on the origin and order of our existence. By Benjamin Seth Youngs. Water-Vliet, near Albany, 30 July 1846' (manuscript).

312. James Harrison Wilson, *The Life of Charles A. Dana* (New York: 1907), p. 40.

313. See *Shakers and Koreshans Uniting* (Mount Lebanon: 1892). The New Lebanon elder was also prominent in a sectional movement to recognize the validity of spiritualism.

314. The founder of Christian Science had lived near the Canterbury community and was doubtless familiar with its tenets.—Edwin Franden Dakin, *Mrs. Eddy. The Biography of a Virginal Mind* (New York: 1930), pp. 13, 193.

315. 'A Mormon interview. Copied from Brother Ashbel Kitchell's Pocket Journal. By E. D. B. [Elisha Blakeman?] August 1856' (manuscript). See also *Doctrine and Covenants, Latter Day Saints Church Book* (1831), Section 49: 1–28.

A comparison may also be made between the *Book of Mormon* (1830) and an inspirational writing produced at the Harvard community, 'A Brief Sketch of this Continent and its Ancient Inhabitants, together with A History of the Opening of the Gospel Among the Indians, In the World of Spirits, By Brother Thomas Iskawaw, An Ancient Indian Preacher. Given by Inspiration in the Church at Harvard; Commenced, March 21, 1842' (manuscript).—Daryl Chase, 'The Early Shakers. An Experiment in Religious Communism' (manuscript), pp. 214–15, 218 Note. In an unpublished doctoral dissertation, Dr. Mario DePillis, University of California, has convincingly documented the influence of Shakerism on Mormonism, with particular attention to the communitarian aspects of the early Mormon faith.

316. Jacobs became interested in the Shakers, published contributions from them in the paper, and later, with his wife Electa, joined the Union Village community. He left the society after a few years, remarking that he 'would rather' go to hell with Electa than to live among the Shakers without her.'—J. P. MacLean, *A Bibliography of Shaker Literature* (Columbus: 1905), pp. 19–20.

Chapter XI

317. After studying seven religious communities—Ephrata, the Rappites (Harmony and Economy), the Zoarites, the Snowbergers (in Pennsylvania), the Ebenezers (Society of True Inspiration), the Jansenists (at Bishop Hill), and the Shakers—Noyes wondered if there was a correspondence between the fortunes of these communities and 'the strength of their anti-familism.' He noted 'a tendency to departure from the stringent anti-familism of the Shakers as one type of Communism after another is sent here from the Old World.' Yet he also noted that the Shakers, 'who discard the radix of old society with the greatest vehemence . . . have prospered most, and are making the longest and strongest mark on the history of Socialism.' It seems probable, he concluded, that 'there is some rational connection between their control of the sexual relation and their prosperity.'—Noyes, *op. cit.*, pp. 139–42.

318. C. 1849. Manuscript in the library of the Western Reserve Historical Society.

319. 'If every out-farm were sold [Evans told Nordhoff], the society would be better off . . . for their success depends upon the assiduous labor of some of our ablest men, whose services would have been worth more at home.'—Nordhoff, *op. cit.*, p. 162.

320. Frederick W. Evans, *Land Limitation. Letters of F. W. Evans and John Marlin* (Mount Lebanon: 1884), and *Shaker land limitation laws* (Mount Lebanon: n. d.). See also Daniel Fraser, *Shaker support for Henry George* (Mount Lebanon: 1886), and *Land Limitation* (Mount Lebanon: n. d.).

According to John Humphrey Noyes, the 'lust for land' had much to do with the failure of American communities. For one thing, it led them away from markets, railroads, and business centers, whereas to succeed such experiments should be kept abreast of the times, in touch with if not in advance of modern progress, and founded on some kind of manufacturing. Farming, Noyes thought, was too uncertain 'as to modes and theories,' too fertile a field for communal discord, and the most arduous road to fortune. In support of his thesis, the founder of the Oneida community called attention to the holdings of forty-five such associations, whose total property of some 45,000 acres gave each a possession of a thousand acres. In 1875 the eighteen Shaker colonies (which did not figure in Noyes' argument) had a combined estate of about 50,000 acres (not counting a 30,000-acre tract in Kentucky belonging to the Watervliet [N.Y.] society)— an average of some 2700 acres per community.

321. Writing in 1905, the Shakeresses White and Taylor complained of the lack of discipline in financial affairs. Too much trust, 'unlimited power' in fact, was placed in the hands of individuals. Misdeeds were condoned and compromises accepted. Their reference to the strict accounting system of the Quakers and Salvation Army carries the implication that the Believers had again become careless in such matters.—White and Taylor, *op. cit.*

322. John Finch, *The New Moral World; and Gazette of the National Society*, V (London: 6 April 1844), 3rd Series, No. 41.

323. Pelham, *op. cit.*

324. See Frederick W. Evans, *Autobiography of a Shaker* (Albany: 1869). Elder Frederick favored contributions on all kinds of subjects to *The Shaker* (later called *Shaker and Shakeress*, *The Shaker Manifesto*, and *The Manifesto*), the monthly periodical of which he and Eldress Antoinette Doolittle were the first editors.

325. Fraser was the author of several thought-provoking pamphlets: *Analysis of human society*, *The divine procedure in the affairs of men*, *The music of the spheres*, *Shaker hygiene*, *Shaker support for Henry George*, *Theocratic government is self-government*, et cetera.

326. For an extended account of the life and work of Bishop Eads, see C. E. Robinson, *The Shakers and their Homes* (East Canterbury: 1893), Chapter XI.

327. Elder Henry Blinn of Canterbury and Enfield, New Hampshire, one of the saintliest spirits in the movement, but milder and less philosophical than Eads, was no less a traditionalist. For an exposition of the divergent views of Eads and Evans, see Eads, *op. cit.*

328. For example, the 'Circular epistle from the ministry and elders at New Lebanon,' dated 1 September 1829, discussed the desirability of a uniform covenant and the 'exclusion of a party spirit.'

329. White and Taylor, *op. cit.*, p. 396.

330. Manuscript, dated 2 July 1825, in the library of the Western Reserve Historical Society.

331. Nicholas A. Briggs, 'Forty years a Shaker,' *Granite Monthly*, LII (Concord: 1920), pp. 463–74; LIII (1921), pp. 19–32, 56–65, 113–21, 150–55.

332. Thus Freegift Wells, serving as first elder at Union Village, by an allegedly unscrupulous use of certain instruments during the period of the 'manifestations,' was said to have defamed the character of the noble McNemar and excommunicated him from the society.—J. P. Maclean, *A sketch of the life and labors of Richard McNemar* (Franklin, Ohio: 1905), pp. 58–9.

333. Everett, *op. cit.*, pp. 100–01. On another occasion, Thomas Brown was laughed at by another member when he was 'under operations.' His co-worshipper 'was mortified by his lack of self-restraint until an elder excused the conduct on the grounds that he had 'a gift for laughing.'

334. 'Mount Lebanon is the center of a system which has a distinct genius, a strong organization, a perfect life of its own, through which it would appear to be helping to shape and guide, in no slight and unseen measure, the spiritual career of the United States.'—Dixon, *op. cit.*, p. 316.

Notes on Sources of the Illustrations

Banns of Marriage, Abraham Standerin and Ann Lees (p. 7).—From the Cathedral Registry, Manchester, England.

Meeting-houses, New Lebanon. First Church in Background (p. 51). Drawn by Benson J. Lossing; engraved by Lossing-Barritt.—From *Harper's New Monthly Magazine* (July, 1857).

Page from First Written Covenant, New Lebanon, 1795 (p. 63).—From the manuscript in author's library.

Title Page of First Shaker Pamphlet (p. 65).—From author's library.

Title Page of First Edition of *The Testimony* (p. 96).—From author's library.

Trustees' Office and Store, New Lebanon. Built in 1827 (p. 105). Drawn by Benson J. Lossing.—*Loc. cit.*

Trustees' Office, Niskeyuna (p. 107). Artist unknown (Joseph Becker?).—From *Frank Leslie's Popular Monthly*, XX (December, 1885), No. 6.

Kitchen, Church Family, Niskeyuna (p. 111).—*Ibid.*

Sisters' Shop (p. 112). Drawn by Benson J. Lossing.—*Loc. cit.*

A Mender of Clothing *and* Cutting Bread (p. 114).—From *Frank Leslie's*, as above.

Herb Shop, New Lebanon (p. 121). Drawn by Benson J. Lossing.—*Loc. cit.*

Shakeresses Preparing Herb Extracts (p. 123). Line drawing.—From a Shaker almanac (New York: 1886).

Shaker Sisters Corking Bottles, Herb Industry (p. 124).—*Ibid.*

Church Family, Shirley Shakers (p. 128). Photo Electrotype Company, Boston.—From Charles Edson Robinson, *A Concise History of the United Society of Believers called Shakers* (East Canterbury: 1893).

Interior of Meeting-house, New Lebanon (p. 129). Drawn by Benson J. Lossing.—*Loc. cit.*

Entrance to Brethren's and Sisters' Rooms (p. 130).—From *Frank Leslie's*, as above.

Square Order Shuffle (p. 139). Drawn by Benson J. Lossing.—*Loc. cit.*

Singing Meeting (p. 140). From a sketch by Joseph Becker.—From *Frank Leslie's*, as above.

The Gift of Love, Evening Meeting (p. 145). Drawn by J. Boyd Houghton. —From *The London Graphic* (1870).—Houghton (1836–75) was the illustrator of the *Arabian Nights*. In America, on assignment from *The London Graphic*, he found his most sympathetic subject in the Shakers.

Solemn March, The Final Procession (p. 146). Drawn by J. Boyd Houghton. —*Loc. cit.*

Ring Dance, Niskeyuna (p. 148).—From *Frank Leslie's*, as above.

The Whirling Gift (p. 154). Line drawing; artist unknown.—From David R. Lamson, *Two Years' Experience among the Shakers* (West Boylston: 1848).

Mountain Meeting (p. 163). Line drawing or woodcut.—*Ibid.*

Revival Song, Shaker Notation (p. 173).—From an early Shaker hymnal, c. 1848, in author's library.

Brethren's Retiring Room (p. 182).—From *Frank Leslie's*, as above.

Dining Room, North Family, Niskeyuna (p. 183).—*Ibid.*

Girls' Clothes Room, Church Family, Niskeyuna (p. 186).—*Ibid.*

Schoolroom, Niskeyuna Community (p. 190).—*Ibid.*

Sisters' Everyday Costume (p. 200). Drawing by Benson J. Lossing.— *Loc. cit.*

Church Family, New Lebanon Shakers, 1856 (pp. 202–03).—Redrawn from a sketch in Isaac N. Youngs, 'A Concise View of the Church of God and of Christ, on Earth' (New Lebanon: 1856. Manuscript in author's library).

Shaker Evans at Home (p. 232). Drawing by J. Boyd Houghton.—*Loc. cit.*

Title Page of Millennial Laws (p. 249).

Index

(Material appearing in the Notes is not indexed.)

Acts, 'Contrary to order,' *see* Millennial Laws
Adgate, Matthew, 33
Agnew, Brant, 87
Agnew, Joseph, 87
Agnew, Miriam, 87
Agriculture, 83, 116-24, 133-4
Albany *Gazette*, 49
Albigenses, xi
Alcott, Bronson, 222
Alfred, Maine, Shaker community at, 39, 197, 290
Allen, Eldress Catherine, 239
Allen, Joseph, 89
Amana community, xii, 82
Anderson, Martha, 239
Apostacies, 193
Architecture, 78, 125-9, 285-6
Arfwedson, C. D., 143
Arts, mechanical, 121-5, 133
Ashfield, Mass., Shakers at, 37, 43, 47, 291
Avery, Elder Giles B., 108, 197, 239

B

Bacon, Asa, 37
Baker, Morrell, 37, 51
Baptists, in Virginia, 137
Baptists (Negro), in Florida, 137
Baptists, New Light, 18, 37-8, 137
Barbe-Marbois, François, Marquis de, 30, 130-31
Barce, Thankful, 25
Barnes, Benjamin, 39
Barnes, Elder John, 39-40, 61
Barnes, Mary, 39
Barnes, Eldress Sarah, 39
Bates, Betsy, 238
Bates, Elder Issachar, 70-71, 79-80, 238; mission to West, 72f.

Bates, Paulina, 175
Bates, Theodore, 108
Bathrick, Eunice, 239
Beaver Creek, *see* Watervliet, Ohio
Beck, Hannah, 209
Beecher, Henry Ward, 233
Beissel, Johann Konrad, xi
Belchertown, Mass., 37
Bennett, David, quoted, 146-7
Bennett, Joseph, 37, 125
Beulah, *see* Watervliet, Ohio
Birch, Joshua, 37
Birkbeck, Morris, quoted, 131-2
Bishop, Abigail, 37
Bishop, Elder Ebenezer, 238, 289
Bishop, Elder Job, 25, 47, 55, 61, 194, 238
Bishop, John, 43, 56, 238
Bishop, Peter, 37
Bishop, Elder Rufus, 238, 289
Bishop, Talmadge, 18, 238
Bishop Hill colony, 223
Bishoprics, 59
'Blackguard Committee,' 42
Blackwood's Magazine, 196
Blanc, Mme Therese, quoted, 115, 182
Blanchard, Elder Grove, 239
Blinn, Elder Henry, 109, 238
Bloomburg, Elder Andrew, 223
Bok, Edward, 233
Bolton, Mass., 35, 37
Bolton-on-the-Moors, England, 5
Bridges, Jonathan, 37
Briggs, Elder Nicholas A., 189-90, 236-7
Brisbane, Albert, 130
Brook Farm, 103, 222
Brown, Thomas, 31, 140, 191-2, 244
Bruce, Benjamin, 108
Buckingham, James S., quoted, 132-3
Bullard, Eldress Harriet, 239
Burlingame, Nathan, 86-7

341

CATALOG OF DOVER BOOKS

Literature, History of Literature

ARISTOTLE'S THEORY OF POETRY AND THE FINE ARTS, edited by S. H. Butcher. The celebrated Butcher translation of this great classic faced, page by page, with the complete Greek text. A 300 page introduction discussing Aristotle's ideas and their influence in the history of thought and literature, and covering art and nature, imitation as an aesthetic form, poetic truth, art and morality, tragedy, comedy, and similar topics. Modern Aristotelian criticism discussed by John Gassner. lxxvi + 421pp. 5⅜ x 8. **T42 Paperbound $2.00**

FOUNDERS OF THE MIDDLE AGES, E. K. Rand. This is the best non-technical discussion of the transformation of Latin pagan culture into medieval civilization. Covering such figures as Tertullian, Gregory, Jerome, Boethius, Augustine, the Neoplatonists, and many other literary men, educators, classicists, and humanists, this book is a storehouse of information presented clearly and simply for the intelligent non-specialist. "Thoughtful, beautifully written," AMERICAN HISTORICAL REVIEW. "Extraordinarily accurate," Richard McKeon, THE NATION. ix + 365pp. 5⅜ x 8. **T369 Paperbound $1.85**

INTRODUCTIONS TO ENGLISH LITERATURE, edited by B. Dobrée. Goes far beyond ordinary histories, ranging from the 7th century up to 1914 (to the 1940's in some cases.) The first half of each volume is a specific detailed study of historical and economic background of the period and a general survey of poetry and prose, including trends of thought, influences, etc. The second and larger half is devoted to a detailed study of more than 5000 poets, novelists, dramatists; also economists, historians, biographers, religious writers, philosophers, travellers, and scientists of literary stature, with dates, lists of major works and their dates, keypoint critical bibliography, and evaluating comments. The most compendious bibliographic and literary aid within its price range.

Vol. I. THE BEGINNINGS OF ENGLISH LITERATURE TO SKELTON, (1509), W. L. Renwick, H. Orton. 450pp. 5⅛ x 7⅞. **T75 Clothbound $3.50**

Vol. II. THE ENGLISH RENAISSANCE, 1510-1688, V. de Sola Pinto. 381pp. 5⅛ x 7⅞. **T76 Clothbound $3.50**

Vol. III. AUGUSTANS AND ROMANTICS, 1689-1830, H. Dyson, J. Butt. 320pp. 5⅛ x 7⅞. **T77 Clothbound $3.50**

Vol. IV. THE VICTORIANS AND AFTER, 1830-1914, E. Batho, B. Dobrée. 360pp. 5⅛ x 7⅞. **T78 Clothbound $3.50**

Social Sciences

SOCIAL THOUGHT FROM LORE TO SCIENCE, H. E. Barnes and H. Becker. An immense survey of sociological thought and ways of viewing, studying, planning, and reforming society from earliest times to the present. Includes thought on society of preliterate peoples, ancient non-Western cultures, and every great movement in Europe, America, and modern Japan. Analyzes hundreds of great thinkers: Plato, Augustine, Bodin, Vico, Montesquieu, Herder, Comte, Marx, etc. Weighs the contributions of utopians, sophists, fascists and communists; economists, jurists, philosophers, ecclesiastics, and every 19th and 20th century school of scientific sociology, anthropology, and social psychology throughout the world. Combines topical, chronological, and regional approaches, treating the evolution of social thought as a process rather than as a series of mere topics. "Impressive accuracy, competence, and discrimination . . . easily the best single survey," Nation. Thoroughly revised, with new material up to 1960. 2 indexes. Over 2200 bibliographical notes. Three volume set. Total of 1586pp. 5⅜ x 8.

T901 Vol I	Paperbound	**$2.35**
T902 Vol II	Paperbound	**$2.35**
T903 Vol III	Paperbound	**$2.35**
	The set	**$7.05**

FOLKWAYS, William Graham Sumner. A classic of sociology, a searching and thorough examination of patterns of behaviour from primitive, ancient Greek and Judaic, Medieval Christian, African, Oriental, Melanesian, Australian, Islamic, to modern Western societies. Thousands of illustrations of social, sexual, and religious customs, mores, laws, and institutions. Hundreds of categories: Labor, Wealth, Abortion, Primitive Justice, Life Policy, Slavery, Cannibalism, Uncleanness and the Evil Eye, etc. Will extend the horizon of every reader by showing the relativism of his own culture. Prefatory note by A. G. Keller. Introduction by William Lyon Phelps. Bibliography. Index. xiii + 692pp. 5⅜ x 8. **T508 Paperbound $2.49**

PRIMITIVE RELIGION, P. Radin. A thorough treatment by a noted anthropologist of the nature and origin of man's belief in the supernatural and the influences that have shaped religious expression in primitive societies. Ranging from the Arunta, Ashanti, Aztec, Bushman, Crow, Fijian, etc., of Africa, Australia, Pacific Islands, the Arctic, North and South America, Prof. Radin integrates modern psychology, comparative religion, and economic thought with first-hand accounts gathered by himself and other scholars of primitive initiations, training of the shaman, and other fascinating topics. "Excellent," NATURE (London). Unabridged reissue of 1st edition. New author's preface. Bibliographic notes. Index. x + 322pp. 5⅜ x 8.
T393 Paperbound **$1.85**

PRIMITIVE MAN AS PHILOSOPHER, P. Radin. A standard anthropological work covering primitive thought on such topics as the purpose of life, marital relations, freedom of thought, symbolism, death, resignation, the nature of reality, personality, gods, and many others. Drawn from factual material gathered from the Winnebago, Oglala Sioux, Maori, Baganda, Batak, Zuni, among others, it does not distort ideas by removing them from context but interprets strictly within the original framework. Extensive selections of original primitive documents. Bibliography. Index. xviii + 402pp. 5⅜ x 8.
T392 Paperbound **$2.00**

THE POLISH PEASANT IN EUROPE AND AMERICA, William I. Thomas, Florian Znaniecki. A seminal sociological study of peasant primary groups (family and community) and the disruptions produced by a new industrial system and immigration to America. The peasant's family, class system, religious and aesthetic attitudes, and economic life are minutely examined and analyzed in hundreds of pages of primary documentation, particularly letters between family members. The disorientation caused by new environments is scrutinized in detail (a 312 page autobiography of an Immigrant is especially valuable and revealing) in an attempt to find common experiences and reactions. The famous "Methodological Note" sets forth the principles which guided the authors. When out of print this set has sold for as much as $50. 2nd revised edition. 2 vols. Vol. 1: xv + 1115pp. Vol. 2: 1135pp. Index. 6 x 9.
T478 Clothbound 2 vol. set **$12.50**

Music

A GENERAL HISTORY OF MUSIC, Charles Burney. A detailed coverage of music from the Greeks up to 1789, with full information on all types of music: sacred and secular, vocal and instrumental, operatic and symphonic. Theory, notation, forms, instruments, innovators, composers, performers, typical and important works, and much more in an easy, entertaining style. Burney covered much of Europe and spoke with hundreds of authorities and composers so that this work is more than a compilation of records . . . it is a living work of careful and first-hand scholarship. Its account of thoroughbass (18th century) Italian music is probably still the best introduction on the subject. A recent NEW YORK TIMES review said, "Surprisingly few of Burney's statements have been invalidated by modern research . . . still of great value." Edited and corrected by Frank Mercer. 35 figures. Indices. 1915pp. 5⅜ x 8. 2 volumes.
T36 The Set, Clothbound **$12.50**

A DICTIONARY OF HYMNOLOGY, John Julian. This exhaustive and scholarly work has become known as an invaluable source of hundreds of thousands of important and often difficult to obtain facts on the history and use of hymns in the western world. Everyone interested in hymns will be fascinated by the accounts of famous hymns and hymn writers and amazed by the amount of practical information he will find. More than 30,000 entries on individual hymns, giving authorship, date and circumstances of composition, publication, textual variations, translations, denominational and ritual usage, etc. Biographies of more than 9,000 hymn writers, and essays on important topics such as Christmas carols and children's hymns, and many other unusual and valuable information. A 200 page double-columned index of first lines — the largest in print. Total of 1786 pages in two reinforced clothbound volumes. 6¼ x 9¼.
The set, T333 Clothbound **$15.00**

MUSIC IN MEDIEVAL BRITAIN, F. Ll. Harrison. The most thorough, up-to-date, and accurate treatment of the subject ever published, beautifully illustrated. Complete account of institutions and choirs; carols, masses, and motets; liturgy and plainsong; and polyphonic music from the Norman Conquest to the Reformation. Discusses the various schools of music and their reciprocal influences; the origin and development of new ritual forms; development and use of instruments; and new evidence on many problems of the period. Reproductions of scores, over 200 excerpts from medieval melodies. Rules of harmony and dissonance; influence of Continental styles; great composers (Dunstable, Cornysh, Fairfax, etc.); and much more. Register and index of more than 400 musicians. Index of titles. General Index. 225-item bibliography. 6 Appendices. xix + 491pp. 5⅝ x 8¾.
T705 Clothbound **$10.00**

THE MUSIC OF SPAIN, Gilbert Chase. Only book in English to give concise, comprehensive account of Iberian music; new Chapter covers music since 1941. Victoria, Albéniz, Cabezón, Pedrell, Turina, hundreds of other composers; popular and folk music; the Gypsies; the guitar; dance, theatre, opera, with only extensive discussion in English of the Zarzuela; virtuosi such as Casals; much more. "Distinguished . . . readable," Saturday Review. 400-item bibliography. Index. 27 photos. 383pp. 5⅜ x 8.
T549 Paperbound **$2.00**

Philosophy, Religion

GUIDE TO PHILOSOPHY, C. E. M. Joad. A modern classic which examines many crucial problems which man has pondered through the ages: Does free will exist? Is there plan in the universe? How do we know and validate our knowledge? Such opposed solutions as subjective idealism and realism, chance and teleology, vitalism and logical positivism, are evaluated and the contributions of the great philosophers from the Greeks to moderns like Russell, Whitehead, and others, are considered in the context of each problem. "The finest introduction," BOSTON TRANSCRIPT. Index. Classified bibliography. 592pp. 5⅜ x 8.
T297 Paperbound **$2.00**

HISTORY OF ANCIENT PHILOSOPHY, W. Windelband. One of the clearest, most accurate comprehensive surveys of Greek and Roman philosophy. Discusses ancient philosophy in general, intellectual life in Greece in the 7th and 6th centuries B.C., Thales, Anaximander, Anaximenes, Heraclitus, the Eleatics, Empedocles, Anaxagoras, Leucippus, the Pythagoreans, the Sophists, Socrates, Democritus (20 pages), Plato (50 pages), Aristotle (70 pages), the Peripatetics, Stoics, Epicureans, Sceptics, Neo-platonists, Christian Apologists, etc. 2nd German edition translated by H. E. Cushman. xv + 393pp. 5⅜ x 8.
T357 Paperbound **$1.75**

ILLUSTRATIONS OF THE HISTORY OF MEDIEVAL THOUGHT AND LEARNING, R. L. Poole. Basic analysis of the thought and lives of the leading philosophers and ecclesiastics from the 8th to the 14th century—Abailard, Ockham, Wycliffe, Marsiglio of Padua, and many other great thinkers who carried the torch of Western culture and learning through the "Dark Ages": political, religious, and metaphysical views. Long a standard work for scholars and one of the best introductions to medieval thought for beginners. Index. 10 Appendices. xiii + 327pp. 5⅜ x 8.
T674 Paperbound **$1.85**

PHILOSOPHY AND CIVILIZATION IN THE MIDDLE AGES, M. de Wulf. This semi-popular survey covers aspects of medieval intellectual life such as religion, philosophy, science, the arts, etc. It also covers feudalism vs. Catholicism, rise of the universities, mendicant orders, monastic centers, and similar topics. Unabridged. Bibliography. Index. viii + 320pp. 5⅜ x 8.
T284 Paperbound **$1.75**

AN INTRODUCTION TO SCHOLASTIC PHILOSOPHY, Prof. M. de Wulf. Formerly entitled SCHOLASTICISM OLD AND NEW, this volume examines the central scholastic tradition from St. Anselm, Albertus Magnus, Thomas Aquinas, up to Suarez in the 17th century. The relation of scholasticism to ancient and medieval philosophy and science in general is clear and easily followed. The second part of the book considers the modern revival of scholasticism, the Louvain position, relations with Kantianism and Positivism. Unabridged. xvi + 271pp. 5⅜ x 8.
T296 Clothbound **$3.50**
T283 Paperbound **$1.75**

A HISTORY OF MODERN PHILOSOPHY, H. Höffding. An exceptionally clear and detailed coverage of western philosophy from the Renaissance to the end of the 19th century. Major and minor men such as Pomponazzi, Bodin, Boehme, Telesius, Bruno, Copernicus, da Vinci, Kepler, Galileo, Bacon, Descartes, Hobbes, Spinoza, Leibniz, Wolff, Locke, Newton, Berkeley, Hume, Erasmus, Montesquieu, Voltaire, Diderot, Rousseau, Lessing, Kant, Herder, Fichte, Schelling, Hegel, Schopenhauer, Comte, Mill, Darwin, Spencer, Hartmann, Lange, and many others, are discussed in terms of theory of knowledge, logic, cosmology, and psychology. Index. 2 volumes, total of 1159pp. 5⅜ x 8.
T117 Vol. 1, Paperbound **$2.00**
T118 Vol. 2, Paperbound **$2.00**

ARISTOTLE, A. E. Taylor. A brilliant, searching non-technical account of Aristotle and his thought written by a foremost Platonist. It covers the life and works of Aristotle; classification of the sciences; logic; first philosophy; matter and form; causes; motion and eternity; God; physics; metaphysics; and similar topics. Bibliography. New Index compiled for this edition. 128pp. 5⅜ x 8.
T280 Paperbound **$1.00**

THE SYSTEM OF THOMAS AQUINAS, M. de Wulf. Leading Neo-Thomist, one of founders of University of Louvain, gives concise exposition to central doctrines of Aquinas, as a means toward determining his value to modern philosophy. religion. Formerly "Medieval Philosophy Illustrated from the System of Thomas Aquinas." Trans. by E. Messenger. Introduction. 151pp. 5⅜ x 8.
T568 Paperbound **$1.25**

THE PHILOSOPHICAL WORKS OF DESCARTES. The definitive English edition of all the major philosophical works and letters of René Descartes. All of his revolutionary insights, from his famous "Cogito ergo sum" to his detailed account of contemporary science and his astonishingly fruitful concept that all phenomena of the universe (except mind) could be reduced to clear laws by the use of mathematics. An excellent source for the thought of men like Hobbes, Arnauld, Gassendi, etc., who were Descarte's contemporaries. Translated by E. S. Haldane and G. Ross. Introductory notes. Index. Total of 842pp. 5⅜ x 8.
T71 Vol. 1, Paperbound **$2.00**
T72 Vol. 2, Paperbound **$2.00**

THE CHIEF WORKS OF SPINOZA. An unabridged reprint of the famous Bohn edition containing all of Spinoza's most important works: Vol. I: The ,Theologico-Political Treatise and the Political Treatise. Vol. II: On The Improvement Of Understanding, The Ethics, Selected Letters. Profound and enduring ideas on God, the universe, pantheism, society, religion, the state, democracy, the mind, emotions, freedom and the nature of man, which influenced Goethe, Hegel, Schelling, Coleridge, Whitehead, and many others. Introduction. 2 volumes. 826pp. 5⅜ x 8.
T249 Vol. I, Paperbound **$1.50**
T250 Vol. II, Paperbound **$1.50**

LEIBNIZ, H. W. Carr. Most stimulating middle-level coverage of basic philosophical thought of Leibniz. Easily understood discussion, analysis of major works: "Theodicy," "Principles of Nature and Grace," Monadology"; Leibniz's influence; intellectual growth; correspondence; disputes with Bayle, Malebranche, Newton; importance of his thought today, with reinterpretation in modern terminology. "Power and mastery," London Times. Bibliography. Index. 226pp. 5⅜ x 8.
T624 Paperbound **$1.35**

AN ESSAY CONCERNING HUMAN UNDERSTANDING, John Locke. Edited by A. C. Fraser. Unabridged reprinting of definitive edition; only complete edition of "Essay" in print. Marginal analyses of almost every paragraph; hundreds of footnotes; authoritative 140-page biographical, critical, historical prolegomena. Indexes. 1170pp. 5⅜ x 8.
T530 Vol. 1 (Books 1, 2) Paperbound **$2.25**
T531 Vol. 2 (Books 3, 4) Paperbound **$2.25**
2 volume set **$4.50**

THE PHILOSOPHY OF HISTORY, G. W. F. Hegel. One of the great classics of western thought which reveals Hegel's basic principle, that history is not chance but a rational process, the realization of the Spirit of Freedom. Ranges from the oriental cultures of subjective thought to the classical subjective cultures, to the modern absolute synthesis where spiritual and secular may be reconciled. Translation and introduction by J. Sibree. Introduction by C. Hegel. Special introduction for this edition by Prof. Carl Friedrich. xxxix + 447pp. 5⅜ x 8.
T112 Paperbound **$1.85**

THE PHILOSOPHY OF HEGEL, W. T. Stace. The first detailed analysis of Hegel's thought in English, this is especially valuable since so many of Hegel's works are out of print. Dr. Stace examines Hegel's debt to Greek idealists and the 18th century and then proceeds to a careful description and analysis of Hegel's first principles, categories, reason, dialectic method, his logic, philosophy of nature and spirit, etc. Index. Special 14 x 20 chart of Hegelian system. x + 526pp. 5⅜ x 8.
T254 Paperbound **$2.00**

THE WILL TO BELIEVE and HUMAN IMMORTALITY, W. James. Two complete books bound as one. THE WILL TO BELIEVE discusses the interrelations of belief, will, and intellect in man; chance vs. determinism, free will vs. determinism, free will vs. fate, pluralism vs. monism; the philosophies of Hegel and Spencer, and more. HUMAN IMMORTALITY examines the question of survival after death and develops an unusual and powerful argument for immortality. Two prefaces. Index. Total of 429pp. 5⅜ x 8.
T291 Paperbound **$1.65**

THE WORLD AND THE INDIVIDUAL, Josiah Royce. Only major effort by an American philosopher to interpret nature of things in systematic, comprehensive manner. Royce's formulation of an absolute voluntarism remains one of the original and profound solutions to the problems involved. Part one, 4 Historical Conceptions of Being, inquires into first principles, true meaning and place of individuality. Part two, Nature, Man, and the Moral Order, is application of first principles to problems concerning religion, evil, moral order. Introduction by J. E. Smith, Yale Univ. Index. 1070pp. 5⅜ x 8.
T561 Vol. 1 Paperbound **$2.25**
T562 Vol. 2 Paperbound **$2.25**
the set **$4.50**

THE PHILOSOPHICAL WRITINGS OF PEIRCE, edited by J. Buchler. This book (formerly THE PHILOSOPHY OF PEIRCE) is a carefully integrated exposition of Peirce's complete system composed of selections from his own work. Symbolic logic, scientific method, theory of signs, pragmatism, epistemology, chance, cosmology, ethics, and many other topics are treated by one of the greatest philosophers of modern times. This is the only inexpensive compilation of his key ideas. xvi + 386pp. 5⅜ x 8.
T217 Paperbound **$1.95**

EXPERIENCE AND NATURE, John Dewey. An enlarged, revised edition of the Paul Carus lectures which Dewey delivered in 1925. It covers Dewey's basic formulation of the problem of knowledge, with a full discussion of other systems, and a detailing of his own concepts of the relationship of external world, mind, and knowledge. Starts with a thorough examination of the philosophical method; examines the interrelationship of experience and nature; analyzes experience on basis of empirical naturalism, the formulation of law, role of language and social factors in knowledge; etc. Dewey's treatment of central problems in philosophy is profound but extremely easy to follow. ix + 448pp. 5⅜ x 8.
T471 Paperbound **$1.85**

CATALOG OF DOVER BOOKS

MIND AND THE WORLD-ORDER, C. I. Lewis. Building upon the work of Peirce, James, and Dewey, Professor Lewis outlines a theory of knowledge in terms of "conceptual pragmatism." Dividing truth into abstract mathematical certainty and empirical truth, the author demonstrates that the traditional understanding of the a priori must be abandoned. Detailed analyses of philosophy, metaphysics, method, the "given" in experience, knowledge of objects, nature of the a priori, experience and order, and many others. Appendices. xiv + 446pp. 5⅜ x 8.
T359 Paperbound **$1.95**

SCEPTICISM AND ANIMAL FAITH, G. Santayana. To eliminate difficulties in the traditional theory of knowledge, Santayana distinguishes between the independent existence of objects and the essence our mind attributes to them. Scepticism is thereby established as a form of belief, and animal faith is shown to be a necessary condition of knowledge. Belief, classical idealism, intuition, memory, symbols, literary psychology, and much more, discussed with unusual clarity and depth. Index. xii + 314pp. 5⅜ x 8.
T236 Paperbound **$1.50**

LANGUAGE AND MYTH, E. Cassirer. Analyzing the non-rational thought processes which go to make up culture, Cassirer demonstrates that beneath both language and myth there lies a dominant unconscious "grammar" of experience whose categories and canons are not those of logical thought. His analyses of seemingly diverse phenomena such as Indian metaphysics, the Melanesian "mana," the Naturphilosophie of Schelling, modern poetry, etc., are profound without being pedantic. Introduction and translation by Susanne Langer. Index. x + 103pp. 5⅜ x 8.
T51 Paperbound **$1.25**

SUBSTANCE AND FUNCTION, EINSTEIN'S THEORY OF RELATIVITY, E. Cassirer. In this double-volume, Cassirer develops a philosophy of the exact sciences that is historically sound, philosophically mature, and scientifically impeccable. Such topics as the concept of number, space and geometry, non-Euclidean geometry, traditional logic and scientific method, mechanism and motion, energy, relational concepts, degrees of objectivity, the ego, Einstein's relativity, and many others are treated in detail. Authorized translation by W. C. and M. C. Swabey. xii + 465pp. 5⅜ x 8.
T50 Paperbound **$2.00**

*THE ANALYSIS OF MATTER, Bertrand Russell. A classic which has retained its importance in understanding the relation between modern physical theory and human perception. Logical analysis of physics, prerelativity physics, causality, scientific inference, Weyl's theory, tensors, invariants and physical interpretations, periodicity, and much more is treated with Russell's usual brilliance. "Masterly piece of clear thinking and clear writing," NATION AND ATHENAEUM. "Most thorough treatment of the subject," THE NATION. Introduction. Index. 8 figures. viii + 408pp. 5⅜ x 8.
231 Paperbound **$1.95**

CONCEPTUAL THINKING (A LOGICAL INQUIRY), S. Körner. Discusses origin, use of general concepts on which language is based, and the light they shed on basic philosophical questions. Rigorously examines how different concepts are related; how they are linked to experience; problems of the field of contact between exact logical, mathematical, and scientific concepts, and the inexactness of everyday experience (studied at length). This work elaborates many new approaches to the traditional problems of philosophy—epistemology, value theories, metaphysics, aesthetics, morality. "Rare originality . . . brings a new rigour into philosophical argument," Philosophical Quarterly. New corrected second edition. Index. vii + 301pp. 5⅜ x 8
T516 Paperbound **$1.75**

INTRODUCTION TO SYMBOLIC LOGIC, S. Langer. No special knowledge of math required — probably the clearest book ever written on symbolic logic, suitable for the layman, general scientist, and philosopher. You start with simple symbols and advance to a knowledge of the Boole-Schroeder and Russell-Whitehead systems. Forms, logical structure, classes, the calculus of propositions, logic of the syllogism, etc., are all covered. "One of the clearest and simplest introductions," MATHEMATICS GAZETTE. Second enlarged, revised edition. 368pp. 5⅜ x 8.
S164 Paperbound **$1.75**

LANGUAGE, TRUTH AND LOGIC, A. J. Ayer. A clear, careful analysis of the basic ideas of Logical Positivism. Building on the work of Schlick, Russell, Carnap, and the Viennese School, Mr. Ayer develops a detailed exposition of the nature of philosophy, science, and metaphysics; the Self and the World; logic and common sense, and other philosophic concepts. An aid to clarity of thought as well as the first full-length development of Logical Positivism in English. Introduction by Bertrand Russell. Index. 160pp. 5⅜ x 8.
T10 Paperbound **$1.25**

ESSAYS IN EXPERIMENTAL LOGIC, J. Dewey. Based upon the theory that knowledge implies a judgment which in turn implies an inquiry, these papers consider the inquiry stage in terms of: the relationship of thought and subject matter, antecedents of thought, data and meanings. 3 papers examine Bertrand Russell's thought, while 2 others discuss pragmatism and a final essay presents a new theory of the logic of values. Index. viii + 444pp. 5⅜ x 8.
T73 Paperbound **$1.95**

TRAGIC SENSE OF LIFE, M. de Unamuno. The acknowledged masterpiece of one of Spain's most influential thinkers. Between the despair at the inevitable death of man and all his works and the desire for something better, Unamuno finds that "saving incertitude" that alone can console us. This dynamic appraisal of man's faith in God and in himself has been called "a masterpiece" by the ENCYCLOPAEDIA BRITANNICA. xxx + 332pp. 5⅜ x 8.
T257 Paperbound **$1.95**

THE SENSE OF BEAUTY, G. Santayana. A revelation of the beauty of language as well as an important philosophic treatise, this work studies the "why, when, and how beauty appears, what conditions an object must fulfill to be beautiful, what elements of our nature make us sensible of beauty, and what the relation is between the constitution of the object and the excitement of our susceptibility." "It is doubtful if a better treatment of the subject has since been published," PEABODY JOURNAL. Index. ix + 275pp. 5⅜ x 8.
T238 Paperbound **$1.00**

THE IDEA OF PROGRESS, J. B. Bury. Practically unknown before the Reformation, the idea of progress has since become one of the central concepts of western civilization. Prof. Bury analyzes its evolution in the thought of Greece, Rome, the Middle Ages, the Renaissance, to its flowering in all branches of science, religion, philosophy, industry, art, and literature, during and following the 16th century. Introduction by Charles Beard. Index. xl + 357pp. 5⅜ x 8.
T40 Paperbound **$1.95**

HISTORY OF DOGMA, A. Harnack. Adolph Harnack, who died in 1930, was perhaps the greatest Church historian of all time. In this epoch-making history, which has never been surpassed in comprehensiveness and wealth of learning, he traces the development of the authoritative Christian doctrinal system from its first crystallization in the 4th century down through the Reformation, including also a brief survey of the later developments through the Infallibility decree of 1870. He reveals the enormous influence of Greek thought on the early Fathers, and discusses such topics as the Apologists, the great councils, Manichaeism, the historical position of Augustine, the medieval opposition to indulgences, the rise of Protestantism, the relations of Luther's doctrines with modern tendencies of thought, and much more. "Monumental work; still the most valuable history of dogma . . . luminous analysis of the problems . . . abounds in suggestion and stimulus and can be neglected by no one who desires to understand the history of thought in this most important field," Dutcher's Guide to Historical Literature. Translated by Neil Buchanan. Index. Unabridged reprint in 4 volumes. Vol I: Beginnings to the Gnostics and Marcion. Vol II & III: 2nd century to the 4th century Fathers. Vol IV & V: 4th century Councils to the Carlovingian Renaissance. Vol VI & VII: Period of Clugny (c. 1000) to the Reformation, and after. Total of cii + 2407pp. 5⅜ x 8.
T904 Vol I Paperbound **$2.50**
T905 Vol II & III Paperbound **$2.50**
T906 Vol IV & V Paperbound **$2.50**
T907 Vol VI & VII Paperbound **$2.50**
The set **$10.00**

THE GUIDE FOR THE PERPLEXED, Maimonides. One of the great philosophical works of all time and a necessity for everyone interested in the philosophy of the Middle Ages in the Jewish, Christian, and Moslem traditions. Maimonides develops a common meeting-point for the Old Testament and the Aristotelian thought which pervaded the medieval world. His ideas and methods predate such scholastics as Aquinas and Scotus and throw light on the entire problem of philosophy or science vs. religion. 2nd revised edition. Complete unabridged Friedländer translation. 55 page introduction to Maimonides's life, period, etc., with an important summary of the GUIDE. Index. lix + 414pp. 5⅜ x 8.
T351 Paperbound **$1.85**

ASTROLOGY AND RELIGION AMONG THE GREEKS AND ROMANS, Franz Cumont. How astrolology developed, spread, and took hold of superior intellects, from ancient Babylonia through Rome of the fourth century A.D. You see astrology as the base of a learned theology, the influence of the Neo-Pythagoreans, forms of oriental mysteries, the devotion of the emperors to the sun cult (such as the Sol Invictus of Aurelian), and much more. The second part deals with conceptions of the world as formed by astrology, the theology bound up with them, and moral and eschatological ideas. Introduction. Index. 128pp. 5⅜ x 8.
T581 Paperbound **$1.35**

AFTER LIFE IN ROMAN PAGANISM, Franz Cumont. Deepest thoughts, beliefs of epoch between republican period and fall of Roman paganism. Contemporary settings, hidden lore, sources in Greek, Hebrew, Egyptian, prehistoric thought. Secret teachings of mystery religions, Hermetic writings, the gnosis, Pythagoreans, Orphism; sacrifices, nether world, immortality; Hades, problem of violent death, death of children; reincarnation, ecstacy, purification; etc. Introduction. Index. 239pp. 5⅜ x 8.
T573 Paperbound **$1.35**

History, Political Science, Americana

THE POLITICAL THOUGHT OF PLATO AND ARISTOTLE, E. Barker. One of the clearest and most accurate expositions of the corpus of Greek political thought. This standard source contains exhaustive analyses of the "Republic" and other Platonic dialogues and Aristotle's "Politics" and "Ethics," and discusses the origin of these ideas in Greece, contributions of other Greek theorists, and modifications of Greek ideas by thinkers from Aquinas to Hegel. "Must" reading for anyone interested in the history of Western thought. Index. Chronological Table of Events. 2 Appendixes. xxiv + 560pp. 5⅜ x 8.
T521 Paperbound **$1.85**

CATALOG OF DOVER BOOKS

THE ANCIENT GREEK HISTORIANS, J. B. Bury. This well known, easily read work covers the entire field of classical historians from the early writers to Herodotus, Thucydides, Xenophon, through Poseidonius and such Romans as Tacitus, Cato, Caesar, Livy. Scores of writers are studied biographically, in style, sources, accuracy, structure, historical concepts, and influences. Recent discoveries such as the Oxyrhinchus papyri are referred to, as well as such great scholars as Nissen, Gomperz, Cornford, etc. "Totally unblemished by pedantry." Outlook. "The best account in English," Dutcher, A Guide to Historical Lit. Bibliography, Index. x + 281pp. 5⅜ x 8. **T397 Paperbound $1.50**

HISTORY OF THE LATER ROMAN EMPIRE, J. B. Bury. This standard work by the leading Byzantine scholar of our time discusses the later Roman and early Byzantine empires from 395 A.D. through the death of Justinian in 565, in their political, social, cultural, theological, and military aspects. Contemporary documents are quoted in full, making this the most complete reconstruction of the period and a fit successor to Gibbon's "Decline and Fall." "Most unlikely that it will ever be superseded," Glanville Downey, Dumbarton Oaks Research Lib. Geneological tables. 5 maps. Bibliography. Index. 2 volumes total of 965pp. 5⅜ x 8. **T398, 399 Two volume set, Paperbound $4.00**

A HISTORY OF ANCIENT GEOGRAPHY, E. H. Bunbury. Standard study, in English, of ancient geography; never equalled for scope, detail. First full account of history of geography from Greeks' first world picture based on mariners, through Ptolemy. Discusses every important map, discovery, figure, travel, expedition, war, conjecture, narrative, bearing on subject. Chapters on Homeric geography, Herodotus, Alexander expedition, Strabo, Pliny, Ptolemy, would stand alone as exhaustive monographs. Includes minor geographers, men not usually regarded in this context: Hecataeus, Pytheas, Hipparchus, Artemidorus, Marinus of Tyre, etc. Uses information gleaned from military campaigns such as Punic Wars, Hannibal's passage of Alps, campaigns of Lucullus, Pompey, Caesar's wars, the Trojan War. New introduction by W. H. Stahl, Brooklyn College. Bibliography. Index. 20 maps. 1426pp. 5⅜ x 8. **T570-1, clothbound, 2-volume set $12.50**

THE EYES OF DISCOVERY, J. Bakeless. A vivid reconstruction of how unspoiled America appeared to the first white men. Authentic and enlightening accounts of Hudson's landing in New York, Coronado's trek through the Southwest; scores of explorers, settlers, trappers, soldiers. America's pristine flora, fauna, and Indians in every region and state in fresh and unusual new aspects. "A fascinating view of what the land was like before the first highway went through," Time. 68 contemporary illustrations, 39 newly added in this edition. Index. Bibliography. x + 500pp. 5⅜ x 8. **T761 Paperbound $2.00**

AUDUBON AND HIS JOURNALS, J. J. Audubon. A collection of fascinating accounts of Europe and America in the early 1800's through Audubon's own eyes. Includes the Missouri River Journals —an eventful trip through America's untouched heartland, the Labrador Journals, the European Journals, the famous "Episodes", and other rare Audubon material, including the descriptive chapters from the original letterpress edition of the "Ornithological Studies", omitted in all later editions. Indispensable for ornithologists, naturalists, and all lovers of Americana and adventure. 70-page biography by Audubon's granddaughter. 38 illustrations. Index. Total of 1106pp. 5⅜ x 8. **T675 Vol I Paperbound $2.00**
T676 Vol II Paperbound $2.00
The set $4.00

TRAVELS OF WILLIAM BARTRAM, edited by Mark Van Doren. The first inexpensive illustrated edition of one of the 18th century's most delightful books is an excellent source of first-hand material on American geography, anthropology, and natural history. Many descriptions of early Indian tribes are our only source of information on them prior to the infiltration of the white man. "The mind of a scientist with the soul of a poet," John Livingston Lowes. 13 original illustrations and maps. Edited with an introduction by Mark Van Doren. 448pp. 5⅜ x 8. **T13 Paperbound $2.00**

GARRETS AND PRETENDERS: A HISTORY OF BOHEMIANISM IN AMERICA, A. Parry. The colorful and fantastic history of American Bohemianism from Poe to Kerouac. This is the only complete record of hoboes, cranks, starving poets, and suicides. Here are Pfaff, Whitman, Crane, Bierce, Pound, and many others. New chapters by the author and by H. T. Moore bring this thorough and well-documented history down to the Beatniks. "An excellent account," N. Y. Times. Scores of cartoons, drawings, and caricatures. Bibliography. Index. xxviii + 421pp. 5⅝ x 8⅜. **T708 Paperbound $1.95**

POLITICAL PARTIES, Robert Michels. Classic of social science, reference point for all later work, deals with nature of leadership in social organization on government and trade union levels. Probing tendency of oligarchy to replace democracy, it studies need for leadership, desire for organization, psychological motivations, vested interests, hero worship, reaction of leaders to power, press relations, many other aspects. Trans. by E. & C. Paul. Introduction. 447pp. 5⅜ x 8. **T569 Paperbound $2.00**

THE EXPLORATION OF THE COLORADO RIVER AND ITS CANYONS, J. W. Powell. The thrilling first-hand account of the expedition that filled in the last white space on the map of the United States. Rapids, famine, hostile Indians, and mutiny are among the perils encountered as the unknown Colorado Valley reveals its secrets. This is the only uncut version of Major Powell's classic of exploration that has been printed in the last 60 years. Includes later reflections and subsequent expedition. 250 illustrations, new map. 400pp. 5⅝ x 8⅜. **T94 Paperbound $2.00**

FARES, PLEASE! by **J. A. Miller.** Authoritative, comprehensive, and entertaining history of local public transit from its inception to its most recent developments: trolleys, horsecars, streetcars, buses, elevateds, subways, along with monorails, "road-railers," and a host of other extraordinary vehicles. Here are all the flamboyant personalities involved, the vehement arguments, the unusual information, and all the nostalgia. "Interesting facts brought into especially vivid life," N. Y. Times. New preface. 152 illustrations, 4 new. Bibliography. xix + 204pp. 5⅜ x 8. T671 Paperbound **$1.50**

GARDNER'S PHOTOGRAPHIC SKETCH BOOK OF THE CIVIL WAR, Alexander Gardner. The first published collection of Civil War photographs, by one of the two or three most famous photographers of the era, outstandingly reproduced from the original positives. Scenes of crucial battles: Appomattox, Manassas, Mechanicsville, Bull Run, Yorktown, Fredericksburg, etc. Gettysburg immediately after retirement of forces. Battle ruins at Richmond, Petersburg, Gaines'Mill. Prisons, arsenals, a slave pen, fortifications, headquarters, pontoon bridges, soldiers, a field hospital. A unique glimpse into the realities of one of the bloodiest wars in history, with an introductory text to each picture by Gardner himself. Until this edition, there were only five known copies in libraries, and fewer in private hands, one of which sold at auction in 1952 for $425. Introduction by E. F. Bleiler. 100 full page 7 x 10 photographs (original size). 224pp. 8½ x 10¾. T476 Clothbound **$6.00**

Art, History of Art,
Graphic Arts, Handcrafts

ART STUDENTS' ANATOMY, E. J. Farris. Outstanding art anatomy that uses chiefly living objects for its illustrations. 71 photos of undraped man, woman, and child are accompanied by carefully labeled matching sketches to illustrate the skeletal system, articulations and movements, bony landmarks, the muscular system, skin, fasciae, fat, etc. 9 x-ray photos show movement of joints. Undraped models are shown in such actions as serving in tennis, drawing a bow in archery, playing football, dancing, preparing to spring and to dive. Also discussed and illustrated are proportions, age and sex differences, the anatomy of the smile, etc. 8 plates by the great early 18th century anatomic illustrator Siegfried Albinus are also included. Glossary. 158 figures, 7 in color. x + 159pp. 5⅝ x 8⅜. T744 Paperbound **$1.45**

AN ATLAS OF ANATOMY FOR ARTISTS, F Schider. A new 3rd edition of this standard text enlarged by 52 new illustrations of hands, anatomical studies by Cloquet, and expressive life studies of the body by Barcsay. 189 clear detailed plates offer you precise information of impeccable accuracy. 29 plates show all aspects of the skeleton, with closeups of special areas, while 54 full-page plates, mostly in two colors, give human musculature as seen from four different points of view, with cutaways for important portions of the body. 14 full-page plates provide photographs of hand forms, eyelids, female breasts, and indicate the location of muscles upon models. 59 additional plates show how great artists of the past utilized human anatomy. They reproduce sketches and finished work by such artists as Michelangelo, Leonardo da Vinci, Goya, and 15 others. This is a lifetime reference work which will be one of the most important books in any artist's library. "The standard reference tool," AMERICAN LIBRARY ASSOCIATION. "Excellent," AMERICAN ARTIST. Third enlarged edition. 189 plates, 647 illustrations. xxvi + 192pp. 7⅞ x 10⅝. T241 Clothbound **$6.00**

AN ATLAS OF ANIMAL ANATOMY FOR ARTISTS, W. Ellenberger, H. Baum, H. Dittrich. The largest, richest animal anatomy for artists available in English. 99 detailed anatomical plates of such animals as the horse, dog, cat, lion, deer, seal, kangaroo, flying squirrel, cow, bull, goat, monkey, hare, and bat. Surface features are clearly indicated, while progressive beneath-the-skin pictures show musculature, tendons, and bone structure. Rest and action are exhibited in terms of musculature and skeletal structure and detailed cross-sections are given for heads and important features. The animals chosen are representative of specific families so that a study of these anatomies will provide knowledge of hundreds of related species. "Highly recommended as one of the very few books on the subject worthy of being used as an authoritative guide," DESIGN. "Gives a fundamental knowledge," AMERICAN ARTIST. Second revised, enlarged edition with new plates from Cuvier, Stubbs, etc. 288 illustrations. 153pp. 11⅜ x 9. T82 Clothbound **$6.00**

THE HUMAN FIGURE IN MOTION, Eadweard Muybridge. The largest selection in print of Muybridge's famous high-speed action photos of the human figure in motion. 4789 photographs illustrate 162 different actions: men, women, children—mostly undraped—are shown walking, running, carrying various objects, sitting, lying down, climbing, throwing, arising, and performing over 150 other actions. Some actions are shown in as many as 150 photographs each. All in all there are more than 500 action strips in this enormous volume, series shots taken at shutter speeds of as high as 1/6000th of a second! These are not posed shots, but true stopped motion. They show bone and muscle in situations that the human eye is not fast enough to capture. Earlier, smaller editions of these prints have brought $40 and more on the out-of-print market. "A must for artists," ART IN FOCUS. "An unparalleled dictionary of action for all artists," AMERICAN ARTIST. 390 full-page plates, with 4789 photographs. Printed on heavy glossy stock. Reinforced binding with headbands. 7⅞ x 10⅝. T204 Clothbound **$10.00**

CATALOG OF DOVER BOOKS

ANIMALS IN MOTION, Eadweard Muybridge. This is the largest collection of animal action photos in print. 34 different animals (horses, mules, oxen, goats, camels, pigs, cats, guanacos, lions, gnus, deer, monkeys, eagles—and 21 others) in 132 characteristic actions. The horse alone is shown in more than 40 different actions. All 3919 photographs are taken in series at speeds up to 1/6000th of a second. The secrets of leg motion, spinal patterns, head movements, strains and contortions shown nowhere else are captured. You will see exactly how a lion sets his foot down; how an elephant's knees are like a human's—and how they differ; the position of a kangaroo's legs in mid-leap; how an ostrich's head bobs; details of the flight of birds—and thousands of facets of motion only the fastest cameras can catch. Photographed from domestic animals and animals in the Philadelphia zoo, it contains neither semiposed artificial shots nor distorted telephoto shots taken under adverse conditions. Artists, biologists, decorators, cartoonists, will find this book indispensable for understanding animals in motion. "A really marvelous series of plates," NATURE (London). "The dry plate's most spectacular early use was by Eadweard Muybridge," LIFE. 3919 photographs; 380 full pages of plates. 440pp. Printed on heavy glossy paper. Deluxe binding with headbands. 7⅞ x 10⅝. T203 Clothbound **$10.00**

THE HUMAN FIGURE, J. H. Vanderpoel. Every important artistic element of the human figure is pointed out in minutely detailed word descriptions in this classic text and illustrated as well in 430 pencil and charcoal drawings. Thus the text of this book directs your attention to all the characteristic features and subtle differences of the male and female (adults, children, and aged persons), as though a master artist were telling you what to look for at each stage. 2nd edition, revised and enlarged by George Bridgman. Foreword. 430 illustrations. 143pp. 6⅛ x 9¼. T432 Paperbound **$1.45**

ANIMAL DRAWING: ANATOMY AND ACTION FOR ARTISTS, C. R. Knight. The author and illustrator of this work was "the most distinguished painter of animal life." This extensive course in animal drawing discusses musculature, bone structure, animal psychology, movements, habits, habitats. Innumerable tips on proportions, light and shadow play, coloring, hair formation, feather arrangement, scales, how anmials lie down, animal expressions, etc., from great apes to birds. Pointers on avoiding gracelessness in horses, deer; on introducing proper power and bulk to heavier animals; on giving proper grace and subtle expression to members of the cat family. Originally titled "Animal Anatomy and Psychology for the Artist and Layman." Over 123 illustrations. 149pp. 8¼ x 10½. T426 Paperbound **$2.00**

PRINCIPLES OF ART HISTORY, H. Wölfflin. Analyzing such terms as "baroque," "classic," "neoclassic," "primitive," "picturesque," and 164 different works by artists like Botticelli, van Cleve, Dürer, Hobbema, Holbein, Hals, Rembrandt, Titian, Brueghel, Vermeer, and many others, the author establishes the classifications of art history and style on a firm, concrete basis. This classic of art criticism shows what really occurred between the 14th century primitives and the sophistication of the 18th century in terms of basic attitudes and philosophies. "A remarkable lesson in the art of seeing," SAT. REV. OF LITERATURE. Translated from the 7th German edition. 150 illustrations. 254pp. 6⅛ x 9¼. T276 Paperbound **$2.00**

THE MATERIALS AND TECHNIQUES OF MEDIEVAL PAINTING, D. V. Thompson. Based on years of study of medieval manuscripts and laboratory analysis of medieval paintings, this book discusses carriers and grounds, binding media, pigments, metals used in painting, etc. Considers relative merits of painting al fresco and al secco, the procession of coloring materials burnishing, and many other matters. Preface by Bernard Berenson. Index. 239pp. 5⅜ x 8. T327 Paperbound **$1.85**

THE CRAFTSMAN'S HANDBOOK, Cennino Cennini. This is considered the finest English translation of IL LIBRO DELL' ARTE, a 15th century Florentine introduction to art technique. It is both fascinating reading and a wonderful mirror of another culture for artists, art students, historians, social scientists, or anyone interested in details of life some 500 years ago. While it is not an exact recipe book, it gives directions for such matters as tinting papers, gilding stone, preparation of various hues of black, and many other useful but nearly forgotten facets of the painter's art. As a human document reflecting the ideas of a practising medieval artist it is particularly important. 4 illustrations. xxvii + 142pp. D. V. Thompson translator. 6⅛ x 9¼. T54 Paperbound **$1.25**

VASARI ON TECHNIQUE, G. Vasari. Pupil of Michelangelo and outstanding biographer of the Renaissance artists, Vasari also wrote this priceless treatise on the technical methods of the painters, architects, and sculptors of his day. This is the only English translation of this practical, informative, and highly readable work. Scholars, artists, and general readers will welcome these authentic discussions of marble statues, bronze, casting, fresco painting, oil painting, engraving, stained glass, rustic fountains and grottoes, etc. Introduction and notes by G. B. Brown. Index. 18 plates, 11 figures. xxiv + 328pp. 5⅜ x 8. T717 Paperbound **$2.00**

HAWTHORNE ON PAINTING. A vivid recreation, from students' notes, of instruction by Charles W. Hawthorne, given for over 31 years at his famous Cape Cod School of Art. Divided into sections on the outdoor model, still life, landscape, the indoor model, and water color, each section begins with a concise essay, followed by epigrammatic comments on color, form, seeing, etc. Not a formal course, but comments of a great teacher-painter on specific student works, which will solve problems in your own painting and understanding of art. "An excellent introduction for laymen and students alike," Time. Introduction. 100pp. 5⅜ x 8. T653 Paperbound **$1.00**

STIEGEL GLASS, F. W. Hunter. Acclaimed and treasured by librarians, collectors, dealers and manufacturers, this volume is a clear and entertaining account of the life, early experiments, and final achievements in early American glassware of "Baron" Stiegel. An 18th century German adventurer and industrialist, Stiegel founded an empire and produced much of the most highly esteemed early American glassware. His career and varied glassware is set forth in great detail by Mr. Hunter and a new introduction by Helen McKearin provides details revealed by later research. "This pioneer work is reprinted in an edition even more beautiful than the original," ANTIQUES DEALER. "Well worth reading," MARYLAND HISTORICAL MAGAZINE. Introduction. 171 illustrations; 12 in full color. xxii + 338pp. 7⅞ x 10¾.
T128 Clothbound **$10.00**

PINE FURNITURE OF EARLY NEW ENGLAND, R. H. Kettell. A rich understanding of one of America's most original folk arts that collectors of antiques, interior decorators, craftsmen, woodworkers, and everyone interested in American history and art will find fascinating and immensely useful. 413 illustrations of more than 300 chairs, benches, racks, beds, cupboards, mirrors, shelves, tables, and other furniture will show all the simple beauty and character of early New England furniture. 55 detailed drawings carefully analyze outstanding pieces. "With its rich store of illustrations, this book emphasizes the individuality and varied design of early American pine furniture. It should be welcomed," ANTIQUES. 413 illustrations and 55 working drawings. 475. 8 x 10¾.
T145 Clothbound **$10.00**

VITRUVIUS: TEN BOOKS ON ARCHITECTURE. Book by 1st century Roman architect, engineer, Is oldest, most influential work on architecture in existence; for hundreds of years his specific instructions were followed all over the world, by such men as Bramante, Michelangelo, Palladio, etc., and are reflected in major buildings. He describes classic principles of symmetry, harmony; design of treasury, prison, etc.; methods of durability; much more. He wrote in a fascinating manner, and often digressed to give interesting sidelights, making this volume appealing reading even to the non-professional. Standard English translation, by Prof. M. H. Morgan, Harvard U. Index. 6 illus. 334pp. 5⅜ x 8.
T645 Paperbound **$2.00**

THE BROWN DECADES, Lewis Mumford. In this now classic study of the arts in America, Lewis Mumford resurrects the "buried renaissance" of the post-Civil War period. He demonstrates that it contained the seeds of a new integrity and power and documents his study with detailed accounts of the founding of modern architecture in the work of Sullivan, Richardson, Root, Roebling; landscape development of Marsh, Olmstead, and Eliot; the graphic arts of Homer, Eakins, and Ryder. 2nd revised enlarged edition. Bibliography. 12 illustrations. Index. xiv + 266pp. 5⅜ x 8.
T200 Paperbound **$1.65**

STICKS AND STONES, Lewis Mumford. A survey of the forces that have conditioned American architecture and altered its forms. The author discusses the medieval tradition in early New England villages; the Renaissance influence which developed with the rise of the merchant class; the classical influence of Jefferson's time; the "Mechanicsvilles" of Poe's generation; the Brown Decades; the philosophy of the Imperial facade; and finally the modern machine age. "A truly remarkable book," SAT. REV. OF LITERATURE. 2nd revised edition. 21 illustrations. xvii + 228pp. 5⅜ x 8.
T202 Paperbound **$1.60**

THE AUTOBIOGRAPHY OF AN IDEA, Louis Sullivan. The pioneer architect whom Frank Lloyd Wright called "the master" reveals an acute sensitivity to social forces and values in this passionately honest account. He records the crystallization of his opinions and theories, the growth of his organic theory of architecture that still influences American designers and architects, contemporary ideas, etc. This volume contains the first appearance of 34 full-page plates of his finest architecture. Unabridged reissue of 1924 edition. New introduction by R. M. Line. Index. xiv + 335pp. 5⅜ x 8.
T281 Paperbound **$1.85**

THE DRAWINGS OF HEINRICH KLEY. The first uncut republication of both of Kley's devastating sketchbooks, which first appeared in pre-World War I Germany. One of the greatest cartoonists and social satirists of modern times, his exuberant and iconoclastic fantasy and his extraordinary technique place him in the great tradition of Bosch, Breughel, and Goya, while his subject matter has all the immediacy and tension of our century. 200 drawings. viii + 128pp. 7¾ x 10¾.
T24 Paperbound **$1.85**

Miscellaneous

THE COMPLETE KANO JIU-JITSU (JUDO), H. I. Hancock and K. Higashi. Most comprehensive guide to judo, referred to as outstanding work by Encyclopaedia Britannica. Complete authentic Japanese system of 160 holds and throws, including the most spectacular, fully illustrated with 487 photos. Full text explains leverage, weight centers, pressure points, special tricks, etc.; shows how to protect yourself from almost any manner of attack though your attacker may have the initial advantage of strength and surprise. This authentic Kano system should not be confused with the many American imitations. xii + 500pp. 5⅜ x 8.
T639 Paperbound **$2.00**

CATALOG OF DOVER BOOKS

THE MEMOIRS OF JACQUES CASANOVA. Splendid self-revelation by history's most engaging scoundrel—utterly dishonest with women and money, yet highly intelligent and observant. Here are all the famous duels, scandals, amours, banishments, thefts, treacheries, and imprisonments all over Europe: a life lived to the fullest and recounted with gusto in one of the greatest autobiographies of all time. What is more, these Memoirs are also one of the most trustworthy and valuable documents we have on the society and culture of the extravagant 18th century. Here are Voltaire, Louis XV, Catherine the Great, cardinals, castrati, pimps, and pawnbrokers—an entire glittering civilization unfolding before you with an unparalleled sense of actuality. Translated by Arthur Machen. Edited by F. A. Blossom. Introduction by Arthur Symons. Illustrated by Rockwell Kent. Total of xlviii + 2216pp. 5⅜ x 8.

T338 Vol I Paperbound **$2.00**
T339 Vol II Paperbound **$2.00**
T340 Vol III Paperbound **$2.00**
The set **$6.00**

BARNUM'S OWN STORY, P. T. Barnum. The astonishingly frank and gratifyingly well-written autobiography of the master showman and pioneer publicity man reveals the truth about his early career, his famous hoaxes (such as the Fejee Mermaid and the Woolly Horse), his amazing commercial ventures, his fling in politics, his feuds and friendships, his failures and surprising comebacks. A vast panorama of 19th century America's mores, amusements, and vitality. 66 new illustrations in this edition. xii + 500pp. 5⅜ x 8.

T764 Paperbound **$1.65**

THE STORY OF THE TITANIC AS TOLD BY ITS SURVIVORS, ed. by Jack Winocour. Most significant accounts of most overpowering naval disaster of modern times: all 4 authors were survivors. Includes 2 full-length, unabridged books: "The Loss of the S.S. Titanic," by Laurence Beesley, "The Truth about the Titanic," by Col. Archibald Gracie; 6 pertinent chapters from "Titanic and Other Ships," autobiography of only officer to survive, Second Officer Charles Lightoller; and a short, dramatic account by the Titanic's wireless operator, Harold Bride. 26 illus. 368pp. 5⅜ x 8. T610 Paperbound **$1.50**

THE PHYSIOLOGY OF TASTE, Jean Anthelme Brillat-Savarin. Humorous, satirical, witty, and personal classic on joys of food and drink by 18th century French politician, litterateur. Treats the science of gastronomy, erotic value of truffles, Parisian restaurants, drinking contests; gives recipes for tunny omelette, pheasant, Swiss fondue, etc. Only modern translation of original French edition. Introduction. 41 illus. 346pp. 5⅝ x 8⅜.

T591 Paperbound **$1.50**

THE ART OF THE STORY-TELLER, M. L. Shedlock. This classic in the field of effective story-telling is regarded by librarians, story-tellers, and educators as the finest and most lucid book on the subject. The author considers the nature of the story, the difficulties of communicating stories to children, the artifices used in story-telling, how to obtain and maintain the effect of the story, and, of extreme importance, the elements to seek and those to avoid in selecting material. A 99 page selection of Miss Shedlock's most effective stories and an extensive bibliography of further material by Eulalie Steinmetz enhance the book's usefulness. xxi + 320pp. 5⅜ x 8. T635 Paperbound **$1.50**

CREATIVE POWER: THE EDUCATION OF YOUTH IN THE CREATIVE ARTS, Hughes Mearns. In first printing considered revolutionary in its dynamic, progressive approach to teaching the creative arts; now accepted as one of the most effective and valuable approaches yet formulated. Based on the belief that every child has something to contribute, it provides in a stimulating manner invaluable and inspired teaching insights, to stimulate children's latent powers of creative expression in drama, poetry, music, writing, etc. Mearns's methods were developed in his famous experimental classes in creative education at the Lincoln School of Teachers College, Columbia Univ. Named one of the 20 foremost books on education in recent times by National Education Association. New enlarged revised 2nd edition. Introduction. 272pp. 5⅜ x 8. T490 Paperbound **$1.50**

FREE AND INEXPENSIVE EDUCATIONAL AIDS, T. J. Pepe, Superintendent of Schools, Southbury, Connecticut. An up-to-date listing of over 1500 booklets, films, charts, etc. 5% costs less than 25¢; 1% costs more; 94% is yours for the asking. Use this material privately, or in schools from elementary to college, for discussion, vocational guidance, projects. 59 categories include health, trucking, textiles, language, weather, the blood, office practice, wild life, atomic energy, other important topics. Each item described according to contents, number of pages or running time, level. All material is educationally sound, and without political or company bias. 1st publication. Extensive index. xii + 289pp. 5⅜ x 8.

T663 Paperbound **$1.35**

THE WORLD'S GREAT SPEECHES, edited by Lewis Copeland and Lawrence Lamm. 255 speeches ranging over scores of topic and moods (including a special section of "Informal Speeches" and a fine collection of historically important speeches of the U.S.A. and other western hemisphere countries), present the greatest speakers of all time from Pericles of Athens to Churchill, Roosevelt, and Dylan Thomas. Invaluable as a guide to speakers, fascinating as history both past and contemporary, much material here is available elsewhere only with great difficulty. 3 indices: Topic, Author, Nation. xx + 745pp. 5⅜ x 8. T376 Paperbound **$2.49**

THE ROMANCE OF WORDS, E. Weekley. An entertaining collection of unusual word-histories that tracks down for the general reader the origins of more than 2000 common words and phrases in English (including British and American slang): discoveries often surprising, often humorous, that help trace vast chains of commerce in products and ideas. There are Arabic trade words, cowboy words, origins of family names, phonetic accidents, curious wanderings, folk-etymologies, etc. Index. xiii + 210pp. 5⅜ x 8. T710 Paperbound **$1.25**

PHRASE AND WORD ORIGINS: A STUDY OF FAMILIAR EXPRESSIONS, A. H. Holt. One of the most entertaining books on the unexpected origins and colorful histories of words and phrases, based on sound scholarship, but written primarily for the layman. Over 1200 phrases and 1000 separate words are covered, with many quotations, and the results of the most modern linguistic and historical researches. "A right jolly book Mr. Holt has made," N. Y. Times. v + 254pp. 5⅜ x 8. T758 Paperbound **$1.35**

AMATEUR WINE MAKING, S. M. Tritton. Now, with only modest equipment and no prior knowledge, you can make your own fine table wines. A practical handbook, this covers every type of grape wine, as well as fruit, flower, herb, vegetable, and cereal wines, and many kinds of mead, cider, and beer. Every question you might have is answered, and there is a valuable discussion of what can go wrong at various stages along the way. Special supplement of yeasts and American sources of supply. 13 tables. 32 illustrations. Glossary. Index. 239pp. 5½ x 8½. T514 Clothbound **$4.00**

SAILING ALONE AROUND THE WORLD. Captain Joshua Slocum. A great modern classic in a convenient inexpensive edition. Captain Slocum's account of his single-handed voyage around the world in a 34 foot boat which he rebuilt himself. A nearly unparalleled feat of seamanship told with vigor, wit, imagination, and great descriptive power. "A nautical equivalent of Thoreau's account," Van Wyck Brooks. 67 illustrations. 308pp. 5⅜ x 8. T326 Paperbound **$1.00**

TREASURY OF THE WORLD'S COINS, Fred Reinfeld. The finest general introduction to numismatics, non-technical, thorough, always fascinating. Coins of Greece, Rome, modern countries of every continent, primitive societies, such oddities as the 50 lb. stone money of Yap, the nail coinage of New England; all mirror man's economy, customs, religion, politics, philosophy, and art. An entertaining, absorbing study, and a novel view of history. Over 750 illustrations. Table of value of coins illustrated. List of U.S. coin clubs. Bibliographic material. Index. 224pp. 6½ x 9¼ T457 Paperbound **$1.75**

HOAXES, C. D. MacDougall. Shows how art, science, history, journalism can be perverted for private purposes. Hours of delightful entertainment and a work of scholarly value, this often shocking book tells of the deliberate creation of nonsense news, the Cardiff giant, Shakespeare forgeries, the Loch Ness monster, Biblical frauds, political schemes, literary hoaxers like Chatterton, Ossian, the disumbrationist school of painting, the lady in black at Valentino's tomb, and over 250 others. It will probably reveal the truth about a few things you've believed, and help you spot more readily the editorial "gander" and planted publicity release. "A stupendous collection . . . and shrewd analysis." New Yorker. New revised edition. 54 photographs. Index. 320pp. 5⅜ x 8. T465 Paperbound **$1.75**

A HISTORY OF THE WARFARE OF SCIENCE WITH THEOLOGY IN CHRISTENDOM, A. D. White. Most thorough account ever written of the great religious-scientific battles shows gradual victory of science over ignorant, harmful beliefs. Attacks on theory of evolution; attacks on Galileo; great medieval plagues caused by belief in devil-origin of disease; attacks on Franklin's experiments with electricity; the witches of Salem; scores more that will amaze you. Author, co-founder and first president of Cornell U., writes with vast scholarly background, but in clear, readable prose. Acclaimed as classic effort in America to do away with superstition. Index. Total of 928pp. 5⅜ x 8. T608 Vol I Paperbound **$1.85**
T609 Vol II Paperbound **$1.85**

Dover publishes books on art, music, philosophy, literature, languages, history, social sciences, psychology, handcrafts, orientalia, puzzles and entertainments, chess, pets and gardens, books explaining science, intermediate and higher mathematics mathematical physics, engineering, biological sciences, earth sciences, classics of science, etc. Write to:

Dept. catrr.
Dover Publications, Inc.
180 Varick Street, N. Y. 14, N. Y.